SKY BURIAL

SKY BURIAL

An Eyewitness Account of
China's Brutal Crackdown
in Tibet

BLAKE KERR

The Noble Press, Inc.
CHICAGO

Printed in the United States of America

Library of Congress Cataloguing-in-Publication Data

Kerr, Blake.
Sky burial : an eyewitness account of China's brutal crackdown in Tibet / Blake Kerr.
p. cm.
ISBN 1-879360-26-8 : $21.95
1. Tibet (China)—Politics and government—1951–
2. Tibet (China)—Description and travel. I. Title.
DS786.K39 1993
951'.5—dc20   92-51080
                                                    CIP
Noble Press books are available in bulk at discount prices.
Single copies are available prepaid direct from the publisher.

The Noble Press, Inc.
213 W. Institute Place, Suite 508
Chicago, Illinois 60610
(800) 486-7737

When the iron bird flies and horses run on wheels, the Tibetan people will be scattered like ants across the world and the Dharma will come to the land of the Red Man.

Padmasambhava, eighth century

Contents

Acknowledgments

I would like to thank Geri Thoma at the Elaine Markson Literary Agency for getting *Sky Burial* published, and Doug Seibold at Noble Press for his editorial expertise. I am also indebted to John Ackerly, Margaret Alice Doorty, Mitch Pacelle, Philip Turner, and Kate Skinner Kerr for their comments and guidance through different stages of the manuscript. Most of all, I would like to thank all of the Tibetans that I have met. Without their courage in the face of adversity, I would not have been able to finish this book.

The events and experiences I recount here are all true. However, the identities of many of the characters in this story, Westerners and Tibetans alike, have been altered in order to protect individuals' privacy and/or security.

Introduction

by Heinrich Harrer

Author of *Seven Years in Tibet*

IN 1991, AFTER the United States government gave permission for an additional 1,000 Tibetan refugees to settle in North America, I came to this country for a fundraising tour. In Washington, D.C., I met Dr. Blake Kerr. When I heard that he had witnessed the fall 1987 uprisings in Lhasa, I was of course interested to hear more. It was the first time I heard a first-hand report from a man who was a reliable witness to the suffering of the Tibetans, who half a century ago had been my generous hosts for seven years. I had lived with them at a time when they were a happy people in a happy country, under the leadership of the Dalai Lama, who so deservedly received the Nobel Peace Prize for 1989.

What attracted me to the author was the love and admiration we share for the Tibetans and their beautiful country. Without hesitation he gave me a number of his and John Ackerly's slides that illustrate the uprising in Lhasa and the courage of the Tibetans. I also learned for the very first time of the latest and most unbelievable cruelty of the Chinese—the sterilization of Tibet's women.

When I first read the manuscript of *Sky Burial*, I was impressed by all its many fine details; but I was also depressed to learn that life for the Tibetans is even worse than I had heard. The writer himself, a young American physician, is in every respect entitled to give us information on what is really happening in Tibet now that the Chinese occupy the country: torture, coerced abortions, and sterilization. Dr. Kerr was witness to the suffering of a people who struggle to be free.

The people of the free world have read many books and seen many pictures testifying to the destruction of 99 percent of Tibet's temples, shrines, hermitages, and monasteries, and have heard of the incredible number of Tibetans who have lost their lives. In *Sky Burial* the reader will suffer with the Tibetans, and understand how desperately they need our help in their struggle to survive.

March, 1993
Liechtenstein

Foreword

....

Tenzin Gyatso
The XIV Dalai Lama

I N THE FIRST days of October, 1987, I was asked by
reporters from around the world about a demonstration that had
occurred in Lhasa. During my thirty-four years of living in exile in
northern India, I had heard of many other such protests in my native
land, but not until months after they had happened. China had been
very successful in keeping information from leaking out of Tiber—until
October 1, 1987.

I remember meeting Dr. Blake Kerr and John Ackerly in mid-
October immediately after they came out of Tiber. They were the first
eyewitnesses of the Octber 1 demonstration with whom I spoke. When
they told me they had seen Chinese police kill unarmed Tibetans who
were peacefully calling for freedom, I was deeply saddened. But I was
also encouraged that my people had maintained their nonviolent resistance, despite China's use of lethal force. On behalf of six million
Tibetans, I wish to thank all of the Western tourists whose hearts, in the
face of truth, went out to the Tibetan side.

Since China's army invaded Tibet in 1950, one million Tibetans—
one-fifth of my people—have died. Over 6,000 monasteries have been
destroyed, and with them much of Tiber's 1,200 years of history,
Buddhism, and art. I believe that Tibetans are currently struggling
through one of their darkest moments. Now more than ever the world
needs to heed Tibet's message of nonviolence and respect for all living
beings.

PART ONE

ON PILGRIMAGE

CHAPTER ONE

TAKE THE NEXT TRAIN TO TIBET

O N A BREAK from Dartmouth College in the summer of 1979, I went mountaineering in Kashmir, Northern India. It was monsoon season, the season of if's, and port-wine clouds followed me up the valleys like bleating lambs until they exploded over the mountains in a frenzy of wind and torrential rain. My guide, Gulam, made rice and vegetables in the evenings and asked about the day's climb. He also inquired about how much money I made, how much money each material possession I had cost, and how much money I had left. Every night.

"I am thinking, Sahib," Gulam said, eyeing my camera covetously.

"Please don't call me Sahib, Gulam."

"As you wish, Sahib. I am thinking that you must be very tired of getting wet like this. You will be going to your home country soon."

Gulam was right. It was too dangerous to climb alone in the rain. But the mountains were beautiful during storms: warm wind heavy with moisture breaking into translucent waves across an ice ridge; waterfalls leaping off the moonscape of sculpted snow; glaciers trembling under the rain's weight. "What does this have to do with my camera?" I asked.

"You are a rich man, Sahib. I am a poor man. So why are you not giving me your camera when you leave? A present for all that Gulam has done for you."

"I need my camera to take pictures."

"You can get another camera in your country, Sahib. A better one. I cannot get such a camera in India. You could be selling it to me."

"No thanks, Gulam."

3

"What is thanks? I am telling you. I am a humble servant of God. All I am asking—"

"If you are a humble servant of God, you shouldn't need material things to make you happy. I am not as fortunate. I come from the most material of worlds. I need my camera to be happy."

"Perhaps there is something else," Gulam continued. "Something that you are wanting very much. Something only Gulam can give you."

"I doubt it."

"For instance, Sahib. I am knowing that the mountains in Tibet are too high for the monsoon. Tibet is a high-altitude desert, I am telling you. It never rains in Tibet." As Gulam kept talking, I remembered reading T. Lobsang Rampa's *The Third Eye* as an adolescent. My mind still harbored vivid images of monks who meditated in caves for years and diagnosed diseases in their incipient stages long before they became manifest. As a boy I knew very little about Tibet, but I had always wanted to go there.

"Gulam is knowing a secret pass."

"How high is the pass?" I asked, trying not to sound interested.

"16,000 feet, Sahib."

"And where might this pass be?"

"Very near, Sahib. Perhaps for your camera, I could be showing this pass to you."

I kept my camera. Gulam kept to himself the location of the pass. Tibet would have to wait.

＊ ＊ ＊

It took years for me to convince John Ackerly that his destiny included going to Tibet with me. While we were students at Dartmouth I first appealed to John's sense of adventure with a copy of Heinrich Harrer's *Seven Years in Tibet*, the epic journey of an Austrian mountaineer who climbed Nanga Parabat in Pakistan during World War II and was imprisoned by the British in Northern India. In what must be one of the greatest adventures of all time, Harrer escaped from prison into the Himalayas five times, spent years with nomads, and became a friend and tutor of the Dalai Lama. John loved the book, but not enough to keep him from going off to American University's law school in Washington,

D.C. After graduating he worked as a civil-rights lawyer in Jackson, Mississippi.

While I, in turn, attended medical school, I found myself longing for some sort of adventure. I relished the memory of John convincing me to withdraw from Dartmouth as a senior in order to hop freight trains across the country. We lived by our wits and ate out of dumpsters, sleeping in missions, boxcars, and by the side of the road. With this in mind, in 1985 I enticed John with a train-hopping mini-reunion from Jackson to New Orleans during a summer break from medical school. Hopping trains would be a celebration: time to exaggerate our memories of the climbs we had done together in the Andes and Yosemite National Park; time to embellish our search for the Great American Hobo; time to plan our next expedition; and time for me to convince John to join me in the Himalayas.

As we rode southwest, southern Louisiana's pine forest yielded to tidal estuary and a windswept ocean of tall grass, brown in the autumn sun. As the train screeched slowly to a halt in a mosaic of cattails, the steady hum of insects replaced the boxcars' clatter. The swamp lost its charm as a cloud of mosquitoes descended upon us. I slapped the first mosquito that buried its proboscis deep into a vein. John was sitting cross-legged in the middle of the open boxcar door. He looked relaxed, more like a *sanyassi* than a lawyer. Insects never bite John when I am around.

"We have to sell plasma, for old time's sake," John said.

The thought of a needle burrowing in my arm made me cringe. Even when we found five-dollar bonus coupons in the local paper, this would only entitle us to twelve dollars each for our blood plasma. I hated selling plasma, and had stopped doing it after getting a golfball-sized hematoma years before in San Antonio. "It's easy money," John said. "We have to do it again, just like in the old days."

"Imagine a yak-intensive pilgrimage to Himalayan cliffs higher than El Capitan," I said, trying to change the subject. "We travel light, like Harrer, moving at night and hiding during the day."

"Where have you been?" John said. "The Chinese are starting to open Tibet. But even if I did want to go to Tibet, I can't leave my practice. Not until I learn how to sue doctors."

"Then how about after I finish medical school?" I said. "That's two years before I can malpractice on you."

"I'll still have clients that depend on me two years from now. I couldn't just up and leave them."

"Of course you could. We're talking about the conditional tense. *Two* years from now. Plenty of time to ease out of your job."

"It's more than easing out of a job," John said. "I've got professional responsibilities."

During the next two years I fueled John's interest in Tibet by appealing to his literary penchant, first with a copy of Alexandra David-Neel's *My Journey to Lhasa*. In some ways her story was even more remarkable than Harrer's. As a mountaineer Harrer was used to the rigors of altitude and travel under inclement weather; David-Neel was an English society woman with no prior experience in the mountains. Nevertheless, she learned Tibetan, dyed her hair black, and traveled disguised as a Tibetan woman, with a revolver stashed under her robes. On one of her first forays into Tibet, she was caught by the authorities and expelled from the country. Like any seasoned, self-respecting traveler, she ignored the expulsion order, outwitted her captors, and proceeded with her journey.

I finally broke John down. In the summer of 1987, he agreed that we would try to climb as high as we could on the Tibetan side of Everest— *if* we acquired warm clothes, shelter, and food as we needed them. During a brief pre-flight stop in New York City, we bought condoms, had our pictures taken with a cardboard cutout of Ronald Reagan, and stopped at the Office of Tibet. A one-way flight to Hong Kong and a high-speed train brought us to Western China. From our first-class compartment we surveyed the lush patchwork of cultivated fields. We also cut the speaker wires in our compartment to avoid being assaulted by a shrill, continuous socialist reveille, courtesy of the Chinese government. Torrential rains followed us from Kunming to the Taklamakan Desert and the caves at Dunhuang. It was still raining when we reached Golmud, the end of the train line and the northeast gateway of Tibet.

If the air-conditioned, Japanese-made tourist bus we boarded next didn't become mired in the flooded plains, and *if* we didn't get killed crossing the Kun Lun or Tanggula mountains, it would take us two days to travel from Golmud to Lhasa by bus. But the seasonal monsoon had migrated north of the Central Himalayas for the first time in forty years. Daily rains turned the 12,000-foot Tibetan Plateau into a jeep-swallowing quagmire. Long lines of vehicles waited on both sides of eroded embankments and engorged rivers. Going into Tibet were buses, jeeps, and Land Rovers from the China Travel Service filled with tourists; trucks loaded with Chinese vegetables, Hami melons, and video cassettes; and People's Liberation Army trucks packed with soldiers. Coming out of Tibet were trucks hauling timber; tourist buses; and more soldiers.

Once we left the salt marshes on the Qaidam Basin to wind into the mountains, seven passengers began vomiting regularly out of the windows. They suffered from a wicked combination of altitude sickness mixed with motion sickness as the bus groaned toward a 16,000-foot pass. I was more alarmed by the foxholes I saw dug into the serpentine bank of a river, the bunkers on the high slopes, and the stone barracks surrounded by barbed wire.

Finally the clouds began to clear. Dawn broke over the mountains in great columns of light, cinnabar and orange, teasing snowcapped peaks and tongues of ice from dark silhouettes. Even through our muddy windows the mountains appeared as cathedrals of light and beckoned for us to hike past the yaks dotting the frozen hills to their serrated tops. A hanging glacier angling up toward the sun's first rays tempted us to imagine different routes to its summit. We did this continually from Golmud to Lhasa; with 6,000-meter peaks alongside the road, neither of us was able to pay attention to the other passengers' infirmities, or to our own aching muscles, cramped from being folded unnaturally into seats designed for Japanese. We had been waiting so long for this first glimpse of sun that we were caught unprepared. How can one prepare for an avalanche of light?

The clouds stole the light back from the mountains as quickly as it had come. Suddenly the bus hit a bump that launched passengers into the luggage racks over their heads. Moans and obscenities in several languages filtered up to our seats in the front of the bus. A Chinese man wearing a full-length green army coat pulled his ashen face inside his window. He looked like he might throw up again at any moment.

Patrick, a loyal British subject on a three-week holiday from teaching English in Yunnan Province, also looked ill. I gave him some aspirin and my water bottle and asked him to offer them to the Chinese man. The man did not take the aspirin, but he wanted to talk. According to Patrick, the government had offered the man work in Tibet at double the wage he could have earned in the mainland. He also could apply for government loans to start a business, and his children would be guaranteed a place in school.

"We should be hitchhiking," John said, staring out the window.

"We got out of shape riding soft-sleeper," I said, referring to China's trains.

"First class!" Patrick said, with the flair of an Elizabethan actor. "That's traveling in a style more befitting gentlemen in your professions." Patrick said the Chinese army was "brilliant" to have built the road we were on with polypropylene, which would withstand the area's temperature extremes.

"The PLA built the 'Friendship Highway' in the mid-1950s to invade Tibet," John said.

"Where did you get that misinformation?" Patrick asked.

"It's in the Tibet guidebook," John said.

"Do you believe everything you read in the guidebook?" Patrick challenged. "I've been in China for a year. The *People's Daily* has frequent articles on a number of socialist reforms and development in Tibet."

John and Patrick argued whether the *People's Daily* was a propaganda tool of the State. I grew tired of the sound of these two Westerners arguing out of ignorance and boredom, fueled as much by being cramped into the same bus for days than by anything either of them had experienced or read. I wondered if after four decades of occupation the Chinese were still "liberating" Tibet; many of the vehicles on the Friendship Highway carried soldiers.

The first bus in our convoy charged up an unpaved section of road and slid, wheels spinning, into the mud. As soon as our forward motion stopped, queasy passengers dashed off the bus to vomit, the typical beginning to a communal bathroom break. Men relieved themselves by the side of the road; women sought what shelter could be afforded behind a tuft of grass or hillock. The second bus swung wider than the first and plowed ten feet farther into the furrows from previous tracks.

After consulting with the two other drivers, our bus driver then veered even farther from the road—and deeper into the mud.

Livid passengers cursed at the Chinese drivers for getting all three buses stuck at the same time. "The *worst* drivers in the world," an Italian man shouted from the front of the bus. A Frenchman wearing thick glasses agreed: "You'd think the Chinese would have learned to drive."

"On the contrary," Patrick said, rising to the drivers' defense. "These men are masters of the sodden road. More times than not they have saved us from becoming mired in this godforsaken baskerville." When the Frenchman shouted obscenities at our driver, Patrick resorted to *ad hominem* attack: "You're blind as a bloody mole with those glasses. I'd like to see you do better."

"Fuck you and your imperialist country."

"Why don't we get out and see if we can help?" Patrick said.

Without anyone's help, the drivers quickly hooked a braided steel cable to the front of the first bus. Patrick directed fifty people to line up on either side of the cable. Another fifty people surrounded the bus. With Patrick shouting encouragement to members of the myriad nations who pushed, pulled, and kicked each bus in turn, none moved.

"Bloody hell," Patrick yelled. "We're all bloody stuck."

When all efforts to extricate any of the buses from the quagmire failed, travelers resumed their verbal assault on the drivers. Patrick continued his defense of the Chinese drivers, populace, and government. Two hours later, two young soldiers who came by in an army truck towed each bus back onto the People's Highway.

We stopped in the late afternoon at Wenquan, the world's highest town at 16,830 feet. Some of the passengers yelled "*Zou! Zou! Zou!*" (Go! Go! Go!). Wind howling through the valley gave a lonely, desolate air to the place. A dog chained to a shelter of corrugated tin barked at two Chinese children, who pelted it with rocks. The dog frothed at the mouth and lunged at the children, only to be jerked back by the chain, which seemed as if it would snap at any moment.

When a Chinese man emerged from a run-down cinderblock building and handed the driver an envelope of money, which the driver counted, he said that we had to pay fifteen yuan (three dollars) each to stay the night. "This is extortion!" Patrick said. "Hotels cost five yuan. We have daylight left. If we stay here, we will never make Lhasa tomorrow." I told Patrick that he could also die at this altitude. Patrick pleaded with the driver to continue to the next village. He became furious when the driver left the bus.

"*Zou! Zou! Zou!*" Patrick shouted. Other passengers joined in, tourists alongside Chinese immigrants, chanting, "*Zou! Zou! Zou!*" which reverberated inside the bus and drew in people from the other buses. "*Zou! Zou! Zou!*" until the sun slipped behind a hill and the temperature dropped below zero. Two Frenchmen pulled out sleeping bags inside the bus. The rest of us paid fifteen yuan each and were led into the hotel's dark rooms, where the bunk beds smelled of mildew.

Outside, near the icy chatter of the river, John and I talked about Robert Ford, the only Westerner living in eastern Tibet when the Chinese invaded. In 1949, Ford sent coded radio messages from Wenquan to monks in Lhasa. His last transmission on March 10, 1949, simply said: "The Chinese are here." Several months later, Ford was captured by the Chinese and accused of being a British spy. He spent the next five years of his life in jail.

John was a talking guidebook, and he shared with me his enthusiasm for the Yangtze River, tumbling out of the nearby glaciers to wind 3,430 miles through China, farther than any other river in the world except for those draining into the Nile and the Amazon. Tomorrow we would be in the Brahmaputra River drainage system, which emptied into the Ganges and flooded the plains from Calcutta to Bangladesh, and the Mekong River drainage system, which fanned out through Laos, Thailand, Cambodia, and Vietnam into the South China Sea.

The next morning three tall, stoic men waited by the bus. They wore long sheepskins and daggers tucked into rope belts. Red tassels braided into their hair and wrapped around their heads enabled John to identify them as Khampas, from eastern Tibet. By reputation Khampas were a hardy people who had waged the most determined armed struggle against the Chinese in the 1960s. John pointed out that Khampas continued their isolated attacks on army convoys even after 1972, when Nixon and Kissinger formally halted the CIA funding of the Tibetan resistance.

After everyone else had boarded, the driver let the Khampas sit in the last row. Altitude sickness, and being launched into the roof each time the bus hit a pothole, had proved too much for five of the Chinese immigrants, who had not gotten back on. The Khampas sang and laughed each time their heads hit the roof. This annoyed some of the other passengers, but I was in awe of these proud people. I also made sure to get off the bus every time they did, to make certain our packs did not disappear. By reputation, Khampas are also bandits.

Rock cairns with strings of faded prayer flags marked the Tanggula Shankou pass, the highest point in our trip. Two more people threw up. I heard Patrick moan as we crossed China's "official" border into the Tibetan Autonomous Region.

Each bend in the Lhasa Valley's patchwork of barley fields awaiting the harvest, each expanse of steel scree and magenta slope beneath an amphitheater of cliffs, each snowcapped mountain that tore at the indigo clouds seemed more magnificent than the last. The cramps from the two-day bus ride were forgotten as we approached the ancient city. Guidebooks appeared as passengers tried to decide which hotel they would try. As if by magic, thunder from the low-lying clouds accompanied our first glimpse of the Potala Palace rising majestically above the cinderblock buildings. Thunder rattled the bus windows and the pit of my stomach, thunder that, we learned later, turned out to be the Chinese Army using artillery to liberate the monsoon from the clouds.

CHAPTER TWO

COUNTERCLOCKWISE AROUND THE JOKHANG

C LIMBING ON TOP of the bus to reclaim our packs, I saw the Potala Palace enthroned in an amphitheater of mountains. The gold on the many-terraced roofs glistened against a sky marbled with thick cumulus clouds. My heart beat faster as I imagined exploring the palace, once the Dalai Lama's winter residence. The Potala surprised me, just as it would in the morning through the mist on the banks of the Kyichu River, above the maze of narrow, medieval streets, or in the afternoon light when seen while we were on day hikes into the mountains. The Potala was a beacon, a reminder of Tibet's grandeur before the Chinese invasion. From the top of the bus I could also see more Chinese people, with their green Mao hats, than Tibetans among the crowds in the street.

The ten-foot barred metal gate of the Kiri Hotel opened into a paved compound. An international assortment of soiled socks and underwear stretched across clotheslines on the second- and third-floor balconies. Iceland poppies and roses in bloom ringed the base of a restaurant centered in the courtyard. A stern Tibetan woman at the main desk made us pay in Foreign Exchange Currency, automatically doubling the price.

Another Tibetan woman, with ruddy cheeks and wearing tight blue jeans, ran screaming into the room holding a clear plastic bag that let out a steady stream of water. This ignited a chase into the courtyard. Exhausted travelers made caustic remarks.

"The toilet is disgusting," an American woman complained when she sat on a squeaky dormitory cot. "The quilts are filthy. Only *two* thermoses of hot water for *ten* people. I demand a double room." As the litany of hygienic atrocities perpetrated against her by the "filthy" Tibetans continued, we stowed our packs under our cots. The woman fit the stereotype that Americans are the most obnoxious travelers. I had to agree in this case. John and I went to the Jokhang Temple, a mecca for Buddhist pilgrims in the heart of the Barkhor, Lhasa's traditional Tibetan section.

There we joined the hundreds of pilgrims from all over Tibet who ritualistically circumambulate Lhasa's most revered temple. Men from Kham stood a foot taller than women from Amdo, in the northeast. Monks sitting cross-legged in maroon and yellow robes chanted scripture in low, grumbling tones, while Tibetan women accosted us with necklaces of red coral and pitted Nepalese turquoise. A bald man with fierce, inquisitive eyes and an enormous metal amulet slung around his neck stretched out, bare-chested, across stones strewn with excrement and worn smooth from centuries of such devotion.

Chinese police in khaki uniforms brushed past us. None of the pilgrims seemed to notice. Tourists sorted through the tables of red felt boots with yak leather soles, skeins of dyed wool, jade talismans, temple artifacts, cymbals, and wooden bowls for drinking butter tea. Everywhere children tugged at travelers' sleeves, asking "*Kuchi kuchi* (please, please), Dalai Lama photo?"

"You're walking the wrong way," a Western woman told us. It had already become obvious that we had been wading against the living stream of people walking clockwise around the temple. "The Chinese do it on purpose," she said. "Tourists do it out of ignorance." The woman, who introduced herself as Carolyn, wore a lavender *chuba*, the full-length Tibetan dress, pulled tight around the waist.

Now circuiting the Jokhang clockwise, we got to know each other quickly, as travelers often do. Carolyn had saved enough money teaching grade school in New York City to travel in Asia for six months. She had also grown up with a Tibetan brother; in the sixties her family had lived in India and adopted a Tibetan boy. Carolyn was staying with his family now.

"How about these?" John said, donning a pair of medieval-looking glacier goggles with bug-like insulated cups protruding from each eye.

"They're fantastic," Carolyn said.

"I'm going to get them," John said. "We'll need them in the mountains."

"Are you climbers?"

"Yes," we both said.

"We want to get as high as we can on Everest," John said.

"In sneakers," I interjected.

"Could I go with you?" Carolyn asked. John and I looked at each other, and then back at Carolyn. We were smitten. Grinning like schoolchildren, we followed Carolyn into a store where she had been bargaining daily for the past week to get a Tibetan rug.

"Sorry," John whispered and slapped me on the back. "She wants me, not you."

"*Tashi delek!*" (hello) a wrinkled old man said when he saw Carolyn. He smiled, revealing a gold-capped incisor.

"*Tashi delek!*" Carolyn replied and they resumed bargaining over a pile rug with a green dragon design. Carolyn joked with the old man, but he did not go down in price. "If only I could bargain like a Tibetan," Carolyn said, leading us back into the street.

"Are you fluent?" John asked.

"Not for someone with a Tibetan brother," Carolyn said. "You're welcome to have dinner with us tonight, but you'll have to be careful. The police watch all of the houses in the Barkhor. They don't like travelers talking to Tibetans."

"What harm can *talking* do?" John asked.

"If tourists see what's happening here," Carolyn said sarcastically, "they won't spend as much money."

Carolyn told us not to talk about things like this on the street. Instead, she started to teach us the Tibetan numbers. We repeated the numbers after her and then, armed with this new knowledge, went off to shop for dinner ingredients. Compared to the description of the market we'd read in the *Tibet Survival Guide*, printed in 1984, Lhasa's market overflowed with produce. In addition to the Tibetan staples—large burlap sacks of *tsampa* (roasted barley flour), fifty-kilo rounds of yak butter sewn into yak stomachs, and freshly butchered yak meat—the market had small mountains of fresh and dried apricots, blocks of tea, sacks of potatoes, rice, imported Hami melons, and an abundance of Chinese vegetables.

"Once you go yak, you never go back," John said to a man wearing a crumpled black felt top hat, who offered him a taste of creamy yak butter at the end of a knife. "It's sweet," John said, surprised not to be scrunching his face at the taste. This inaugurated our enjoyment of the market's sensual feast. We bought a half-kilo of yak butter, a loaf of round barley bread, oranges, a cabbage, string beans, and two Chinese vegetables we could not identify.

Carolyn stopped at a table of yak meat. Nearby, mongrels sat with their gaze fixed on the blood dripping onto the cobblestones from the pile of maroon flesh. The woman laughed at my repeating how much half a kilo of yak meat cost in Tibetan, and she laughed at John swatting flies off the meat.

"What's so funny?" I asked. The woman kept laughing.

"She says I'm lucky to have *two* good men," Carolyn said.

John saw NBC News anchor Tom Brokaw, wearing a safari shirt and mirrored glasses, walking against the flow of pilgrims circumambulating the Jokhang. "NBC is doing a six-part special on China," Carolyn said. "Maybe they'll title this episode 'Counterclockwise Around the Jokhang.'"

* * *

Carolyn's Tibetan brother's parents greeted us with the sort of affection Westerners reserve for long-lost relatives. Dikey, a large, barrel-shaped woman, seated us on a Tibetan pile rug covering a bench and disappeared into the kitchen to fire up the kerosene stove. Rinchen, her husband, appeared frail in comparison. He poured us cups of *chang* (barley beer), touched his own cup to his forehead, and drank the beer in one gulp, with more than a little dribbling onto his cheeks. Carolyn downed her cup. John and I followed. Thereafter Rinchen refilled our cups after each sip.

Rinchen also shared with us his enthusiasm for playing *Tok*. The object of *Tok*, it appeared, is to hopscotch all of your pieces in a clockwise direction around a leather pad and yell "*Tok!*" as loud as you can when you slam the dice cup on the pad. Rinchen hopscotched our cowrie shells, washers, and coins with amazing alacrity for a man who had drunk so much *chang.* I swiftly forgot that we had only a few words in common.

"*Tok!*" Rinchen exclaimed, and we all drank.

"Rinchen used to be rebellious," Carolyn said, "before he started drinking. I don't blame him. Two of his brothers were killed by the Chinese. One died in combat. One committed suicide in prison. Don't worry, he doesn't understand English." Carolyn raised her glass to Rinchen and took a sip. "I love them as my own family," Carolyn continued. "They don't have running water or electricity. None of the houses in the Barkhor do. The Tibetan section of town is a ghetto compared to the new apartment buildings for the Chinese immigrants."

Dikey brought in a tray heaped with five steaming plates of vegetables cooked with yak meat, then helped an uncooperative Rinchen stand and negotiate his way to the toilet on the roof. Moments later, Dikey returned with a fresh thermos of *pe cha* (butter tea). She made fun of my bloodshot eyes. Carolyn joined the laughter. A sudden, warning flash of stomach pain accompanied my first sip of butter tea.

"Do you know what the loudspeakers all around Lhasa are broadcasting day and night?" Carolyn asked. "They extol the merits of the Chinese 'liberation' of Tibet. They say that the Dalai Lama is trying to split the Motherland. The Chinese never refer to the Dalai Lama respectfully. This infuriates the Tibetans."

"*Dalai Lama, yakbudoo* (The Dalai Lama is good)," Rinchen said, slurping a full cup of *chang.*

"We could cut the speaker wires, like we did on the Chinese trains," I said.

"That's a great idea," Carolyn exclaimed. John gave me a dirty look.

Another knifing pain in my stomach made me bolt up to the roof toilet. Two filthy children on the next roof watched in wide-eyed fascination as I sprinted to the hole in the mud roof microseconds before a liquid stream initiated a new round of sphincter roulette, a game that would rile my intestines throughout Tibet. I was overwhelmed by the stench, and promptly lost the elation I had gained from having made it to the toilet in time.

Exhaling my first breath, I noticed that the children on the next roof were laughing at my plight. All of my experience traveling has not inured my stomach to the different foods I encounter on the road. I had no doubt been poisoned by some pathogenic strain of *E. coli* in the *chang*. Perhaps it was the dreaded *Entamoeba histolytica* in the water, which at this altitude could never be boiled long enough to kill the germs. It was too dark to see if I had passed any blood. Tibetan toilets, I was learning, can have a marked sobering effect.

A lone, primal howl came from the alley. The howl was joined by another, punctuated by frantic, high-pitched barking from a pack of Lhasa Apsos, Tibetan spaniels, and terriers that seemed to be fighting to the death. Dogs ruled the Barkhor at night. Alone and in packs, their individual and collective yelps ebbed and swelled in a canine chorus. The same frightening crescendos prevented us from sleeping much that night.

* * *

The next afternoon, John, Carolyn, and I drank cold Chinese beer in the hot sun on the Kiri restaurant's roof-garden while we listened to Patrick and Dawa argue. Dawa was a charismatic, angry young Tibetan man we'd met who had engaged us in conversation immediately. "Do you know why they won't sell tickets to Nagchu?" Dawa asked.

"I waited in the line for two bloody hours," Patrick complained. "Then the man had the audacity to tell me that I could not buy a ticket. There was an outbreak of the plague in Nagchu. The plague! Tibet is still in the middle ages."

Dawa smiled sardonically and said, "Plague is a standard lie when the Chinese don't want foreigners to see things. Like troop movements, or shipments of nuclear weapons. Did you know that Helmut Kohl is in Beijing selling West Germany's nuclear waste to China? Do you know where they want to dump it? In either the Gobi Desert or Northern Tibet."

"Where did you read that?" Patrick challenged.

"In the *New York Times* before coming here," Dawa said. "As a Tibetan, I can tell you that Tibetans don't want nuclear waste dumped anywhere in Tibet. You know what really angers me?" Dawa continued uninterrupted. "I can't be understood speaking Tibetan in Lhasa's stores. In the government supermarket today, the 'Friendship Store,' the clerk spoke to me in Chinese. 'Speak Tibetan,' I told her, 'you're in

Tibet.' She didn't understand a word I said. It's the same at the post office, the bank, even the schools! All higher education in Tibet is in Chinese."

Dawa told us that he himself had grown up in exile. This was his first trip to Tibet and he had just spent a month visiting his parents' home in Kham. Dawa had become depressed seeing how few adult men there were in eastern Tibet. Every family he met had lost someone who had died either as a result of fighting the Chinese or after a harsh imprisonment.

"If it were not for the Chinese," Patrick said. "Tibet would remain underdeveloped for centuries."

Dawa glared at Patrick. "Before the Chinese came to Tibet we had a road from Lhasa to Nepal. And a telegraph. You should know that! The British built the telegraph. Since the Chinese invaded we are *less* developed. The truckloads of Tibet's forests and minerals traveling east into China—copper, uranium, oil, lead—*that* is China's development of Tibet. Much of China's mineral wealth has recently been discovered on the Tibetan Plateau. Do you know where it's going? To China! The Chinese are developing Tibet for themselves, not for the Tibetans."

Fists clenched, Dawa leaned closer to Patrick. John tried to ease the tension by pointing out that Heinrich Harrer and Peter Aufschnaiter had helped the Tibetans build a dam and small hydroelectric plant before the Chinese invaded.

"I take this personally," Dawa said. "I'm Tibetan. There are only six million of us left. The Chinese have already killed over one million Tibetans."

"An outrageous statistic," Patrick said.

"The British Parliament accepts these statistics," Dawa said.

"This conversation needs more Chinese beer," Patrick said and stood up.

"Let's go to the Lhasa Hotel," Dawa said. "It's the only place in town you can get whiskey."

"That's the first sensible thing you've said all afternoon," Patrick replied.

* * *

We cycled almost eight miles through the rain on rented one-speed bicycles. When we arrived at the Lhasa Hotel gate, a Chinese guard stepped in front of Dawa's bicycle and held out his hand. "Stop. Tibetans not allowed."

"What do you mean?" Dawa shouted.

"Tibetans not allowed," the guard yelled. Dawa stepped closer to the guard and said that he had no right to discriminate against Tibetans. The guard yelled back, "Tibetans not allowed." Dawa was a foot taller and eighty pounds heavier than his Chinese adversary. He could have knocked the guard out with one punch. Instead, Dawa argued that it was the Chinese military that should not be allowed in Tibet. Dawa pushed the guard to his limit before he produced his passport. Seeing that Dawa was a Nepalese national, not a Tibetan, the guard stepped aside and let him pass.

Dawa led us defiantly into the Lhasa Hotel foyer and up its wide swing of stairs. Our sneakers made squashing sounds with each step and rain dripped off our unkempt garb. As soon as we sank into the pink, marshmallow-like couches next to a string quartet, Dawa began a diatribe against the hotel itself, Holiday Inn's joint venture with the Chinese government. According to Dawa, the Lhasa Hotel catered to rich tourists and businessmen investing in the Chinese occupation of Tibet. Dawa despised the rooms that had oxygen to combat acute mountain sickness at a mere 12,000 feet; the restaurants that served sterilized yak burgers; and the glitzy shops that sold stolen temple artifacts. However, Dawa also liked to smoke Marlboro cigarettes and drink Johnnie Walker Black in the hotel lounge.

"I was born in exile," Dawa said. "This is my first trip to my country and here I'm treated like a second-class citizen. The Chinese are the most racist people on earth. Not only to Tibetans. They hate all minorities. Their word for foreigner means devil."

"The United States is no stranger to racism," John told him. "I grew up in Boston. After law school, I was the first white person to work in this all-black law firm in Mississippi. I couldn't believe how blatant the local officials were. At a poll watch, I caught officials throwing out just enough of the black votes to have the white candidate win."

"The biggest problem Tibet faces now is Chinese colonization," Dawa continued. "It's a deliberate government policy that has already smothered China's other minority areas. In Manchuria, there are thirty-five times more Chinese than Manchurians. In Mongolia, it's nine to one. Right now there are one million more Chinese in Tibet than Tibetans."

"More outrageous statistics," Patrick said.

"You can't deny there are more Chinese in Lhasa than Tibetans," Carolyn said.

"That may be true of the larger cities," Patrick said. "What about the large tracts of land outside of the cities?"

"The new buildings going up?" Dawa continued. "They're all for Han immigrants. Soon there will be ten times as many Chinese as Tibetans in Tibet. I'm talking about the *real* Tibet, before the Chinese gave two-thirds of the country to Western China. What China calls 'The Tibet Autonomous Region' is a joke."

Just then Tom Brokaw entered with an entourage and sat at an adjacent couch. Dawa stood up and engaged Brokaw in candid conversation for twenty minutes. We all said amongst ourselves that we wished we had the courage to get up and talk to Tom Brokaw. No one did. What would we say to him? That he had walked the wrong way around the Jokhang?

*　*　*

The next evening Dawa invited Carolyn, John, and me to his relatives' house. Dawa's aunt looked 108 years old; she was actually fifty-eight. She spoke Tibetan with Carolyn and filled and refilled our cups with *chang*. Dawa engaged us in conversation with his relatives by translating questions that he initiated.

Dawa's brother Tenzin showed us a fox fur hat that Dawa had given him, and a postcard of the Dalai Lama standing by the banks of the Kyichu river with the Potala Palace in the background. John pointed out that the picture had been retouched, because the Dalai Lama had escaped Tibet as an eighteen-year-old boy in 1959 and had not returned since. Dawa retorted that the postcard represented a vision of His Holiness's return to Lhasa.

Tsering, Dawa's youngest cousin, had lines of indecision marked in his face. He had excelled in the two primary subjects taught in high school, Chinese and mathematics. Because Tibetans in the top 5 percent of their class were sent to China to continue their higher education, Tsering was to be sent to a university in mainland China. He did not want to go; he had heard that the Chinese treated the Tibetans there like savages. Tsering wanted to study Tibetan, but this was impossible after grade school.

Dawa skipped his uncle in the introductions. When I asked what his uncle did, Dawa replied dismissively, "He drinks *chang*."

"*Chang yakbudoo*," the bleary-eyed uncle said, and gave an impromptu lesson on making first *chang*, which we were drinking. After boiling barley and letting it cool to room temperature, he mixed in yeast and let it stand for ten days. Cold water poured over the barley stood for three more days. The clear liquid poured off was first *chang*. Second *chang* was made from a second batch of water, and was not as strong.

The homemade barley beer had a remarkable clarity and effervescence. It was making me tipsy. Seeing Carolyn having an animated conversation with Dawa's aunt made me want to learn Tibetan.

On our way out, Dawa said, "Tomorrow I'll take you to see a monk who spent twenty years in prison."

* * *

The next morning, Patrick looked longingly at our collection of supplies for the mountains: pleated wool pants with cotton liners that we had tailored for us on the street; wool sweaters; and bags of dried apricots, roasted barley, peanuts, Chinese hard candies, fruit rolls, Lucky chocolate bars, and 721 Bars. These last were high-energy People's Liberation Army rations. We had an assortment manufactured from 1984 to 1987. "Gentlemen," Patrick announced with his usual flair. "If you wouldn't mind the company of a domesticated old goat such as myself, I would like to accompany you as far as I can to Everest before I have to return for fall semester."

"We'd love to have you," John said.

"By the way," Patrick said. "Where are your crampons and ropes?"

"We're going to try to get as high as we can without climbing gear," John said.

"Carolyn outfitted us with our most precious items," I said. "Wool socks for John, and a silk top for me."

"What exactly is it you and Carolyn have been doing?" John said. "Details!" Patrick exclaimed, his eyes narrowing. I evaded their inquiries.

Layers are the best way to keep warm in the mountains. We had found everything we needed in Lhasa: blue nylon running pants with white stripes down the sides from the Chinese vendors on the sidewalk, and thick, cotton turtlenecks and down coats from the Friendship Store. Dawa would have disapproved of our buying anything Chinese, but at least the sleeves on the turtlenecks and coats were long enough for our arms.

"What's this?" Patrick asked when he discovered eleven cans with a picture of a pig on the label.

"The Chinese equivalent of Spam," John said. "I used to love Spam when I was a kid. Sliced thin, fried until the edges are crispy."

"I don't see any stove," Patrick said.

"We decided against bringing a stove," John said. "Or a tent, for that matter. We want to experience the mountains directly."

"What are we going to cook on?"

"A tin can," John said.

"I'm not even going to ask what type of fuel you plan on using," Patrick said, waiting for an answer.

"Yak dung," John said matter-of-factly. "It's supposed to impart a tangy flavor to the food."

* * *

Later that day, Dawa glanced over his shoulder and took an unexpected left into the main street and the anonymity of crowds. "We're being followed," he said.

"I don't see anyone," John said.

"On the sidewalk behind us," Dawa whispered. "One Tibetan. One Chinese." Dawa had warned us that we could not be seen visiting the underground monk, who spent from 1959 to 1980 in Chinese prisons. If we were caught talking with the monk, the police could send him back to prison.

An hour later, our separate circuitous routes finally brought us together in front of an easy-to-miss temple. Dawa talked to an acolyte in maroon and yellow robes who escorted us into a quiet room. A hippopotamus-like monster with bulging eyes and fangs was carved over the door jamb. I found myself feeling at ease; the closed wooden shutters kept the room dark, and a young acolyte refilled our cups of butter tea while we waited for the older monk.

The acolyte jumped to his feet when the elderly monk stepped into the room. The monk had the brown leathery skin of someone who had spent most of his life outside, but his forehead and face were remarkably free of wrinkles. He greeted each of us and motioned for Dawa to sit next to him on the bench. Dawa and the monk talked and held hands. After several minutes, Dawa translated that the monk welcomed us to the monastery. Dawa referred to the monk as "*Geshe-la*," an honorific title denoting a monk who had passed the examinations for a doctorate of theology.

Large scars were evident on the monk's chest as he leaned toward us expectantly. I pointed to the scars and he showed us a burned mark on his leg, a prominent bulge on his wrist from a poorly set bone, and scars around his ankles and wrists from being shackled.

"Because Tibetans were political prisoners," Dawa translated for us, "they were beaten regularly. No one was allowed to talk to the person next to them. The prisoners were made to carry loads of rocks and dirt from sunup to sundown, seven days a week. Of the 360 Tibetans in one prison, only six survived. At first *Geshe-la* ate anything to supplement a starvation diet of *tsampa* and water: bits of leather, worms in his feces, putrid flesh picked from a carcass. With so many people dying from consumption, he learned about edible plants from a Tibetan doctor who was also a prisoner."

Asked how he had survived the beatings and torture, the old monk said that he found a way to see the good side of his captors, who were in a difficult position. He also practiced *thumo* (heat yoga) to aid his powers of digestion. In the evenings, when the prisoners had to memorize Mao's Little Red Book, he secretly meditated to bring more heat to his stomach.

The worst part of prison was not the physical torture or seeing his friends die all around him; it was the way the Chinese tried to change how he thought. After working all day, he had to attend "struggle sessions" until midnight, seven nights a week. Political prisoners were beaten regularly during struggle sessions if they did not recite the proper creed of the Motherland: Tibet is part of China; Tibet has always been part of China; the Dalai Lama is an enemy of the Motherland. "*Geshe-la* says that no matter what the Chinese did to him, he never said anything bad about the Dalai Lama," Dawa told us.

John asked if monks were still in prison. Without asking the monk, Dawa stated that Lhasa had hundreds of political prisoners. This monk had been gathering a secret list of names of Tibetans serving political sentences.

"How can you tell if a prisoner is political and not a common criminal?" John asked.

"Political prisoners get prolonged sentences for crimes like gambling, or being drunk. If you come back before you leave Lhasa, *Geshe-la* will give you a list of prisoners' names to take to the Tibetan government in exile."

The monk unfolded his hands from his lap and talked for some time before Dawa translated that all this was in the past. These days *Geshe-la* was more concerned about the lack of religious freedom in Tibet. Monks had to be approved by a Chinese Committee on Religious Affairs. The committee only appointed enough monks to take care of the tourists. The Potala Palace, which had more than a thousand rooms, was assigned only thirteen monks. Money donated by pilgrims and tourists didn't go to the monks; it was deposited in an account in the Bank of China. *Geshe-la* received a salary of sixty yuan a month (twelve U.S. dollars). Acolytes were paid twenty yuan, barely enough to live on.

When John asked about the restorations that had taken place, Dawa said that only six of Tibet's 6,000 monasteries had been restored, for tourism purposes. The Chinese had not given this particular monastery enough money even to build a washroom. The restoration that we had witnessed was all done by Tibetan volunteers. When that was finished, the Chinese government would take full credit.

I was surprised by the lack of animosity in the monk's eyes when he said that the young monks were initiates, not monks. Under the present conditions they would never be able to prepare for the *Geshe*. With their duties in the fields and taking care of the tourists, the older monks were not able to teach the young monks. They felt this was the greatest crime committed against them. It took twenty years of memorization to prepare for the *Geshe*, and teaching was considered subversive. Although some of the older monks taught secretly at night, they had to be careful. Every monastery had monks who reported to the police.

There was also the problem of books. The few books that tourists saw in monasteries were decorations. The majority of Tibetan texts had been stolen or destroyed. Tibetan monasteries had always been centers of culture and learning, more closely resembling universities than cathedrals. Some monasteries had hundreds of buildings, including medical schools, libraries, painting studios, and printing presses. "Soon all the old *Geshes* will be dead," Dawa said. "There will be no one left to teach the young monks. The old knowledge will vanish. *Geshe-la* considers himself a custodian for the tourists. These are his exact words. He is a 'custodian for the tourists.'"

"There must be something positive since the Chinese officially eased up in 1980?" I asked.

Dawa looked annoyed but translated my question. The monk laughed. "Things are getting a little better," Dawa said. "Until a few years ago saying "*Tashi delek*" was punishable by death. This is why some of the older Tibetans do not respond when you greet them."

"There must be something else?"

The monk thought for a moment before answering. "There is one thing," Dawa translated. "The higher-up Chinese officials are getting nervous. They want to go back to China while they are still young enough to get another job and retire in peace."

*   *   *

A week later Carolyn and I went to the *Mendzekhang*, Lhasa's College of Tibetan Medicine and hospital. After being paid the equivalent of eight cents, a third-year medical student named Yoden offered to give us a tour. "I am not English speaking well," she told us, taking two stairs at a time. Carolyn said that she was not "Tibetan speaking" well either, and complimented Yoden on her English. I asked Yoden what it was like being a Tibetan medical student, hoping this would slow her down. It did not.

"We are woken at 4:00 in the morning to memorize while the mind is fresh," Yoden said. "The four root texts alone are 1,140 pages in length. At seven our instructors quiz us on what we have learned, and we have our first cup of butter tea. Then all students gather in the assembly hall for prayers." Before we had even reached the top of the stairs, I learned that Western and Tibetan medicine had at least one thing in common: long hours of study and memorization.

Yoden bowed before entering the library and asked us to remove our shoes and put on sandals. Except for a few Tibetan manuscripts—unbound stacks of printed parchment wrapped in yellow silk—the bookshelves were empty, the library bare. "Most of our medical texts were destroyed during the Cultural Revolution," Yoden said. "Others were claimed as Chinese medicine. It is ironic. Now we are getting some of our original texts back from China, but we have to translate them from Chinese back into Tibetan."

I asked how much room and board cost for one year. Yoden said this was very expensive: "One hundred U.S. dollars. The tradition in Tibetan medicine is to treat the patient for free. We only charge a fee for the price of the medicine. We have 150 students and doctors at the *Mendzekhang*. Three hundred beds. In a normal day, we see 600 to 800 patients, including clinics and house calls." I told Yoden that most Western doctors did not do house calls anymore, and asked if many Tibetans went to the Chinese hospitals.

"The Chinese divide Tibetans into six categories according to their economic and political status," Yoden explained. "The few Tibetans who have jobs with the Chinese government receive socialized medicine. Most Tibetans are poor village people. They cannot afford to pay for Western medicine at the Chinese hospitals."

As with the elderly monk we had met, Yoden's tone and demeanor bore no ill will toward the Chinese. She was merely telling us what had happened. I opened a recently published encyclopedia of Tibetan medicine to a medical *thanka* (painting) that depicted the metamorphosis of the human embryo from primordial to amphibian to mammalian form. "This medical *thanka* describes the weekly development of the fetus," Yoden explained, "including the nature of its consciousness. There are techniques for determining a child's sex before birth, medicines to accelerate labor, reduce pain, and guard against post-partum infection. But all of the writing is in Chinese. Only the captions are in Tibetan."

I asked how much the book cost. "I am afraid this book is too expensive. More than a hundred yuan." I bought one to mail home and Yoden said, "You are lucky to come from a rich country."

After putting our shoes on, Carolyn and I found an unlocked door and snuck onto the roof, where we saw a spectacular view of kites and prayer flags flying over the sea of Tibetan rooftops. My heart raced as we looked out over the Barkhor Square. At the far end, thick clouds of juniper obscured the Tibetans prostrating in front of the Jokhang. Carolyn and I held hands. Yoden's cheeks flushed crimson as she struggled with what she wanted to ask next.

"How do Western women prevent babies?" she finally got out. Carolyn mentioned the diaphragm, the birth control pill, the IUD, and the condom. She left it to me to explain how they worked. Yoden was full of questions, like, "What effect does the birth control pill have on the fetal consciousness if a baby is formed?"

* * *

At Drepung Monastery, once the world's largest cloister with 10,000 monks, the caves in the surrounding limestone cliffs bore mute witness to the handful of reconstructed buildings. Ceilingless fragments of still-standing walls crumbled into rubble. In the ruins there was beauty: a Buddha's red robes faded to pink on a piece of wall; Iceland poppies were tucked next to a foundation; a Tibetan snow finch sang from a scrub pine. Although I savored the ruins' magnificence, I could not escape the realization that the destruction of Tibet's monasteries translated into the loss of a monumental portion of Tibetan religious and medical texts, literature, philosophy, art, and history.

Confronted by so much destruction in one monastery made me feel suddenly afraid. What if Yoden had exaggerated about Tibetans receiving inferior health care compared to the Chinese immigrants? What if Dawa had lied about his relatives being killed by Chinese soldiers? What if he made up everything he had said about Tibetans not learning their own language and the lack of religious freedom? Perhaps the Tibetans had better health care now than before the Chinese came. In my zeal to see the "real" Tibet, I had believed everything Tibetans had told us during our first week in Lhasa; I was so moved that I had suspended my own healthy skepticism, and now doubts were cropping up to haunt me.

I was most uncertain about Yoden. She spoke in the calm, detached manner I associated with Western doctors discussing a patient's illness with their peers; yet I did not even know what kind of medicine she practiced. What if her gentleness were a facade for an inner cruelty? I discussed this with John while walking past piles of *mani* stones with the words *Om Mani Padmi Om* (Praise to the Jewel in the Heart of the Lotus), the mantra of Avalokiteshvara, Tibet's bodhisattva of compassion, carved into them in Tibetan script. I realized that I had become afraid of trusting my perceptions. In my heart I believed Dawa, the underground monk, and Yoden. Their stories were consistent; to imagine that they were lying was to assume a conspiracy of impossible proportions. If I could not trust my perceptions then my life, and this trip, would be meaningless.

We came upon an aged monk on a path that wound through a boulder field. A pack of dogs followed him in anticipation of being tossed some of the pre-rolled balls of *tsampa* mixed with yak butter tea tucked in his robes. He stopped often to touch a *mani* stone and pray, to finger the rosary of beads between his thumb and forefinger, to toss a *tsampa* ball to each dog he came upon, and seconds to the faithful who followed along with him. A light rain sent the monk and the dogs along a well-worn shortcut to the monastery. John explained to me that Tibetans believed dogs to be reincarnated monks who had erred in their previous lives. That explained why we saw so many of them everywhere we went in and around Lhasa.

A small boy appeared, extending an elongated metal pail into a three-foot waterfall that sluiced off a rock. "*Tashi delek!*" he greeted us. Remarkably, the boy did not ask us for a Dalai Lama picture. He pointed to a boulder with a larger-than-life-sized Avalokiteshvara painted on the rock, two other boulders with freshly painted Buddhas, and a fourth boulder lying upside down farther down the hill. "*Yakbumindoo* (bad)," the boy said and extended index fingers from clenched fists. He mimed soldiers with guns herding monks from the monastery to the boulders.

Without warning the boy shook his hands violently and yelled, "Tatatata."

John gave the boy a picture of the Dalai Lama. The boy smiled widely, touched the picture to his head, then tucked it into a dusty fold in his robe. With the aid of a tumpline, the boy shouldered the pail and disappeared quickly down the path. I was left wondering if he had been pantomiming a rendition of monks being executed, and if this boy were old enough to have seen such violence through his own eyes. I was left pondering how vividly the horrors of war are imprinted on the minds of children.

* * *

In the style befitting overland travelers who expect to be afflicted with diarrhea for the next month, we descended on the Lhasa Hotel's Sunday buffet to indulge in helpings of beef and lamb curries, vegetables sauteed with yogurt and ginger, rice pudding, and cakes. Patrick toasted Mallory and Irving, two British climbers who disappeared attempting the Tibetan side of Everest in 1924.

"Did you know that Irving had no climbing skills whatsoever?" John said. "Mallory dragged him up Everest to bugger him at 28,000 feet."

"How dare you defile one of mountaineering's greats with your prurient slander," Patrick said.

Carolyn did not go to the Lhasa Hotel with us. She had decided to stay in Lhasa until her Tibetan brother returned from Kham later that month. We had not even left and I already missed her. We had just begun drinking cinnamon tea in Moslem restaurants and taking walks together late at night.

A balding, middle-aged Frenchman with unwashed, shoulder-length hair brought a plate heaped with food to our table. "I have not eaten in four days," he said, and did not utter another word until he had licked every grain of rice from his plate. "I hiked from Ganden to Samye. After the first pass, it snowed for thirty-six hours. I had only one bread, one *saucisson*, and one chocolate. For two nights I was too wet and cold to sleep. Many times I became afraid for my life. Once I slipped on ice next to a river. I had only sneakers. I almost lost my toes to frostbite."

"Didn't you realize what you were doing?" Patrick exclaimed. "You could die going unprepared into the mountains."

John and I smiled at each other. The Frenchman continued: "I did the same hike last year. The storm was a fluke. You will not understand until you go into the mountains with just enough clothes and food to survive. It is a religious experience."

CHAPTER THREE

ON PILGRIMAGE

T HE SMELL OF hashish mingled with the smell of the drenched travelers who had waited in the rain for two hours at 4:00 in the morning for the bus that would take us to Gyantse, the first city in the direction of Everest. I was crammed in the back of the bus between a blond-haired German man wearing red felt Tibetan boots with thick yak soles, and a PLA soldier in uniform. The German passed a pipe of hashish past the soldier, who did not notice, to Patrick.

"I have never tried hashish," Patrick said excitedly. "What will it do?"

"It makes the mountains come alive," the German assured him. After smoking it, Patrick stared out the window at barley fields lush with the monsoon's promise of bumper crops against barren slopes of red clay.

"There's a dragon in the clouds," Patrick said. "Do you see it?"

The German saw the dragon. I did not, more out of principle than from not really seeing it. I wanted to lose myself in the moment. Watching air condense out of flared yak nostrils was in itself completely satisfying, as were the subtle hues of vermilion shimmering on eons of sedimentary rock, and impossibly blue Lake Yamdrok Tso.

From the fifteenth to the nineteenth centuries, Gyantse exported caravans of yak and sheep wool to China and Nepal. Gyantse's pre-eminence as a trading center ended in 1904, when Younghusband led a British military expedition into Gyantse in order to force the Tibetans into a trade agreement. The damage done by Younghusband, however, was negligible compared to that done more recently by Chinese artillery. Now the fort on top of the ridge that looked out over the town lay in ruins, and only three of the Palkhor Monastery's buildings had been reconstructed. When the bus driver would go no farther than the Chinese hotel on the outskirts of town, we trudged through sneaker-stealing mud past a military compound of one-story barracks surrounded by barbed wire.

"If you want to know the truth about Younghusband," Patrick said, "he was sent here to see if the Russians had invaded."

"Bullshit," I said, and prepared for battle. "The Brits just used the Russian threat as an excuse to have wool socks made for their navy."

"I read Younghusband's account of the expedition," John said. "After killing over 600 Tibetans, the British gave medical assistance to the wounded. This dumbfounded the monks. The Tibetan generals wanted to surrender but the local monks wouldn't let them! They ordered the generals to fight. The monks got creamed."

"What does that tell you about the peace-loving Tibetans?" Patrick asked. "They were ruthless."

"More ruthless than Younghusband?" John asked. "Younghusband recorded the deaths of eighty coolies in the fighting under the heading 'animal casualties.'"

"*Kuchi kuchi*, Dalai Lama photo," we heard from a swarm of bare-foot urchins, who tugged on our shirt-tails with hands covered with layers of filth and excrescence. "*Kuchi kuchi*, Dalai Lama photo," we heard, as we squished through mud furrowed by wagon wheels. "*Kuchi kuchi*," as men whose clothes blended with the mud stared at us. "*Kuchi kuchi*," beginning to annoy me as I watched a woman pick nits from another woman's head. I felt like an astronaut in the midst of a Tibetan western.

An audible rumbling preceded the sight of Patrick dropping his spotless red Karrimor pack in the mud and running into an alley to drop his pants. Cheers heralded Patrick's return. Blushing and bowlegged and clutching his stomach, Patrick said, "I'm bloody melting. Doc, what do you have for the shits?" I suggested that Patrick stick to a diet of boiled rice, yogurt, and black tea, and abstain from beer for a few days. "What kind of medicine is that?" Patrick replied, resuming a brisk pace. "I'll just have to bloody well melt, then."

* * *

That evening John climbed up a rock shoulder to the base of the fort. Climbing, he reasoned, would be safer than encountering the dogs on the streets at night. Patrick and I tried to follow. "I'm going back for a torch," Patrick said below me.

"You'll be killed by the dogs," I said.

"The hell with the dogs," Patrick said. "I'm going—" A sudden visceral growl behind Patrick made both of us scream, and I heard John laughing above us. "You're a real comic," Patrick said. "I almost soiled myself."

"Hurry up," John said. "There's a pack of mongrels behind you."

"Like hell there is," Patrick said, flicking his lighter, only to illuminate six pairs of eyes staring back at him. Patrick yelled and scampered up the slab until he reached the base of the fort, where he could sit on the tourist path. Patrick eyed John suspiciously and inspected the fifteen-foot-high stone wall rising above them. Without any jokes about rotten mortar or landing if he fell, John made three swift moves up the wall and disappeared over the top.

"Come back!" Patrick yelled. No answer came from the other side of the wall. I was scared too, not for John, but for myself. John had already done the crux; I had to follow. "You're both crazy," Patrick yelled, as I tried to grab a handhold and pulled a loose piece of slate from the wall.

"Rock," I yelled down. Luckily, none of my other handholds broke off. I made it over the top and saw John up ahead, climbing a moonlit ribbon of quartz to the shadowy fortress. When I caught up with him, I was glad to see that he was out of breath, too. "We're crazy," I said.

"Better for it," John said.

As is always the case, downclimbing triggered more adrenaline than our climb up. When we made it back to Patrick, he was ecstatic to see us alive, and later bought us several rounds of beers to celebrate our safe return at the Tibetan hotel.

We returned the next afternoon to explore the devastated fort's stooped hallways and courtyards, discovering that many of its carved wooden beams and frescoes were still in excellent condition. The top of the hill offered a depressing view of the Palkhor Monastery. An outer wall and three reconstructed buildings were all that remained. The famous "temple of a thousand images" had been blown into smithereens.

On the way down the hill, a small window let us enter a locked room of the fort containing five well-preserved Tantric *mandalas*. We studied these ancient symbols of the universe for hours. Each had two central figures depicted in graphic sexual union, ensheathed in layers of eternal flames.

* * *

At 6:00 the next morning we returned to the Palkhor. Three generations of monks chanted sutras in the central court, which was festooned with numerous *thankas*. I felt myself immersing in the experience. The rumbling of the baritones resonated deep inside my skull. The rise and fall of the young tenors lapped like waves on the shores of my subconscious. I felt weightless among the multicolored silk banners, and gradually began to feel my mind's eye rise above the floor. This phenomenon had happened to me many times as a child lying in bed. It had always seemed frightening at first, seeing the room get smaller and fearing to venture out too far in case I could not return.

Suddenly I was transported back to my first trip to India in 1979. Determined to come to terms with my strict Catholic upbringing, I had gone alone into the mountains with the Bible, the Koran, the *Bhagavad Gita*, the *Upanishads*, Lao Tzu, and the *I Ching*. As fortune would have it, I came upon an elderly, bearded man on a pilgrimage to Amarnath Cave. The man wore only sandals and a sheet. He carried a three-pronged staff of Shiva and blessed pilgrims who put coins into his hand. I accompanied him across a fleeting glacier, long enough to see him drop the coins for others to find. We could not communicate with words, but we picked wild flowers before approaching the cave. Reading the religious texts and meeting this pilgrim helped me see that the world's great religions all share core doctrines of love, and fascinations with ritual.

A group of tourists walked counterclockwise around the inside of the monastery. They talked loudly and took pictures of the fearful deities on the wall, the vulture hanging upside down from the roof, the monks slurping their butter tea and blowing their noses in their sleeves. The monks did not seem to mind when the tourists pointed at them. But when a German man came in and began doing prostrations next to the initiates, I felt self-conscious and left.

* * *

In the infinite wisdom of the China Travel Service, our getting off the bus at Gyantse meant that we could not get back on the same bus at a later date. Patrick asked Chinese truck drivers for a ride to Shigatse when they stopped at one of the town's matchbox restaurants. After two hours of rejections, and no luck trying to hitchhike, John sat down to read Gu Hua's *A Small Town Called Hibiscus*. Finally, a Tibetan driver skidded to a halt next to us. "Shigatse?" John asked. The driver nodded and said, "*Gomo nga*" (ten yuan, two U.S. dollars). We paid the driver ten yuan each, and the dozen other Tibetans in the back of the open truck helped pull us and our packs aboard. Turquoise nuggets and over-sized red coral beads dangled from the men's earlobes.

"I'm not paying in advance," a British man who'd appeared beside us said, and looked to me for support. "What if he doesn't take us to Shigatse? What if his truck breaks down?" The driver started the engine. When the Brit saw that the truck was leaving without him, he threw a ten yuan note into the cab and climbed in the back with us and the grinning Tibetans. Patrick opened a bottle of Chinese brandy and yelled in pure *satori*, and all of the Tibetans cheered when he passed the bottle.

Knowing that there were no military checkpoints between Gyantse and Shigatse gave us the same surge of freedom I associated with hopping a freight train. The landscape and the altitude and the brandy were intoxicating. Great curtains of light swept across the harvested fields. The Tibetans sang. The obnoxious Brit turned out to be a medical student, and he shared his flat bread with us. With a second bottle of brandy came more singing and political discussions about who was more of an imperialist, Ronald Reagan or Margaret Thatcher.

* * *

In 1447, the Fifth Dalai Lama is credited with having built Shigatse's Tashilhunpo Monastery, the historical seat of the Panchen Lama, Tibetan Buddhism's second highest lama under the Dalai Lama. The last Panchen Lama spent ten years in Chinese prisons during the Cultural Revolution before he was forced to reside in Beijing. Foreigners often accused the Panchen Lama of being a puppet of the Chinese. Although the Chinese wrote and announced his public declarations, which counseled Tibetans to denounce the Dalai Lama and accept the Motherland, the Panchen Lama also managed to give many pro-independence statements. His most recent and most vociferous appeal for Tibetan independence came two weeks before he died in January of 1989 on a visit to the Tashilhunpo Monastery. The Chinese press said that the Panchen Lama had died of a heart attack. To verify this the government sent a plane-load of cardiologists from Beijing to Shigatse. It struck me as excessive to send so many cardiologists to examine the Panchen Lama after his death.

Tucked into the monastery's complex of narrow alleys and prayer halls were marvelous gilded roofs, monks engaged in debate, a printing press, and enormous copper cauldrons of butter tea stirred with six-foot ladles. One might even glimpse monks blowing on conch shells or long brass trumpets. From all outward appearances, the Chinese had lavished money on the Tashilhunpo's reconstruction. The crescent moon and sun, ancient symbols of universal consciousness, still topped each *stupa* (shrine). Banners of colored silk and fantastic *thankas* adorned the main halls. Tibetan pilgrims offered *tsampa*, money, and strands of hair beneath a picture of the Dalai Lama, and spooned yak butter from greasy skins into the monastery's butter lamps.

But the golden corners of the roofs turned up in the Chinese style, instead of the traditional rectangular Tibetan lines. The printed books were censored. The bulk of the monks' duties lay in the fields, and tourists were ushered in and out of the monastery with rude efficiency.

* * *

Patrick organized a farewell party in his own honor at the Tibetan hotel in Shigatse. He had extended his sightseeing as far as he could if he was still to make it back to Yunnan for the start of his second year teaching "the Queen's English" to Chinese university students. The party made for a fitting end and beginning. On the first cloudless night we had seen in three weeks of rain, we played Chinese checkers and drank warm beer and brandy. This made Patrick long to continue with us into the mountains. "You bloody wankers better write," Patrick said. "I've never had as much fun as hitchhiking in the back of that truck."

"Come to Sakya Monastery with us," John said. "Sakya is the seat of the Red Hats. The monks there were allowed to marry and drink alcohol. We'll become monks!"

John and Patrick argued for the last time. They started somewhere in the thirteenth century with Kublai Khan's Mongolian empire. Patrick said the Han Chinese were listed as the lowest racial hierarchy, following Mongols, Turks, and Manchus. John said that Kublai Khan had adopted Tibetan Buddhism as Mongolia's state religion, and that therefore the Tibetans conquered the Mongolians, not the other way around.

"I don't know about religion," Patrick said, "but I have a lot of respect for the Chinese after living in Yunnan. The Chinese are a wonderful people."

I would miss Patrick's unfailing respect for everything Chinese. He provided a worthwhile counter-balance to our pro-Tibetan sentiments. In the West we are raised to believe that the solution to two opposing views usually lies somewhere in the middle. However, in the case of Tibet, we were beginning to believe the truth was closer to the Tibetan view. John and Patrick continued playing checkers under the stars while I began to nod off. Before I fell asleep, I heard Patrick argue that China's development of Tibet would eventually benefit the Tibetans: "It's the trickle-down theory. You should know about that with Ronald Reagan as your president."

* * *

According to travelers we met who had been trying to hitchhike out of Shigatse for a week, a pilgrim truck was to leave for Sakya from the Tibetan truck stop across from the Tashilhunpo's main gate at 6:30 the next morning. We walked quickly down the wide, dark boulevard through the sprawl of three-story cinderblock buildings that housed Shigatse's predominantly Chinese population. Mongrels charging us from the shadows made it difficult to appreciate the outline of a dilapidated fort on the ridge against the backdrop of pre-dawn stars. Their barking continued as we sat down next to a metal gate where pilgrims were sleeping. The Tibetans gathered up their bedrolls moments before a truck with no lights came barreling out of the gate. We ran with the pilgrims and helped women throw their bedrolls and children into the back of the truck. They in turn pulled us up.

Traveling with Buddhist pilgrims at last! Each time the truck hit a bump we were thrown into the air and landed hard on burlap sacks of barley. There were twenty-eight pilgrims, including seven women and five babies. It took me a long time to notice that there was a young British couple among them, wearing sheepskin coats turned inside out. They almost looked Tibetan with their dark tans and the turquoise nuggets that hung from their ear lobes. They did not say a word to us, but they shared their large plastic bags of *tsampa* and pretended to sing Tibetan folk songs with the pilgrims. Everything became an excuse to laugh: the idea of these Westerners trying to sing Tibetan folk songs, and landing on top of someone else with each new bump. How strange John's and my pleated wool pants and down parkas looked next to the sheepskins. I noticed that the same shades of orange and dun that colored the horizon were settling on us. We were being baptized by Tibetan dirt.

"Fuck you," the British woman said, when one of the pilgrims pinched her.

* * *

Vertical red and white stripes distinguished Sakya Monastery's blue fortress walls from the contiguous sprawl of Quonset huts. We headed for the houses across the river, where Tibetan work crews secured stone walls with wire mesh to prevent the river from claiming any more of the homes being built for newly arrived Chinese settlers. Painted blue and striped like the monastery, the new houses had sticks piled on their rooftops for fuel. They stood in stark contrast to the barracks-like housing for the workers.

Across a flimsy bridge that spanned the torrent, a Tibetan boy wearing Western clothes and a Mao hat followed us into an alley. We jumped puddles of urine from unattended cows, saw a dog lying stiff-legged with rigor mortis, and passed yak-dung patties molded like large peanut butter cookies on the adobe walls. Other children, wearing rags, paid no attention to us; they were too busy carrying the largest rocks they could muster to divert runoff around their homes.

The recent monsoon had done little damage to the Tibetan neighborhood compared to the adjacent monastery, which had been razed by Chinese artillery. Demolished houses and fragmented walls blended with other ruins that predated Sakya Monastery by several centuries. A single *stupa* remained among the rubble.

The boy produced a note pad from his back pocket that contained sentences written in Tibetan, Mandarin, and English. He pronounced each word carefully, and badly: "My name is Tenzin. How are you? I am well." We exchanged the Tibetan for English names of things we could point to, like "*ta*" (teeth), "*ka*" (mouth), "*mic*" (eyes). Tenzin led us to his house, where his mother welcomed us into a smoky room. Tenzin had a younger brother and sister, two and four years old, who sat in our laps and pulled at the hair on our arms while Tenzin passed us reed baskets of *tsampa, chorro* (a small, bittersweet curd), dried peas, and cubes of dried yak cheese. "*Pe cha, yakbudoo!*" (butter tea is good), we said, as the mother churned the golden liquid and insisted that we fill our pockets with peas and barley and help ourselves to handfuls of "*Chorro, yakbudoo!*" We delighted the mother with our appetites, and by drinking many cups of *pe cha*.

At my inquiring if the *chorro* were from a *ya* (yak) or a *dzo* (yak-cow cross), the mother ordered Tenzin out of the room. He returned leading a small cow on a rope. The mother shrieked with laughter. Next, she had Tenzin fetch a bag of vintage *tsampa*, which we mixed with butter tea into balls. When we were sated, Tenzin played a four-string guitar, danced, and sang folk songs. Tenzin's lilting tenor accompanied a familiar cement feeling in my stomach. Too many "*chorro, yakbudoo,*" "*pe cha, yakbudoo,*" and "*ya ma, yakbudoo. To che che,*" (yak butter is good, thank you). I became acutely aware of the blackened fingers with which Tenzin's mother had expertly kneaded the yak butter into *tsampa* balls for us to eat.

* * *

The next afternoon, six Japanese tourist buses stopped at Sakya Monastery for two hours. Since none of the buses were full, I assumed that one would be willing take us a half-day drive to Tingri, from which we would hike to Everest. Each driver leaned on his horn while anxious stragglers pushed through the swarm of "*Kuchi kuchi*" kids. I waded into the tugging chorus and asked a German woman if we could pay for two seats to Tingri. "We can do whatever we want," the woman said. "We chartered this bus ourselves. But we are having a problem with the driver." As if on cue, people at the front of the bus screamed at the Chinese driver in French and Italian. The driver stared out the windshield. The woman looked at us apologetically. "I am sorry. There is nothing I can do."

Sakya was an afternoon stop on their way from Lhasa to the Nepalese border. Once foreigners chartered their own bus, they became possessive. I walked to the driver's window and constructed a formal greeting from sentence fragments I had learned from Patrick: "Hello. I am a Western doctor. We are going to Everest! Thank you."

"*Mei yuo,*" (don't have) the driver said, still leaning on the horn. If we had learned anything on this trip, it was never take the first *mei yuo* for granted. But the bus left us behind, even though there were enough empty seats to take us. I cursed the buses for abandoning us to another night among the bedbugs at the Tibetan hotel. We were stranded in Sakya, where the only Chinese restaurant in town specialized in greasy stir-fry soup. I was ready to leave behind its dirt alleys and puddles and urchins.

I almost missed Sakya's charm completely. The next day, when no tourist buses arrived to refuse us, we hiked up the nearest mountain. Each new rise looked like the summit, and it took us longer to get there than we expected. Finally, we rested on a small outcrop of red shale that clung to the steep scree. Sakya's town and monastery looked miniature next to the river.

A *CRACK* resounded through the hills. Another *CRACK* and sheep scattered across a steep ravine. We saw two moving forms that turned out to be children. If they fell they would die. *CRACK* and we watched the children move with amazing quickness across a slope. Wide-brim felt hats and beige cloaks gave them an appearance of supernatural grace. *CRACK* resounded through the mountains, and finally I noticed the slings the children were using to throw rocks with deadly accuracy.

We worried at first that the boys were caught in an avalanche. Then, realizing that all the noise was an acoustical illusion created by the echoing sound of the slings, we relaxed. When the boys showed us how to use their slings, it no longer mattered if we left Sakya that night or next week. The children showed us how you put stones the size of walnuts in the widened section of the black and white sling, and then swung it over your head like a giant propeller. Once it started whirring, you released one end and the rock shot out in the intended direction with a thunderous *CRACK*. Our stones flew out erratically and made the boys take cover. The boys themselves were experts; they could hit a sheep on the run from fifty yards. When they tired of teaching us how to throw rocks, they ran after the sheep they were tending.

We ran down the scree in giant, moon-walking bounds. At lunch, we added canned mackerel and ramen noodles to our stir-fry soup, and talked about the legal aspects of mountaineering in off-limits areas with a heterogenous group of Europeans we came upon, who had liked Sakya so much that they had stayed an extra day. They offered to give us a ride.

A mud shower sprayed us as we walked to the bus the next morning. Three Tibetans peered down on us from above the half wall on a three-story roof. Seeing them prompted me to pick up a Tootsie-Roll-sized donkey turd and throw it back at them as hard as I could. The turd almost hit one of the men's heads, and we were engaged in battle. The men threw mud at us. John and I whipped turds back at them.

"*Kuchi kuchi. Dalai Lama photo*," I said to a girl clutching a Dalai Lama postcard in her hands. The girl screamed. I tugged on the postcard and repeated my request. Uneasy laughter spread among the younger children, who had toilet-training splits in the back of their pants. "*Kuchi kuchi*," I said grabbing the smallest boy's belly with my enormous white hand. The children shrieked with laughter. When we had arrived at Sakya I had cursed these urchins. Now they were my *kuchi kuchi* kids.

* * *

At Xegar, six French trekkers waiting by the side of the road pushed onto our bus and demanded that we take them to Tingri. They had just hiked from Everest and had to return to Tingri for their equipment. The group's arrogant tone incurred the collective wrath of the chartered passengers. The trekkers argued until the passengers let them stay—if together they paid 108 yuan to travel the next twenty-six kilometers.

"Cons! For that price we could go to Lhasa."

"Then go to Lhasa!"

"This is preposterous."

The driver settled the argument by charging each trekker five yuan, a fair price. We were moving again. A tall, unshaven man with water dripping off his stringy, unwashed hair sat down next to me. "Two weeks we are trekking to Everest and the whole time rain," the man said. "We come 12,000 miles for a glimpse of this mountain. We wait in Base Camp three extra days, and still only monsoon. Not seeing Everest is the biggest disappointment of my life!" I tell the man we are headed toward Everest and he says, "You will never see Everest."

* * *

Wisps of smoke traced magical lines from the prayer flags on Tingri's rooftops to the heavy clouds that sealed the valley. As we walked to the Tibetan hotel, a flock of urchins pressed fistfuls of *tsampa* into our hands, ran metal hoops in circles around us, and splashed each other in the hotel's flooded central courtyard. The magic faded when we realized that there would be no effective boundary between the monsoon and our room. The straw mats were the dirtiest I had yet seen in Tibet, and smelled of mildew. A sordid history unfolded as I examined the soiled sheet: the first corner had been used as a dish towel for spaghetti sauce; the second to wipe blackened soot from a pot; cigarette burns marked the third corner; crusted snot clung to the fourth.

"Don't touch that mattress!" shouted another Frenchman, with a half-smoked Gauloise protruding from his scraggly beard. "*Les puces de lits.* Bedbugs. They attacked me last night." Seeing the Frenchman scratching made me scratch. "This is a godforsaken place. I am going to Everest. Today I wait all day for a stupid yak man. We made an agreement yesterday. I paid him and he never came back. They are thieves, these yak men."

We went in search of a yak man and found five of them drinking *chang* in the hotel's smoky restaurant. An ancient woman poured the turbid liquid from a black kettle into our cracked porcelain cups.

Tsarang, the tallest and most inebriated of the yak men, wore black pants cut off at mid-thigh. He offered a toast, *"Dalai Lama, yakbudoo,"* and downed the contents of his cup, which the woman promptly refilled. We followed suit. The homemade beer looked like dishwater but was pleasantly bubbly, and it breached the language barrier. We were going to Everest, or "Chomolungma." They were yak men. Each wanted to take us.

As the self-appointed spokesman for the group, Tsarang traced the arc of the sun on the table with his finger three times—three days for the trip to Chomolungma. The other yak men nodded their heads in agreement. Tsarang held up fifteen fingers (fifteen yuan, three U.S. dollars) for himself for each of the three days, and ten fingers each for the two yaks, if burly fingers marching across the table were meant to represent yaks.

"They are cheating you," yelled the Gauloise-smoking Frenchman, who had joined us at the restaurant.

The yak men did not understand the Frenchman's English, but they understood his derogatory tone. John protested that three days was too long; the guidebook said that you could hike from Tingri to Everest in two days. John traced two arcs to Chomolungma. Tsarang shook his head no. I sided with Tsarang. An extra day would help us acclimatize slowly to the change in altitude from 10,000 to 17,000 feet. John stubbornly raised his cup to Chomolungma in two days. Tsarang added a third arc and the yak men laughed.

"He's cheating us," John said when Tsarang ordered another kettle of *chang.*

I reminded John that Tsarang needed an extra day to get his yaks back, and that we did not have a tent or a stove. The yak men laughed when they understood from my tracing of a tent and a stove that we had neither. Tsarang waved them in free. John calculated 105 yuan to be a fair total price for the three days, if it also included kerosene. "And three more for the Dalai Lama," I said, holding up three fingers, invoking 108, Tibetan Buddhism's symbolic number for enlightenment. "Chomolungma, *yakbudoo,*" we toasted, and Tsarang refilled our cups.

"You are fools," the Frenchman said.

"Dalai Lama, *yakbudoo,*" I said.

"Dalai Lama, *yakbudoo,*" the yak men said and touched their cups to their foreheads before downing the *chang*. Tsarang stood up abruptly, mumbled something unintelligible, and left. "He will never come back," the Frenchman told us. Tsarang returned in two hours with a horse cart for our packs. On the way out of town we bought a case of Chinese *pijou* (beer) and a whole quarter of one of Tibet's scrawny sheep. I also plucked a wide-brimmed, beige felt hat off a Tibetan man selling cheap, colorful clothing in front of our hotel. He wanted forty-five yuan but took twenty-five.

"It's filthy," John said, inspecting the sweat-stained brim for infestation.

"Broken in," I corrected.

"Be careful he does not steal everything," the Frenchman yelled after us. I left Tingri thinking that if I were a yak man, I would have stolen the Frenchman's choice food items.

The rain clouds broke and left us standing in a green valley with Cho Oyu lifting the horizon. Cho Oyu was the largest mountain we had ever seen. We could not imagine "knocking the bastard off," as Sir Edmund Hillary said of Everest. Although we had climbed 20,000-foot peaks in Peru, they were mere foothills compared to Cho Oyu's 27,000 feet, and Everest at over 29,000 feet. We were mere inebriated specks in the vast Himalayas.

Tsarang drank only *chang* during our three-day trek. We tried to get him to drink water, but he handed us back beer instead, which we accepted as part of an unwritten social contract. Despite frequent stream crossings and numerous *chang* stops to toast "Dalai Lama, *yakbudoo*!" we crossed the valley in only two hours. Tsarang had the largest house in the village we found there, with hay stacked on its roof as is the custom throughout western Tibet.

There I tried to milk a *dzo* in a corral, to the encouragement of Tsarang's teenage brother, but after milkless minutes the *dzo* kicked me into the dung with its hind foot. Undaunted, I went inside for another yak-byproduct overdose. Tsarang's grandmother looked at us through thick cataracts and asked how much we were paying Tsarang. We mimed the original transaction that led up to 108 fingers. This sent the grandmother into hysterics. Everything we did made her laugh: eating whole boiled potatoes, tossing *tsampa* onto our cheeks instead of into our mouths, dancing with Tsarang while he sang and played a four-string guitar. After a refreshing stop, we were soon back under way again.

"Chuh!" Tsarang yelled at Khampa and Sera, our yaks, who stood motionless and snorted steam from their nostrils in the frigid morning air. "Chuh!" Tsarang yelled again, and threw a softball-sized rock with frightening speed that thumped against Khampa's flank. At each river crossing Khampa tried to buck the case of beer. Sera had the reddish coat and white marking of an Irish Hereford. She had enormous brown eyes and preferred to graze, until a swift kick to the hind quarters made her bolt to the next patch of grass. Such was our skittery introduction to chasing the unruly beasts.

* * *

Dokale was not a town like the map said, but nothing more than two black, yak-hair nomad tents. Unlike these nomad tents, which opened at the top to let the smoke out and fresh air in, Tsarang's ripped, canvas tent let snow in and kept the smoke from escaping. Soon everything we owned smelled like dried rabbit dung, which Tsarang fired red-hot with a bellows under a boiling pot. The smoke, and the sight of John and Tsarang devouring greasy boiled lamb and butter tea, nauseated me. I tried to eat *tsampa* to thwart an impending intestinal eruption. It was too late.

"What are you doing?" I yelled when John poured the water from the boiled lamb into a water bottle.

"Didn't they teach you nutrition in medical school? All the nutrients are in the water. We'll need all the energy we can get."

Seeing the greasy water and bits of lamb in the wide mouth of the water bottle sent me running out of the tent to the nearest hillock. A fine snow covered my tracks by the time I returned, and every other occasion I was forced to sprint from the tent in order to avoid defiling myself. Snow covered our blankets, until daylight illuminated a fairy-land with thick gray clouds and yaks on the hills. That morning it took Tsarang two hours to find Khampa and Sera, who had wandered off in the night. How Tsarang ever found them amazed me. On a distant hill all yaks look alike, and there were hundreds of them. Yaks also do not come when they are called.

Being afflicted with diarrhea in the mountains was infinitely better than having diarrhea in a populated area. The mountains did not care if you dropped your pants while struggling toward a high pass or descending through a valley that narrowed into a gorge. By afternoon the diarrhea, nausea, and a headache made me fall behind Tsarang and the yaks. John stayed close by to humor me through my frequent rest stops.

"Seriously," John said, opening a can of unnaturally pink, greasy meat. "Have some Spam."

* * *

"We've been robbed!" John said when he discovered that our case of Chinese beer was actually nonalcoholic cider. Tsarang had hurried back down the mountain at the onset of a torrential rain, but we had decided to take refuge at what remained of Rombok Monastery. "I paid seventy-five yuan," John lamented. "Twice as much as this cider is worth." I had the worst headache of my life and cared more about avoiding the rain pouring through the slate roof.

A teenage monk in dirty robes entered the room and handed us a thermos of butter tea for which he wanted five yuan, an exorbitant price. Hoping to get rid of him, I paid the money. He proceeded to pull from his robes a freeze-dried shrimp dinner, a can of Cadbury chocolate powder, and an assortment of electrolyte drinks. He insisted that we buy something.

John offered a bottle of cider to the pseudo-lama for the chocolate powder. The monk shook his head no and pointed to the word *pijou* written in Chinese on the case. Of course. The monk did not drink alcohol. John took a sip and demonstrated that we had indeed brought a case of nonalcoholic *pijou*. The monk traded the chocolate for three bottles of cider. Just as John was feeling good about his bargain, the monk demanded ten yuan from each of us for the room.

The rain continued through the evening. We drank cider and moved our sleeping bags to avoid each new leak that sprang in the roof. A reconnaissance of the monastery revealed a solitary, hourglass *stupa* amid the remnants of buildings that had been destroyed during the Cultural Revolution. Sleep was out of the question. John and I stayed awake discussing the ill-fated Everest expedition of Mallory and Irving.

"The climbers in the Mallory expedition used to make fun of the monks at Rombok Monastery," John said. "The monks believed that each rock, plant, and animal on the mountain had its own spirit, and that to disturb anything was to invite death. The British climbers ridiculed the monks for being superstitious and unkempt. The expedition was held up for two months by inclement weather. Finally, the climbers sought the blessing of the old abbot who presided over Rombok. In an ornate ceremony, the abbot pled their case before the ruling spirits. Apparently, the ceremony was not a success; the abbot warned Mallory and Irving that inauspicious portents boded ill for their expedition. But the weather cleared the next day, and the mountaineers were determined to press on. Mallory and Irving climbed to their death."

CHAPTER FOUR

CHOMOLUNGMA, GODDESS MOTHER OF THE WORLD

W E WERE PILGRIMS in a wilderness of catastrophic light and sound. Glacial melt from the Kangshung and East and West Rombok Glaciers thundered through the valley as we hiked the last seven miles from Rombok Monastery in full view of Everest. The snow-covered leviathan appeared weightless. Light bounced off a thousand facets on the mountain ice. Cirrus clouds pulled their fine silk threads across the steep North Face.

We had finally arrived at Everest Base Camp, but we were ill-prepared to stay. Distant tent clusters were the only evidence of life on a moraine criss-crossed by hundreds of gurgling channels. With neither tent nor stove nor extra food, and sneakers and summer sleeping bags instead of hiking boots and winter bags, we offered ourselves like idiots to the elements. Yet this was our challenge; if monks could subsist on barley and water in caves for years, we could scrounge enough food from the pseudo-lamas to hang out a few days at Everest Base Camp.

"We'll offer to carry loads in exchange for food and clothing," John suggested. I reminded John that I was a doctor and that it would not be seemly for me to perform manual work. John failed to see the humor in this and headed toward a far-off group of red and blue tents. I headed toward a separate group of tents beneath a glacier's dirty edge. While imagining the choice food items a well-financed mountaineering expedition might have to offer, I stepped knee-deep into an ice-blue channel.

A sign reading "NO FOOD, KEEP OUT" guarded an enclave of tents, from which fifteen pairs of Japanese glacier goggles eyed the water line on my pants. "How's the weather?" I asked. "No food," said a man bundled in an enormous parka. I introduced myself as an American physician and the same man volunteered that two of their climbers had gotten pulmonary edema. Their doctors were evacuating them to Kathmandu. Daily precipitation had made it too dangerous for their team to get onto the West Ridge. They had tried for one month. I tried to conceal my delight and offered my services. Fifteen pairs of glacier goggles shook their heads no. They had everything they needed. I had the moraine to myself.

I found John next to a similar sign, "NO TREKKERS, NO FOOD!" John had engaged Rod, the base camp manager of an American North Ridge team, in an animated conversation. It turned out that Rod knew Mark Sonnenfeld, our climbing mentor in college, and we took turns recounting epic anecdotes of the young Mark Sonnenfeld being helicopter-rescued in the Canadian Rockies, and breaking his wrist in a fall off Dartmouth's administration building. Clouds suddenly swept Everest from view. "You better set up your tent," Rod said.

"Don't have one," John said. "We were hoping we could carry loads. Blake's a doc."

"*You're* a doc?" Rod said, looking at my wet sneakers and pants. I explained that I had accidentally stepped in a stream, and Rod stuck out his hand in greeting. A Chinese man in his early twenties walked toward us and Rod introduced Mr. Tang, the Chinese Mountaineering Association liaison officer. Rod explained that we were both climbers and would be joining their expedition.

"No more trekkers," Tang said.

"They're *climbers*," Rod replied.

"They not on list," Mr. Tang shouted, becoming red-faced. Rod said that we were staying and Mr. Tang had a tantrum. The more he screamed, the more Rod insisted, until Mr. Tang stomped off toward the Japanese Camp.

"Don't worry about Tang," Rod said as he led us to the team's communal tent. "Tang never agrees to anything. We do what we want." Once inside the tent, it became impossible not to stare at the empty Stroh's beer cans, fruit rolls, bags of hard candy, herb teas, Pepperidge Farm cookies, and an enormous block of cheddar cheese. After weeks of consuming little but yak byproducts, the assortment of junk food seemed irresistible.

"These guys know Sonnenfeld," Rod said when introducing us to Steve, the sickly looking expedition leader, who was sunken into a beach chair next to a radio. He did not offer us any of the food. The radio clicked. "Camp One to Camp Three," Steve said into the receiver.

"Tom at Three. The North Col avalanched this morning. Misha's porters fell 2,000 feet. Hurt bad. One torn knee. One wrenched back. Doubt they'll make it down tonight. Sending Mike with them, over," came the transmission.

"We'll be waiting. Did the yaks arrive? Over."

"Got in a fight with the yak drivers. Their rocks against our ice axes." Sounds of a struggle interrupted the transmission before, "Send *women!*" came screaming through the receiver. Steve jerked the microphone away from his ear.

"Is that you, Strange?"

"I'm so horny the yaks are nervous."

"So is Greg," said Tom's voice, after more wrestling sounds. "He's got diarrhea—I think it's giardia. Send some antibiotics."

Steve looked at us apologetically. "I would carry the medicine up myself, but I pulled an intercostal muscle." Steve demonstrated his wet, hacking cough. Rod said we could "hump" loads for the team and it was agreed. "I'm sending up two trekkers with a load to Camp One tomorrow," Steve said. "Over."

"Do they have nice asses?" came the reply.

Steve saw me staring at a bag of BBQ corn chips and handed me the bag, saying, "Now that you're humping loads, help yourself." Steve explained that Pepperidge Farm cookies were the expedition's favorite, mainly because the company had sent them three times the amount Steve had requested. Ten trekkers who had paid $5,000 each for the privilege had accompanied the team to Base Camp; only one remained. Steve spoke in brief sentence fragments and quickly tired of banter. It had been raining for four weeks. If the rain kept up, they would never get a summit attempt.

"At least we're doing better than the Spanish expedition on the North Face," Rod said. "Poor bastards. They have one of the best Sherpas anywhere. He's summited Everest three times. But it doesn't look like they'll summit." Rod sounded cheerful when he said this.

* * *

We joined some of the team members in a hackysack game, in which a circle of players juggle a small, leather sack with their feet without letting it touch the ground. Even Mr. Tang joined in. Tang looked diminutive in his oversized down expedition parka. He scowled at us and often said that he hated mountains. But eventually I grew fond of Mr. Tang. Like any twenty-one-year-old man on his first trip away from home, Mr. Tang longed to return to his family and friends in Beijing. He turned out to be a natural hackysack player. Years of studying martial arts enabled him to send either foot in a roundhouse to retrieve wayward sacks back into the game. The longer we played, the more I admired his skill with his feet.

"He can't play," Mr. Tang said of Yongdup, a bare-chested yak man who strode up to our circle wearing yak-soled boots. Even in his parka, Mr. Tang looked puny next to the well-muscled Yongdup. "He steal water jugs!" Mr. Tang complained. "And cooking pot. You must search his tent."

"Bullshit," Rod said, and tossed the tiny leather sack to Yongdup. Yongdup kicked the sack twenty yards into the moraine. "You can't trust him!" Mr. Tang shrieked. Yongdup stepped up to within inches of Tang's face. Mr. Tang had no concept of compromise, which left him in jeopardy of either losing face in an argument or else being beaten up by Yongdup. John distracted Yongdup by retrieving the sack and lobbing it back to him. Again, Yongdup kicked the sack defiantly back into the scree. There was no limit to Yongdup's laughter, just as there was no getting him to play by our rules.

* * *

The next morning I got up early with Brack, a cardiothoracic surgeon who was part of the team, in order to examine the two Sherpas injured in the avalanche the day before, who were now lying quietly in a tent across the moraine. One man had a grotesquely swollen knee. The right side of the other man's back was tender and swollen. The Sherpas were incredible. They had fallen 2,000 feet in an avalanche and then walked fourteen miles down a glacier.

"They're lucky to be alive," Brack said, with the confidence of a man who himself had participated in eight Himalayan expeditions. He gave the men some pain pills and directions in Nepalese. Outside the tent, Brack said, "The older man has a grade-four tear of the medial collateral ligament in his right knee. Unless he gets an operation in Kathmandu, he'll never climb again. But he can't afford to go to Kathmandu. Maybe it's just as well—the operation also could do him more harm than good."

Brack smiled when I asked him if he had seen many cases of pulmonary and cerebral edema, where in reaction to shifts in altitude the lungs or brain become engorged with fluid. "I've never seen a single case," he said. "I guess I'm lucky."

*   *   *

John and I met Misha on the terminal moraine in full view of Everest. We were in a tremendous mood. Rod had loaned us down sleeping bags rated to forty degrees below zero. We would be carrying a load to Camp One tomorrow, which meant that we would be eating with the team for the indefinite future. And the music of the Doors was blaring on the largest cassette box we had ever seen.

Talking to Rod, we learned he was an amiable wealth of information about the three American teams on Everest that season. A British climber named Doug Scott was leading an expedition that was expected any day. They would try the Northeast Ridge, where the British climbers Joe Tasker and Pete Boardman had disappeared at 27,000 feet in 1982. As with their legendary countrymen Mallory and Irving, their bodies had never been recovered. "Shit," Rod said, noticing a man with a mane of unkempt Medusa hair bounding toward us across the expanse of moraine. This was our first glimpse of Misha.

Misha had wild, eccentric blue eyes. He walked to within inches of Rod's face before screaming, "I not paying Sherpas. They are laziest goddamned Sherpas I ever had."

Rod looked Misha directly in the eye and said, "You're lucky they didn't get killed in that avalanche."

Misha clenched his fists and yelled, "Sherpas lie. There was no avalanche! Sherpas steal my cameras! Sherpas steal everything." Misha turned to John and said, "I am Misha, famous Russian filmmaker. Maybe you see one of my mountain films on German television?" Misha snapped his head back to Rod and softened his tone. "I need to use your ropes."

"Why did you send your Sherpas up in an avalanche?" Rod asked.

"I lose all my equipment because of fucking Sherpas."

"You can't use our ropes," Rod said.

I thought Misha would punch Rod, but he stormed across the moraine like a spoiled child in the direction of his tents. "You'll never meet nicer people than these Sherpas," Rod said, as Misha stomped away. "They're honest. They do most of the dangerous climbing on most Himalayan expeditions. Misha doesn't do any hard climbing. He sends his Sherpas to fix all of his lines before he goes up. We don't have any Sherpas. We want to do everything ourselves."

● ● ●

At sixty-five years old, Charlie was the expedition's youngest spirit. We hiked with him to Camp One, at 18,000 feet, where one of the climbers from Camp Three would come down from 21,500 feet to ferry more choice food items back up to where the expedition was beginning its technical climbing. Charlie's white, Santa Claus hair and beard gave away his age; Buddy, his mountaineering teddy bear, dressed in its own miniature wool pants, down parka, and glacier goggles and strapped on top of Charlie's pack, belied it. After Rod finished packing our loads, we learned that twenty-five pounds felt twice as heavy at this altitude as it did in the flatlands.

As the three of us started across the moraine, Charlie stuttered, "Well B-Buddy, are you r-ready?" I wondered if Charlie always trekked with his teddy bear, or if the altitude had done this to him. He told John and me, "You go right ahead, gentlemen. I'll hike slower than both of you. Don't wait for me."

"We wouldn't think of hiking without you," John said. John wasn't threatened by Charlie's talking to Buddy, but I couldn't help thinking that there must have been something wrong with a grown man who consulted his teddy bear before each drink of water, snack, or rest. Hiking at my own pace in front of Charlie and John, I questioned Charlie's sanity as the trail wound through house-sized boulders and tall dirt columns sculpted by rain and runoff. Everest disappeared from view once the trail turned up a side valley that carried the East Rombok Glacier. I should have waited for John and Charlie, but I was impatient and hiked ahead.

Endless switchbacks wound ever higher above the trickle of glacial melt sparkling in the sun. As my heart beat louder and my mind moved slower, fear tugged at the base of my brain. Was my body acclimatizing quickly enough to compensate for the changes in altitude? Was water oozing through my alveolar membranes to fill my lungs with pulmonary edema? Was my brain swelling like a wet sponge to herniate against the base of my skull? The symptoms of Acute Mountain Sickness summed up how I felt at the moment: headache, dizziness, nausea, no desire to eat or drink. I collapsed to rest when I arrived at a cairn of rocks. A marmot barked at my approach. Charlie and John arrived with a refreshing breeze that blew cool air off the end of the glacier.

* * *

At Camp One, Tom, Steve's radio correspondent, bounded off the ice and immediately gulped down two liters of the grape drink we had brought. Between gulps, Tom told us that he had hiked down from Camp Three, approximately ten miles, in just over two hours. With luck, he would make it back to Three in time for dinner. Tom had just finished his internship in Seattle, where he had arranged to postpone his residency in anesthesiology until January so he could go on this expedition. For future reference, I asked how he had finagled a break between internship and residency. "Ever hear of the Hornbine Couloir on Everest?" Tom said. "Well, the famous Hornbine happens to be my residency director."

Tom filled his pack with our loads and, before stepping onto the glacier, handed me a stamped letter from his back pocket. "I almost forgot. Would you mind giving this to Rod? It's a letter to my wife and kids."

"R-Ready, B-Buddy?" Charlie asked, as he prepared to join Tom on the hike back up to Camp Three, and I thought how precious the human body is, how delicate the balance between life and death.

With Tom and Charlie gone, John and I ate as much of the expedition food as we could. We deserved it after carrying our loads. Triscuits and sardines with mustard sauce naturally led to potato chips and cheddar cheese and quarts of grape drink, granola bars, mixed nuts, raisins, and fruit rolls. I ate so much my stomach felt full for the first time in over a month. Without warning, the stream five hundred feet below suddenly seemed noticeably louder. I shortly thereafter succumbed to four bouts of projectile vomiting.

"Hold still!" John yelled, hurrying to position his camera. "O.K. Now do it again."

* * *

Back at Base Camp later that evening, Yongdup unzipped the door of the communal tent and stepped brazenly inside, accompanied by two yak men who gawked at the incredible array of food and equipment. Their smiles reminded me of my own first sight of the tent. "No," Rod said to Yongdup, who was helping himself to a bag of pretzels. "No," to one yak man, who found a bottle of rice wine. A still louder "No!" to the other yak man, who grabbed a case of Pepperidge Farm cookies. Suddenly the three men turned on Rod. I was afraid for myself and pushed my beach chair against the wall of the tent. Rod traded handfuls of pretzels in exchange for the rice wine and cookies, and herded the yak men out. "Expeditions breed this kind of relationship," Rod said.

* * *

Two days later, cough or no cough, Steve was determined to get to Camp Three. Rod hiked slowly with Steve. If all went well, Charlie would be waiting to meet us at Camp Two, and would then return to Base Camp with us. John and I did not know the route to Camp Two, but we did not want to wait for Rod and Steve. A trail of sticks with red plastic flags led us back onto the lip of the East Rombok Glacier. We moved cautiously around holes in the ice, beneath which a freezing river raged through dark caverns. We took care to see that the other was not getting too tired or had lost his sense of humor, early warning signs of altitude sickness.

I got a headache that afternoon. John tried to get me to eat more sardines, the idea of which made both of us laugh until our stomachs hurt. A trail zig-zagged across the glacier to a steep scree slope on one side of the valley, then back to the other side. The sun had slickened the icy jaws of the trail that opened into the river. Twice great sprays of rocks and car-sized boulders rained down from the cathedrals of rotten stone at the valley's rim. Twice we sprinted in terror before realizing that we were a safe distance away. The higher we climbed, the thicker the glacier became, until the ice beneath our feet was hundreds of feet thick. As the valley narrowed and steepened, the glacier threw countless creaking ice pinnacles into the path of the wind. We were insects in a giant's world. The higher we climbed, the smaller and more insignificant we became.

One foot fell in front of the other. Thoughts acquired a weight of their own: the Sherpa's discombobulated knee; climbers fighting the yak men; Rod fighting with Misha; everyone fighting with Mr. Tang. Mountains emphasize the best and the worst in each of us.

Camp Two's tents sat on their own ridge of lateral moraine, a safe distance from avalanches, dwarfed beneath vertical oceans of scree and the energetic sweep of the glacier. Charlie cradled Buddy like a nursing baby. "B-B-Buddy and I are g-glad to s-see you," he said. He looked tired but he talked enthusiastically about the North Col, where the Sherpas had been avalanched off the mountain. In the morning Rod wasn't feeling well and decided to hike back down to Base Camp with Charlie, John, and myself. A rejuvenated Steve climbed alone to Camp Three.

* * *

We took three days to recuperate from humping loads to Camp Two. Then tragedy struck again. We met death in a boulder field. A solemn procession of Japanese climbers with glacier glasses and zinc oxide over their sun-charred faces carried a corpse lashed to a stretcher of ski poles.

Twenty-four climbers followed. The funeral procession passed as quickly as it had come, and I found myself wanting to know how the climber had died, as though knowing would help me avoid a similar situation.

"I've never seen a dead body," John said, resting on a boulder. "My grandfather had a closed casket. No one else in my family has died."

I told John about an autopsy I had done on a man who had left a bar without paying and driven at high speed into a tree. The car exploded and burned for half an hour before the firemen could pull him out. I couldn't even identify the man's race; his cooked flesh smelled sweet, like barbecue.

"That's disgusting," John said.

"He had *liters* of beer in his stomach. Smelling *that* was disgusting."

"You sound so removed," John said. "How old were you when your dad died? *That* must have been hard on you."

I had seen my father die from lung cancer when I was fourteen, then a close friend drown the following spring. Eventually I'd seen several friends die in climbing accidents, and many people die in hospitals. John wondered if the climber had a wife and children, if there was a God who cared about each of us, if one of us would get hurt. I told him that we were cosmic fertilizer.

＊　＊　＊

The next day, a group of yak men loaded their shaggy beasts and beat them into a line across the moraine long before the sun had chiseled the prehistoric chill from the valley floor. John was carrying two fifteen-pound oxygen bottles. I carried a twenty-five-pound tape deck and five pounds of batteries. Rod filled his pack with choice food items. Once the yaks hit the switchbacks, it would be too dangerous to try to pass all fifteen of the behemoths. With no incentive to catch up, we took frequent rests. Hiking slowly would give our bodies more time to acclimatize and help us avoid getting sick during the fourteen-mile hike from Base Camp to Camp Three. If all went well, we would stay at Camp Two that night, and continue to Camp Three tomorrow.

On a switchback above us, a yak bucked a blue barrel that careened down a steep dirt embankment toward the river. As the barrel tumbled faster down the slope, I hoped that it didn't contain anything choice, like Pepperidge Farm cookies. I did not see the ton of charging mane and horns until it was upon me. "Chuh!" I shrieked, and threw a rock at the yak. The beast kept coming and I leapt off the trail after the barrel.

An unfamiliar yak man ran down the trail after me. He pretended to throw a baseball-sized rock at my head. Only then did I realize that the yaks were from the Spanish team coming down, not from our North Ridge team going up. The yak man had seen me throwing a rock at his yak, and blamed me for his load bounding toward the river. He looked crazed, like he wanted to kill me. I ran far enough down the slope that John became an easier target.

"*Tashi delek*," John said, "*To te che*" (thank you), his hands folded as if in prayer. The yak man pretended to throw the rock at his head. "Hello-thank you," John pleaded and pointed to me, "He did it."

* * *

A loud *CLAP* came from the rotten amphitheater of cliffs a thousand feet above us. *CLAP-CLAP* and our heads snapped up to see yak-sized boulders careening off an ancient buttress. The boulders seemed to fall for a long time before they hit the shoulder of scree, and exploded into perfect waves of shattered rock that fanned toward us. The expanding waves seduced us with their beauty, this glimpse of death. We ran from them as much for fun as from any real danger.

At Camp Two, Brack and another climber drank soup outside their tents. Brack looked pale. His eyes were sunken and listless. He introduced us to Paul, a short, stocky man who spilled Knorr leek and potato soup into his beard. "Paul got pulmonary edema during the night," Brack said authoritatively, even though he looked worse than Paul. "He's doing well now. As soon as we finish our soup, we'll continue to Base Camp."

"It's funny," Paul said. "Last night I woke up drowning in my own juice. Now I'm drinking soup."

"I didn't need a stethoscope to diagnose this one," Brack said. "Paul got better with sitting up and oxygen. I didn't have to use Lasix. We hiked down at daylight. With a bit of luck, we'll make it to Base Camp in time for dinner." Brack spent all of his breath talking and paused to sip his soup. Paul looked sternly at Brack, who grudgingly continued, "That's only half of it. This morning I vomited bright red blood, twice."

"I'm going with you," Rod said.

"That won't be necessary," Brack said.

"It's mountain etiquette," Rod said. "I grew up in the mountains. It will get dark before you get off the glacier."

"We'll be fine," Brack said gruffly, and wobbled to his tent.

Bad judgment is a classic sign of mountain sickness, something climbers have to be vigilant for in themselves and their partners at all times. I followed Brack to a rock with a view of the ice sails billowing down the frozen river in front of us. I was a recent graduate from medical school with no independent experience, and Brack was a cardiothoracic surgeon and veteran of eight Himalayan expeditions. All of this made me hesitate before saying the obvious: Brack had a bleeding ulcer and was too stubborn to admit it. He did not speak for some time and appeared to be in the throes of indecision. "We'll make it to Base Camp tonight," Brack said. "The question in my mind is whether I should go straight to the American Hospital in Kathmandu. I don't want to go."

"You have two choices," I said. "You can stay in Base Camp and worry. Or you can do what you would tell one of your patients to do."

* * *

That night, alone at Camp Two, John and I listened eagerly to the evening's radio communication. "Rod at Base to Three, over."

"Tom at Three. How's Paul?"

"Paul's lungs are clear. He's eating soup and loving it. Brack's resting in his tent. He didn't vomit any more blood. I did orthostatics on him. He's fine, just tired."

"Glad to hear it. We're all rooting for him. Will he evacuate to Kathmandu?"

"Doesn't want to."

"Have the Japanese doc look at him tonight."

"Already did."

"Good job," Tom said. "I'm sleeping by the radio tonight. I'll turn the radio on every two hours for one minute. Call if there's a problem.

Everyone carried full loads to Camp Four today. If the weather holds, we'll establish Camp Five next week."

"Here's the latest on the Japanese death," Rod said. "He was their best climber. He was exhausted, descending from 23,000 feet to rest at Base, and drowned crossing the river."

Vertical oceans of scree and the energetic sweep of the glacier dwarfed Camp Two's tents. John won the toss for Rod's expedition sleeping bag and slept soundly. I spent the night shivering in everything I had: thermodactyl long underwear, warm-up pants, Carolyn's silk top, a wool sweater and wool pants, balaclava, three pairs of socks, and two summer sleeping bags. John and I had experienced many sleepless nights in snow caves, on cliff ledges, in boxcars, and on the side of the road. Shivering as Orion crawled across the sky, I realized that for the first time since I had arrived in the mountains, I felt healthy.

Snowfall obliterated the trail to Camp Three. The morning's radio communication confirmed "heavy dumping." As Yongdup broke camp and drove the yaks ever farther up the glacier, we spent the day playing rummy and foraging through Camp Two's extensive cache of peanut M&M's, Cadbury chocolate, and quarts of hot Jello, vegetable soup, and macaroni and cheese.

At noon, we ventured onto the folds of Changtse's Glacier. We explored wind tunnels and climbed flying buttresses of blue ice. A bare-handed ascent up the back of a gently sloping serac led to an adrenaline-filled descent through feathery crust. That night we gorged ourselves on junk food and played rummy for six hours. I slept soundly in Rod's expedition bag.

Carrying our packs even a short distance the next morning gave fresh insight into the climber's expression, "humping loads." I sang songs in my head, even songs that I hated, to keep myself from going insane with boredom as the spectacular ice highway turned into an endless series of rises. This eventually led to cursing in foreign languages: *"Ya kelb, yebne kelb"* ("You dog, son of a dog," in Egyptian); *"Ta tum kalooch. T'un pisc que ho disc. Vay ood jarack varie"* ("Squash head. You're not wearing any underwear. You smell horrible," in Armenian); *"Va tu faire foutre, grand merde"* ("Go fuck yourself, big shit," in French); and *"Como caca. No come las uvas"* ("Eat shit, don't eat the grapes," in Spanish). Even John looked mad. "Fuck Everest," I said to the Northeast Ridge that unfolded before us for hours without end. "Fuck climbing," I said to the fresh snowfall. "Fuck," I said to myself, 1,008 times.

* * *

We swaggered into Camp Three with the Doors blaring on the tape deck at peak volume. John and I thought it made for an appropriate way to introduce ourselves to the expedition members we hadn't met yet. It took several minutes for the climbers to crawl from their tents.

"You made great time," said Steve, whose cough had gotten worse. "Looking good," said Tom, the expedition's remaining doc. "Let's party," said the other Steve, who everyone referred to as "Strange." We remembered him from our first radio transmission—he was the one who'd inquired about the comeliness of our asses. Strange sang along with us to Jim Morrison, "Break on through. Break on through. Break on through. *YEAAAA-AHHHH!*"

It must have been Strange's ebullient nature that inspired me to add a quarter-cup of fresh black pepper, ginger, cinnamon, and ten cloves of garlic into that night's meal, a salmon curry. Jeff, the only Canadian on the team, talked incessantly with us about how many loads everyone had carried and how their performance related to their chances of gaining the summit. He also put out the fires when kerosene dripping from the Nepalese stove ignited. "Pete summited Everest once from the Nepalese side," Jeff said. "He's strong as a yak. So is Tom, but he's the only doc left and has to stay low. That leaves four out of ten who've been able to hump loads to Camp Four. Greg tried once and left his pack on the ridge. Do you believe that? A real sap. Mike's a businessman. He hasn't carried a load yet. But he donated $40,000 to the expedition. He can climb with me anytime."

Once eleven people were crammed into Camp Three's smaller version of Base Camp's communal tent, Strange announced, "This curry's hot enough to burn the ass hairs off a yak. I like it." All of the climbers who had humped loads to Camp Four agreed.

"It's too hot for me," Greg said. Those who had not carried loads nodded.

"It's time for the game you've all been waiting for," Strange announced, and then pulled his knees to his chest to accentuate his rear. "'The Lowest Common Social Denominator.'"

"Take cover," Pete yelled and pulled his fishing hat over his face.

Ripples of discontent erupted from the non-load carriers as Strange lit a match and sang, "*Break on through!*" He held the match to his backside, and an instant later a jackhammer fart belched orange flames from his rear.

"That's disgusting," Greg said.

"The yak men almost killed us," Strange told John and me. His bushy black eyebrows quivered as he recounted how Yongdup had refused to drive the yaks the last thousand meters to Camp Three. A shouting match between the yak men and the climbers escalated into a battle. The yak men armed themselves with rocks. The climbers clutched their ice axes nervously. Luckily, no one got hurt. For an extra ten dollars, the yak men agreed to drive the yaks the remaining distance. John recounted our own epic conflict with the yak men from the Spanish team.

"I'd like to go down to Base Camp tomorrow and rest," Mike said. "But with the route going up so fast, I'm afraid to be away. I might miss the summit."

"Don't strain yourself worrying," Strange warned. "We hardly have Camp Four established. It's a long way to Six." Strange turned to the man with the fishing hat. "Goddamnit, Pete. If you hump loads any faster we'll get heart attacks trying to keep up."

"I can't believe Misha sent his Sherpas to fix the North Col with heavy avalanche danger," Pete said. "It had snowed for three days straight. Those men are better climbers than all of us put together. Misha sent them to their death."

"I say we disembowel Misha and feed him to the vultures," Strange said. "And Tang. That son of a bitch fought us every step of the way. He was a nightmare flying our gear from Beijing to Lhasa. Chop them both into little bits. We'll have a Tibetan sky burial."

I had seen pictures of a Tibetan sky burial: people hacking flesh from human corpses and mixing it with *tsampa* to feed to the vultures. Like us, the expedition members unanimously despised China's destruction of Tibetan culture, just as the United States had exterminated native American cultures. But here we were, subsidizing China's occupation of

Tibet with our tourist dollars. Eating salmon curry and Pepperidge Farm cookies in enormous expedition sleeping bags on the slopes of Everest, Tibet seemed light-years away.

"I'm going to Antarctica next year," Greg said. "I want to be the youngest person in the world to climb the highest mountain on each continent. I've already got North and South America and Africa. Antarctica is easy. But it costs $12,000 for the air fare from Patagonia to Antarctica. The airline has a monopoly. Anybody want to come?"

"Hand me the cough medicine," Strange bellowed. "A toast to Brack, the concocter of this medieval brew."

"Give it to me next," Greg said.

"Don't let Mike have any," Strange said. "He's addicted." Mike did not say anything. Codeine, I learned, after taking a sweet vermilion sip, was the anti-tussive ingredient Brack had used in mixing up this home remedy—enough codeine for my mind to feel unsteady in my body when I tried to fall asleep in the warm expedition bag.

* * *

The next morning I crawled out of the tent not knowing if I were going to vomit or defecate. I felt dizzy. A pounding headache made it impossible to appreciate my first view of the North Col's 3,000-foot curtain of ice and a foreshortened view of the summit. John made me eat Fig Newtons with powdered milk and I soon felt well enough to hike to the top of the East Rombok Glacier. Jeff pointed to the team's fixed ropes up to the ridge, then the two miles of ridge to Camp Four, illustrating how camps Five and Six were weeks away. Their approach to the summit through the steppes was clear of snow, thanks to the jet stream scouring the rock clean with 200-mile-an-hour winds.

A cornice broke off the rim of the North Col above us and blossomed into a spindrift avalanche. I held my breath. There was nowhere to run. The avalanche was miles away, but distances were deceiving. Jeff pointed out where the Sherpas fell from the North Col, then looked longingly at the summit. "I'm twenty-two years old. I'll never be in better shape. I want the summit. You've got to want it. I want it bad."

* * *

Rod looked well when we passed him on the glacier below Camp Two. Tom, Greg, and Mike were coming down with us to Base Camp for a rest. We joked with Rod that he should treat himself to an extra day at Camp Two. Rod insisted that he could make it from Base Camp to Camp Three in two days. This was fast, going from 17,000 to 21,500 feet, but Rod had just carried a load to 19,500 feet without problems. Then, the next day, he missed the morning radio call. At noon a barely audible voice was heard asking for help. It took precious minutes for us to discern that Rod had awoken with a "killer" headache. He had not been able to see or move for hours.

"What have you done so far?" Tom asked.

"I crawled to the oxygen tank. I took a Fiorinol. My headache's a little better."

Tom looked at each of us to see if we understood that Rod had cerebral edema, and his brain was being squashed against his skull. "No wonder his headache feels better," Tom said with the receiver off. "He took a narcotic." Clicking back on, he said, "Keep nursing the oxygen. How's your vision?"

"Better."

"Who else is in Three?"

"Just me. Everyone left to carry loads to Four."

"Jesus," Tom yelled again with the receiver off. "How do five people leave camp and not see that Rod could die any moment?" Click: "You're going to be fine, Rod. It sounds like the worst is over. Hike down when they get back. Bring someone with you. There's oxygen at Two. We'll talk again in one hour."

That night Rod and Steve arrived in Base Camp in time for another gourmet treat: pressure-cooked turnips sauteed with onions and cabbage and too much fresh black pepper (but never too much garlic), topped with a roux of yak cheese and powdered milk. A sumptuous feast in celebration of Rod's being alive.

"This is fantastic!" Rod said, smacking his lips. "I'm not a religious man, but I thank God last night is over. I had the most intense headache of my life. I tried to call for help but I couldn't move. I couldn't see or hear. By morning everyone had left to hump a load. I couldn't call out. I knew I had cerebral edema."

"We were worried about you," Tom said.

Rod laughed. "I was worried about me, too."

* * *

A clanking reverberated across the moraine from a convoy of Chinese Army trucks, which had brought generators, gravel, steel, and a small army of tents. "Chinese expedition," Tang said proudly, and described how the construction of new cement platforms was only the beginning. Concession stands would be completed within the year.

"Another humongous Chinese assault on Everest," Rod said. "In 1960, the Chinese attacked Everest from Tibet with 214 people. They claimed that three climbers made it to the summit. But they did it at night, and couldn't take a picture."

"Three Chinese climbers made the summit," Tang shouted. Rod said that the Nepalese were so mad at China for trying to appropriate their holy mountain that Gurkha soldiers with fixed bayonets lined the road all the way from the airport to the city when the Chinese Premier arrived in Kathmandu. "Three climbers made the summit," Mr. Tang shouted again.

Rod and Mr. Tang continued to argue against the backdrop of the clanking generators. As much as I had been enjoying our encounter with the American Everest team, I longed to return to Lhasa. I began to focus on the garbage surrounding us, abandoned by hundreds of previous expeditions: piles of rusty cans, broken bottles, batteries, medical waste, and high-tech plastics with a half-life of 100,000 years, all tucked in middens across the terminal moraine.

Two days later we paid 150 yuan each to a Tibetan truck driver who took us to the main road. It was an exorbitant price, but we were too tired for the two-day walk. Crammed into an open truck with a dozen other trekkers, I contemplated the unanswered questions left in my mind after our encounter with the North Ridge expedition. Would Brack hemorrhage on the way to the hospital in Kathmandu? Would any of the climbers make it to the summit? What would the world's highest concession stands do to Everest Base Camp?

PART TWO

SKY BURIAL

CHAPTER FIVE

THE FORBIDDEN CITY

RIDING BACK TO Lhasa, I saw young lovers sitting in a field of purple nycothiums. They reminded me of Carolyn. So did the Tibetan women spreading barley out to dry. I wondered if Carolyn was still in Lhasa, and if she had missed me during our month-long excursion into the mountains. The driver kicked us out at the edge of a desolate valley. We shouted obscenities at him when he drove off. We did not realize our mistake until we walked around a small hill that had concealed the Xegar checkpoint from view; if the driver had been caught with passengers, he could have been fined and lost his license.

Two unarmed guards stood at the checkpoint. Confident that we were unrecognizably dirty, we walked past the guards toward the adjacent truck stop. The guards shouted after us, but then retired to their hut. We wanted food and our first showers in a month, but we soon learned that the truck stop had not had food for a week and that it could spare us no more than a thermosful of hot water. John opened a map and a can of Chinese Spam. He held up a chunk of smoked pink flesh and made a toast: "In the spirit of epic adventure, may Everest pale compared to our next and even greater expedition."

Two German men in their thirties were waiting on the Lhasa side of the checkpoint. Hans had a crew cut and wisps of blond beard. He looked like a young Anagarika Govinda, the German monk whose decades-long pilgrimage through Tibet, as recounted in his book *The Way of the White Clouds*, explored Tibetan Buddhism's spiritual horizons. His friend Otto had stringy, shoulder-length hair and a penetrating gaze. "We come from Kathmandu," Otto said. "The border is shit. Three days we hike across landslides. More than a hundred people die this monsoon season." Otto spoke in German to Hans and they laughed. "It is unfortunate only twelve tourists die, and no Americans," he translated for John and me. John liked Otto's defiant attitude, but I was leery of him. He had the demeanor of a Khampa, which made me wary of my valuables.

A rising plume of dust on the horizon streaked toward us. Watching the approaching dust devil, I imagined a monk bounding across the 12,000-foot plateau in effortless, exaggerated strides. In Tibet some monks are known to cover large distances at superhuman speeds. While I believed that such things were possible, I was not surprised to see a bus materialize at the head of the dust plume. It took two hours for the guards to check everyone's passports and let the bus through. When the bus finally pulled up in front of us, I assumed it was to pick us up. I did not see its flat tire. Otto pushed past an ashen man fighting to get out of the bus in order to vomit. A horrible smell accompanied the gauntlet of harsh stares from other passengers as John and I headed toward the two remaining seats in the back.

"Whuh," I gagged at chunks of dried vomit in a topographical relief on the seat. John's suggestion that we clean it up brought more harsh stares from the passengers who had sat next to the mess. Outside in the fresh air I realized there was no way I could get back on the bus. Even if we didn't get sick trying to clean the seat, we would have to endure that smell for the days it would take us to get from Xegar to Lhasa.

Just then an army jeep skidded to a halt at the checkpoint. The driver was Tibetan. A PLA soldier sat in the passenger side. I said hello in Tibetan and Chinese: "*Tashi delek*" and "*Ni hao*," and asked, "Lhasa?" The driver nodded. I ran back into the bus, and found John's face hostage to the same contortion as the other passengers. "Fuck America," Otto yelled out the bus window after us as we climbed into the jeep.

John handed a pack of Marlboro cigarettes to the front of the jeep for Tenzin, the driver, who never smiled, and Zheng, the soldier, whose uniform was two sizes too big. Tenzin threw the wrapper out the window and accelerated onto the dirt road. Just as I was beginning to fantasize about reaching Lhasa and having a hot bath, the jeep hit a pothole that shot us against the roof. The joy of having a 360-degree view of the mountains faded as Tenzin barreled over and into more potholes.

The jeep broke down regularly. Fortunately, Tenzin was a mechanical wizard. He replaced an old alternator belt with a larger one from a tractor in a nearby village. Dust in the fuel line was sucked by mouth out of the tube. Radiator leaks were plugged with a rag. The jeep broke down so many times that I stopped counting after twenty.

I think Zheng tried to tell us his life story, but neither John nor I spoke enough Chinese to understand him. Like Mr. Tang, the Everest expedition's liaison officer, Zheng was in his early twenties and hated mountains. He had been stationed in Tibet for several years and longed to return to the mainland. He also disliked Tibetans, which explained why Tenzin never smiled.

Rain the second day made the jeep stick fast in the muck in addition to breaking down. We became covered in mud after wedging stones under the wheels and pushing it out of ruts. Then Tenzin drove forty miles an hour off the road. Miraculously, no one was hurt. With oil, water, and gas leaks, we broke down every fifteen minutes. I stopped counting after fifty.

Ironically, we ran out of gas twenty-five miles from Lhasa. Many army trucks passed us, but none would stop for the Tibetan driver, for the Chinese soldier, or for the American who yelled "Fuck you" at receding taillights. At first I was angry that we would have to spend one more night outside. I noticed that the electricity lines that paralleled the road did not branch up to a nearby Tibetan village. Tibetan homes were lit by butter lamps, as they had been for centuries; they had neither electricity nor showers. At dawn Zheng flagged a driver who let us siphon enough gas to get to Lhasa.

* * *

The well-dressed tourists at the Lhasa Hotel's main desk eyed us suspiciously. I explained to the manager that we had just come from Everest. He smiled uneasily, but he took my American Express card. We took two baths each and still could not wash the blue dye from our cheap pants off our legs. John looked thin; he had lost ten pounds. I was emaciated, having lost twenty-five. We ate five meals in a row without leaving the premises: copious amounts of stainless steel eggs and cold toast, overcooked yak burgers and greasy fries, beef stroganoff and sugary desserts. The food didn't taste very good but we wanted to satisfy our cravings for Western cooking before we resettled in a Tibetan hotel.

"Are you staying *here?*" Otto shouted when he discovered us in the lobby. Otto and Hans sported a motley assemblage of dirt that offended the sensibilities of the hotel's refined clientele—the same dirt that had covered us less than twenty-four hours before. "The Lhasa Hotel is fucked," Otto bellowed, loud enough to attract the manager's attention. John said we were leaving. Otto berated us "soft Americans" for taking a luxurious jeep while he stayed on the bus.

"Change money for me," Otto demanded. "I lose my passport." Otto retrieved a 500-mark note from a sack hung around his neck. I took the bill to the main desk and the manager said that German marks had to be changed at the bank. Otto glared at me and shouted, "They would change American dollars. Chinese treat Tibetans like shit. FEC's (foreign exchange currency) are fucked. The Lhasa Hotel is fucked."

Lhasa had changed since we had left a month before. Squads of police goose-stepped in the streets while roving loudspeakers denounced the Dalai Lama as an enemy of the Motherland. It took two days for me to find a letter from Carolyn on the Tibetan hotel bulletin board. She had stayed for another two weeks after her brother returned from Kham, then went on to Nepal. She would be at the Tibet Hotel in Kathmandu.

Otto was soon arrested for stealing a government stamp. After a policeman refused to authorize a special visa to Bhutan, Otto stole the government stamp. No one witnessed the theft, but when Otto returned from his trip and heard that the police had searched his room, he gave himself up. For five days no one knew what had happened to him. Even I began to miss him. Then Otto reappeared one evening at a Chinese restaurant.

"I was in Drapchi Prison," Otto announced.

"Did they beat you?" John asked seriously.

"It was like a hotel!" Otto said. "I had my own room. In the morning, the guard asked me what I wanted to eat, then sent someone to the market. The guards were O.K. until the last day. The bastards charged me forty FEC." John asked if Otto had seen any other prisoners. Otto said that he had not.

"Was it worth it?" John asked.

"I gave government back their stamp," Otto said, "but first I make two visas."

* * *

"We have to see the Potala," John said once we had settled into the third floor of the Banak Shol Hotel. "That is, *if* you can handle being a tourist for a few hours." John put a colorful, postcard-sized sticker of the Tibetan national flag on his black shoulder bag. I admired the colorful sticker of two facing snow lions with red and blue rays streaming from a rising sun. John gave me one. He had gotten two at the Office of Tibet in New York, and had forgotten about them until now. I put the sticker on the cover of my journal. We rented bicycles from the hotel and raced them through the streets to the Potala Palace.

I had imagined that the Potala's thousand small rooms would be adorned with *thankas* that portrayed alternately enlightened or horrific manifestations of the human subconscious against a backdrop of colorful silk brocade, with the walls blackened by eons of accumulated soot and floors slippery from centuries of spilled yak butter. John veered his bicycle around a dog with a mutilated haunch that stared at two men unloading yak quarters from the back of a truck onto the dirt alley.

At the palace we locked our bicycles and walked up the long switchback of stairs; dwarfed by the palace's white walls rising into a cobalt sky, I thought of standing at the base of Half Dome in Yosemite with John three years ago. We had climbed the Northwest Buttress in one day instead of the usual two. In order to lighten our loads we did not bring extra equipment or clothing. We carried one quart of water each during the eleven-hour ascent, and each lost fifteen pounds. A lightning storm approached the cliff as we summited, and we ran down the back of the dome without touching the metal handrail.

Six Chinese soldiers with AK-47s slung over their shoulders smoked cigarettes at the entrance. I wondered if the police were there to arrest the monks for subversive activity. Surely they were not sightseeing. "*Tashi delek,*" I greeted the soldiers in Tibetan. They did not respond. We paid our entrance fees and passed through a large wooden gate into a courtyard with red and green trim on the wooden balcony.

A Chinese woman standing on the steps leading into the Potala's East Wing spoke to a tour in English. "Before Tibet's peaceful liberation from its feudal past," the woman said, "serfs had no rights. Brutal warlord monks tortured their serfs in human sacrifices. Now, thanks to the People's Government, the monks at the Potala Palace enjoy total religious freedom. I have arranged for you to meet a Tibetan monk who will tell you how happy the Tibetans are in the Motherland."

"These Tibetans are barbaric," an overweight man said. He was breathing hard and had the crimson face and distended neck veins that precede a massive coronary. John and I looked at each other in stunned disbelief; no one had questioned the tour guide's version of Tibetan history.

I noticed a beckoning side door next to the stairs that was slightly ajar. The soldiers had entered the courtyard but were not paying attention to the tour. John saw me moving toward the door and grinned enthusiastically. Without saying anything, we walked through the side door. Shouts followed us down a corridor that opened into rooms piled with carpenters' tools and stacks of slate shingles. The voices almost caught up to us as an unlocked wooden door led us into a red courtyard. There were no visible handholds on the steep maroon walls. A half-wall on one side looked out over the valley floor 500 feet below. We were trapped. The voices were upon us.

Terrified of being caught, I climbed over the half-wall, lowered myself gently onto a two-foot-wide slate roof, and crawled as fast as I could beneath the locked wooden shutters that lined the wall. John followed. No soldiers ventured onto the roof after us, but I continued to crawl farther away from the yelling. The houses on the valley floor looked diminutive next to the winding banks of the Kyichu River. "Slow down, you crazy bastard," John called after we rounded a bend. I did not stop until I found a shutter that opened. When our eyes eventually adjusted to the darkness, we explored the Potala not open to the tourists.

We lost track of time, how many floors we hiked up or down, and where we were in the palace labyrinth. Lit matches cast eerie shadows on padlocked doors and clay hearths blanketed by dust. We tried to climb to the highest roof, but locked doors and dead ends forced us down into the Potala's depths. We negotiated stairwells clogged with broken timber, trash, and excrement, which left us silent for long periods. I thought of how easily the tourists had believed the tour guide and became angry at myself for not challenging her.

John wedged a copy of a U.S. Congressional resolution on human rights violations in Tibet, which he had gotten in New York prior to our departure, into a padlocked door. The resolution, dated June 7, 1987, stated succinctly that 1.2 million Tibetans had died from execution, imprisonment, and starvation in Tibet's thirty years of military occupation; that 6,254 monasteries had been destroyed, and only thirteen rebuilt; and that Tibet was being colonized by Han immigrants. "I had forgotten what a hard-hitting document this is," John said. He stopped to admire the piece of paper, which stood out like a flag from the door frame.

I asked John what he expected to accomplish by leaving the resolution, and how he thought the Chinese police would respond. John said that he had not thought about it. He disliked the fact that Tibetans got no information other than the Chinese party line from the *People's Daily*. I became angry at John in a way that I never had been before. As long as I had known him he had loved to indulge in these sorts of quixotic adventures; but leaving this resolution behind could get Tibetans in trouble. I started to yell at John for being reckless, but as usual his easy grin and humor disarmed me. We both realized that no one was likely to see the piece of paper for years, and we laughed at the idea of such an effete gesture.

Sunbeams straying into a corner of the dark hallway drew us to a room with a crack in its shutters that opened easily. I was surprised to see the late afternoon sun on Chokpori Hill, where Lhasa's most prestigious college of medicine once stood. The Fifth Dalai Lama had Chokpori Medical College built in the seventh century. Physicians from all over Mongolia and Tibet were educated there, until Chinese soldiers bombed it to the ground with artillery. Now all that remained was a television tower on a barren slope.

John leaned out the window and looked down two stories to a sloping ramp of trees. The cracks in the ancient mortar looked as though they could provide finger-width holds to the ramp. "We can downclimb this!" John exclaimed. As we made our way down the wall he talked about sharing the resolution with fellow travelers. He suggested that we leave the shutters unlocked; we could come back another night with other travelers and have a Potala party.

"We have to *do* something," John said.

I agreed with John that something had to be done about Tibet's plight. But I still needed to recuperate from Everest. I coveted my breakfasts of yogurt and fried eggs wrapped in pancakes with chocolate sauce at a Chinese restaurant. My afternoons were devoted to drinking cold beer in the hot sun and writing exaggerated postcards home at the Lhasa Cafe, a new restaurant in the Barkhor, where an Austrian chef made apple strudel, bratwurst, and potato salad. In the evenings I wanted to enjoy six-hour dinners with other travelers.

*   *   *

"How's the intrepid traveler?" John inquired as I sprinted out of bed and down the hall to the hotel's communal toilet. This particular toilet was a noisome reminder of other hygienic atrocities I'd experienced around the world. I held my breath.

Dysentery was not new to my travels. I had my first bout in 1979, mountaineering in Peru with John. After eating salad on our descent into the lowlands, I became stricken with diarrhea. Then, in 1983, after a month of not getting sick on rancid yak butter tea in Ladakh, in northern India, I considered myself immune; in the capital, Leh, I thought I could drink the water with impunity. One should never think one can drink or eat anything in Leh with impunity.

Squatting and holding my breath like this at 12,000 feet made me lightheaded. I envied John's intestinal fortitude. He ate ravenously and rarely had to run for a toilet, as I often did. John made fun of how I hoarded bits of newspaper, the small Tibetan currency notes worth two cents, even bus tickets. No scrap was too small, no parchment too rough that it could not be used in an emergency. I had eaten nonstop for two weeks and was still unable to gain weight, which made me wonder what sort of parasites I was hosting.

*   *   *

We met another American woman in the market. Julie had saved enough money working as a nursery-school teacher in Colorado to travel for six months in Asia. She traveled with a "male friend" from India to Pakistan, crossed the Karakoram Highway to Kashgar, and continued along the old silk road to Urumchi and Turfan before they split up. He went to Beijing. She came to Tibet. Both John and I told her we were glad she came to Tibet. Julie smiled. She planned to stay in Lhasa for a few weeks, then hitchhike to Everest. She also asked if we wanted to play hackysack in the Barkhor Square. We became an attraction among the chanting monks and Khampa dancers. John and I tried to outdo each other, intent on impressing Julie.

A Tibetan woman lunged for the Tibetan National Flag sticker on John's camera bag. "Watch it!" John warned. The woman lunged again for the sticker and berated John in Tibetan. I could not understand everything the woman said, but I recognized her hand in the shape of a pistol pointing to the sticker and back to John.

That night we ate dinner at Julie's favorite restaurant, the Sunflower Cafe, which was run by a cantankerous Chinese man who thought Tibet should be free. Lu served warm beer and charged too much for his mediocre food, which had to be eaten while sitting on miniature stools around miniature tables. But the atmosphere was appealing, and we became regulars.

One night Lu closed the restaurant after the other customers had left. We were drinking warm beer and blasting Dylan on Lu's tape deck, and John was talking about politics. We thought Lu was getting ready to push the six small tables together and get his bedding out from the kitchen, but instead he handed everyone at our table another can of beer, and said gruffly, "On the house for my American friends."

"You won't make any money if you give away beer," John said.

"Americans are good business!" Lu said. He smiled his rotten-teeth smile, then scrunched up his face. "There was a public execution in Lhasa today. Two Tibetans killed at the People's Stadium."

"Did you see it?" John asked.

"Had to. A representative from every business is required to go, then report back to others. China has executions every year before the People's Congress. This year, 15,000 people come." Everyone at the table strained to discern Lu's thick Chinese accent over the blaring tape deck. "The police tie prisoner's wrists behind back. After prisoner's crimes are announced, police pull up on wrists to break elbows. Then each prisoner is shot with one bullet in back of head. They charge family five dollars for bullet."

"That's on a par with the Khmer Rouge," Julie said. John and I agreed.

"Used to be worse," Lu said. "Before, they cut prisoner's tongue out. Otherwise Tibetans screamed, 'Free Tibet,' before they shot." Lu leaned forward to ask, "Why do my American friends think execution at this time?" Lu looked inquisitively at us, sitting in stunned silence. "Dalai Lama in United States now," Lu said. "He make political speech to U.S. Congress. China wants to show the world they will not be push around by U.S. government."

"How do you know this?" John asked.

"The Chinese broadcast it on the street," Lu said.

Two nights later Lu said there was a rainbow over Potala; that same night, all of us felt three subtle seismic tremors. "I am not religious," Lu said. "But I believe everyone should be free to practice religious. Rainbows and earthquakes are auspicious signs for Tibetans."

*   *   *

At 9:00 the next morning, September 27, 1987, one dozen monks from the Sera Monastery carrying homemade Tibetan flags began a circuit of the Jokhang Temple. The monks chanted, "Free Tibet," and "China out of Tibet." All business activity ceased as Tibetans left their shops and homes to march with the monks. By the third circuit there were 300 people marching and chanting. A dozen police arrived in jeeps and beat the monks with rifle butts, but they were vastly outnumbered, and the demonstrators continued toward the Cultural Palace.

A hundred yards ahead I saw a flash of maroon and yellow robes surrounded by men in green uniforms with raised truncheons. John, Julie, and I ran with Chinese, Tibetans, and tourists alike down the wide boulevard. On the sidewalk to our left, two policemen beat a Tibetan woman to the ground with their truncheons. Hundreds of people had stopped to watch but did nothing. I could not believe what I was seeing. I was also unable to intervene, and in the mayhem I briefly lost sight of

John. Julie and I ran toward the police jeeps that blocked the main intersection in front of the Cultural Palace.

Five young cadets stood at attention while a group of older police beat a Tibetan couple. The audible *crack* of a truncheon slicing a hunk of flesh from the man's head registered as terror on two of the young cadets' faces. Another cadet winced as the man fell to the ground. The cadets laughed nervously as their elders beat the woman on the head, back, and legs. A pair of policemen grabbed the man's wrists and ankles and swung his limp body onto the back of an open truck. The police continued to beat the woman as she climbed onto the truck to stay with the man.

Hundreds of people saw the Chinese police beat the Tibetans. No one tried to stop them. I counted eight monks thrown into the truck before it drove off. With the monks gone, the police raised their truncheons and dispersed the crowd still converging in front of the Cultural Palace. Suddenly, the three of us were holding hands and running down the wide boulevard away from the police.

CHAPTER SIX

....

ARREST

....

"JOHN'S BEEN ARRESTED," Julie said, when she found me eating *thukpa* (noodle soup) at a Tibetan restaurant the next day. "Two policemen saw John's sticker of the Tibetan flag. They interrogated us for hours. John got the police to let me go. You have to get all of your books out of your room—"

"*John's* books," I corrected her. The Tibetan woman in the market had warned John to take that damn sticker off, but he kept it, insistent on making a point—on not being intimidated. Julie immediately got up to leave. "Where are you going?" I asked.

"To clean my room before the police do. You'd better, too."

I thought of racing back to the room to retrieve John's books and my journal. Sitting there, I envisioned the police catching me when I tried to leave the room with the incendiary publications. I decided to finish my *thukpa* and then walk slowly back to the hotel. When I arrived, five policemen were already crammed into our tiny cubicle. John was with them.

"We have some trouble with your friend," a Chinese police captain said in English. "Wait outside." John looked with forlorn eyes at the books, papers, our passports, and my journal on the night table. Two Tibetan men in plainclothes sat next to John on his bed. One man was balding and had a paunch. The other was a teenager trying to grow sideburns. Two Chinese policemen in uniform sat on my bed. Our possessions lay strewn about the room. "Wait outside!" the captain said again.

I did not have to be told a third time. To my surprise no one fol-

lowed. Long, panicky strides took me down the stairs to my bicycle and
the street. If the police found John's resolutions where they were hidden
in the ceiling, he could go to prison. I did not think the police would
physically hurt him, but he could be learning Chinese the hard way for
an indefinite period of time. I was sure I too would be arrested once they
read my journal. Although I had liked the individual Chinese people we
had met, every page of my journal mourned some aspect of China's
occupation and colonization of Tibet. I resolved to eat as much as I
could while I remained free.

* * *

A stiff hand on my shoulder interrupted my second steaming bowl of
thukpa. "We got the stickers in Hong Kong," John whispered quickly.
"They don't know about the resolution yet."

"I told you to take that damned sticker off," I whispered back, before
seeing the two Chinese policemen behind John. "*Ni hao,*" I greeted the
first man in Chinese. He led me out of the restaurant and prevented
John from getting into the jeep that had brought them. I dropped my
bicycle key out the window for John before the police and I sped off
through the cobblestone streets.

The jeep's screeching siren warned the pedestrians and bicyclists,
who fled from its path. I felt a visceral sense of helplessness that reminded me of when I had been arrested twice, in New York City, when I
worked on the United Farm Workers grape boycott in 1976. Still an
idealistic teenager, I had been arrested for posting colorful "BOYCOTT
SCAB GRAPES AND LETTUCE" stickers in the subway, then a week
later for singing, "We Shall Overcome" in a supermarket that sold scab
grapes. Both times a judge heard my case and released me within twenty-four hours.

A Chinese woman selling preserved apricots outside the Banak Shol
hotel jumped as the jeep skidded to a halt inches from her stand. A
Swedish couple registering at the desk paused to watch us. I had no
thought of fleeing as the police led me up the stairs.

"You will call me Mr. Chen," the police captain said, standing at
attention. He had a hard face and eyes that gave nothing away. He
picked up my journal with its sticker of the Tibetan national flag and

said, "First we have trouble with your friend. Now we have trouble with you. Where did you get this flag?"

"It's not a flag," I said. "It's a sticker."

"It is Tibetan flag!" Mr. Chen screamed. "Tibet is part of China!"

Even if the five policemen and I had been friends we would have been uncomfortable in such a cramped space. I opened a pack of Marlboros and offered one to Mr. Chen. He refused automatically, refused a second time, then finally accepted a cigarette. So did the Chinese deputies and the undercover Tibetans.

"You don't smoke?" Mr. Chen asked.

"It's bad for your health," I said.

Mr. Chen proceeded to attack me with a barrage of questions: Where did I get the flag? How many did I bring into Tibet? Who did I give them to? Where? Why? I tried to answer each question correctly. None of the police seemed to mind when John walked in and sat down next to me. After an hour, Mr. Chen grabbed my journal and our passports. The deputies took the stack of evidence. "You are forbidden to leave your room tonight," Mr. Chen said. "You will report to the police station tomorrow morning at ten."

After they left, John said, "The young Tibetan trying to grow sideburns and the Chinese mute took Julie and me off the street at gunpoint. I had a resolution in my camera bag. They took us to the police station and interrogated us for three hours. The deputies kept looking at the Tibetan flag. They inspected it, fondled it. In a way I think they were fascinated by it. I was terrified they were going to open the bag and see the resolution."

A grin broke across John's face. "It didn't take long to figure out how to try to get rid of the resolution. I stood up and grabbed the bag. They were as surprised as I was. Then I pretended that I had explosive diarrhea. One of the policemen led me to their bathroom. He tried to watch me go. 'No way!' I shouted, and slammed the door shut. Then I dropped our resolution into the black hole."

The siren from the departing police jeep drove us to the window. The two deputies had been stationed as guards at the hotel's front door.

"Thanks for getting me arrested," I said.

"We wouldn't be if you had cleaned the room before the police came. Didn't Julie tell you?" he replied. For a second John became livid with anger, then said, "What does Chen mean by having us return to the police station at ten? Let's find Julie and get some beer," John said.

"What about the deputies?"

"You must be flustered," John chided. "If the chance to see Julie doesn't make you want to sneak out of here now, think what miserable company you'll make in prison."

Even when I was mad at John, I couldn't stay mad at him for long. John's good humor had enabled me to rappel twenty pitches in a blizzard off El Capitan, to almost enjoy shivering all night in a boxcar going east when we wanted to be going west, and to tease that Julie wanted me, not him.

That night I could feel myself losing the ability to distinguish fantasy from reality, paranoia from fear. I lay awake worrying that the police would read my journal and discover that I despised the Chinese occupation of Tibet. What I had seen in Tibet affected me deeply. The Tibetans were tourist attractions in their own country, the way native Americans are in parts of the United States.

The next morning, John assembled paper, pen, money, cigarettes, and condoms on his bed in preparation for our trip to the police station. For John, going to jail was another adventure, like hopping trains or climbing Everest. I asked if he thought we were going to summer camp. John didn't take the bait. Looking out the window and seeing that there were no guards and no jeep to drive us to the police station, he said, "If they won't drive us, I'm going to take my time getting there." I put water purification tablets in my left sock, antibiotics in the right.

We pedaled slowly through the park behind the Potala toward the station. The smell of rotting leaves made me homesick for New England's fall explosion of color—anywhere but this windswept desert. Then John stopped his bicycle next to a beautiful Tibetan girl and motioned for her to get on. She hopped sidesaddle across the back of the bicycle and wrapped her arms around his waist. Her long black hair swayed as John wobbled to a start. Soon the three of us were laughing as we wound our way through the park.

* * *

Under different circumstances the Tibetan rugs and couches that decorated the station might have lent it a pleasant air. Mr. Chen stood up from his desk. His face looked stern. "Sit down," he ordered, pointing to the couch near his desk. "You will begin by telling me your professions, and where you live."

"We are students," I said.

"You are not student!" Mr. Chen shouted. "Mr. Ackerly. Where are you from?"

"Washington, D.C." John said.

"Washington!" Mr. Chen yelled. "Home of CIA! What is CIA doing in China?"

"We are tourists," John protested.

Mr. Chen slapped the table and screamed. "Tibet is part of China! You are not tourists! You work for CIA. You come to China to make trouble." The jugular veins on Mr. Chen's neck bulged as he repeated the same questions that we had already answered. John maintained that we had gotten the flags from a street vendor in Hong Kong, and that neither of us could remember what the man looked like or where his shop was. In spite of Mr. Chen's yelling, John remained pleasant and calm. He also tried to appease Mr. Chen.

"What does 'national' mean?" Mr. Chen yelled, holding John's camera bag with the sticker of the Tibetan national flag inches from John's face.

"We have the same thing in our country," John said. "Each state has its own flag. It represents its own distinct area, the way Tibet is a distinct part of China."

"National means independent. Tibet is not independent. What does 'national' mean?"

"In the United States," I said, hoping to distract Mr. Chen, "native American Indians used to live all across the country before the Europeans came. Now there are relatively few Indians left."

"Yes!" Mr. Chen exclaimed. "What would you say if your Indians cried, 'Free America?'"

"They still cry, 'Free America,'" I said.

"Tibet is part of China."

"Just since your military invaded—" I interrupted. John kicked me under the table.

"Tibet has never been independent," Mr. Chen screamed. "Tibet will never be independent. Tibet is part of China." Mr. Chen did not hit me, but I think the thought crossed his mind. Instead of yelling at me again, he said, "In China, we have ways of changing your attitude." He walked to a back room to yell first at his deputies and then into a phone.

"Do you *want* to get your passport back?" John hissed. "I forgot to tell you—they found the picture of us with that Reagan cut-out."

"No wonder they think we're CIA."

"They thought Reagan was for real," John said. "I didn't say anything. I wasn't sure if it would help us or hurt us." After a long silence, John said, "China doesn't put U.S. citizens in prison."

"They will if they read my journal."

John laughed. "I'd be worried too if I had written what you did. So *don't* argue with Chen," he whispered, as Mr. Chen emerged from the back room.

"China signed the Geneva convention in 1981 regarding the acceptable treatment of prisoners," John announced. "I would like to see the statutes that we have violated. In English. It's international law."

Mr. Chen pointed to a poster behind his desk that I had been too scared to notice. "'Article Five,'" Mr. Chen said. "'Aliens are forbidden by Chinese law to endanger the national security interests of China, harm its public interests, or disturb its public order.'"

"How have we endangered China's national security interests?" John asked.

Mr. Chen slammed his fist on the table. For a second I thought I might get to kick John. John's face turned the same shade of red as Mr. Chen's, but he managed to suppress his anger.

Our interrogations took on a regular pattern. Mr. Chen repeated the same series of questions. John tried to placate Mr. Chen and kicked me under the table when I argued. I began to sense that underneath Mr. Chen's hard police exterior, he himself was seeking answers to the questions that he asked. John's training as a lawyer gave him remarkable grace under the pressure of interrogation. Before law school, John had been defenseless when anyone yelled at him. As for me, I was a victim of passion and mood, which had just been made worse by medical school.

A group of French trekkers came into the station to get Alien Travel

Permits. Mr. Chen retreated into the back room while one of the deputies issued the permits. John produced a deck of cards and played solitaire. I became so curious about the back room that I meandered over to the slightly open door. Mr. Chen stood over the Tibetan trying to grow sideburns; both men were intent on my journal. Seeing this—even more than John kicking me under the table—prompted me to stop arguing with Mr. Chen.

"The Dalai Lama say many things to your government," Mr. Chen said when he returned. "China get bad press. We don't know what we're going to do with you. But we're going to punish you." Mr. Chen let the seriousness of our situation register on our faces before he continued, "Report here tomorrow morning at 10:00. You must write self-criticisms and bring them with you."

After being interrogated for eight hours, John and I were allowed to ride our bicycles back to our hotel without a police escort. We should have been elated, but we continued to argue. I said we should consider trying to leave Lhasa immediately. John said he wasn't going anywhere until he got his passport back.

* * *

"How's this for a self-criticism?" John said, reading from a page in his journal later that night. "'I apologize for any trouble I may have caused the People's Republic of China. I have always been an admirer of the People's Revolution, and supported the People's Republic of China. It was not my intent to harm anyone by bringing postcards of the Dalai Lama to Tibetans. I am sorry for the trouble that this careless deed has caused me, and for the shame it has cast upon my ancestors.'" John looked up with glee. "They'll love the line about bringing shame to my ancestors," he said. "The Chinese really relate to that kind of stuff. What did you write?"

"Nothing."

"But Mr. Chen—"

I interrupted John by asking if he still had his map of the Dalai Lama's escape route in 1959. "Now you're talking like the old Blake," he said. John retrieved the folded paper from his pack and surveyed the route from Lhasa across the Himalayas to Bhutan. "It took the Dalai

Lama several weeks to cross the Himalayas," John said. "It's a direct route. If we're considering an overland escape, I think we should cross into Nepal near Everest, where we already know the route. It's almost October: if there's a storm, if we choose the wrong pass, we could freeze to death. We'll have to avoid being seen the whole time. The border will be intense. We could say that we lost everything in an avalanche."

This John, the one I knew and loved, disappeared again after only a moment, replaced by the poised lawyer. He refolded the map. "The more I think about sneaking out of Tibet," John said, "the more it makes sense to stay. Mr. Chen will return our passports tomorrow. He has to. China has to officially notify any foreign national's government within forty-eight hours of his arrest."

* * *

"Our superiors in Beijing have decided to release you," Mr. Chen announced at four the next afternoon, after we had spent six hours that day in the station. "You will pay $200 each for a flight to Beijing tomorrow."

"We don't have enough money for a flight anywhere," John lied.

Mr. Chen disappeared yet again into the back room. I knew that John was pushing him, testing the limits. This time it worked. Mr. Chen returned our passports and John's camera bag and said that we had four days to leave by bus. John argued that we should have at least ten days, and got the extra time. My journal was brought out next. It had a clean rectangular patch in the center where the sticker had been torn off. The police, it appeared, had not been able to decipher my handwriting. Mr. Chen sat next to John and opened my journal to the last page.

"What is this?" Mr. Chen yelled, his voice sounding enraged.

"It's nothing," John said, easing my journal from Mr. Chen's hands and dropping it into my lap. "It's just about the demonstration. Everyone's talking about it. It's no secret."

I said that I had only written about the demonstration on the last page. Noticing Julie's name in the paragraph before the demonstration, I pointed this out and said, "This is about, you know . . . sex." Mr. Chen blushed when I moved my index finger in and out of my fist. He

approved when I tore the offending pages out, and struggled to maintain his composure while I shredded the pages into the ash tray. Soon
after John and I were racing our bicycles down the street, away from the
station.

* * *

Lu let us cook dinner in his kitchen that night. Julie and I chopped garlic and ginger while John stirred the wok. Otto supervised. We played
rock and roll too loud on Lu's rickety tape deck as I put eleven cloves of
garlic into the stir fry and Julie poured in a healthy splash of warm beer.
My arm tingled expectantly when it touched hers as we worked side by
side in the kitchen. Earlier, as we had walked to Lu's place from the
hotel, Julie and I had first discussed the prospect of spending the night
together.

"Tomorrow is Chinese National Day," John said to no one in particular.

"Like Fourth of July in America?" Otto said. "Lots of boom-boom.
Tomorrow I make my own boom-boom. Today I bought a Chinese flag
to burn."

"They'll shoot you," John said.

"Is no problem," Otto said and waved his hand. "In Germany, I
burn already ten, eleven American flags at demonstrations. Tomorrow I
burn one Chinese flag. No problem."

Lu stormed into the kitchen. He looked disgruntled. "I had trouble
with police," Lu said. "Three come in earlier. They want to eat free. I let
them eat, but not for free."

"Won't that cause trouble for you later?" Julie asked.

"Everything cause trouble for me later," Lu said.

CHAPTER SEVEN

CHINESE NATIONAL DAY

ON OCTOBER 1, Chinese National Day, no one had any idea that Lhasa would erupt in the largest nationalist uprisings witnessed by Westerners since the Chinese invasion of Tibet in 1950. As they had four days before, a handful of Buddhist monks circumambulated the Jokhang Temple at 9:00 that morning. The monks carried outlawed Tibetan flags and chanted, "China out of Tibet." Pilgrims stopped prostrating. Urchins stopped tugging on tourists' sleeves. Monks stopped chanting scripture. Women stopped hawking necklaces of cheap turquoise. All business activity ceased as Tibetans left their shops and homes to follow the monks.

At the completion of their third circuit around the Jokhang, hundreds of chanting Tibetans faced seven jeep-loads of police. The police beat the demonstrators with shovels and rifle butts. In the time it took the police to drag twenty monks into a nearby police station, the crowd outside swelled to about a thousand. Gunfire inside the building apparently made the crowd of Tibetans believe that the police were killing the monks.

I learned all of this from Julie, when she returned to find me breakfasting on sweet tea and yogurt on the third-floor balcony of our hotel. Julie had gotten up and gone out early, and had seen the crowd grow so fast that she knew something horrible was going to happen. By the time she returned I had already seen the column of black smoke rising above the Tibetan rooftops in the distance. John had come by fifteen minutes earlier to tell me he was going out on his bicycle, convinced that something important was going on. He had kept us up late the night before talking in legalese about how China's "liberation" of Tibet was a euphemism for colonialism and violated international law. Now it seemed that Tibet's unrest under Chinese domination might be erupting into violence. The thought of treating wounded demonstrators terrified me. As a newly minted physician I had never treated patients on my own. I stuffed bandages and antibiotics into my shoulder bag.

Julie and I held hands as we ran among the hundreds of people flocking to the Barkhor Square. The streets were so crowded that people had climbed on top of the metal fence around the Tibetan Medical Institute to look into the square. I searched the crowd for John; he was probably in front of the Jokhang. A police line kept us from crossing the open square, where a single overturned police jeep poured smoke into the air. A soldier raised his AK-47 to strike a Tibetan woman who tried to step through the line.

"Should we go back to our hotel?" a couple obviously from the Lhasa Hotel asked us from where they stood at a bus stop. "Isn't this exciting! What's happening?"

A shrill cry came from a Chinese man twenty feet away who was being beaten by a crowd of Tibetans. Blood spurted from his head amid a swarm of fists. He cried for mercy as the Tibetans beat him with stones and stripped the film from his camera. I felt a wave of revulsion for the Tibetans. No one deserves to be beaten. Desperately flailing his arms, the man broke free and ran toward a group of Chinese watching from a distance.

A troupe of "*kuchi kuchi*" children chased another Chinese man who was trying to ride his bicycle through the mayhem. The children threw rocks that thumped against his back. One rock hit the man's head and sent his bicycle reeling. The children shrieked and threw more rocks. They treated the Chinese man the way they might have tortured an insect.

The crowd parted for a fire truck that I assumed would be used to extinguish the burning jeep. Instead, soldiers on top of the truck aimed the hose into the crowd. Sixty soldiers goose-stepped toward the crowd from behind the truck. The sound of coordinated boot steps striking the cobblestones punctuated the soldiers' collective yell. Instead of stopping to extinguish the burning jeep, the fire truck headed toward the Jokhang.

Defiant fists rose out of the crowd of Tibetans guarding their most holy temple. They threw a volley of rocks that shattered the fire truck's windshield. The truck made a U-turn and the soldiers followed. The Tibetans cheered. Julie and I took the opportunity to sneak past a policeman who had turned to watch the fracas. We sprinted in a wide arc around the burning jeep, wider around the truck and retreating police, and joined the thousand-strong crowd of Tibetans who were cheering and crying in front of the Jokhang.

Tibetan women alongside the monastery's outer wall were pounding the street's cobblestones into baseball-sized pieces, which the children in the crowd scattered at everyone's feet. A monk standing on the Jokhang's roof raised his fists and yelled down into the square. The woman next to me screamed, "They're killing our monks." I looked around for John and saw another crowd forming in front of the police station. More overturned vehicles clogged the alley.

The Tibetans next to me stoned a Tibetan man who had been taking photographs of the crowd. The man dropped his camera and fought for his life. The Tibetans are killing their own people, I thought; had they gone mad? Suddenly it dawned on me that this Tibetan must be an undercover policeman, like the other man with a camera. Their developed film would have been used to identify and arrest people later.

Julie was gone. I called her name and looked frantically around the crowd. I needed to find her, John, a familiar face. A crackling sound stampeded the crowd. I found myself stooped over, scurrying toward the burning vehicles. I ran past an overturned jeep with a young boy squatting next to a puddle of leaking gas. I spotted a policemen on the roof and jumped into an alcove where several families had taken refuge. Most of the people looked frightened. Two of the Tibetan men in the alcove stepped out into the alley, threw rocks at the policeman on the roof, and ducked back.

The two men laughed. They seemed deranged, and they presented easy targets for the police. A withered Tibetan woman with a baby in her lap motioned for me to come farther inside as the men stepped into the alley to throw another rock. When they returned to the alcove amid a burst of firecrackers, their faces were frozen in terror.

I peered around the corner and saw a woman shouting at the head of a crowd in front of the police station. Five Khampas with red tassels wrapped around their heads ran up to the station and climbed in through the broken first-floor windows. Other men followed. Soon every window had Tibetans climbing into them. Office furniture and police files were thrown out of the windows and piled at the station's front door. Boys lit the pile using gasoline-soaked rags. The flames quickly engulfed the mountain of furniture and paper and reached up to the police on the roof. A nearby explosion paralyzed me, and I felt my heart thundering in my chest. A tire had exploded on one of the vehicles; I felt my arms and legs to make sure they were all there.

More fireworks from the rooftop drove home the sickening realization that the sounds I was hearing were actually weapons fire. I thought for a second about how easily human flesh is torn, took a deep breath, and ran out of the alcove and back to the Jokhang. I found Julie holding a Tibetan woman's hand in front of the two-story pillars at the Jokhang's main entrance. The three of us embraced. Tears rolled off the woman's ruddy cheeks. She said something that neither Julie nor I understood and we started crying. I cried for the Tibetan children throwing rocks at the Chinese and for what it must have been like to grow up in Lhasa. I also cried for the Tibetans still inside the police station, and for John, who I hoped was not hurt, or worse. But mostly I cried for the fear of losing my life.

"John's taking pictures in front of the police station," Julie said. "I'm running film for him. It's a miracle Otto hasn't been shot. He's at the front of the crowd, throwing rocks at the soldiers."

◆ ◆ ◆

Four running men carrying a monk on their shoulders materialized out of the smoke. The men ran as fast as they could and seemed to transport the monk effortlessly. Bullets strafed the wall over the men's heads. They ducked and kept running toward us. Even at a distance, I could see the monk was badly burned. A policeman on the roof took a bead on the men with his pistol as they ran. Everyone around me was crying.

"*Amchi yin*" (doctor am), I said, and the crowd let me squeeze closer to the monk. He appeared to be unconscious. The skin on his arms, face, neck, and head was covered with second- and third-degree burns. Large sheets of flesh hung from his scarlet arms like onion skin. I could see in an instant that he needed intravenous fluids, antibiotics, and sterile bandages, none of which were available. Instead, the crowd lifted the monk overhead. He opened his eyes and raised a clenched fist. Everyone cheered.

The sweet smell of the monk's cooked flesh made me gag. I could do nothing for him except document what I had seen. The crowd headed toward the soldiers at the far side of the square. The soldiers fidgeted with their machine guns. They looked nervous, as though they did not know how to respond to the angry Tibetans.

A Tibetan man came toward me carrying a small boy in his arms. Blood poured from the boy's mouth and soaked the left side of his shirt. The man stared straight ahead. The boy looked up at me with weak eyes as I examined where the bullet had entered through a small hole near his heart and exited through his back. The boy needed a trauma surgery team. I pressed my hand onto the wounds as life faded from his eyes. His dazed father kept carrying the boy through the maddening crowd. There was nothing I could do. I looked for a weed or tuft of grass with which to wipe the blood from my hands.

Six men carried another man on a table through fifty yards of machine-gun fire on the ground in front of the police station, dodging single rounds from snipers on the roof. Even before they arrived I could see that the man on the table was dead. Pink foam oozed from his nose and mouth. His neck was warm but he had no pulse. Like the boy, he had been shot through the chest from the front, but this bullet had gone through his heart.

Eight small children hiding behind an overturned jeep used slings to throw rocks at the police in front of the burning station. They used the same slings that the shepherd boys had shown us in the mountains, but they were not old enough to make them *CRACK* when the rock shot out. The police fired back over the children's heads. I doubted the kids understood that they could be killed by the police. "Stop," I yelled at the children, but they didn't listen.

A group of Tibetans huddled in the middle of the square. My first *"Amchi yin"* got me close enough to see a woman in a lavender *chuba* cradling the head of a sixteen-year-old boy. The bone structure and soft tissue on the right side of the boy's face had been completely caved in by multiple blows with a blunt object. A Tibetan man wearing a business suit told me in broken English that the police had beat the boy inside the station. I watched the woman pour water from a chalice into her son's unresponsive mouth. The boy was dead.

A war cry rose from a line of soldiers at the far end of the square. Their cry continued as they ran toward the Jokhang. Tibetans in front of the temple raised their fists in the air. The thought of fleeing did not occur to me. I picked up rocks along with the hundreds of Tibetans all around me. In a desperate reaction to the killing I became part of the violence myself. "Motherfuckers," I yelled at the oncoming soldiers. "Die, motherfuckers," I screamed with the first volley of rocks.

To my amazement, the soldiers turned in mid-stride and fled before our mob. We chased the soldiers off the end of the square and down the wide boulevard toward the Cultural Palace. This ignited cheers from the Tibetans, as though for a day they had reclaimed Lhasa.

* * *

At dusk I stared at the smoldering remains of the collapsed police station. I still had not found John or Julie. Besides the few Tibetans who were sifting china cups and other such prizes from the rubble, I was surprised to see how quickly the pilgrims had resumed their circumambulations of the Jokhang. Amazingly, tourists were browsing among the stalls, most of which had already been set up again. A young man I had never seen before approached me and asked, "Are you the American doctor?" in an English accent. He introduced himself as Andrew and asked if I would come with him to treat a man he knew of who had been shot in the ankle. During the riot Andrew had put a pressure dressing on the wound, and had gotten directions to the man's home.

Between the two of us we confirmed six deaths that we had witnessed personally: two monks in their twenties shot with AK-47s; one ten-year-old boy shot through the chest; a thirty-six-year-old woman shot in the head; a thirty-five-year old man shot in the heart; and a sixteen-year-old boy beaten to death inside the police station. Andrew recorded each detail in a notebook.

Snapping his head from side to side as though he were still under fire, Andrew led me along the shadows from the two- and three-story Tibetan buildings, where darkness hid the dirt but not the smell of the excrement spread onto the streets. I walked quickly behind him, carrying a rock in each hand. After throwing rocks at the police I was nervous about carrying them now, but I was afraid of being attacked by mongrels. Lhasa's dogs were out in force.

Headlights swept toward us across the cobblestones and we ducked into a side alley. A Lhasa Apso barked ferociously, and just got louder after I pretended to throw a rock at it. The dog continued to bark while a Toyota Land Cruiser filled with Chinese police drove slowly past the alley. We crossed a well-lit area that cast an eerie glow over a pack of mongrels heaped in confusion against a wall. Piled on top of each other they looked like adorable children; I counted fourteen of them before we rounded the corner.

"This is it," Andrew said in front of a large wooden door. He knocked using its serpentine brass ring and shouted in Tibetan that he was with a Western doctor. Two men appeared in the alley and I turned to the wall and pretended to urinate. Andrew continued to knock and yell—too loudly, I thought. I became convinced that the whole neighborhood could hear him. He didn't even know for certain if this was the man's house.

Footsteps approached from inside. Andrew started speaking in Tibetan, then in Chinese. "Shit," he said, walking away. "When I was talking in Tibetan, she said this was the right house. But my Chinese is better than my Tibetan. Once I switched she said that the man had already gone to the hospital."

Andrew said that he knew of another man who had been shot in the leg. "He's somewhere near here," he said. After we first knocked loudly at two wrong doors, a woman let us into her home.

"Thank you for coming," the woman whispered before closing the wooden shutters. "I know how dangerous the streets are after dark." She wore a colorful striped apron over a turquoise *chuba*. "My name is Pema. I am sorry that we have to be so secretive." Pema smiled as she said this and I noticed that she spoke fluent British-accented English. In the dim light she motioned for us not to make a sound. We followed her up wooden stairs that were so steep I had to use the handrail.

"There are informers in every compound," Pema whispered. "One of the neighbors will report us if they see us coming in or out." The darkness scared me, but I was more afraid of not being able to help anyone who had been shot in the leg.

"I'm pleased to meet you," Pema's brother said, lifting a heavy hand to greet us. He said his name was Tsering. They were Nepalese Tibetans who had come to visit relatives in Lhasa. Tsering pulled the sheet back to reveal dirty, blood-soaked gauze wrapped too tightly around his right thigh. Most of the blood on the bandage had dried. Both of his feet had good pulses and color, which meant that the bullet had not severed an artery. I asked Tsering if he could move his toes, which he did, slowly. He could also move his foot and raise his leg.

Andrew asked a series of questions to find out what Tsering had seen. A Tibetan doctor had stitched Tsering up and discharged him before the police surrounded the *Mendzekhang.* Tsering went on to say that he had heard of wounded Tibetans who went to the People's Hospital, the only place where Tibetans had access to Western medicine, and the doctors there sent them to prison.

Tsering looked more relaxed than I felt. I couldn't remove bullets without hemostats or injectable anesthetic; I had only bandages and antibiotics. Butter lamps beneath an eight-by-ten-inch color photo of the Dalai Lama lent an air of calm to the room. Pema poured cups of butter tea and my stomach shuddered. I sipped the tea anyway and found it to have a fresh, clean taste. I thanked Pema in Tibetan and she refilled the cup to the brim after the first sip.

"You speak Tibetan well," Pema said.

I smiled back. Tibetans always said this no matter how little Tibetan you spoke. I asked if she had any boiling water with which to wash my hands.

Pema shook her head yes from side to side the way Indian and Nepalese people do. "I am familiar enough with Western medicine to know that you would need lots of boiling water."

Pema poured hot water over my hands and the dried blood coming off my fingers unleashed mental images of the riot: the burned monk, the boy beaten to death inside the police station, the man shot in the heart. Tears blurred my vision for an instant. Pema offered me a filthy towel, but I air-dried my hands instead.

"Did the bullet go in here?" Andrew asked as I dabbed gauze on the bloody, fingertip-sized holes in Tsering's thigh.

Tsering beamed. "In one side. Out the other."

"Where were you when you were shot?" Andrew asked.

"I was standing in the alley next to the police station," Tsering said. "The police were shooting pistols and machine guns from the rooftops and the street. I was looking right up at the policeman on the roof who was aiming down at me with his machine gun. A monk next to me was hit first. Then something hot ripped through my leg and I knew I was hit."

"What happened to the monk?" Andrew asked.

Tsering turned his head to stare straight up at the ceiling. A single tear rolled down his unshaven cheek. "The bullet blew the back of his head off. Blood got in my eyes. I couldn't see anything after that. Someone dragged me back."

I cleaned the entrance and exit wounds with hydrogen peroxide, imagining the tunnel of macerated flesh through the thickest part of Tsering's thigh. He needed intravenous antibiotics in a hospital. If an infection set in he could die, or at least need to have his leg amputated. By adding a mere squeeze of antibacterial cream, I was just putting a Band-Aid on an abyss. After rewrapping Tsering's thigh with a clean roll of gauze, I asked if his leg hurt.

"No," Tsering replied, and we both laughed. I knew he was lying. It was an odd moment to laugh but it made me feel better.

"You're a lucky man to have such a wonderful woman taking care of you," I said, and paused for their full attention before asking if Tsering had ever had a bad reaction to Western medicine before. I explained how to take the antibiotic pills and Tsering reached up and squeezed my hand. After effusive thanks and a few last sips of butter tea, Pema hurried us out into the dark hall. Before entering the street, Pema thanked us for saving her brother's life. I said that I would bring more antibiotics later.

"Please don't come back," Pema said. "It is too dangerous. If the police see you . . ."

"Wait," Andrew said, as I left to go off in search of John and Julie. "I need your help at a meeting."

CHAPTER EIGHT

LHASA BY NIGHT

ONE HUNDRED FOREIGNERS who had witnessed the riot had gathered in a dormitory room at one of the Tibetan hotels. I was so glad to see John and Julie sandwiched on a bed with eight other travelers that I didn't hear Andrew yelling from the middle of the room. John said he had spent the entire day in front of the police station. He photographed Tibetans besieging the police station and burning it to the ground; police taking pictures and video of the crowd from the rooftops; and police firing AK-47s and automatic pistols from the rooftops and the street. Julie had hidden three rolls of John's film.

"The telex and trunks have been down for three days," Andrew shouted. He held a clipboard as he spoke to the throng of people still buzzing with a cacophony of Asian and Indo-European languages. "There are no press here as yet. Which makes it imperative that we accurately record confirmed, first-hand accounts of what happened for the press when they do arrive. Before we start, I will state for the record that the purpose of this gathering is wholly nonviolent. As a group, we must condemn those individuals who threw rocks at the police."

"I throw rocks at Chinese police if I want," Otto shouted from a bunk bed in the back of the room. Other travelers who had participated in the demonstration hurled insults and profanity at Andrew. The meeting swiftly disintegrated into mayhem. I wanted to tell John and Julie what I had seen but I was mute. Even though I was a physician I felt unable to save anyone from dying. Throwing rocks at the police was the only thing I could do to try to stop the killing. Andrew gave up insisting that the rock throwers should be condemned and moved on to the next item on his list.

Andrew was a great organizer: he had to be in order to extract useful information out of the chaotic meeting. In less than an hour he confirmed that an additional six Tibetan men, women, monks, and children had died from gunshot wounds or beatings. "I'm afraid the police are taking the wounded to prison," Andrew said. "Now, an American doctor who treated a man who was shot has something to say."

Unexpectedly, I faced the crowd. I had always been afraid of speaking in public. I mentioned the wounded hiding in their homes who feared arrest if they went to the Chinese-run hospital. I estimated that there were ten times the number of wounded to the number of dead, and said that we needed more bandages and medicine. Julie volunteered to make the rounds of the Tibetan hotels later and collect medicine.

"The police are coming!" a voice outside the window called. People stampeded through the only door. I peered out the window and saw a Tibetan boy who worked at the hotel standing in the shadows. There were no police in sight, but I had no doubt that the meeting had been too loud.

*   *   *

Hours after the meeting, Julie and I fell asleep in each other's arms in her room. Lobsang, a Tibetan man who worked at the hotel, awoke us at six the next morning with homemade *momos* (yak meat dumplings) and tomato-egg soup. "Very good," Lobsang whispered excitedly to Julie. "Thank you for your help. Any wounded Tibetans, I am sending to you."

"No tourists with sore throats," I said.

"Yes," Lobsang said, smiling broadly. "Don't forget—I am not English-speaking. If the Chinese find out, I am finished." Lobsang excused his still-smiling self and we organized the assortment of medicine that Julie had collected into piles of antibiotics, pain medicine, antiseptics, and bandages. We had one pair of hemostats to use removing bullets, but no sterile gloves or injectable anesthetic. The different kinds of antibiotics we did have could provide broad-spectrum coverage for infections. This could save lives.

Andrew came in with a handsome blond couple. Heidi was a Swedish woman who, like me, had just graduated from medical school. She and I talked about not being able to do anything really helpful, and doing more harm than good if we were caught. Mark had a full beard and wore wool Tibetan pants and a vest. He looked like Saint Nicholas and turned out to be a lawyer from Australia who had lived in Tibet for the past eight months. He spoke good Tibetan and Mandarin. His dress and gentle demeanor stood out in marked contrast to Andrew, who wore a green army coat.

"You look tired," Julie said to Andrew.

"I was up all night," Andrew said, "trying to find someone at the Lhasa Hotel who would take a roll of film to Hong Kong. Let's get started, shall we?" Andrew opened his clipboard and said that he had met a Norwegian orthopedic surgeon who would act as a back-up if anything happened to Heidi or myself. The five of us would work as a team.

"This room will be our temporary base of operations," Andrew said. "Mark, you and Heidi comb the Barkhor for contacts to more wounded. Stick to people you can trust, like elders and monks. Blake and I will meet you at ten in front of the Jokhang. I met a monk yesterday who told me there were many wounded monks hiding inside the monastery. I set up a meeting. Julie, you stay here and coordinate incoming messages. We should all meet back here at noon."

* * *

At ten, when we all met at the main entrance to the Jokhang, a group of Chinese and Tibetan men were looking intently at two posters glued to the monastery walls. One poster was printed in Tibetan, the other in Chinese. I stepped closer to read them and two of the men raised their truncheons. I had to jump back to avoid being hit. Apparently, the men were police.

"Keep walking," Mark said. As we continued on he explained, "Those are posters from the underground. I saw them go up early in the morning before the undercover police staked them out. They say, 'Ten to twenty people died yesterday. Ten to twenty more may die. It does not matter. The Chinese have been here for thirty years. Now is the time to act.'"

By now, circumambulating the Jokhang had almost become second nature. Not only did I recognize individual vendors selling jewelry, but also monks who had stayed in the same place reciting scriptures for weeks. One pilgrim stood out more than the rest. Regardless of the time of day he was naked from the waist up and did prostrations around the Jokhang. At first his spasmodic movements and piercing stares had frightened me. Today he smiled, and I felt an unspoken kinship with him.

Convinced that a side door near the Jokhang's main entrance would open, Andrew stationed himself next to fifty older Tibetan men and women doing full-length prostrations. Like inchworms moving in place, they stretched out over the stones and then stood up, raising their clasped hands to the sky. Andrew devoted his undivided attention to the wooden door, which was obviously bolted on the outside. A small eddy of onlookers gathered in the stream. Even the Tibetans were wondering what he was doing. Andrew was a menace; I was sure he would get us all arrested. Heidi slipped a hand under Andrew's arm and gently coaxed him away.

Mark led the four of us past the prostrators into the temple's main entrance. Five somber Tibetan monks with well-muscled arms blocked the stairwell. Mark explained that Heidi and I were Western doctors and we were led up the steep stairs to the roof. Strings of prayer flags ran from the tips of the many-terraced roof to the tops of its golden spires, and carved wooden dragons jutted out from the corners like medieval gargoyles. We crossed several terraces, ran twice across open stretches, and climbed down some steep stairs to a dank room permeated by the smell of rancid yak butter and incense.

Our first patient told Mark that he had been shot in the stomach. He pulled up his shirt to reveal bloody gauze wrapped around his abdomen. Fortunately, the laceration skimmed but did not enter his side. "Kelsang was standing in front of the police station when a policeman on the roof shot him," Mark said. I had been so absorbed with Kelsang's wound that I had not heard him talking the whole time.

"How many demonstrations has Lhasa had?" Andrew asked.

"Since 1959," Mark translated, "there have been many major demonstrations that these monks know of, all as large as yesterday's riot. Yesterday was different only because Western travelers witnessed it."

A dozen pus-filled craters dotted the next monk's forehead. The oily salve he'd put on it made his burns look worse than they were. He held out a wide-mouth jar for us to examine the preparation of ground herbs it held. In my fledgling Tibetan I said, "Tibetan medicine is good." The monk nodded and stared deep into Heidi's beautiful cerulean eyes. Heidi told Mark to explain how important it was for the monk to avoid touching his face, and to wash his hands regularly with soap. I doubt the monk heard a single word Mark told him.

"Sonam here was one of forty-seven monks taken into the police station," Mark translated. "At first the police used rifle butts and cattle prods to beat all of the monks. Lobsang Gyatso, a twenty-one-year-old monk from Sera Monastery, was beaten on his head with a shovel and fell to the ground inside the police station. Sonam did not see him get up. After the police station began to burn, everyone was taken into the back rooms. The place was getting very hot and Sonam saw a Tibetan policeman let some of the monks escape out a side window. A Chinese policeman saw this and shot the Tibetan policeman in the head with his AK-47. At this time Shue Chuntan, the head police officer, ordered another Chinese policeman to shoot one of the monks in the forehead. His name was Lobsang Deleg, and he was killed instantly. Buchong, a twenty-two-year-old monk from the Jokhang, was also shot. The bullet went in the front and out the back. Both monks were killed with AK-47s. The police told the monks that they had killed a total of eleven people inside and outside the police station. Sonam says the number is really much more, because that doesn't include the Tibetans who will die in prison."

Sonam talked so vehemently that the corners of his mouth were bleeding. This made him look grotesque. He seemed more interested in Heidi's eyes. Heidi realized that the monk had a crush on her and held his hand. Andrew checked to make sure that he had recorded each monk's name, age, and monastery correctly.

"If it weren't for Champa Tenzin," Mark said, referring to the grotesquely burned monk who ran with Sonam inside the burning police station and engaged the police in hand-to-hand combat, "Sonam thinks the police would have killed more people. Sonam and Champa Tenzin created so much commotion that others escaped. The police threatened to shoot anyone who did not exit one of the side windows and run back to the police lines. But after jumping out the window into the side alley, they took a chance and ran toward the Tibetans. He says his face was burned during his escape, and that his burns were minor compared to Champa Tenzin's. This does not bother him compared to a rumor that he has mentioned several times.

"Sonam keeps saying that the police have killed two of the Jokhang monks with lethal injections. The police use two types of injection on the prisoners. One makes the prisoners talk freely. Another makes them crazy, if it does not kill them. He says the injections scare him more than being tortured."

Walking down the main street the next day, I felt as though someone was staring at me and I turned around. People were running to get out of the path of an army convoy of twelve trucks. Each truck had machine guns mounted on its top and cab. At least thirty-five soldiers with fixed bayonets peered menacingly over the side rails of the trucks. Tibetans on the sidewalks made derogatory hand signals and uttered curses under their breath. The caravan of special forces had been sent from Golmud to quell any future uprisings. They had traveled across the Friendship Highway, as we had. With the arrival of reinforcements, snipers appeared on the rooftops around the Jokhang Temple. The soldiers enforced a 10:00 P.M. curfew.

* * *

"We were mentioned on the front page of the *New York Times*," John said. "Two days in a row: 'Two Americans arrested in Tibet.'" I had not seen John for two days and thought he was kidding. "I've never been more serious. That piece of paper I sent out with our names and passport numbers got on the wire service. Today I talked to correspondents from the *New York Times*, the *Washington Post*, the *Christian Science Monitor*, the *Far Eastern Economic Review*. So many I can't remember. And they all want to speak to the young doctor who is sneaking out to treat the wounded. Andrew is pissed."

John explained that three plane-loads of new arrivals to Lhasa had arrived from Chengdu. The passengers on each plane consisted of military officers and reporters; both groups were trying to look inconspicuous to the other. John said the Chinese were dumb to let the reporters in at all. The reporters didn't sound that smart either—they were all staying at the Lhasa Hotel.

"Can you believe a French magazine is paying an American photographer $600 cash to sneak into Sera Monastery?" John said. "I'd sneak into Sera for free. We should go there tonight. You could treat patients and see a sky burial."

"Do you know what Chinese soldiers did in Sera last night?" I asked.

"No! Do you?"

"They broke in at two in the morning to beat the monks with cattle prods and clubs with nails driven through the ends. The soldiers tried to force the monks to renounce the Dalai Lama and Tibetan independence. After half an hour many of the monks were bleeding profusely. Blood was everywhere. One monk lost his right ear. Several were executed."

"How do you know this?" John asked. "Did the monks tell you? I'd give anything to be able to talk to an eyewitness."

We talked about our respective "tourist" and "medical" undergrounds. John told me about his epic ride back from the Lhasa Hotel at 4:00 A.M., well after curfew, while dogs attacked him.

"I was hoping things would calm down after the riot," John said. "It's just getting worse. All the buses leaving Lhasa this morning were turned back."

Some of the reporters traded bits of information ruthlessly, the way one might trade futures on a commodities exchange. Our story was valuable as an exclusive, if we had not spoken to any other information junkie. If we had, it was worthless. There were also reporters like Ed Gargan of the *New York Times* and Dan Sutherland of the *Washington Post*, who worked hard to get information on the streets instead of at the Lhasa Hotel bar. Tibetans and Westerners working to gather information and help the wounded felt deeply indebted to these and many other reporters whose presence, we felt, protected us.

* * *

A man named Adam who said he was from the State Department arrived in Lhasa with the reporters. Adam was tall, young, and blond, dressed in the khaki pants and upturned collar of an Ivy League preppie.

He bumped into us on the street "accidentally." We talked, and John asked if he could get word to our parents that we were safe. Adam said that he could, if we signed a release of information. I didn't trust Adam. "I advise both of you to leave Lhasa as fast as you can," Adam said. "If something happens, we can't do anything for you. The State Department has no jurisdiction in China."

"We'll be fine," John said. "We've got a week before we have to leave."

"None of my patients are fine," I added, and I told Adam about the twelve confirmed deaths, how wounded Tibetans were afraid to seek medical care at Chinese hospitals, and how monks said that the police were using injections to debilitate recalcitrant prisoners.

"I'll make a note of it in my report," Adam said.

"What is China's official statement about the riot?" John asked.

"The Chinese said that a few splittists staged a small demonstration," Adam said. "They said that Tibetans were angered by what they saw, took guns from the police, and shot the Tibetan demonstrators. The Chinese estimate that one Chinese policeman was killed."

"No police officer was killed," John said. "To the best of my knowledge."

"Leave Tibet now," Adam said. "It's for your own safety."

"What is the State Department's position on the riot?" John challenged.

"China is very sensitive about Tibet," Adam said. "We hope they resolve this incident as soon as possible, but it's not for us to get involved."

* * *

The next afternoon two of our arresting officers, the young Tibetan trying to grow sideburns and the Chinese mute, followed Andrew and me into the market. We were on our way to see a ten-year-old boy who had a fever from an infected gash in his scalp, which he'd gotten when a policeman had struck him with a bayonet during the riot. "I see them," Andrew said after I tipped him off, walking faster. The police were fifty feet behind us. Standing a head taller than the Chinese and Tibetans in the market, we were an easy target for our pursuers. "Follow me,"

Andrew said, zig-zagging between Chinese women selling vegetables. "Shit," Andrew exclaimed, as he splashed through a fetid orange puddle that spanned an alley. We ran down another cobblestone alley where human excrement seeped onto the street from a second-story toilet. A side alley let us sprint around a horse-drawn cart loaded with cabbages. We lost the police and resumed our search for the boy.

Andrew found the boy's house at the back of a construction site, but a stout woman in a purple *chuba* would not let us in. Andrew pleaded with her in Tibetan and Chinese, but she closed the door. I did not blame the woman for not trusting us, but I could not face the boy's dying from infection.

We saw sixteen patients on our second visit to the Jokhang, in a room where beams of light from windows near the high ceiling sliced through the dusty air. The monks were between seventeen and thirty-five years old; all had been beaten severely. After the riot, the police had rounded up twenty Tibetan men, women, and children and took them to an empty schoolhouse. They were beaten for two hours before being released with a warning: "If you demonstrate again, we will kill you."

A pattern to the beatings was obvious: bruises covered each person's head, spine, kidneys, and all the major joints. Nightsticks left long purple bruises on the back and arms. Stones left large, irregular, macerated blotches on the skin. Gun butts left raised triangular patches on the scalp. The external bruises did not bother us as much as the probability of internal bleeding. Even a slow bleed inside the head would increase pressure on the brain until it herniated and the person died. All of the monks complained of headaches, but they were alert, had clear speech, and their pupils responded to light. I knew that several nights later some of them would begin to slur their speech and lapse into coma; I also knew that I was powerless to do anything except document what I had seen.

In exchange for mild pain relievers and reassurance, we were overwhelmed by effusive thanks. Unlike the other monks we had seen inside the Jokhang, no one knew or would tell us the whereabouts of others who had been wounded. As we prepared to leave, I wondered how many more wounded were hiding in Lhasa's homes and monasteries. It was already four days after the riot. People with bullet wounds were dying from infection. Antibiotics were the only lifesaving thing I had to offer.

A nervous young monk came up to Mark and spoke earnestly. Mark translated, "His name is Lobsang. He is concerned about Jokhang monks who were arrested after the riot. He wants us to take their names to the Dalai Lama. Their names are Gyantsen Tharchin Champa Tenzin . . ."

"How many names is that?" Andrew asked.

"One name," Mark said. "You know him. He's the badly burned monk who ran in the police station with Sonam. He was arrested several days after the riot, along with Gampel Sengya, Donyo, and Gamyang Chodon and taken to Sangyip Prison." How could I forget the image of the burned monk, which woke me up in the middle of the night crying?

"Lobsang says that special torture teams from mainland China arrived in Lhasa's prisons after the demonstration. The monks are bound by metal cuffs on the wrist, which get tighter if they move. The cuffs are pounded while the police force the monks to say that Tibet is not free, and find out who organized the demonstrations. Each monk was stripped naked and beaten with clubs with nails driven through the ends, rifle butts, electric cattle prods, and truncheons. Lobsang says the police beat the monks into unconsciousness, then revived them with cold water. No food has been given to them for two days. 'Tibet's freedom will be your food,' one of the policeman yelled at them. Lobsang also says that their testicles were crushed by policemen standing on them."

"How does he know this?" Andrew asked.

"Lobsang tried to visit them in prison. He did not see the monks, but one of the Tibetan guards told him."

"Ask about the special torture teams," Andrew said, taking notes.

Mark translated after he talked with Lobsang for a while: "In addition to their beatings, the prisoners are hung by their thumbs, hung by their ankles upside down with a heater under their head until they pass out, tied to electric beds, and submerged in a tub of ice water. Lobsang says that these tortures were not done before the riot. He also says that he learned that the Austrian secret police helped train the Chinese police."

* * *

"You're under arrest!" a deep voice boomed as the door to my room was kicked open. I sprang into midair with nowhere to run as Julie stepped in. I told her she sounded like she had been taking voice lessons from Tantric chanting monks. Within minutes we were playing hackysack on the Barkhor Square in front of the Jokhang. Hundreds of Tibetans gathered around to witness the spectacle. Julie kicked the hackysack high into the air, to the crowd's astonishment, then let the sack bounce on her raised thigh and down to her feet, where she juggled it with the inside of each foot before passing it to me. The crowd cheered and pushed closer.

A handsome Tibetan Khampa with baggy burlap pants and untied boots stepped into our circle. Julie passed the sack to him and he kicked it hard over her head. The crowd cheered and a flock of children ran screaming after it. The largest boy returned the sack to our circle. He dropped the sack on his foot, juggled it three times expertly, and passed it to Julie. She juggled the sack a few times and passed it to the Khampa. The crowd cheered again as the sack soared over Julie's head.

I realized that we were as much of a spectacle to the Tibetans as the chanting monks were to us. I passed my overturned felt hat. Several Tibetans extricated small, crumpled bank notes worth one cent from folds in their clothes and put them into the hat. One Tibetan woman gave us a two-cent note. A father gave his child a coin to hand to us.

This inspired Julie and me to bring a Tibetan woman into the circle. She juggled the sack several times until the Khampa strode boldly over to her, grabbed the sack, and kicked it back into orbit. The crowd cheered and more crumpled, well-worn notes dropped into the hat. One woman with an infant on her back gave us five cents. The same woman pointed to me and made throwing motions with her arm. Several Tibetans in the crowd mimicked with approval. They must have seen me at the riot. I felt uncomfortable taking any money from a woman with a child on her back, but she wouldn't take it back. It was impossible to get the crowd to step back and give us enough room for more than a minute, impossible for the Khampa not to kick the sack as hard as he could each time he had the chance, impossible not to be awed by Julie's agility. In half an hour we had enough money for a round of beer.

＊ ＊ ＊

Mark pulled me off the sidewalk later that afternoon. It was the first time I had ever seen him looking distraught. He said he had just heard my name on Xinhua radio, in Chinese, broadcast from Beijing; it was said that I was a "splittist agent of the Dalai Clique," and that I had urged Tibetans to throw rocks at the police. It was also said that I had been arrested with another foreign instigator and we were being taken to Beijing for further questioning.

"I'm sorry I have to tell you this," Mark said. "I think you should know that Andrew told a reporter and a wire service that you threw rocks at the police during the riot. I couldn't believe he could do such a stupid thing. The damage is done."

I was stunned. I wandered away, and I'm not sure if I even said good-bye to Mark. Telling reporters that I had thrown rocks at the police jeopardized my being able to sneak out for medical rounds. Andrew had no reason to give anyone my name, unless he wanted to hurt me. I could feel myself exploding as my hotel loomed larger in front of my eyes. I found Andrew on the third-floor balcony, talking with John and a core group of travelers I recognized from the first meeting after the riot. Andrew didn't wait for me to reach him before leaving the meeting. "Let's talk in your room, shall we?" he said.

"Did you tell the reporters I threw rocks?" I exploded as soon as we were in my room.

"No," Andrew said, sitting down calmly on the bed.

"Don't lie to me," I shouted. "Did you tell reporters I threw rocks at the police?"

"Who told you this?" Andrew said, as though talking to a child. I yelled at him and he moved farther back on the bed.

John came in then and told Andrew, "Blake is easily excited. You should have seen how hyper he got when we were arrested." He asked in a nonjudgmental tone if Andrew had told a reporter that I had thrown rocks. Andrew squirmed.

"Did you?" I yelled before John could intervene.

"Well . . ." Andrew stammered, ". . . yes, I did."

"*Why?*"

"Because you *did* throw rocks."

■ Tingri, the staging point for all travelers approaching the Tibetan side of Mt. Everest.

■ Cooking inside the tent of Tsarang, one of the yak men who helped lead us to Everest.

■ Our trip to Everest, like all of our travels in Tibet, was a yak-intensive experience.

■ Enjoying a few of the choice food items available to the American
Everest climbers we encountered, 20,000 feet up at Camp II.

Looking up at the North Col on Everest from Camp III at 22,000 feet—
the start of technical climbing.

The Potala, winter palace of the Dalai Lama.

JOHN ACKERLY

■ The streets of Lhasa.

JOHN ACKERLY

■ Overturned police vehicles burning during the October 1 protests in Lhasa.

■ Thousands of Tibetans filled the streets of Lhasa during the October 1 protests.

■ A twenty-five-year-old Tibetan man shot through the heart by Chinese police during protests.

■ A man carrying his ten-year-old son after the boy was shot in the chest during the protests.

■ Two monks running into the burning police station to rescue others trapped inside during October 1 protests.

■ Tibetans escaping from the side of the burning police station.

■ Champa Tenzin, a monk whose dramatic escape from the burning police station inspired the protesting crowds.

JOHN ACKERLY

■ John Ackerly (right) and myself with the Dali Lama in Dharamsala, northern India, seat of the Tibetan government-in-exile.

BLAKE KERR

■ Champa Tenzin in the Jokhang Temple in 1991, holding his prized photo of the Dali Lama meeting with George Bush.

"Don't you see how that jeopardizes Blake's staying in Lhasa?" John interjected.

It became clear why Andrew wanted me out of the picture. The reporters had been more interested in talking to us than to Andrew, the self-proclaimed leader of the "tourist underground." He was jealous. This was a brilliant way to get rid of me. My right fist tightened into a knot. I thought how good it would feel to punch Andrew, especially with his glasses on. "I'd like to punch you in the mouth," I told him.

"Are you threatening me?" Andrew asked.

"No—yes, goddamnit! I could be arrested again."

"Well, calm down," Andrew said. "We have to work together. We have to get medicine to Champa Tenzin."

CHAPTER NINE

SKY BURIAL

TERRY'S PARTIES WERE well known to Lhasa's overland travelers. An alcoholic and polysubstance abuser who smoked opium to wean himself from intravenous heroin, Terry cultivated the appearance of a suicidal clown: black eye-liner running into hastily applied rouge, electric lavender and orange pajamas, and a shawl draped protectively around his shoulders. He was fastidious about ensuring that he acquired all of the essential ingredients for a successful bash. Tonight he was proud to be offering forty liters of Tibetan *chang*.

Because of the 10:00 P.M. curfew, people began arriving before dark and filled the hall at the Banak Shol's rear perimeter. German punk, Japanese new wave, and English rock and roll blasted out over the Tibetan homes in the Barkhor. From a balcony I surveyed the moonlit clotheslines of socks and underwear in the courtyard and the hallway that led to our rooms. I was convinced that the police would come to arrest us, and that I would have to climb over the hotel's rear wall. John said I was being histrionic. I no longer found any glamour in the idea of an overland escape.

"Come in before you freeze to death," John said from inside the hall. I didn't answer. He and Otto climbed out the window to join me on the balcony, and I listened to them discuss a demonstration John had seen today at the post office. Eighty monks from Drepung Monastery dressed in civilian clothes marched all the way into town before being discovered. Four trucks of soldiers drove past them on the way to the monastery. When the soldiers arrived at Drepung and realized their mistake, they raced back into town. According to Otto, the soldiers found the monks in front of the post office, beat them with cattle prods and rifle butts, and carted the limp bodies away in the trucks. John said that he hadn't seen anyone unconscious.

"I was afraid to take pictures," John said. "A woman next to me got her film taken."

John's description of the demonstration prompted toasts to the Tibetan freedom fighters. "We will have a travelers' demonstration," Otto said.

"No more politics tonight," Terry said from inside the hall. "We have forty liters of *chang* to drink."

John's story of the beaten monks blended with the details of my day: another boy dying of sepsis whose parents were afraid to let us into their home; a forty-seven-year-old woman shot in the breast; and a sixty-eight-year-old man who had been shot from a rooftop. We also learned of an imprisoned monk who had suffered a compound fracture of his right arm during a torture session.

"The Chinese are even crueler than the Americans," Otto said. "I would like to shoot the police. Maybe I steal an AK-47."

I heard the sound of glass shattering as a rock crashed through a window above the tape player. This didn't stop the blaring music. Like Otto, I had thought of killing. During the riot I had imagined getting a gun. When I was charging at the police, I don't know what I would have done with a gun if I had gotten one, but I knew that I had wanted to kill. This realization frightened me more than the idea of being shot. My life and training as a physician had taught me to respect all life. Now I feared I was becoming obsessed with the thought of taking life.

"A toast to Otto," John said. "We won't see him again if he's shot by the Chinese police."

More toasts, and curses at the rock thrower, accompanied the music that continued to bombard the Barkhor. It occurred to me that the stone thrower may have been hiding someone wounded during the riot; perhaps they just wanted to sleep. I wanted to enjoy myself at the party and felt jealous that I could not relax. I also felt repulsed by Westerners enjoying themselves while Tibetans were dying.

From the balcony we watched as, across the courtyard, four of the five policeman who had arrested John and me—the mute, two deputies, and the young Tibetan trying to grow sideburns—walked down a hall and knocked at our door, which John had padlocked. "Now do you believe it?" I challenged John.

We saw a young Tibetan man sprint conspicuously along a third-floor balcony above the police, slide down a corrugated metal roof, and lower himself into the courtyard. The brilliant moon illuminated his frenetic dash through the clotheslines and his ascent up a ladder to our balcony. He moved with the awkward intensity of an animal that was about to be slaughtered. Breathless, he told us his name was Namgyal. I wondered if he was working with the Tibetan underground.

"Very bad men," Namgyal said, flipping his pinky up. *Chang* perfumed his breath and slurred his speech.

"Why are the police here?" John asked.

"All foreigners must leave Lhasa. The police have developed their film of the riot. They will arrest everyone involved. Everyone." Namgyal left as frantically as he had come, reversing his route down the ladder into the courtyard. The police were sure to see him.

"Let's leave," I implored John.

"You can leave if you want to," John said. "We're getting more *chang.*" Otto and John climbed back inside, leaving me alone to brood out in the cold.

"You're under arrest!" a deep voice boomed. I jumped and looked around frantically—there was nowhere to run on the balcony. Then Julie appeared, smiling, climbing out the window. "Nice trick," I said, shivering. She covered me with a blanket and we hid in the shadows. The four police officers came four different times to our room, and four times an acid knife gouged at my stomach as they pounded and yelled at the door. But for some reason they never tried to break in, nor did they come to look for us at the party. "They're afraid of us," John boasted later, but I wasn't inclined to take unnecessary chances. I cursed him for staying here tonight, and for making me realize that I could not leave, either. When the police finally left the hotel at four, Julie and I went into our room, made love, and fell asleep, while John and the others partied through the night.

* * *

"The police came to our hotel last night. They were checking visas," Mark said at the next morning's medical meeting. He sat next to Heidi, their arms and legs touching. "I didn't care that my visa had expired," Mark said, "but all of our extra medicines were under the bed. I stayed under the covers and pretended to be sick. I said I had been vomiting and had violent diarrhea. They ordered me to leave as soon as I could travel. I'm going to sleep at a safe house tonight. You are all welcome to stay there if you want."

Mark described the house of a Tibetan friend of his. It reminded me of the home of Carolyn's Tibetan family, but nothing about it sounded safe—especially when Andrew said that he would stay there. That night Julie and I snuck into a different hotel's dormitory for a catnap and left before the hotel employees woke up. If we were caught, I reasoned, it would be better for the hotel if we had not registered.

Mark and Heidi met a man named Tenzin in the Barkhor, who led me to Lodi, another gunshot victim from the riot. Tenzin was so nervous that he made me nervous. His pinstriped suit seemed an anachronism in the Barkhor. When we got to Lodi's house, Tenzin said that after Lodi was shot in the calf, the police had taken him to the People's Hospital, where a Chinese surgeon removed the bullet. I told him that I had not heard of any wounded Tibetans receiving medical care at the People's Hospital.

"After the surgeon finished sewing the wound," Tenzin replied, "Lodi ran away. Otherwise the police would have taken him to prison."

Lodi sat in a chair with both legs on a stool. I later learned he was twenty-six years old, but a fever and taut facial muscles made him look much older. Lodi looked so ill that I barely noticed a petite Tibetan woman with us, who I assumed was his daughter. Lodi's wound was badly infected. The sutures had to be cut and the abscess drained or he would die from sepsis.

Lodi laughed and I asked what was so funny. "Lodi says he must have very bad luck," Tenzin said. "He sprained his good ankle when he was running away from the police."

"Lodi has good luck not to be in prison," I said.

Lodi repeated three times that he would have done anything to avoid going to prison. He had heard about the special torture teams that had come from Chengdu to Lhasa's Gutsa Prison, which used new electrical devices on Tibetan prisoners. He asked why I washed my hands, and I gave him a graphic description of great "Kali germs" that destroy all neighboring flesh unless you take "special pills" that His Holiness also takes when he gets sick.

"*Dalai Lama yakbudoo,*" Lodi said as I cut his sutures, to a rush of foul-smelling pus.

"*Dalai Lama yakbudoo,*" I said. Lodi winced as I irrigated the pus from the wound. I explained how the "special pills" circulated in the blood, and why his daughter had to wash her hands before she changed his bandage.

Tenzin said that the nineteen-year-old "daughter" was Lodi's wife, Kunyang. She had a terrible skin infection that had not gone away for over one year. The Tibetan doctors at the *Mendzekhang* had tried many different medicines. None had any effect, until they tried penicillin. Now the infection was improving. I asked Kunyang how many children she had and she looked down in shame. I looked to Tenzin to see what I had said wrong. He looked away.

With tears in her eyes, Kunyang talked softly in Tibetan. Tenzin translated: "Last year, Kunyang was six months' pregnant. The work unit leader saw that she was showing and ordered her to go to the People's Hospital for a checkup. Inside the hospital, the Chinese doctor said that she needed an operation to save her life. Kunyang insisted that she was healthy. She argued with the doctors but it was no use. The nurse injected her belly with something that made the baby come out. She heard the baby cry. Then the nurse gave an injection into the soft spot on the baby's forehead. The next day Kunyang was forced to have an operation. She says she cannot have any more children."

* * *

"Give me your medical bag," Andrew demanded the next afternoon. He looked delighted. "It's not fair to your patients. You're too high-profile. The police have come to your room two days in a row. The streets are teeming with army and undercover police."

I gave Andrew my shoulder bag. Instead of yelling at him I wanted to cry. The truth was that it would be a relief not to sneak out to see patients. Like the wounded Tibetans I had snuck out to treat, I had also become a fugitive. I was afraid to stay in Lhasa and afraid to go back to my hotel in case the police were there. I was afraid of my patients dying from infection and afraid to go to their homes in case we were seen. Stripped of my medicine bag, I could no longer hide behind the brave image of a physician helping the wounded.

More than explicit violence, I was afraid of the implicit violence in Tibet's military occupation: the wounded being sent to prison; the routine torture of prisoners; women entering Chinese hospitals for checkups and being forced to have abortions and be sterilized. I was also afraid for those Tibetans who remembered their country before the Chinese invaded, and for the two generations of children who had grown up in fear.

* * *

On what I thought might be our last night together, Julie and I went to an after-hours bar packed with other Westerners who had decided to stay in Lhasa as long as they could. We held hands under the table. Heidi had her arm around Mark. John cuddled a puppy in his lap. "Her name is Rangzen," John said. "I found her on the street. Rangzen means freedom in Tibetan."

"Him," I corrected, inspecting the dog's genitals.

John stroked the puppy affectionately. "I wonder where Rangzen and I will sleep tonight."

"I saw a man get dragged out of his house this afternoon," Julie said. "On the main street. Six policemen beat him unconscious with their rifles. I heard his head crack."

"This afternoon I saw a Tibetan man swerve his bicycle in front of a police jeep," Mark said. "The driver had to swerve and slammed on the brakes. He jumped out and beat the man to the ground with a truncheon. Then a fat man got out of the jeep with his pistol drawn. He stepped on the Tibetan's neck and put the pistol to his head, the whole time yelling in Chinese. 'Shoot me,' I yelled, 'Shoot me, you bastard,' until the police got back in their jeep and drove off."

"We have to get out of here," John said.

"You've got to get your film out," Julie said.

"The first scheduled commercial flight to Kathmandu is leaving in two days," John said. "A bus leaves from the Lhasa Hotel to the airport at four in the morning. We could dress in clean clothes. The police won't expect us to be mixed in with the Holiday Inn tourists, and that crowd doesn't get searched."

An Australian man at an adjacent table pulled a lubricated condom over his head, which squashed his eyes shut and flattened his nose. He gulped air through his mouth and exhaled through his nose to inflate the condom like a balloon. His table of fellow Australians stamped their feet and banged their fists and their countryman's neck and cheeks turned scarlet, as the tip of the condom swelled to basketball size and exploded.

Out on the empty street, John ripped the latest in a series of official announcements off a wall:

The No. 3 Announcement by the People's Government of the City of Lhasa

In order to ensure the smooth implementation of the opening *police*, to promote the development of tourism industry in our region, to increase our economic and technical exchange and co-operation with different countries in the World, to avoid appearance of displeasure in foreign affairs's work, the city announces as follows:

1. We extend welcome to friends from the different countries in the World who come to our region for sightseeing, tour, visit, work, trade discussion and economic cooperation.
2. Who ever comes to our region must *respects* our State sovereignty, abide by the *lows* of our country. They are not allowed to interfere in internal affairs of our country and engage in activities that are incompatible with their status.
3. Foreigners are not allowed to crowd around watching and photographing the disturbances manipulated by a few splittists, and they should not do any distorted propaganda concerning disturbances, which is not in agreement with the facts.
4. In accordance with our *lows*, we shall mete out punishment

to the trouble-makers who stir up, support and participate in the
disturbance manipulated by a few splittists.

Mark, Heidi, Julie, Otto, John, Rangzen, two fellow inebriated trav-
elers, and I all proceeded to rip down every Chinese poster in the
Barkhor, in defiance of the local *lows*. We stopped outside the Kiri
Hotel's two-story metal gate, which had been locked for the night.
Climbing the gate would have been a formidable task when sober.
Instead we played hackysack under the streetlight.

A rock skidded through our group. We could barely make out three
silhouettes fifty yards away next to a vehicle. I stopped the next rock
with my foot. They couldn't throw far enough to hit us directly. John
picked up a rock. So did Otto, Julie, and the two travelers. "One, two,
three," I whispered, and we launched a collective volley with no thought
of the consequences. Our rocks, too, fell far short of our target. The silhouettes jumped into the vehicle, which backlit their dome-shaped helmets. We froze in the approaching headlights.

The two travelers ran down a side alley. Julie and I scrambled over
the gate and sprinted across the courtyard. Mark, John, Heidi, and Otto
followed. The vehicle stopped outside the gate. The police got out and
yelled for the gatekeeper as a flashlight beam probed the dark recesses of
the courtyard. Julie and I hid in the toilets. The gatekeeper would have
to let the police in. They would wake up every traveler and tear the hotel
apart. How could we have been so stupid? I held my breath and stared
between the horribly stained porcelain foot pads. I never thought I
could have hidden in a Tibetan toilet, even if it meant avoiding prison. I
was naive. Julie and I huddled there for hours, unsure if the police had
left. We did not see the others again until morning.

* * *

I felt no animosity toward Andrew when we met for the last time to talk
about our patients, only sadness for how little I had been able to do for
the wounded. As a direct result of gunshot wounds and beatings during
the October 1 riot, we had confirmed twelve deaths. We also had documented fourteen Tibetans with bullet wounds, two monks with burns,
and fifty Tibetans with multiple contusions from severe beatings.

Andrew fastidiously recorded the name, sex, and age of each patient, the location of entrance and exit wounds, course of treatment, and prognosis. He also recorded details about four monks who were still missing from the Jokhang, two monks believed to have been killed by lethal injection, and the eighty monks from Drepung Monastery who were clubbed with cattle prods and AK-47s before being taken to prison.

Andrew thanked me for what I had done and said that he would stay as long as he could to collect the names of Tibetan prisoners. At that moment, standing in the street and wishing Andrew luck, I realized the importance of his forty-five-page handwritten document for the press. I admired his tenacity and his obsessive attention to detail. Andrew smiled and excused himself abruptly.

"There's a monk dying in the Jokhang," Julie said the next afternoon. "A monk approached me in the market. He said the police hit his friend many times on the head during the riot. Two days ago he started losing coordination. The monks didn't think anything of it. Then his speech became slurred. Now he's unconscious."

What Julie described was called a subdural hematoma. The police had hit the monk's head hard enough to break a blood vessel in his brain, which continued to bleed. The monk needed a hole bored in his skull to relieve the pressure. The thought of the monk's brain being squeezed against the inside of his skull made me shudder. So did the thought of trying to perform a trephination with a Swiss Army knife. "There's nothing I can do," I said. "Even if—"

Julie pulled a Dalai Lama postcard from the back pocket of her jeans. "If he can still see, we can hold a picture of His Holiness as an offering," she said. Julie was right. I felt embarrassed for hesitating. I was so tired that the thought of getting arrested seemed appealing; at least then I could relax.

We walked arm in arm through the Barkhor Square, where snipers with binoculars and telephoto lenses occupied the rooftops. Before completing a circuit around the Jokhang, we slipped into a close-by construction site. Chinese workers stopped laying bricks to giggle at the two lovers stealing up a bamboo ladder into the depths of an unfinished building. We continued to a back window that let us onto one of the Jokhang's rooftops. After crossing several terraces, we dropped onto Lobsang's balcony.

Lobsang jumped when we stepped into his room. It was reassuring to see his face. Shadows from seven butter lamps leapt across the walls as I used my rudimentary Tibetan and sign language to describe Julie's unconscious monk. Lobsang did not understand and left us alone in his quarters. Sitting quietly on the hard bench, I realized that I was bored. So much had already happened to us in Lhasa that I now needed the adrenaline rush I had become used to getting on a regular basis.

Lobsang returned with Tashi, a monk from Amdo who spoke English. "No one has heard of an unconscious monk," Tashi translated. "The police are preparing to storm the Jokhang. They have done this many times, sometimes killing monks. It is dangerous for you here. You have to leave. Lobsang wants you to take a message to His Holiness."

Lobsang looked at me quizzically and laughed. I asked why and Tashi said, "He's waiting for you to take notes." I pulled a four-by-four-inch bandage wrapper from my pocket and tried to write fast enough to keep up with Tashi's translating. "Puchong was shot through the left chest inside the police station on October 1," Tashi said. "Lobsang went to get the body with some of the other monks two days ago. When he asked for the body, the police demanded 650 yuan. Lobsang said monks did not have that kind of money. The police wrote their names down in a book and said if they didn't bring the money the next day they would all go to prison.

"Lobsang came back with the money," Tashi continued. "Puchong's hands were still tied behind his back. One bullet went through his chest. Another went through the stomach. The back of his head was crushed. Large bruises covered his kidneys. There were many bruises and cuts on all limbs. Puchong's body went to Sera for sky burial. Do you have all this down?"

Writing down what Tashi translated wasn't the problem. Reading it would be. Lobsang stopped talking and Julie asked if he had heard of any women in prison. Lobsang started talking again at high speed.

"For participating in the October 1 demonstration, Namla was taken to Gutsa Prison on the same day. She is only twenty-three years old, from Garu nunnery. The police stripped her and beat her with sticks with nails in the ends, rifle butts, and electric sticks. They also beat her while she was hanging from her ankles with a heater placed under her head, for hours. The police tied her to an electric bed, and tied an electric belt around her breasts." Tashi stopped translating and giggled with embarrassed discomfort. I asked what was funny and he said, "The police jabbed the electric stick into Namla's vagina."

I asked Tashi how Lobsang had come to know all of this. He said that Lobsang knew the woman's sister well. I looked for another scrap of paper to write on and Lobsang unfurled two white silk *khatas* and put them over our necks.

"Lobsang thanks both of you for what you have done for the Tibetan people," Tashi said. "He says that he will never forget you. He asks you to please tell the Dalai Lama what is happening to his country."

* * *

Like many Westerners who had seen the riot, Julie had decided not to leave, but to stay as long as she could to gather more information. The mobile loudspeakers broadcast in the streets that the authorities would be "lenient" with Tibetans who participated in the demonstration. Criminals who didn't give themselves up would be "punished." Julie and I planned to meet again somewhere, in Nepal, India, or back in the States. We told each other how much we wished we had more time together. We exchanged addresses and phone numbers and wept on each other's shoulders as we hugged.

John and I took showers, shaved, and washed our clothes, the better to blend in with the tourists at the airport. Before walking to the bus, which left at 2:00 A.M., John hid rolls of film in his dirty socks and underwear and scattered condoms throughout his pack, in an attempt to distract soldiers at the airport customs. We fought continuously during the hour-long walk to the Lhasa Hotel, but we agreed to pretend that we did not know each other at the airport; if the police held one of us back, the other would try to keep going. Four soldiers got on the bus with us.

At 6:00 A.M. the bus droned steadily up the Lhasa valley. The Tibetan homes and fields of barley in the valley seemed impossibly far away from the tumult of the demonstrations. A donkey stood unattended in a stream. Smoke curled out of an adobe house. A British couple complained that the bus was taking too long, and then we had to wait in line while soldiers checked each passport individually. I went before

John. Two male soldiers perused my passport and handed it to a woman, who noticed the canceled visa. She yelled at the men for what they had missed.

"Why canceled?" she demanded angrily.

"I made cheese out of yogurt to sell to tourists," I said. "I had to pay a fine."

"How much fine?"

"Fifty FEC."

The woman's professionally angry demeanor cracked. She smiled as though this had been an appropriate punishment and said, "I hope you learn from this lesson." She waved me on. "Stop," a soldier yelled. I spun around and the woman pointed to the airport tax counter. I was so happy to pay the airport tax that I didn't even mind waiting for John to get through customs.

John looked nervous when he handed his passport to the male soldiers. Once again, they both missed the canceled visa and the woman yelled at them. I imagined John being led away. He said something I couldn't hear and they waved him through. "They didn't even search me," John said after he paid the airport tax. "She asked me why my visa was canceled. Naturally, I told her the truth, that you had thrown rocks at the police—"

"John!" I exclaimed loud enough to startle a couple next to us.

"You would make a terrible secret agent," John said. "I told her I had changed 100 FEC for yuan on the black market. She wanted to know how much I was fined. I said thirty FEC and she said that wasn't bad. Someone else was fined fifty FEC for selling homemade cheese to tourists."

We waited another hour for the rest of the passengers to be processed through customs, another hour for a bus that took us to the plane, and thirty minutes standing on the tarmac while soldiers walked up and down the line, intimidating each passenger. Amid this final display of force, I noticed three sleek black helicopters with exaggerated blades stationed farther down the runway.

Instead of being ecstatic when the plane took off, John and I sat on separate sides of the cabin. As the snowcapped Himalayas passed beneath us, I wondered how many Tibetans were trying to escape across the mountains at that moment. What would happen to the burned monk? How many wounded Tibetans would die in their homes? How many people were being tortured in prisons? I felt defeated thinking of the ten-year-old boy who would die soon from infection. Up to now in my life I had always thought that living would be better than dying, no matter what. I had never seen children slaughtered in the street. I had never met monks tortured in prison and women sterilized against their will. In a moment of despair, I wondered if the Tibetan boy would be better off dying than living under Chinese military occupation.

I looked back at John and saw him staring out the window. I cried in fitful, uncontrollable sobs, and envisioned the body of a dead monk lying on a boulder. It was Puchong, Lobsang's friend. Large, ugly bruises covered the corpse, which had been shot once in the chest and once in the abdomen. The wrists were still tied behind the back.

When the sun hit the rock, the body breakers stopped drinking *chang* and began to hack flesh from the corpse. They chopped the body into small pieces and crushed the bones. Vultures waited patiently at the crest of the hill. Clotted blood spilled onto the rock and over the hands of the body breakers, who worked quickly, without pause, to prepare their celestial offering. In Tibet's high-altitude desert, with little wood for cremation and burial reserved for criminals whose souls should not be reborn, sky burial was a practical solution to the problem of death's decay. Once the flesh and bones were mixed with barley flour, the sky became dark with enormous black wings as the vultures descended upon their corporeal feast.

CHAPTER TEN

WHAT DO WE TELL THE CHILDREN?

KATHMANDU WELCOMED US with an extravagance of foliage, colors, and smells that was a stark contrast to desert-like Tibet. The taxi's two-tone horn parted the sea of pedestrians as we sped past glass shelves heaped with pies, chocolate cakes, cookies, and slabs of dark chocolate. Indian, French, Mexican, Italian, Greek, Vietnamese, and Tibetan restaurants beckoned. Rock-and-roll bars provided a backdrop for street urchins, skeleton-like cows, and a legless man pushing himself on a skateboard.

The desk manager of the Tibetan Hotel gave us a room for half price when he learned we were the "American doctor and lawyer arrested in Tibet." He also said we could make overseas calls at the hotel's rate. Before our calls to our families went through, though, we had a visitor.

"Dr. Kerr and Mr. Ackerly?" said a large, distinguished-looking man wearing a white linen suit. "Please allow me to introduce myself. My name is Kedar Man Singh. I am Kathmandu's official Associated Press representative. I am also the Association Francaise Presse correspondent."

Singh shook his head from side to side as he talked. "You are famous, really. The whole world is waiting for your story. I would like to take your picture and send your story on the AP wire as soon as possible."

Neither John nor I knew what to say. Singh kept talking. "There is much for you to do in Kathmandu. I am personally knowing the BBC man here. He is a very good fellow who also wants to take your photo and interview you. Tibet is a big issue in your country right now. You were in all the papers and magazines."

"We're in more trouble than I thought," I whispered to John, mimicking Singh's accent and shaking my head from side to side. "I have 108 hours of sleep to catch up on."

Singh wanted us to wear our packs for the picture. I also wanted to wear my wide-brimmed felt hat that smelled of yak butter and carried the many hues of the Tibetan landscape. We compromised and took two pictures, one with packs and hat and one without.

"What is happening in Tibet now you will not see mentioned favorably in our press," Singh said. "The Nepalese are afraid of China. We have had border disputes with China since 1962. It is an explosive issue. And why is Nepal so afraid to say the least little bit of criticism about China? Nepal has very big mountains, but it is a very small country. And China's army is so big!"

* * *

"I'm so happy you're alive," my mother said, crying through the long-distance crackle on the other end of the phone. I said that we were safe in Kathmandu, and that I would be home once I gained thirty pounds. "We heard you were arrested. Then the police station burned down. I thought you were killed." Her voice faded into sobs.

"It was a different police station," I said, trying to sound reassuring.

"I'm so glad you're safe. I'll call the Ackerlys right away." My mother explained that Michael Van Walt, the Dalai Lama's lawyer, wanted us to testify at a congressional hearing on human rights violations in Tibet. We had to fly to Washington, D.C., as soon as possible. John's parents and my mother would meet our flight. "I don't suppose you brought a suit, so we'll bring them. You and John are heroes to the Tibetan people. That's what Rinchen Darlo, the U.S. representative for the Dalai Lama, said." I didn't feel like a hero, or able to cope with any new impositions on my life.

Then she added, "The Dalai Lama wants to see you. Do you have a pen? I'll give you the numbers of the Kathmandu and Delhi offices of Tibet. They are hoping to hear from you as soon as possible."

"John!" I yelled. "The Dalai Lama wants to see us!"

* * *

Paljor Tsering, the Tibetan government-in-exile's representative in Nepal, sent a car to bring us to the Tibetan Consulate. Hidden from the street behind a high brick wall, a grapefruit tree on the spacious lawn had so much ripe yellow fruit that each branch bowed to the ground.

"I would like to get your impressions of what you have seen in Tibet on video while they are still fresh," Paljor said. He offered us tea. "Perhaps tomorrow. His Holiness will see the video before you meet him. I have already telexed Delhi. They are preparing for your arrival. His Holiness is very interested in what happened in the riots and the demonstrations. He wants to thank you personally for all you have done to help the Tibetan people."

"How was the riot portrayed in the Nepalese press?" John asked.

"I saved all the articles," Paljor said. "Many mention you. The Chinese government says that you are splittist agents of the Dalai clique. They said you threw rocks at the police and urged the Tibetans to attack the police station."

"What about the police shooting unarmed people?" I asked.

"The articles didn't mention that."

"That's ridiculous," John said.

"Of course it is. The Nepalese press says whatever China tells it to say. This is a difficult time for Tibetans. You have seen for yourselves what happens to Tibetans in Tibet who demonstrate for independence. Until the riots China was very successful at preventing any information from getting out of Tibet. Tibetans in exile wait for tidbits of news.

"Even in Kathmandu," Paljor continued, "I am not free to say what is really happening in Tibet. The Nepalese government is angered by what has come out in the press. Two days ago an article accused a Tibetan youth organization of threatening to bomb the Nepalese Embassy. This is of course not true. I am in a difficult situation. That is why we are so happy to see the two of you. You are free to say what is really happening in Tibet. But even you have to be careful. The Nepalese may kick you out of the country if you make political statements."

* * *

The next three days were packed with lengthy video interviews with Paljor Tsering and French and Dutch television, talking long-distance to CBS News, and sending a detailed, fifty-minute telex concerning the riot and the individuals killed and wounded to the Senate Foreign Relations Committee. Nightmares and being woken up by an otherwise pleasant woman from National Public Radio at 2:00 A.M.—twice—precluded my getting more than two hours of consecutive sleep. We were so busy we forgot to get our Indian visas until the day before our press conference in Delhi.

When we got to the Indian Embassy, thirty Westerners were waiting impatiently at the visa window. When John asked for visa applications, the guard said, "Come back tomorrow." John persisted and got two applications, which we filled out and handed back. "You see these people?" the guard said. "You have to bring your application back tomorrow, like these people have done. The day after that you will get your visas. Not before."

"We have to be in Delhi tomorrow," John pleaded.

"Show me your tickets."

"We don't have them yet," John said. "We were going to get them after we got our visas."

"There is nothing I can do."

"What if we get our plane tickets and come back?" John asked.

"It is no use. Come back tomorrow."

"We have a press conference in New Delhi tomorrow," John said.

"You are not looking like a press conference. This is a civilized country we are living in. I am telling you, tomorrow is tomorrow."

"Why can't you take our applications today?" John demanded.

"It is no use arguing. Nothing can be done. I assure you."

Two prior trips to India had taught me the futility of getting mad at government officials. The country's institutionalized inefficiency made Westerners like John and me go berserk. The trick was to discover something that the official wanted; money usually sufficed as a last resort. I approached the man calmly and whispered, "We are coming from Tibet."

"Why didn't you say you were coming from Tibet?" The guard walked down a freshly raked gravel path through a garden to a building surrounded by Gurkha soldiers and manicured lawn. He returned promptly. "My superior officer will see you now."

"I will be honest with you if you will be honest with me," a large army officer said, stretching his pudgy hands to the edge of the desk. He wore a green khaki uniform with the collar unbuttoned. "As you men know, the Nepalese are interested in China's military presence in Tibet. Naturally, with you just coming from Lhasa, you have seen things that would be useful to us. I will get right to the point. If you write down everything you saw about China's army and air force at Gonggar Airport, I will arrange to have your visas ready by five o'clock."

The officer leaned forward to inspect my crude drawing of a sleek helicopter with exaggerated propellers. "Sikorsky helicopters from America!" the officer exclaimed. "Write it all down. Come back at five."

"I don't trust him," John said outside the consulate. "He told us to come back an hour after they close.

"Relax," I said, mimicking John. "A few drawings and troop estimates and we meet the Dalai Lama. Jesus—what are we going to call him?"

* * *

"Who started the riot?"

"Why did you throw rocks?"

"Are you working for the CIA?"

These were three simultaneous questions from reporters at the New Delhi press conference. We were trapped at the back of a room where eighty reporters were clamoring to ask us questions. The air conditioning didn't work. The room was so humid that beads of water trickled down the wallpaper. Forgetting that we were in a hotel in Delhi, where even the air could give me dysentery, I guzzled ice water.

"Are you a military expert?" shouted one reporter, whom we later learned represented the city's communist paper.

"Were you ever in the military?"

"Did the Tibetans have guns?"

"Why did you even talk to Tibetans?"

I was so nervous I spilled my glass of water into a nest of wires, microphones, and tape recorders on the white tablecloth. Two waiters in white coats brought fresh glasses of water and towels to mop up the spill. No one was electrocuted. John and I forsook our prepared statements and tried our best to answer the aggressive barrage:

"How many people were killed?"

"How many were wounded?"

"Why did the Tibetans kill a Chinese policeman if they're pacifists?"

"What about the public execution? First the Chinese said three were executed, then two."

"How many foreigners were in Lhasa at the time?"

"How many saw the riot?"

"There were hundreds of Westerners in Lhasa," John said, trying to keep up. "Dozens of foreigners must have witnessed the riot. It was widely felt that there would have been a massacre if the foreigners had not been present in such great numbers in the crowd."

"Why did you throw rocks at the police?"

"I did not throw rocks at the police," John said. "I took photographs."

"What is China's military presence at the border?"

"We flew over the border," I said.

"What is the condition of the Tibetans versus the Chinese?"

"The Tibetans live under military occupation," I said. "Chinese is the official language of government and industry. Monks do not have religious freedom. Children don't learn Tibetan in schools. Protesters are tortured."

"Mr. Ackerly, what is your view of the whole thing?"

"What the Chinese are doing in Tibet has already happened in Inner Mongolia and Xinjian, the old East Turkestan," John said. "It's a racial situation. No matter how you feel about Tibet's autonomy, the Tibetan language and culture have always been separate from China's. Some of the policies of the Cultural Revolution are still going on, and Chinese colonization in Tibet is a serious threat to their culture."

"What will happen to Tibet?"

"As long as the Tibetans are treated as second-class citizens in their own land, there will be revolts."

One hour of questions whizzed by and we found ourselves being served a sumptuous feast of chicken and lamb curries, dal bat, yogurt, and salad. Everyone shook our hands and assured us that we had done a good job.

* * *

We played rummy on the floor of the Old Delhi train station while waiting for the 5:00 A.M. train to Dharamsala, home of the Dalai Lama and the Tibetan government-in-exile. Hundreds of skeletal Indians slept on the platform surrounding us, their gaunt cheeks and hollow eyes at peace for a few hours. The fortunate had a blanket or piece of cloth to lie on. A deformed boy held my hand as we played. My arms were bigger than his legs. Two of my fingers were wider than his arm. He had no neck and his jaw rested on top of his chest, which was pinched forward into a grotesque prow. We let him shuffle the cards and deal.

We glimpsed the Indian countryside on the train from New Delhi to Petan Court. As the sun burned through the layers of mist that blanketed the fields, we saw Indians squatting on cracked, parched earth. Children splashed in a muddy trickle of water that meandered through a desiccated river bed. Deprived of this year's monsoon, India was left hot but not humid; the rains had gone north of the Himalayas to Tibet. The papers also reported a 99.9 percent crop failure in India's southern provinces. The bleak forecast of famine in a country where 15 million children starve to death every year had a sobering effect on our journey.

* * *

A young Tibetan had been sent from Dharamsala to pick us up at Petan Court train station. We left the arid plains and started winding toward the snowcapped foothills of the Himalayas. I had wanted to meet the Dalai Lama for fifteen years, but never thought it would be possible. I am neither an avowed Buddhist nor a statesman. My lifestyle is far from holy. The prospect of meeting the Dalai Lama made me so nervous I decided to write down questions to ask him. I got stuck on the first one: What do you think about foreigners in Tibet throwing rocks at the police?

"Are you sure you want to tell the Dalai Lama about throwing rocks?" John said, ever the lawyerly strategist.

"With all the media attention we're getting, he has to know who he's dealing with."

"Just because you have a guilty conscience doesn't mean you have to tell him everything. This won't be a confession."

"If I don't tell him I'll regret it later."

Dharamsala had changed since I had visited the old British Hill station seven years earlier during a trip to India. The mountains still leapt off the subcontinent, but more houses covered the hillside. Deep cuts from erosion scarred the mature pine forest on the hillside.

We stopped for a troop of monkeys sitting on the road, their red rumps high in the air as they sauntered across the strip of asphalt intruding on their forest. Young monkeys clung upside down to their mothers' fur as tenaciously as the trees clung to the steep scree slope. The largest male berated our jeep with a bone-chilling cry, stared it down to a standstill, then dragged his pendulous red testicles into the trees.

＊ ＊ ＊

Thubten Samphel greeted us at the Information Office with cups of sweet tea and effusive thanks. "We do not wish to impose on your time," Thubten said, "but many of the younger Tibetans at the children's village have never seen Tibet. You have seen more of their country than they have, and they are Tibetan. We have 800 children eight to seventeen years old. We didn't used to have so many. Ten years ago many of our children were orphans. Their parents were killed by the Chinese army in Tibet, or else while trying to escape. Sometimes women come out of Tibet to have their baby here, then return; if they do not, their families will be suspect.

"We try to give the children Tibetan and Western educations," Thubten continued. "They study Tibetan, English, religious texts, science, and mathematics. Soon we will be getting a computer. If you would share your impressions of Tibet with some of the organizations in Dharamsala, it would mean so much to them. Many of the older Tibetans are anxious for any news of their homeland. We will provide you with a jeep and driver."

John and I both smiled at the thought of a jeep to drive us around. "It would be our privilege," John said.

Thubten beamed. "Then tomorrow you will give a talk at the Tibetan Children's Village at ten in the morning. In the afternoon, if you are not too tired, you will address the Tibetan government-in-exile and staff at two? The Tibetan Institute of Performing Arts has arranged a special performance for you tomorrow night. After this the Welfare Office would like to take you out to dinner. Your audience with His Holiness has been scheduled for the day after tomorrow at 9:00 A.M. After that the monks at His Holiness's monastery would be most grateful if you could also talk with them. All Tibetans are very happy that you two made it out of Tibet and came here to tell us what you have seen."

Before leaving the Information Office, Thubten loaded our arms with books about Tibet's religion, culture, medicine, struggle, and reconstruction, the XIV Dalai Lama, and dialectics in Buddhist education. "It is the least we can do," he said.

"Do you have *Seven Rivers and Six Ranges?*" John asked.

Thubten rummaged through a cabinet crammed with papers and books and produced two copies of the cherished memoirs of a Khampa resistance fighter.

"I have been trying to find this book for years," John said.

* * *

That evening as the sun melted into the Indian plains, we had drinks with Tenzin Choegyal, His Holiness's youngest brother, on the porch of the Kashmiri Cottage Guest House. "As you can see, I'm the bad sheep of the family!" Tenzin said, introducing himself with a tray of Indian XXX brandy and cold bottled beer. Tenzin's wild laugh put me at ease. Sitting on the patio overlooking the scorched plains, Tenzin said, "Now tell me what *really* happened during the demonstrations."

John extricated a handful of bullet casings from his pocket and asked Tenzin if he could identify them. "Seven and nine millimeter automatic pistols," Tenzin said. "The large one's from an AK-47. Where did you get these?"

"On the rooftop of the police station," John said. "I paid children one yuan for each casing they would bring me. You can have these if you want. I have a whole pocketful."

I started telling Tenzin about the carnage. He jumped up when an American man appeared on the porch. "You rascal," Tenzin said, pinching Avedon affectionately. "Did you meet anyone in the hills? A young woman?" Tenzin introduced us to John Avedon, the author of *In Exile from the Land of Snows*. Avedon was in Dharamsala for a week-long symposium on the brain with five Western scientists and His Holiness. He was full of energy, and playfully tried to pinch Tenzin back.

"Tibet is finally getting some attention from the U.S. Congress," Avedon said. "I testified at a Senate hearing in Washington last week on human rights violations in Tibet. At last Tibet is getting looked at; since Nixon and Kissinger opened relations with China in 1972, Tibet has been aggressively ignored."

"If your CIA hadn't stopped economic and military assistance to the Tibetan freedom fighters," Tenzin said, "Tibet might be a free country today."

"How was your testimony received?" John asked.

"They grilled me because I haven't been there," Avedon said. "China is about to undergo a massive industrialization. The Chinese market has overwhelming appeal to international business. That's what Tibet is up against."

"We better get this over with," I said. John rolled his eyes and I continued, "I threw rocks at the police during the riot."

"They are freedom fighters!" Tenzin exclaimed delightedly. "How many rocks?"

"Several," I admitted, explaining my rage reaction.

"A toast to the freedom fighters!" Tenzin said. "I wish I were your age. I'd love to go to Tibet again." Tenzin was so good-natured and easy to talk to that I felt comfortable asking him why so many Tibetans were named Tenzin. "You see," Tenzin said without any mischief in his face. "My older brother's name is Tenzin Gyatso. So naturally every Tibetan child who is taken to His Holiness is named Tenzin." He laughed again and did his best to pinch Avedon.

"What if Congress finds out about Blake's rock throwing?" John asked. "It will bolster the Chinese charge of foreign instigation."

"You shouldn't have anything to worry about," Avedon said. "You have great reputations: the American physician and lawyer who were arrested in Lhasa for helping the Tibetans."

"What if they ask direct questions?" John asked.

"Whatever you do," Avedon said, "don't ever lie to a congressional hearing, and don't let anyone fluster you, even if they harp on one point. Just stick to your personal experience and explain why you did what you did."

Tenzin successfully pinched Avedon, which ignited cackles of laughter from both of them. Avedon continued, "The State Department has just released a report assessing the status of all minority peoples in China. Ninety percent of the report is on Tibet. The irony here is amazing. The report was published on October 1, the same day as the riot. It states that the Chinese are improving the human rights of the Tibetans.

"You can imagine how embarrassed the State Department was to read that the largest anti-government rioting since 1959 coincided with the publication of their report. The report puts the Chinese population in the Tibet Autonomous Region at 70,000. They also laud the wealth of economic and social improvements.

"The question that interests me now is what effect all this publicity will have on China. Tibet has gotten more media attention in the last two weeks than since the PLA invaded in 1959. Tibet is a thorn in the Chinese side. Tibet represents the threat of a civil and human rights movement in China. But it remains to be seen whether any of this media attention will budge China."

* * *

I was afraid to go into the Tibetan Children's Village auditorium, packed with 800 students, and then have to describe to them the atrocities we had seen. At the Delhi press conference we had eluded the reporters' accusations of throwing rocks. I would have no defense against the acumen and brutal honesty of these children.

Two young boys kicked a clay ball wrapped in plastic with a feather top. John and I made a circle and other children joined in. The children kicked the ball expertly several times from one foot to the other before passing it to the next person. Soon more than fifty children crowded around our circle of hackers. An adult yelled for us to get inside.

Two hundred teachers sat in chairs. Six hundred students sat cross-legged on the floor. Everyone turned to stare as we walked from the back of the hall to a table on the stage. After a brief introduction by the school principal we were left alone with an older student who would translate. Unlike the press conference, we made it through our prepared statements before questions. I said that I had a favorable impression of China and the Chinese people until we got to Tibet. Before discussing the riot I apologized for having to describe horrible things and said that it was important for students to know what was really happening in Tibet, even if it was bad. John covered our arrest, how there was little freedom in the monasteries or schools, and the demonstrations.

"These are the biggest health problems in Tibet," I said, raising bullet casings. Sixteen hundred silent, watery eyes stared back. Many of the children cried during our talk, before their questions were written on scraps of paper and passed to the front of the room. They were questions only children could ask: Do the Tibetans in Tibet hate the Chinese? Will Tibet ever be free again? What happens to our Tibetan brothers and sisters who are taken to prison?

After two hours the jeep whisked us to another hall, where 300 men and women in the Tibetan government-in-exile and staff waited. I had managed to hold back tears in front of the children. Large drops tumbled down my cheeks and splashed on the table as I described the ten-year-old boy who had been shot during the riot. The children were more interested in the current conditions in a Tibet they had never seen. The Tibetan government and staff focused on Tibet's future and the possibility for a free country. For the second time that day we talked and answered questions for two hours.

* * *

I felt numb as we were driven on the narrow ribbon of asphalt to the Tibetan Institute of Performing Arts. We were ushered in next to four Mongolian abbots in the front row. I fell asleep on one of the abbot's shoulders as the M.C. talked about Genghis Khan encountering the Tibetan army in the sixteenth century. Instead of fighting the Tibetans, Genghis Khan adopted Tibetan Buddhism as the state religion. Contemporary Chinese scholars draw on Tibet's succession of military control from Tibet to Mongolia as prima facie evidence that Tibet was part of China; they fail to mention that the same reasoning can be used to show that China was equally a part of Mongolia.

Loud music and acrobatic folk dancing suddenly woke me up, to the abbot's mirth. The dancers slapped their feet loudly and somersaulted across the stage in whirls of color. The men danced and sang and played their guitars for the amusement of the women, who were alternately seductive and independent. Their operatic rendition of nomad life among the spirited yaks left me exhilarated as we stepped out under the stars.

"The Welfare Office wants to take you to dinner at your hotel," Thubten reminded us after the show. For the first time in my life I understood how someone could be killed with kindness. We couldn't refuse. Every Tibetan we met was desperate for news of the their homeland. "The Chinese will do anything to keep information from coming out of Tibet," Thubten explained.

The members of the Welfare Office were waiting to ask the same round of questions we had already answered in detail twice that day. At least, I thought, we were getting practice speaking in public. After dinner we met a stooped Tibetan man who had been waiting in the hall. He unrolled white *khatas* to drape around our shoulders. Tears streamed down his face. Thubten translated, "This man spent twenty years in a Chinese prison. He heard you speak this morning at TCV. He wants to thank you for telling people what is really happening in Tibet. He hopes you will continue to tell the people in your own country."

"It will be our privilege," I said, for the first time realizing our responsibility to speak out against the Chinese disinformation campaign. My training as a physician had prepared me to document the atrocities; traveling in Tibet introduced me to the collective ills of a people.

* * *

We decided to call the Dalai Lama "Your Holiness," the standard greeting. I caught myself holding my breath as the jeep took us to his residence. John tapped his fingertips on his knees, a sure sign of nervousness.

A towering Gurkha soldier with an antiquated rifle and fixed bayonet stood at attention beneath a rounded arch. His piercing gaze sent chills down my spine as we were led to a waiting room where an enormous Hindu couple sat on a bench. A man in a suit recorded our full names, addresses, and passport numbers, after which we were escorted up a hill to a second waiting room filled with Tibetan artifacts in glass cases.

"We had an audience with His Holiness last year," the man said, showing us a picture of them standing next to the Dalai Lama. "I am not saying we are Buddhists. We are Hindus. But His Holiness is a living God! And the blessing of any God, whether he be Hindu or Moslem or Buddhist, can only help in the next life." I hoped that this pair would not accompany us during our precious minutes with His Holiness.

Tenzin Geyche, His Holiness's personal secretary, escorted the Hindu couple out of the room. John tapped his fingers. I stared at a *thanka*. Time slowed to a standstill. I was too nervous to talk when Geyche returned with the beaming Hindu couple. He led us up the path to a porch where His Holiness stood in the door. The Dalai Lama was much taller than I expected. He wore maroon and yellow robes.

"Welcome, my friends," His Holiness said, looking each of us in the eye. We unrolled our *khatas* awkwardly into his outstretched arms. He laughed and returned a firm handshake. We were seated next to him on a couch beneath a topographical map of Tibet that filled the wall. Sunlight warmed the dragons depicted on the Tibetan rugs and *thankas* decorating the room. Geyche sat across from us.

"On behalf of six million Tibetans," His Holiness said, "I want to express my gratitude to both of you. As a human being who very much believes in truth as a human value, I also want to express my deep thanks. When tourists saw the true situation, their hearts went toward the Tibetan side. This really gives us some kind of inspiration and courage."

"Do you mind if I use a tape recorder?" Geyche asked. "There are so many things we must ask you."

"One thing," His Holiness said. "During the event that took place in Lhasa, how many Tibetans came from eastern Kham and Amdo?"

"We couldn't tell," John said. "The Khampas cut off their red tassels."

His Holiness's deep, jolly laugh was infectious. We couldn't help laughing when he asked us how we had come to Tibet, and John said that we had hiked to 22,000 feet on Chomolungma in sneakers. We chatted for fifteen minutes before His Holiness asked again about the demonstrations.

"Did any Tibetans fire guns?" His Holiness asked. John said that a Tibetan child picked up a machine gun after a Chinese policeman was hit on the head with a rock. The gun was passed over several Tibetans' heads, then smashed on the street. His Holiness was intent on learning the individual details of each man, woman, monk, and child who had died, the numbers of Tibetans and Westerners at each demonstration, and whether the police had shot deliberately.

"You see," His Holiness began, "reporters are asking for news. From Delhi, we hear some whispers that something happened in Lhasa. The radio explained little bits. Actually, you see, we also were taken by surprise." He showed us a photograph of a few monks carrying a Tibetan national flag. "The people around them are looking passive," he said, describing the picture. "So besides the monks, were the Lhasa people fully . . ."

"Involved?" I interjected.

"That's it," His Holiness said. "Were the Lhasa people fully involved?" John gave me a look I hadn't seen since our interrogation by the police. I couldn't help interrupting. We had no idea how much time we would have to speak with the Dalai Lama.

John said that there were approximately a thousand travelers and tourists in Lhasa, and several times that many Tibetans during the October 1 riot. "Dozens of Westerners actually witnessed the event. When the Chinese refused to treat wounded Tibetans, Blake snuck out to treat them. I worked with twenty other foreigners who gathered information for the press," he added.

We identified the picture His Holiness had shown us as having been taken during the September 27 demonstration. "On October 1, the people were ready," John said. "The mistake the Chinese made was to put the monks in the PSB right next to the Jokhang. That became a focus for the crowd's anger. It wasn't a riot in that there was undirected anger. The violence was very much directed at the station in the hope of freeing the monks. And that's exactly what happened. The monks were able to escape."

"Some," I interrupted, and mentioned the three monks who had been shot while trying to escape.

His Holiness asked how many Tibetans were involved with the Chinese police, and if the Tibetan policemen fired on Tibetans. He was particularly interested in people's reactions to Tibetans who worked with the Chinese police. John said that no one had seen a Tibetan policeman fire a weapon, and that initially the Chinese police appeared to fire warning shots over people's heads.

"How many bullets?" His Holiness asked.

"Thousands," I said. "The police fired machine guns and automatic pistols for several hours."

John pulled out his handful of bullet casings and gave some to His Holiness. His Holiness felt the weight of the AK-47 casing in his hands. "I have never seen bullets like these. How did you get them?"

"I paid children one yuan for each one they would bring me from the rooftops of the buildings," John said.

Once again, His Holiness's laughter caught me off guard. "You see," he said, marveling at the size of the AK-47 casing, "some people bring me flowers. You bring me bullets . . . Is it true that monks threw rocks at the police?" I looked at the tape recorder nervously. "Would you feel more comfortable if we turned the tape recorder off?"

"Yes," I said.

"I think people were mostly throwing rocks at the burning police station," John said, giving me a look.

"After seeing several people killed from bullets," I said, unable to contain myself any longer, "and one boy beaten to death by the police, I threw rocks at the police. I didn't know what else to do to stop the police from shooting unarmed people. I was so angry I wanted to kill. This still bothers me very much."

"You must not hate the Chinese for what they are doing," His Holiness said. "The Chinese are wonderful people. It is their government that makes trouble."

"How do you feel about monks throwing rocks?" John asked.

"You see," His Holiness said. "Buddhism is a religion that respects all life on the planet. We try not to even slap mosquitoes, but we don't always succeed. Just because a monk takes vows and wears robes does not mean that he stops being human. For a monk to throw a rock at a policeman is very sad. But I understand how throwing rocks could be a natural response to an extreme situation. Tibetans have been living under very sad conditions for more than forty years.

"The Chinese are very good at preventing information from leaking out of Tibet," His Holiness continued after a long pause. "Even if I had known what happened during the demonstrations, there are so many constraints on what I can say. The Indian government has been very generous to the Tibetan people, but still I am not free to make any political . . ." His Holiness looked again to Geyche for help with word choice.

"Statements?" I interjected. John kicked me under the table.

"Yes, that's it. It is the same in every country I visit. I am always told not to make any political statements. It is a difficult position. What am I to do?" His Holiness smiled benevolently.

John said, "When we were arrested we found out a little of what Tibetans go through when they are arrested. The Chinese tried to get us to denounce you and say that Tibet had always been a part of China."

"The monks are tortured in prison," I said, and described the monks who had bones broken in prison and were refused medical treatment, and that at least one monk had died from beatings during and after the riot. "The monks are especially afraid of lethal injections."

"We must always be thinking of solutions," His Holiness said. "For some time now I have had this idea of, how should I call it . . . Buddho-communism. You see, Buddhism and communism have many things in common. If the conditions of my people are ever going to improve, there must be some compromise. This compromise is Buddho-communism."

"Do congressional resolutions put pressure on China to stop human rights abuses?" John asked.

"Everything helps. Tibet is getting more publicity now than ever before. So far China has not changed."

"We should boycott goods made in China," I said. "As long as the State Department is primarily interested in big business, we have to organize grass roots organizations."

His Holiness looked at me quizzically. "Even in your State Department you will find people who are sympathetic with oppressed people all around the world."

"Blake generalizes easily," John said.

"One of the great things Tibetan Buddhism has to offer to this world is the Bodhisattva ideal," His Holiness said. "In Tibetan Buddhism, we do not believe in gods. We believe that perfection is possible in this lifetime. Ever since Sakyamuni, Bodhisattvas have shown that it is possible to reach enlightenment." His Holiness laughed again and I felt lighter. "This is lucky for me. You see, with so many things to do for my people, I have not had time to keep up with my meditations."

Sensing that our audience was about to end, John asked, "Is it true that West Germany and Switzerland are negotiating with China to dump nuclear waste in Tibet?"

"I have read something to this effect in the Western press," His Holiness said, and continued to discuss his concern that nuclear waste on the Tibetan Plateau could pollute all of Asia's great rivers. I didn't interrupt him when he occasionally paused to search for a word. This surprised John.

"Do you have any difficulty answering the press?" His Holiness asked suddenly. He looked worried. John said that the historical record was clearly in Tibet's favor. I was pleased that the Dalai Lama sought our advice, even if we could not answer his last question: "Do you know anyone close to Ronald Reagan who is a good human being?"

CHAPTER ELEVEN

DHARMA AND THE RED MEN

AFTER RETURNING HOME, I did not need another physician to diagnose that I had a mild case of post-traumatic stress disorder. I cried when I described the explicit violence I had witnessed in Tibet to my family and friends. Loud noises made me duck as though I were under fire. I continued to wake up crying in the night. With patience and help from my family—and with regaining the thirty pounds I had lost—I began to recover. More than anything, writing about my experiences helped me to cope.

My mother waited for several days after my return, until I had begun to settle down, before telling me what had happened to her during the turbulence. The initial press reports out of Tibet said that we had been arrested, and that an angry mob had burned the police station to the ground. "For ten days I thought you were dead," she sobbed. "I didn't dare leave the house in case I missed a call with news of your whereabouts." My mother explained that while the unrest had raged the phone rang day and night. She took forty pages of notes on a legal pad from her conversations with parliamentarians, government agencies, and concerned people around the world, which included many requests for press interviews and speaking engagements at universities and human rights organizations.

* * *

John and I had a week at home to recuperate before undergoing a live interview for CNN. Bernard Shaw introduced us as "eyewitnesses" in

Tibet and asked what the Dalai Lama's reaction had been. John said the Dalai Lama was a nonviolent man and was sorry for the deaths. I began explaining the escalation of events, from the Dalai Lama's proposing his Five-Point Peace Plan to—

"We couldn't get any reports," Shaw interrupted. "Why did you subject yourself to that kind of physical jeopardy?"

"There were no reporters in Lhasa," John said. "This was an historic moment for Tibet. We felt we needed to take pictures and document what was happening, and to get those reports out to the West."

"What did you see?" Shaw asked. "What did you hear? What did you feel?"

John said that he watched a group of Tibetans overturn a jeep and light it on fire, and that he couldn't believe this was happening.

"What were you doing physically?"

"I was in the Tibetan crowd," John said. "Taking pictures, trying to stay undercover between streetlight posts and tables. Tibetans kept begging us to take pictures and show them to the Dalai Lama."

"One effect of this is you sometimes wake up crying?"

"That was me," I said, angered by the question. I held up the bullet casings and said that twelve people had died.

"Were you aiding the victims?"

"Definitely," I said. "I tried to stop profuse bleeding. Most of the time I could only document how someone had died."

"Based on what you saw, what do you make of the situation in Lhasa, in Tibet, as it relates to the Chinese and the policies affecting the Tibetans?"

"Tibetans have been living under Chinese military occupation for thirty-seven years," I said, talking as fast as I could. "China is committing genocide in Tibet. Colonization is the biggest threat to Tibetan autonomy." I knew I had only seconds left, and suddenly recalled the woman who was sterilized after the nurse gave her newborn a lethal injection.

＊ ＊ ＊

The next day we addressed the Congressional Human Rights Caucus, co-founded by Tom Lantos (D-CA) and John Porter (R-IL) to make human rights concerns a bigger part of U.S. foreign policy. Lantos spoke eloquently of his own experience with Nazi Germany's attempt to exterminate the Jews, and said that Tibet was another holocaust. Charlie Rose (D-NC), a large, impressive gentleman, said in a Southern drawl that China's occupation of Tibet sickened him. He gave his full support to the cause of Tibetan independence.

"Before I went to Tibet," I said, "I expected Tibet's biggest health hazards to be intestinal . . . I lost thirty pounds while consuming mostly yak byproducts." People laughed and continued eating. "But I learned that these are the biggest health hazards in Tibet," I said, raising the bullet casings. People stopped eating as I described the killing and the wounded Tibetans who feared imprisonment if they went to a Chinese hospital.

John spoke in terms of human and civil rights. His words sounded removed from our experiences, but the congressmen paid attention to phrases like "restrictions on freedom to practice religion" and "arrest and imprisonment without due process." He mentioned that the Tibetans' living conditions were substandard compared to those of Chinese immigrants who received higher wages and better jobs, that Chinese was the language of commerce and industry, and that massive population transfer was conspicuous in Lhasa.

As at the New Delhi press conference, we were treated to a sumptuous feast and assured that we had done well. We met representatives from Amnesty International and Asia Watch and reporters for the *Christian Science Monitor*, the *Washington Times*, the *Washington Post*, and the *American Medical News*.

* * *

I felt puny standing in the State Department's marble lobby of skyscraping columns and country flags. We had requested a meeting with Bart Flaherty, the head of the "China Desk," in order to discuss the Tibet section of the department's annual "country report." Flaherty listened politely while John showed slides of the escalating violence: the police beating monks, Tibetans burning the police station, the ten-year-old boy shot through the chest who died in my hands, Champa Tenzin coming out of the burning police station with third-degree burns. Flaherty squirmed.

"What is the department's position on the demonstration?" John asked.

"The State Department recognizes that the People's Republic of China perpetrates a number of human rights violations throughout China," Flaherty said. "We also believe that Tibet is an internal affair of China's."

John looked stunned. It was as though we were talking to Mr. Chen, our Chinese jailer. Unable to conceal my anger, I shouted, "What about people being slaughtered?"

Flaherty became red-faced and pushed his chair back. "The State Department is expressing its concern through the appropriate diplomatic channels."

John opened the State Department's country report on China, which was dated October 1, the same day as the riot. In reference to the assessment that the Tibetan Autonomous Region had 30,000 Chinese immigrants, John estimated that Lhasa alone had at least 70,000 Chinese, more than the number of Tibetans. He showed a panoramic photo he had taken from the Potala's rooftop of the newly constructed cinderblock buildings in the valley.

"You can't determine population from a few photographs," Flaherty said.

"Tibetans are being tortured in prisons as we speak," I shouted. Flaherty moved his chair back.

"Did you see anyone being tortured?" he asked. I said that I had met monks beaten with cattle prods during interrogation.

John pressed Flaherty to justify the State Department's reversal on Tibet as of 1972, when the U.S. China policy changed. "It's pure politics—it's not based on historical realities or what's right or wrong," John charged. He supported his points with slides and a calm demeanor, while I tried to argued with Flaherty, who kept moving his chair back. After three hours, Flaherty had moved his chair to the wall and could retreat no farther.

At one point another man came into the room and said, "It looks like there's going to be a demonstration in Ithaca tomorrow. The Chinese ambassador is visiting Cornell University." I did not mention that Ithaca was my home town, or that I had accepted an invitation to speak at the demonstration. They would find out soon enough.

"It's genocide," I said, exasperated. Flaherty repeated that the State Department considered Tibet an internal affair of China's.

"The U.S. could stop selling arms to China that are used against the Tibetans," John said.

"We should boycott goods made in China," I said.

"I'm going to be frank," Flaherty said. "The State Department empathizes with the plight of the Tibetans. We recognize that China is committing human rights violations throughout mainland China and Tibet. However, it is the department's position that Tibet is an internal affair of China's."

PART THREE

RETURN TO TIBET

CHAPTER TWELVE

WHY ARE THEY LAUGHING?

L HASA'S INDEPENDENCE DEMONSTRATIONS
in the fall of 1987 alerted the world to Tibetan nationalism.
China promptly responded by closing Tibet to reporters, parliamentarians, and international human rights organizations. A trickle of
overland travelers brought out stories of brutal torture and repression,
and of continued demonstrations occurring throughout the country.
Although the world press reported the Chinese atrocities in "Shangri-
La," their interest in Tibet's plight was fleeting. Even more distressing
was the Reagan/Bush Administration's tolerance of Chinese oppression.

What John and I had witnessed in Lhasa changed our lives. John
went to work for the International Campaign for Tibet in Washington.
I postponed my residency to write a narrative account of our trip. Two
years went by quickly. Devoting ourselves full-time to advocacy work,
we wrote a dozen articles for magazines and newspapers. We presented
testimony to several congressional committees and the German parliament, and gave fifty talks to university and human rights groups in
North America. To help foster new Tibet support groups after our talks,
we developed a pamphlet with useful information for fledgling activists
on fundraising, literature tables, sample letters to elected representatives, and civil disobedience.

At times, both of us wondered if our memories of the explicit violence that we had witnessed in Lhasa were becoming exaggerated, and if
the violence implicit in the daily lives of the Tibetans had subsided. If
the Tibetans continued to live under extreme repression, we felt that we

owed it to ourselves and to the Tibetans to document these conditions to the best of our professional abilities.

In the fall of 1988, John and I traveled separately to India to interview Tibetan refugees. We had developed a questionnaire to investigate prison conditions and China's family-planning policy in Tibet, and hoped to write a report if we gathered enough information. I also wanted to know more about Tibetan medicine. I already had established a written correspondence with Namhla Takla, the director of the *Mendzekhang* in Dharamsala. Now I would have the chance to speak with her in person.

*   *   *

Mrs. Takla's office at the *Mendzekhang* looked out over forested mountains that rolled onto the arid Indian subcontinent. Mrs. Takla served tea and explained the major problems facing the *Mendzekhang*. First, there was a lack of money. Second, they did not have the facilities to make enough medicine. Third, they had a difficult time getting the necessary herbs; the Chinese had pressured the Nepalese to forbid all exports of herbs.

"Musk comes from Tibet," Mrs. Takla explained. "The Chinese are taking all the musk that enters Nepal for themselves."

Mrs. Takla also said that Tibetans in exile needed to train more *menlops* (Tibetan medical students). They were currently building accommodations for visiting scientists, doctors, and medical students. "The older doctors are very traditional and stubborn," she said. "I often have to side with the younger doctors, which makes trouble for me."

Mrs. Takla smiled broadly as Dr. Choedak stepped into the room. This was the Dalai Lama's personal physician, a slightly stooped man in his sixties. "His ears must be ringing," Mrs. Takla said to me. She explained to Dr. Choedak in Tibetan that I had treated wounded in Lhasa. Dr. Choedak held my hands as he talked. Mrs. Takla translated the information that Tibetans had excellent medicines for asthma, hypertension, adult-onset diabetes, arthritis, cancer, and multiple sclerosis.

Dr. Choedak was equally forthright about the shortcomings of Tibetan medicine. Newly trained Tibetan doctors didn't focus as much on diet and behavior. Even before 1959, there was less focus on meditating, massage, and medicine baths. These things needed to be revised. Western and Tibetan doctors should do research together and take the best from both systems.

"All of this depends on training the young *menlops*," Mrs. Takla said. "Most of our medical students learn to speak English at the Children's Village, but they do not know the Western medical terms. Dr. Choedak would be honored if you would stay here with us, and give a series of lectures on Western medicine to the students while you are here."

Dr. Choedak took me to my room. It had the simplicity of a monk's quarters, with bare walls, a bed, and a desk. I sat down to begin outlining my first lecture and he returned in a few minutes with Lobsang, a young monk who had just arrived from Lhasa. Neither Dr. Choedak nor Lobsang could speak English, and my Tibetan was still restricted to the social amenities. I drew a crude map of the world in my journal with the U.S. and Tibet prominently featured. I asked Lobsang how he left Tibet and he answered "Yes," as he did to all subsequent inquiries. Although it was frustrating not being able to communicate, I was struck by how forcefully he spoke. Half an hour and many cups of butter tea later, I realized that I needed a translator.

* * *

At Dharamsala's Office of Information I met Norbu, a Tibetan who had grown up in Switzerland. Norbu was the most staid Tibetan I had ever met, and spoke English with a Swiss-German accent. He agreed to translate during my three-week stay, during which I would be interviewing Tibetan refugees. On our way to have tea we met Kelsang, the Jokhang scribe I had treated the previous year. He was taller than I remembered. He also had sixteen stubbleless scars on his shaved head.

Kelsang was brimming with details of the special torture teams that came to Lhasa in the fall of 1987. Individuals were first stripped and beaten. The torturers screamed, "Tibet's freedom will be your food," as they crushed one man's testicles; another man died from being beaten with a bayonet. Hearing about these victims of torture brought back a flood of horrific memories. I wanted desperately to leave, even before I'd started the work I'd come for, but struggled to record all of the details.

"Kelsang was inside the Jokhang Temple during the March 5, 1988, demonstration," Norbu translated. "At 11:00 A.M., 700 Chinese police stormed the monastery. They used ladders to climb the walls. Nine hundred Tibetans were sheltered inside, including a hundred women and children. Another thousand Tibetans stood outside the main door. The police used tear gas and beat everyone with clubs. Many people were bleeding. Nine people died in the first hour. Kelsang does not know how many died in prison afterward. Sixty-four people were taken to prison. Tibetans attacked a Chinese policeman taking photographs from the roof. They hit him on the head with stones and threw him down onto the street. He died in the ambulance on the way to the People's Hospital.

"Kelsang was bleeding profusely from wounds all over his body," Norbu continued, speaking without emotion. "He went to the *Mendzekhang* in an ambulance, and spent two months there. The police came in every day to interrogate and photograph the wounded. They wanted to take Kelsang to prison but the doctors complained that Kelsang was too ill to move. Then the doctors discharged him secretly. When he went back to the Jokhang the Chinese police tried to capture him and he escaped."

Besides the scars on his scalp and the rest of his body, Kelsang still had headaches and had not regained his previous energy level, but he smiled as he told me this and posed for pictures. "He has a message from Champa Tenzin," Norbu said. "Champa Tenzin was in the *Mendzekhang* for one month, then the police kept him in Sangyip Prison for four months, but he is alive. He sends his regards."

● ● ●

I heard many eyewitness accounts of other demonstrations throughout Tibet. Twenty-nine nuns from the Shongsey and Garu nunneries were arrested for demonstrating outside the Jokhang on March 4, 1988. The next day fifty-three monks from Ganden Monastery started another demonstration that resulted in the police using tear gas and bullets to break up the crowd. Although the estimates of deaths and arrests varied, it appeared that the police used increasing force to quell each successive uprising. I also found the individual Tibetans I interviewed to be credible.

Individual descriptions of torture at Lhasa's Gutsa, Sangyip, Titchu, Utitod, and Drapchi prisons were remarkably similar. The prisoners were beaten while their captors forced them to denounce the Dalai Lama and Tibetan independence. Women were raped with cattle prods at several facilities. The most severe treatment involved attack dogs ripping flesh from prisoners' legs and genitals.

I struggled through each interview. One man who had fought in the resistance told me that he had seen Chinese soldiers kill his wife and three children. He fought in Tibet until 1959 and left with the Dalai Lama. He became bored with life in exile and enlisted in a special regiment of Tibetans in the Indian army who were known for their endurance and determination.

"The Indians lost six battalions trying to free Bangladesh," the man said. "The Gurkhas also failed. Our commander told our regiment that the Chinese were in the swamps. We waded through those swamps with our rifles over our heads. In a month we liberated Bangladesh."

* * *

Dr. Dorje Gyalpo took me to give my first lecture to the *menlops* the following morning. I knew that Tibetan medicine had a detailed knowledge of fetal development, and I had outlined a lecture on human embryology. At first my room at the college had seemed very comfortable, but something biting my ankles had prevented me from sleeping. I slapped but heard nothing. Something bit my neck. Again I slapped, but no culprits could be found. This biting and slapping continued until dawn.

That morning I faced sixty Tibetan medical students sitting upright at their desks with the sort of undivided attention I had never seen in U.S. schools. Dr. Gyalpo sat in the front row with Mrs. Takla and Dr. Namgyal, the head of the pharmacy. "The Buddha taught that a questioning mind is a lifelong endeavor," Dr. Gyalpo said in concluding his introduction to my talk, asking the students to save their questions for the end.

I began with an evolutionary perspective: "One billion lifetimes ago, one-celled organisms formed in the oceans. As these organisms became more complex they developed specialized organs for things like eating, locomotion, and reproduction. After millions of years amphibious beings crawled onto land." I drew pictures to illustrate the phylogenetic explosion of plant and animal species, including dinosaurs, on the chalkboard. This thoroughly confused and interested everyone. "All of the animals on the planet have much more in common than we might think, and all come from the union of cells," I said.

Dr. Gyalpo excitedly handed me a box of multi-colored chalk. "Where do babies come from?" he asked. The *menlops* laughed nervously. Dr. Gyalpo listened politely to my answer that human beings came from the union of the father's sperm and the mother's egg. The students talked while I drew egg and sperm cells and said that the fertilized egg evolved through amphibious and mammalian stages before it developed into human form.

"What is the nature of the developing fetal conscience?" Dr. Gyalpo asked.

"How are they joined?" Mrs. Takla asked.

"Why is it dangerous for a pregnant woman to take an X-ray?" Dr. Namgyal asked.

I answered each question to the best of my knowledge, which led to more questions. It was decided that I would give a lecture every other day. My one-hour lectures to the *menlops* evolved into a dependable three hours; no matter what I started talking about, the students inevitably asked two hours of questions. Most of the males asked about sex. Many passed me notes: "If I do whole night intercourse, about five to six times, is it possible to recover sperms on that particular night?" "In Tibetan medicine, food is the essence of sperm. Is it the same in Western medicine?" "If someone licks sperm, is it good for the body? (DON'T ASK WHO HAS ASKED THIS QUESTION)" "What is the difference between 1) taking sperm purposefully *without* a partner 2) sperm coming while having sex *with* a partner? I have heard that the first one is not good, whereas in the second case the male gets some nutrient from the female."

One man, Dokpa, looked like a beatnik astrology student with his crew cut and goatee. He asked the most difficult questions, such as, "What are the merits and demerits of the Tibetan and Western medical systems? Please state them honestly." I replied that both systems had excellent pharmacopoeias. I added that because Western doctors relied heavily on technology, they relied less on their clinical skills to diagnose an illness. Dokpa also offered his own intriguing insights. During a talk on the central nervous system he likened the function of the brain to a bird on a tree. "When the tree falls," he said, "the bird flies away."

"Exactly what is adrenaline?" Dokpa asked in the middle of my explaining about our endocrine glands. "How can we know its effects?" I could not resist whispering, "Do you want to know what adrenaline does?"

"Please tell us," I heard Dokpa say. I waited for the *menlops* to lean forward and become silent. Then I screamed. The *menlops* jumped back in terror, knocking over chairs and tables. Fortunately, no one was hurt. For once I, who often seemed to strike them as an inexhaustible source of amusement, was able to laugh at them.

* * *

I spoke with a Tibetan nurse named Chimi who had worked for three years at Lhasa's People's Hospital. She explained to me China's family-planning policy for urban Tibetans. Chimi had learned English well and we were able to speak without a translator.

"Tibetan women are allowed to have two children," Chimi said, "but if they have one this is considered best. The work unit leader is in charge of enforcing the central government's policies. In public meetings that everyone is required to attend, women are told that it is best to have one child. If they are sterilized after the first child, praise will be given for being a good citizen.

"If a woman has a second child," she continued, "the child will have rights. But this is discouraged. Sterilization is done automatically on many women delivering their second child at Chinese hospitals.

"Having a third child is strongly discouraged. An illegal child has no ration card for the monthly allotment of Tibetan dietary staples at government stores: seven kilos of *tsampa*, one-half kilo yak butter, and cooking oil. Without a ration card a child cannot go to school, do organized work, travel, or own property.

"In villages there are thousands of illegal children. Tibetans would rather have their own way." When asked how these children survived, Chimi said that such "illegal persons" had to do things like collect dung.

"Women also are fined for having a third or fourth child," Chimi said. When asked if she could list individuals' names, Chimi said that she did not know any women in Lhasa who had more than two children. Since 1983, there had been a new policy that all women living near Chinese hospitals had to deliver their babies in the hospital birth-control units.

When asked if there were differences in the way Chinese and Tibetan patients were treated, Chimi first said that Tibetan and Chinese women were treated equally. Then, in her next sentence, she outlined two systems of health care: "There are two sections in the hospital: one for government officials and people with good jobs, another for ordinary people. The difference is better food and a cleaner environment. Most Tibetan women have babies at home. The Chinese officials and their friends always get the best food, the best medicines, and the best care. The Chinese also have the best jobs and look down on the Tibetans, who have menial jobs, smell, and are not clean."

My stomach felt queasy as Chimi described how "unauthorized" pregnancies were routinely terminated with lethal injections. Chimi said that she herself had given hundreds of these injections.

"There must be *some* improvements in health care since the Chinese came?" I asked her.

Chimi shook her head. "The Chinese brought tuberculosis, for which Tibetans have no natural resistance and Tibetan medicine has no cure. Unemployment and alcoholism are also higher, especially among young Tibetans. Infant mortality is one in six babies, one of the highest in the world. Life expectancy for a Tibetan is ten years less than for a Chinese living in Lhasa."

Chimi seemed on the verge of politely excusing herself. I thanked her and asked if she would list women she had seen get abortions or sterilizations at the Lhasa People's Hospital. In less than an hour, Chimi furnished me with a list of the names, ages, dates, procedures, and complications of twelve women who had abortions by D&C during the first trimester; four women given injections to induce abortion during their second and third trimesters; and six women who had been sterilized.

Before leaving, Chimi asked if she could keep the list. She knew of more women but did not have time to write them all down.

Two nights later Chimi handed me three sheets of paper that listed fifty-three women who were sterilized after an abortion. I asked how she could remember so many names and dates from four years ago. She replied that both of her parents were doctors and taught her to have a good memory. I quizzed her on individual details until I was convinced that they were internally consistent. This appeared to insult her.

"Even if a woman is forced to have an abortion," Chimi said, "she will feel guilty for the rest of her life. We are seeing families break up because of this. For these reasons, Tibetans have nicknamed the People's Hospital 'The Butcher's Place.'"

* * *

Unidentified insect bites continued to plague my nights. I could not sleep until I had scratched each bite raw. After ten nights I finally found my first bedbug. It was as large as a raisin and made a splotch on my pillow. A second bedbug clinging to the wall next to my head also made a stain. I soon found dozens of plump, raisin-sized bedbugs clinging to the underside of the bed's wood frame. I dragged the mattress to the far side of my room and slept soundly.

In the morning I told Mrs. Takla my first complete Tibetan sentence: "Nga nangla deshik manpo do" (There are a lot of bedbugs in my room). That afternoon I returned to find all of my possessions, mattress, and bedding airing out in the sun. "The *deshiks* (bedbugs) will not be returning to your room," Mrs. Takla said. "We sprayed everything with DDT."

* * *

Norbu arranged for a Land Rover to take us to the Bir refugee camp, a four-hour drive from Dharamsala. The Tibetans at the camp had come from all parts of Tibet, and most had left their native land within the last year. They would be excellent sources of information, Norbu reasoned. Chimi came along, but she refused to get into the passenger seat. "The doctor must be comfortable," she said and squeezed into the back seat next to Norbu and two other Tibetan travelers. A hefty woman who joined us also refused my offer to share the spacious front seat and squeezed on top of Norbu's lap. Norbu's polite smile belied a strained expression.

"What are you doing?" Norbu shouted as I forced my way into the entanglement of elbows and knees and moans. I said that either someone had to sit in the front seat with me or I would ride with everyone else in the back seat. This was not altogether altruistic; if an accident on a steep mountain road didn't kill me, I would have been crushed by their weight.

"*Amchi-la, neumba*" (crazy doctor), the driver said, and pulled the woman off Norbu's lap to sit in the front seat with us.

British volunteer teachers at Bir welcomed us and passed the word that an American doctor was documenting torture and sterilization. Anyone who had something to say about this should come to the meeting house. Young Tibetans started lining up outside the door. We interviewed refugees sixteen hours a day for two days. An average interview took two hours. Most provided me with hard first-hand information.

For an hour one young nun named Dechen would talk only about her nun friend who was taken to Drapchi Prison for participating in the October 1 demonstration. "Tamdy is twenty years old," Dechen said. "I visited her in prison." I interrupted to ask how she had been allowed to visit a prisoner. She said that prisoners were occasionally allowed visits by family and friends.

"Tamdy received daily beatings and torture," Norbu translated. "The police forced Tamdy and eleven other women to run for hours while they beat them with cattle prods. The dogs attacked Tamdy many times. The dogs must have had very sharp teeth because there is one place in her right thigh with a large hunk of flesh missing."

I asked for more details about the torture, and for the names of the police who beat Tamdy. Dechen looked insulted and would not answer questions for a long time. I apologized for asking so many questions, and explained that they were essential for my report.

"After the October 1 demonstration," Norbu said when Dechen began talking, "the police came to Dechen's workplace and took her to the police station. There they produced a thick book that she was told contained all of her crimes. The police never opened the book. She told the police that she had not done anything bad. She was then taken to a different room where they touched her mouth with an electric stick many times. This felt as though her mouth had exploded. She lost consciousness.

"Later Chinese policemen stripped her. She cried as the men ripped her clothes off with the help of women police. She was beaten over her body with the electric stick on her breasts, mouth, and head, and lost consciousness many times. She feels that since this she has had difficulty remembering things and learning new words. She thinks this is from the electric sticks. This lasted three days at Drapchi Prison. The male police were Chinese. The women were Moslems, from Pakistan or Kashmir. They had been living in Lhasa for a long time."

Before being released from Drapchi, Dechen was told not to say anything about what had happened to her in prison. She was also warned that if she ever participated in another demonstration, she would be treated much worse.

* * *

The next day we interviewed Jigme, a Tibetan policeman from Lhasa who said that he had tortured his own people. I began by asking about China's family-planning policy and was surprised to hear him say that it was the birth-control teams, not the police, who were responsible for bringing recalcitrant women to the hospital for abortions and sterilizations.

"As soon as a woman gives birth," he said, "she has to register the baby with the local police. The police say, 'Be careful you don't get pregnant again. If you do, you won't get a ration card for the child.'"

I changed the subject and asked why he became a police officer. Jigme said that he thought police training would teach him to be versatile. He learned how to drive a motorcycle, jeep, and truck, to fire pistols and machine guns, and to detect and interrogate criminals. His face saddened. "If he did not do what he was told, the officers would ostracize him at public meetings. The police are very nationalistic," Norbu said.

Jigme answered questions about his police work. "For political reasons," Norbu translated, "the police have a special unit called the *gowanchu* that arrests suspects and takes them to prison. A separate unit, the *gentsayan*, does interrogation. Most officers in both units are Chinese. In general, the *gentsayan* finds out if the prisoner is involved in the underground or demonstrations. They extract confessions and get prisoners to denounce the Dalai Lama.

"Political prisoners are put in a cold, dark cell," he continued. "Depending on the case, prisoners are chained at the ankles and wrists. They often are kept for more than three months. During Jigme's time they used an electric cattle prod with a battery. If they touch the head for fifteen minutes the person will be unconscious. There is also a special rope to tie the wrists and ankles that becomes tighter if the prisoner moves."

Jigme described how the treatment given to prisoners depended on how they cooperated with the police. His face bore no emotion when Norbu said, "If a prisoner is adamant and says that Tibet is independent, he will be stripped and beaten. If the prisoner dies during the beatings the police are not responsible. It is the prisoner's fault if he dies. The police have the upper hand and are free to beat the prisoners to death."

Jigme also said that he tried to do "good things." He gave food and clothes in secret to the prisoners. Sometimes he was able to warn a family before they came to arrest someone.

"There is a special Chinese doctor for prisons," Norbu said. "If a prisoner is about to die the doctor gives just enough treatment to keep him alive and lengthen the torture. If the prisoner dies easily, he cannot be tortured for long." I asked Jigme if he had seen any torture techniques. Tears streaked his cheeks. He spoke in choked sentence fragments about how he had beaten Tibetan prisoners with electric sticks, hung them by their thumbs and ankles over a heater, suspended them in ice baths, and given injections to make them "*neumba*" (crazy).

I asked about the dogs and Jigme said the *owlies* (attack dogs) were trained to bite prisoners on command. He laughed and said that prisoners told him many things at this time. "The dogs eat better than the soldiers," Norbu translated. "They are allotted 300 yuan a month, more than a Tibetan makes in one year."

Jigme said that the reason he left Tibet was to help the Tibetan cause. He felt that he had to tell the Dalai Lama what he had done. Perhaps this could help his people.

* * *

The most outrageous account came from a monk named Tashi who described a mobile birth-control team that came to his village in Amdo in 1987. "When the barley turned brown," Tashi began, "I watched a mobile birth-control team set up their tent next to my monastery. First the villagers were informed that the team had arrived, and that all women had to report to the tent or there would be grave consequences, like fines of 1,000 yuan to women who did not comply. The team also said that sterilization was part of a world constitution; women all over the world have this done. The women who went peacefully received medical care. Women who resisted were rounded up by the police and taken by force. No medical care was given."

"All pregnant women were taken to the tent for operations," Tashi continued. "Women nine months' pregnant had their babies taken out. I saw many girls crying. I heard their screams as they waited for their turn to go into the tent, and I saw the growing pile of fetuses build outside the tent, which smelled horrible. I saw this in two villages. I arrived in my own village too late. The birth-control team had already been there."

As a physician I believe that a woman has the right to choose if she wants to have an abortion. Such forced abortions and sterilizations were an outrageous breach of human conduct. What Tashi described was a mass sterilization that seemed designed to control the Tibetan population.

"The mobile birth-control teams were initiated in 1982," Tashi continued. "Since 1987 there has been an increase in the number and frequency of the teams that move to remote towns and nomad areas. The mobile birth-control teams do not do abortions and sterilizations on Chinese women. Few Chinese live in these areas. Many Tibetans have been shamed by what has happened. All of the Tibetans in Amdo are talking about this. We are outraged that China is trying to end the Tibetan race. At the same time, we are helpless to prevent it."

* * *

It took John and me one year to get our report of torture in Tibet published. We had wanted to include information about family planning, but we had not gotten enough first-hand accounts of abortion and sterilization. We had recorded eight first-hand accounts of torture. This was not a large enough number to provide a comprehensive accounting of Chinese prisons in Tibet, but it established that Tibetan political prisoners are routinely tortured, a point China had previously denied.

We sent a draft of our report to Physicians for Human Rights, a Boston-based group that had already published reports on human rights abuses in Chile, Czechoslovakia, Iraq, Israel, Kenya, Panama, and the Republic of Korea. After sending the manuscript to their external readers and board of directors, PHR published *The Suppression of a People: Accounts of Torture and Imprisonment in Tibet* in November of 1989.

The Dalai Lama received the Nobel Peace Prize that same month. Suddenly the world press exhibited a new concern for Tibet. The Dalai Lama's extensive travels and speaking around the world increased awareness of the cultural genocide being committed in Tibet. It also made me realize that the torture and imprisonment of Tibetans was generally acknowledged by human rights organizations and the United Nations, as it was by the governments of more than a hundred countries around the world. At the same time these institutions seemed inured to the issue of torture. The issue of forced abortions and sterilizations, which I was determined to explore further, was potentially much more powerful; it was still very poorly documented.

I developed a questionnaire on family planning with help from Rinchen Kandala, the head of the Tibetan Women's Association in Dharamsala. Mrs. Kandala volunteered to find and interview women. Nevertheless, the project had to be postponed for a year. The two years since I had graduated from medical school had slipped away; if I did not do my internship, I would not be able to get my license to practice medicine.

I chose Saint Vincent's Hospital in New York City's Greenwich Village at which to do my internship, because it offered one of the few programs in the country that trained general practitioners with rotations in obstetrics, pediatrics, psychiatry, surgery, internal medicine, radiology, cardiology, intensive care units, and the emergency room. I also liked the nuns who ran the hospital, and appreciated their mission to serve the poor and the indigent.

During my internship I worked a hundred hours a week, with thirty-six-hour shifts every second to fourth night, for one year. Even when I was exhausted I still felt grateful for the times I could get away. I loved staying up all night in the emergency room surrounded by life-saving technology and highly skilled personnel. I learned to appreciate the nuns even more, especially when they let me do an extra month of trauma surgery. Nowhere is Western medicine as intense as it is in the resuscitation of people with multiple trauma. Although I was impressed with our incredible array of medical technology, I never forgot the Tibetans, whose health-care needs were more basic: freedom.

After my internship, I started to work part-time at a walk-in clinic that provided primary care to eastern Long Islanders. I was determined to revise my nonfiction account of traveling to Tibet (which eventually became this book) and to investigate China's family-planning policy in Tibet.

* * *

In December of 1990, the Dalai Lama gave the Kalachakra teachings at Sarnath, Northern India, where the Buddha gave his first sermon after his enlightenment in 600 B.C. The Kalachakra is the initiation into what Tibetan Buddhists call the "path of compassion." Historically, these teachings are given by the Dalai Lama only a few times during the course of his life, usually during periods of great strife. Tenzin Gyatso, the Fourteenth Dalai Lama, has already given more than twenty Kalachakras.

A quarter of a million Tibetans came to Bodh Gaya, the site of the Buddha's enlightenment, when the Dalai Lama gave the teachings there in 1985. In 1990, only 2,000 Tibetans from Tibet managed to evade Chinese border patrols in order to attend. Sarnath, nevertheless, was overwhelmed when more than 100,000 Tibetan refugees arrived from settlements in India and Nepal. For lay Tibetans and monks the Kalachakra was an opportunity to see a living god. For me, it was an opportunity to interview recent arrivals on China's family-planning policy in Tibet.

Traveling overland on a low budget meant that I could not afford to pay a translator. Then I met a boy named Tenzin on the train to Varanasi, the nearest city. He was a shy eighteen-year-old, a recent graduate of the Tibetan Children's Village in Dharamsala, who volunteered his services when he found out that I was going to interview women about China's family planning in Tibet. He turned as red as the betel-nut juice the Indian men spit on the floor when I wrote down a list of relevant medical terms he would need to use. "Personally," Tenzin told me, "I am not knowing the vagina."

Tenzin turned out to be an excellent translator. Because he had grown up in Lhasa, he spoke fluent Tibetan and Chinese. As an exile, he learned English at the Tibetan Children's Village. His mother worked for the Tibetan Women's Association, and she let us sleep outside her temporary office at the monastery in Sarnath.

Tenzin and I went to the new arrivals' camp twice a day for two weeks. Our first visit proved to be a good orientation. We found the reception committee inside the registration tent. Wearing coats and ties, they were easy to distinguish among the horde of new arrivals who were ecstatic to have made it to India. Namgyal, the head of the committee, offered to screen all women for first-hand knowledge of China's family-planning policy. He also led us to a women's tent, where twenty-eight women shied away from us when we entered. Namgyal introduced us to a woman with dozens of well-scratched bites on her face, arms, and bare feet beneath her soiled *chuba*. He announced that it was her duty to tell us if she had ever experienced abortion or sterilization.

The woman demanded to see our identification and her friends started yelling at Namgyal. Tenzin explained that the woman wanted to return to her family and that she was afraid to talk with us; if any Chinese "spies" saw us together, she and her family would be in danger. I sensed that she wanted to talk with us, but that her friends clearly did not.

"Perhaps tomorrow," Namgyal said.

Tenzin started walking back to the monastery. He complained that the reception officers were not working hard enough and said that he wanted to see if his friends from school had arrived. I said that we would get our best interviews on our own and likened the process to a hunt. Tenzin liked this metaphor. He said hello to the monks we passed and stopped to help a man draw a bucket of water from a well. At the end of a row of army tents we passed a couple boiling tea. The woman was obviously pregnant. Within minutes we were drinking tea and hearing at length about the Nepalese police who had extracted bribes at eight different checkpoints.

"Yangzum was five months' pregnant when she went to the hospital for a check-up," Tenzin translated. "The Chinese doctor told her to have an injection to kill her baby. Yangzum refused. 'The hospital does not have the authority to force me to have an abortion,' she told them. She went home and escaped before the police could bring her back to the hospital."

* * *

Tenzin's mother found a Tibetan woman, Dolma, who was an obstetrician from Amdo and had undergone an abortion herself. Because Dr. Dolma had been educated in Chinese and worked in a Chinese hospital, she spoke Chinese better than Tibetan. Tenzin conducted her interview in Chinese. When Dr. Dolma became pregnant for the second time the head of her hospital told her to have an abortion or lose her job. She had the abortion.

She described her abortion in medical detail: the dilation of her cervix; the insertion of the curette; the scraping of her uterus; the fetal parts clogging the suction tube. The doctor who performed her abortion was Chinese. No medicines were prescribed for her because she did not experience any complications other than back pain for one month. She returned to work the next day.

Tenzin was in tears. He had never heard of these things before, and his weeping clearly embarrassed him. At this moment I realized how much my medical training had changed me. Just like Dr. Dolma herself, I was distant from her pain. I had to be in order to treat critically injured and sick people.

Besides the D&C abortion, which was virtually identical to the technique used in the West, Dr. Dolma said that women from four to nine months' pregnant were sometimes given an injection directly into their abdomen to induce abortion. During the five years that she had worked at the Chinese hospital, she said that she had seen 1,600 abortions by D&C, 400 by injection, and 800 sterilizations.

Tenzin laughed unexpectedly as he translated Dr. Dolma's account of how the doctor performing a sterilization makes a small cut in a woman's stomach. Dr. Dolma gave him a stern look. "They make a bigger cut if the woman is fat," he said. It took longer for Tenzin to learn the medical terms for sterilization than it took Dr. Dolma to perform such an operation: fifteen minutes. When I asked how the operation could be done so quickly, Dr. Dolma replied that everything was done under local anesthetic. This was painful, but the woman could walk home afterward.

*   *   *

Tenzin chopped vegetables for our dinner on the dirty cement floor while *ama-la*, as he called his mother, sat on the bed. Her feet were tired from going to each camp to make sure the Indian officials brought people water. *Ama-la* and grandmother-la let *amchi-la* (doctor), as they called me, sit on the bed and write my notes. "Varanasi was closed today," *ama-la* said. "There were two murders in the student quarter last night. I tried to go to the Ganges this morning but it was impossible. There is a curfew after the sun goes down."

The grandmother watched me writing in my journal. Even though she could not read English I still felt self-conscious. A cockroach scurried across the floor. Without thinking I raised my foot to crush the insect. The grandmother shrieked and jumped up and grabbed my leg before it could come down on this defenseless creature. Tenzin and his mother broke into hysterics as the grandmother berated me.

That night, lying on a bed of straw, I wrapped a sheet around my head to tune out the mosquitoes' buzzing. A truckload of Ladakhis who arrived in the middle of night kept everyone at the Sarnath Monastery up with their yelling and screaming. Between the Ladakhis and the mosquitoes I was kept awake worrying that I would not get enough interviews. This fear proved to be unfounded.

*   *   *

As the time approached for the Dalai Lama to deliver the Kalachakra, Tenzin lost his fear of talking to officials and asking women intimate questions about their reproductive anatomy. Busloads of jubilant refugees arrived every night. Although the majority of new arrivals were monks, and most left the camp after breakfast to see the sights in Sarnath, we easily obtained eight first-hand accounts from women who had experienced abortions and sterilizations. One woman who worked in a Chinese bookshop had been given two abortions because she had not waited three years after her first baby. Two women were sterilized after they delivered a healthy baby, only to see a nurse kill it with an injection in the soft spot on the forehead.

Some of the reasons women gave us as to why they were sterilized included not wanting to pay a fine; coming from a poor family; having to obey the Chinese rules; and having husbands who worked in Chinese cadres and were not allowed to have more than one child. Regardless of the reasons, the emotional toll this policy wreaked was reflected in increased numbers of divorces and families separating.

From my perspective, it was apparent that all of these women attributed their abortions and sterilizations to social, economic, and political sanctions against unauthorized children that were coercive in nature and existed on a pressure continuum. Regional variation accounted for differences in the amounts of fines, the numbers of children urban and rural families were allowed, and the length of time women who worked in a cadre had to wait between their first and second children. However, the individual accounts were similar in their details, and these accounts were drawn from women who came from throughout Tibet.

Many of the interviewees said their local Chinese officials were corrupt, and gave examples of Chinese women who paid bribes to get ration cards for extra children. Tibetans could also bribe officials, but most of them thought this was easier for the Chinese immigrants.

As with any investigation, questions led to more questions. All of the six Tibetans I interviewed who were from Amdo (northeastern Tibet) knew of or had seen mobile birth-control teams; the question now was whether these teams operated outside of Amdo. While all of the refugees said that Chinese hospitals had a dual system of health care, this was difficult to prove. Without an on-site investigation, it was impossible to discern how extensively China was implementing enforced family planning in rural Tibet.

* * *

A train with people sitting on its roof ran over an Indian beggar as it passed the new arrivals camp one morning. Tenzin and I saw the one-legged beggar hobbling toward the tracks on homemade crutches. He did not seem to be paying any attention to the oncoming train—but I never would have thought he would attempt to cross the tracks. The conductor did not slow down or blow the horn. The man did not make a sound as he flew through the air, landing with his arms and leg crumpled in unnatural positions.

Hundreds of people ran to him simultaneously, including a Tibetan doctor from the clinic. Massive lacerations covered the man's head. Part of his upper lip and nose were gone. Both arms were twisted backward like chicken wings. The remaining leg was severed below the knee, except for a shred of muscle that held the calf to the thigh. I put a tourniquet on the leg, which would have to be amputated. The Tibetan doctor wrapped gauze around the deeper lacerations. Tenzin recruited a rickshaw and five Indian men climbed aboard with the mortally wounded man and drove off. The man would probably die on the way to the hospital. I felt guilty for not going with him, but I had urgent work at the new arrivals camp.

We had our busiest day ever. In addition to a first-hand account of a mobile birth-control team, which took women by force for abortions and sterilization, we interviewed one woman who had been sterilized after her second child, and another who had an abortion because she had not applied for permission to have a child. Two nuns from Chudson nunnery in Lhasa recounted in horrid detail how dogs bit them at Gutsa Prison in April of 1988. Tenzin and I took turns staring blankly out of the tent over the parched fields.

Then, as we were about to leave, one of the nuns told us that she had been gang-raped. Immediately after her release from Gutsa she had returned to her nunnery, but they refused to take her back. Five Chinese men were waiting for her when she left the nunnery at dusk. Two of the men held her down while the rest took turns raping her. They put her clothes over her eyes so she could not see them. She was afraid to tell the police because she feared they might send her back to prison.

* * *

The Dalai Lama's arrival was postponed from 11:30 in the morning of December 20 until late that afternoon. By noon 100,000 people lined the streets from Sarnath to Varanasi. The Indian police beat the crowd back with bamboo *lakhis* to clear a passageway for the Dalai Lama's entourage. People fought to glimpse His Holiness waving from inside his car. The Dalai Lama's arrival meant the end of my work. All of the Tibetans would be at the Kalachakra during the day. At night everyone would want to eat and tend to their own needs.

Some day, I thought, I too would hear the teachings on the path toward compassion, but first I had to finish my report on sterilization. I longed to return home to my family for the Christmas holidays. Dust hung in the air like fog, a product of the overcrowding and lack of rain. Every day more Tibetans needed more water, food, shelter, and latrines. The tiny hamlet of Sarnath had turned into a disaster area. Soon contaminated water would begin causing widespread hepatitis and dysentery.

The man at the Potala Tours travel agency booth in Sarnath said that all of the train seats to Delhi had been booked for weeks. With Tenzin's help, I learned that indeed all of the seats had been booked, but also discovered that a fifty-rupee service charge could get me a second-class sleeper on the Super Deluxe train to Delhi that left at 8:00 that night. It would be a race to get back to the monastery for my things and then return to the Varanasi station for my train.

In the midst of my goodbyes to Tenzin's family, a heavy-set Tibetan man carrying bags of apples and bananas walked into the room. At first I did not recognize him, but it turned out to be Tsering, the Nepalese man I had treated in Lhasa who had been shot through the leg. He was thirty pounds heavier than when I had last seen him—we both were. I had not been able to do anything about the bullet that had torn through his leg, but my antibiotics had saved his life. His uncle had recognized me in the recent arrivals camp. His mother insisted that he bring us the fruit.

"You look younger," Tsering said, and I repeated the same to him. He said that he had no residual problems with his leg and jogged regularly. He also told me I had a place to stay in Kathmandu any time. Tsering recounted how he had spent three more months in Lhasa. "My sister filed a lawsuit against China for shooting me," Tenzin said. "The court confiscated my passport. It took months for them to find that I had been hit by a stray bullet. I had to write an extensive self-criticism before they let me go."

Just as I was leaving for the train station, Tica Broch was arriving from Switzerland. I recognized her from the hearing at the German Parliament where I had testified. Tica lobbied for Tibet at the United Nations and became excited about the prospect of my report on coerced abortion and sterilization.

"Everyone in Geneva has copies of John Ackerly's report on the suppression of religion," Tica said. "China threatened to pull out of the anti-Iraq coalition because of it. Just wait until they get wind of this sterilization report. If you can get it to me by February, it could make an international scene at the United Nations High Commission on Human Rights. Your article in the *Washington Post* on the mobile birth-control teams in Amdo infuriated China. The United Nations refused China's report on human rights in Tibet because of it."

Tenzin gave me the gift of a *khata* as we ran first to the wrong end of the train, then all the way back to the front car as the train started moving. People fought to get on and push their luggage through the windows. The aisle was so crowded that it took me ten minutes to maneuver to my sleeping berth, where a family from Calcutta was already ensconced. Despite the derogatory remarks directed at me from everyone in the compartment, I was invigorated to know that a man I had treated three years ago had lived, and that my article on human rights violations in Tibet had put pressure on China. Individual travelers can make a difference.

CHAPTER THIRTEEN

RETURN TO TIBET

J OHN SPENT FIVE weeks in Tibet in the summer of 1991 interviewing Chinese officials and Tibetans in eastern Kham (western Yunnan and Sichuan provinces) and Amdo (western Gansu and Qinghai provinces). Three weeks later he submitted a report on religious freedom, education, and population transfer to the United Nations High Commission on Human Rights. I had finished my report on China's family-planning policy in Tibet, entitled "Tibetans Under The Knife," but the refugees' accounts of coerced abortions and sterilizations that it contained lacked the veracity of John's on-site investigations. It was as though John and I were climbing. He had completed a new lead; I had to follow. John loaned me his hand-held video camcorder to use on my second trip to Tibet, this time in the winter of 1991.

I funded the trip with my savings from eight months of full-time work as a general practitioner, and hired another physician to staff the clinic during my absence. I planned to first travel overland for two months in Kham and Amdo before heading to Lhasa. Irony permeated my planning of the trip. I knew that all of the money I spent in Tibet would essentially subsidize the Chinese occupation. Also, four decades of Chinese colonization in Kham and Amdo, and the profusion of different Tibetan dialects, made it more practical for me to have a translator who spoke Chinese rather than Tibetan.

A friend at the International Lawyers Committee for Tibet recommended that I hire Jan, an American woman who had lived in China for seven years, written her graduate thesis at Berkeley on China's "minorities," and currently worked as a Chinese translator in San Francisco.

During a brief phone conversation I told Jan about my previous experience in Tibet, and promised her that we would not get arrested. She agreed to join me.

In Hong Kong, an extra $10 paid to a discount Kowloon travel agent expedited our receiving a three-month Chinese visa the next day. The hundreds of soldiers directing travelers around Chengdu Airport in western China set the tone for our first contact with the mainland. Most were young and unarmed and laughed often among themselves. One woman soldier stopped giggling long enough to check our visas, and then we were whisked to a cab. This gave me a false sense of confidence, until the manager at the luxury hotel we had selected saw the two of us coming through the marble lobby with our backpacks. I asked in English for a room. Predictably, none were available. Jan asked again, this time in the most polite form of Mandarin, and we miraculously had a suite on an empty wing, where two hall-monitor types kept up a twenty-four-hour watch.

At the hotel bar, Chinese men in gray suits whispered into obvious wires on the lapels of their coats as they surveyed the prostitutes, American military contractors, and businessmen who filled the room. We had a drink with a French travel agent named Pierre. Within minutes of introducing himself, and after learning that Jan and I were "cousins," and not a couple, he was offering to fly us illegally into Tibet.

"I am going to fly five Italians to Garze Monastery by helicopter," Pierre said. "It is a fantastic place. I would like to stay there for months. The Italians are arriving from Hong Kong tomorrow. I have arranged a deal with a general to let us rent a military helicopter that has just arrived from the United States. When the general heard that they were paying $5,000 each, he agreed to take a cut. This is our test flight. You are welcome to come with us for free," he added, smiling lasciviously at Jan.

I would have gone on the helicopter, but Pierre's assurances turned out to be less than reliable. The hotel's three travel agents all said they could arrange a jeep to drive us through Kham, but this was "*tai gui*" (too expensive), and every town I wanted to visit was a "minority area," which meant that it was closed to travelers.

It took me another day to learn that the hotel's Golden Dragon travel company was really run for profit by the military. In a back room I inadvertently glimpsed a man putting a two-inch stack of hundred-dollar bills into a wooden drawer. He wore a gray business suit. Seeing us, he introduced himself as the general in charge. He did not seem to realize that I had seen the money. Jan asked in Chinese if he had been stationed in Chengdu long. She listened with interest when he said that he had been the first Chinese man to cross the Karakoram Highway. We also learned from him that Golden Dragon could issue us any permit we wanted—for a price.

The general led us to an adjacent room and introduced us to the manager, who insisted that we use her English name of Lois. "Several months ago," Lois said, "an American couple caused trouble for us." Lois described at length how the Americans had brought "shame" on Golden Dragon for interviewing Tibetans and writing "untrue" things in the press. I presumed that the Americans she was referring to must have been John and his translator. I promised to not cause trouble and started bargaining. Lois wanted $200 for every day we rented a new Toyota jeep, which came with an obligatory driver and guide. "*Tai gui*," Jan said.

After an hour of negotiation, I signed a contract agreeing to pay $1,080 for ten days in a military jeep. Lois called at seven the next morning. She had gotten our travel permits, but informed me that I would have to pay an extra 100 FEC (thirty U.S. dollars) for three non-driving days that we would have the jeep. Jan and I immediately headed to the Golden Dragon office, where we started arguing with Lois. "I did not calculate exactly," Lois said. "There is no profit in it for me."

"That's your problem," I said, and then reminded her of our contract.

"I have not actually gotten your permits," Lois said.

Jan tried to intervene, but then I unleashed the ultimate insult: "By being dishonest, you are losing face," I shot at Lois.

Lois screamed at me in Chinese. I did not need a translation to know that she had canceled our trip. I explained to her contritely that I didn't care about the extra money, but the principle. I took a perverse pleasure in repeatedly taking Lois to the limit, apologizing, and then resuming my attack. Later that afternoon we finally signed another contract.

* * *

Our Chinese driver, Mr. Chu, had an untamed mop of thick, dark hair that seemed permanently windblown. He had learned Tibetan as a child when he had accompanied his father, who was also a driver, on trips all over Tibet. He told us that he had many Tibetan friends, and that Americans gave the best tips. Neither Mr. Chu nor our guide, Zhou, minded Jan's request that they not smoke in the vehicle. I felt an immediate affection for both of them, despite the obstacles they might represent for my work.

Zhou was twenty-two years old and had never been to any of the towns where we would be traveling. He also spoke fluent English, which made me suspect that he was a policeman. A few minutes into the trip we struck a bond when he said that his mother, father, and older sister were all obstetricians. He had decided to become a guide, he told us, because doctors had to work too much.

I was surprised to see so many construction projects on the fertile plains, with thousands of people shoveling sand and gravel along the river as we wound into the barren mountains. I counted the trucks that came barreling down the steep, winding road carrying what appeared to be old-growth logs. There were 200 of them before I stopped counting. When Jan asked where all the logs were coming from, Zhou said, "From the West."

"You mean Tibet," I said.

"Tibet is part of China," Zhou corrected.

We drove through hundreds of kilometers of Kham's denuded valleys. Dust choked the air, a product of fallow fields stripped of their root systems. Scarce stands of mature pine were the only reminder of the region's once-great forests. The lone trees on the ridges stood out like fossilized dinosaur spines. Again I started counting trucks carrying timber to the mainland, and again I lost track after reaching 200.

* * *

After a few days Jan got bronchitis from the dust. The prospect of Jan being ill made me realize how dependent I was on her language skills to find and interview Tibetans, as well as to negotiate for food and places to stay. Unfortunately, none of the local Police Security Bureau (PSB) officials knew we were coming, as Lois had promised, so we had to deal with prolonged bouts of intrusive questioning. Because we were traveling in "closed" towns, Jan had to put up with a lot of "*mei you*" (don't have) before finding any hotels that would take foreigners. Invariably, our rooms looked out over construction sites where stone-crushing equipment clanked until 4:00 A.M. When the cacophony finally stopped, the roosters would start crowing. This pattern primed us for our first fight with Zhou.

"I have to be with you at all times," Zhou said when we first tried to take a walk alone through a Tibetan town. "You are not allowed to leave the hotel without me. You are not allowed to talk to Tibetans about anything political."

Jan, nervous and worn out from her illness, burst into tears upon hearing Zhou's reprimand and walked away. Zhou did not know how to respond. At a loss, he yelled for her to come back, but she kept going. I felt sorry for him. Jan had given his male ego a good beating. "Now you've done it," I said sardonically, slapping Zhou on the back. I left in the opposite direction. Zhou retreated to his room to sulk.

I hurried into town and met up with Jan in the market, where we agreed to take advantage of the opportunity and go to the local People's Hospital. "If Zhou finds out," Jan said, "I'll tell him you needed medicine for the *douza* (diarrhea)."

We made it to the hospital at noon and waited for an hour in an anteroom while the doctors had their lunch. A pale, elderly Tibetan man patted the bench next to him and we sat down. Dirt caulked the cracks in his trousers and calloused hands. He was obviously a farmer and communicated with us through his twenty-four-year-old daughter, who spoke Chinese. I learned that he came from a nearby village, and he said that he had been suffering from a cough and pain in his right chest for a month, which was why he was here at the hospital. He also told us that he had seven children between the ages of eighteen and forty-two years old.

Jan asked how it was that he could have had so many children. He explained that the Chinese didn't start family planning in Tibet until 1989. Now there was a 2,000-yuan fine for extra children. Our brief conversation confirmed what I had learned from interviewing refugees: there was regional variation in many aspects of China's family-planning policy in Tibet. Jan was reluctant to ask the father and daughter about abortions, but she did. Both of us were surprised when the daughter said casually that all Chinese hospitals did abortions and sterilizations, and that most of the women in her village had been sterilized.

Within minutes of entering the People's Hospital I came upon a room with four Chinese women internists huddled around a pot-belly stove. Jan introduced me as a *meiguo daifu* (Western doctor). I said that in the United States internists were the most intelligent doctors. Jan translated this and the women smiled; apparently, this was also true in China.

The two-child policy for minority women had been changed this year, the internists told us after they stopped giggling. Now minority women who lived in towns could have only one child, just like Chinese women. I asked them about contraceptives and the doctors said that Tibetans didn't like interfering with conception. Abortion for any reason was anathema to their religious beliefs.

"For these reasons," Jan translated, "many Tibetan women would rather be sterilized than have an abortion or use contraception." The implications of their statement saddened me; the coercive nature of this policy had even more profound implications for the Tibetans than I had assumed.

* * *

The day after our confrontation, Zhou could not look Jan in the eyes. During the night Jan and I had worked out a strategy to become super tourists. Our plan was to wear Zhou down with sightseeing at the next few towns so he would want to leave us alone, enabling us to conduct our interviews. We dove into our roles with enthusiasm.

Several nights later, while resting at a truck stop, Mr. Chu, Zhou, Jan, and I drank rum and warmed our hands over the electric wire heater we used for boiling tea. Zhou's face reddened after one sip of rum. He soon asked me to arm wrestle. I pretended at first not to be interested, then beat him handily. He pouted until I challenged him to do pull-ups on the door jamb. Zhou did three. I stopped at fifteen.

A local PSB officer barged into the room. I offered him a mug of dark rum. He sucked the black liquid enthusiastically through his decaying teeth and told us that he was fifty years old. Twenty years ago, when the army first sent him to this outpost, Tibetans wore animal skins without undergarments. I thought we were in for a lecture on the backward Tibetans, but the official said that he took pride in the local customs and had learned the local dialect. He encouraged us to return in late July and early August for a festival at which thousands of nomads congregated for horse races, dancing, and drinking.

After gulping his second rum he expressed his exasperation that a foreigner who had traveled here the previous year had written an article about how backward the area was. This had hurt him because he had seen how the local economy had improved. The official stood up and left as suddenly as he had entered. Although he did not return, his intrusion fed my growing fear that we would never have enough privacy in Tibet to do our research.

Mr. Chu said that some Tibetans had picked up bad Chinese habits, like cheating other people. He attributed this to Tibet having been taken over by China. Tibetans, he said, were compassionate, kind people. They seemed backward to those Chinese who didn't have religion. The Chinese who had experienced contact with the Tibetans were richer spiritually.

Hearing both this Chinese official and Mr. Chu tell us that they genuinely liked the Tibetans enlivened me. The Chinese were learning compassion from the Tibetans. Zhou smiled broadly and offered us the use of the jeep, "for free," for an extra day's drive to Lanzhou. "I will personally show you the sights," he told us.

Mr. Chu agreed and we all drank. I said that when I was Zhou's age I had realized that my own government could not always be trusted. I mentioned Watergate as an example.

"Irangate," Zhou added confidently. "About Tiananmen Square, I don't know what the truth is."

"A lot of demonstrators were killed," I said.

"We can discuss these things among ourselves," Zhou said. "Not with foreigners."

＊　＊　＊

Hundreds of thousands of yaks and sheep grazed on the plains as we crossed into Amdo a few days later. We spent an entire day driving on a dirt track and stopped often for yaks to get out of the way. Noble-looking men and women with one child on the back of their horses tended expansive flocks. Zhou was in a good mood and shared a large bag of cookies with the Tibetan families we passed riding yaks and walking barefoot through the fresh snow.

We were snowed in for three days in a small town. The fashionable Tibetans there wore leopard collars around their sheepskin coats. Zhou reluctantly agreed to accompany us to the local Tibetan hospital, where we found a Tibetan physician in his office on the second floor. He wore long underwear and a sweater beneath his soiled white coat.

Jan asked questions in Chinese. The Tibetan doctor's name was Tenzin. He represented the seventh generation of physicians in his family, a heritage that had been passed from father to son. Before 1980, when the Chinese built the hospital, sick Tibetans had come to the doctor's home. Now every township in Amdo had a Chinese-built hospital. Tenzin dreamed that in ten to fifteen years the Tibetans would have a major teaching hospital where local doctors could hone their skills. Although there was a Tibetan medical school 30 miles away in Aba with thirty students, most of the Tibetan physicians still learned medicine from their fathers.

By the time we finally got around to discussing family planning, Zhou was completely bored. In rural villages Tibetans were allowed to have three children, one more than the women from the local Hui and Chiang minority communities. As in Kham, many Tibetan women chose to be sterilized rather than face a fine of 2,000 yuan.

Tenzin surprised me by saying that many Tibetans had developed a greater sense of reproductive responsibility. They understood that with the privilege of being able to create life came a responsibility not to have more children than the environment could support. I asked him if Tibetan medicine had any birth-control pills and Tenzin replied that they did, but they were not 100-percent effective. Most Tibetan physicians advised their patients to abstain from intercourse from the twelfth day of a woman's cycle to the end of her next period.

After we left I asked Zhou if he had a preference for a male child. He laughed. "When I was in university," he said. "I joked with my friends that having a girl was bad. But I did not really feel that way. In cities everyone wants their child to prosper. This means having only one.

Otherwise there will not be enough resources to go around. In urban areas people understand this. In villages they have backward beliefs. This is a matter of education."

Later that same day Jan and I snuck back to the hospital on our own. This time we met two Chinese women obstetricians in a room identified as the "Family Planning Office." Jan introduced me to them as an American obstetrician and the three of us compared the contraceptive techniques used in our respective countries. The doctors said they had prescribed both IUDs and birth-control pills. They also sometimes used hormonal implants that prevented ovulation for from three to six months, but these also caused side effects like giddiness and blood clots. They also told us that most Tibetan women chose to be sterilized in order to comply with the family-planning policy.

The women doctors sat up proudly when Jan translated my statement that Chinese women had more options for family planning than Western women. In China, the doctors explained, they could do D&C's up to four months after conception, and injections of levanor, which induces abortion, up to eight months. They claimed that they routinely performed tubal ligations that took no longer than fifteen minutes.

"What happens if the infant comes out alive?" I asked.

"They are given an injection of alcohol into the anterior fontanel [the soft spot on a newborn's forehead] or submerged in water," Jan said. "In China, this is considered abortion."

* * *

We spent our last evening roasting yak meat on the heater and drinking *baiju* (rice wine). I turned the television on at ten, when the news was broadcast in English, and was surprised to hear the commentator denouncing George Bush. "The People's Republic of China condemns George Bush for interfering in China's internal affairs," she said. "Today the U.S. president signed the State Department Appropriations Bill that recognizes Tibet as an occupied country."

Mr. Chu and Zhou were excited about finally returning from the countryside to their homes. Mr. Chu stopped often to purchase freshly killed rabbit, three pheasant, and quail. Zhou refused to take a 200-

yuan tip I pressed on him when we got back to our hotel in Lanzhou. "We are friends," he insisted, holding my hand in his fist. We embraced, and I forced the money into his pocket. Mr. Chu gladly took the money I offered him and volunteered to drive for us again anytime. Jan organized the farewell photo. She messed Zhou's and my hair. There was no need to mess Mr. Chu's hair.

* * *

We soon learned that no permits were needed to travel in Gansu province. I was glad to hear this, because China had instituted its eugenics program in Gansu, where mentally handicapped women were sterilized to improve the "quality of the race." Here I began using John's video camera. I had an aversion to pointing a camera in anyone's face, and I knew I would be in situations where I wanted to film people discreetly. I worked on shooting the camera from the hip, obscuring it under a loose shirt or jacket. I practiced on slogans painted in six-foot characters on the town's adobe walls: ABORTION IS NOT OUTSIDE OF FAMILY PLANNING; AN OVERGROWN POPULATION CAN BE OPPRESSIVE; FAMILY PLANNING IS EVERYONE'S RESPONSIBILITY.

Jan was sick again when we arrived at our hotel and needed to rest. This left me at a real disadvantage, but I tried to buoy my spirits with the thought that every hospital we had visited so far had contained at least one physician who could speak English. I had also learned how to introduce myself in Chinese as an obstetrician, and how to ask essential questions.

I went to the local People's Hospital and met Dr. Chang, a friendly young pediatrician whose English improved the more we talked. I said in Chinese that I treated babies, and he showed off for me all of his patients: three infants, all less than a year old, all admitted for rehydration. The children were plugged into well-used intravenous lines. I shuddered later when I saw the nurses refill the glass bottles with boiled water; if the children survived their rehydration, they could very well die from disseminated yeast and bacterial infections spread by way of the IV lines.

For an hour Dr. Chang translated into English the captions to the pictures in the pediatrics textbook in his office. I had not realized at first that he was Tibetan, and that though he could speak Chinese, and even a little English, he could not speak his native tongue. Jan confirmed this the next day when she returned with me. Dr. Chang had been sent to Lanzhou at the age of five, where he had lived until he had graduated from medical school two years before. He was twenty-three.

He did not realize that the video camera I had placed an arm's length away from him on his desk was filming him as he explained China's two-child policy for Tibetans. I realized that filming anyone without their consent could be seen as unethical. I also felt strongly that China's coercive family-planning policy, like its oppressive occupation of Tibet, had to be exposed before it could be stopped. Dr. Chang blushed when I asked what happened to babies who were still alive after an abortion. I rephrased the question and he shook his head. He would not answer.

The next day, when a recovered Jan told him that I was an obstetrician, Dr. Chang took us to a conference room and recruited a tall friend of his who was also an obstetrician, as well as an internist who chain-smoked cigarettes, to talk with us. Each of the three were mesmerized when Jan spoke, enough so that none of them noticed the sound of the video camera's small lens turning automatically as it focused. I aimed at the obstetrician when he said, "In cities they can offer IUDs. In minority areas sterilization is the only form of birth control." When he bragged that he could do a tubal ligation in ten minutes, and had once done forty in one day, I could not resist looking down at the camera to make certain it was recording. I was mortified to see that it was not.

The chain-smoking internist explained in English that family planning was more lax in distant villages, where Tibetans were known to have three or more children, while in big cities like Lanzhou, women could have only one child. Most of the people in this area were minorities: Hui, Tu, Chiang, and Tibetans.

"What do you do with handicapped women?" I asked.

"Eugenics is part of China's national family-planning policy," the internist said. "The national government says that women who are diagnosed as being mentally ill are to be sterilized." When asked how he diagnosed mental illness he replied, "We ask questions in simple terms in order to determine their intelligence."

Before our meeting ended, I did not get to find out if a Tibetan

woman who could not read or speak Chinese was at greater risk of sterilization. I also had not yet witnessed a procedure. Still, I should have
known better than to return to the same hospital for a third time. Dr.
Chang was not as pleased to see me, but he helped me look for an obstetrician. We found the head of the obstetrics department in the hall. He
said that Dr. Chang's friend was away visiting small villages today. Dr.
Chang asked if I could see a tubal ligation and the chief berated him.
"This hospital does not do operations," Dr. Chang said sadly. "I'm
afraid you are not allowed here. You must leave immediately."

* * *

We took his advice. Luckily, the bus driver stopped for anyone on the
road who hailed him, regardless of how packed the bus had become. I
was squashed next to a Tibetan woman and her cherubic daughter, who
wore matching enormous corduroy overcoats. This left half of me hanging out into the aisle, battling hands and elbows. Jan had brought along
a washboard to insulate her feet from the freezing metal floorboards; we
had known setting out that since we would now be traveling by bus in
rural Tibet, we would need to employ more sophisticated survival techniques.

The first pass offered vistas of distant curtains of rock. Herds of yaks,
sheep, and wild horses grazed freely on the hills. We followed a red dirt
track into a canyon. In one adobe settlement our Chinese driver had to
slow down for a group of Tibetan women herding sheep through the
road. He leaned on the horn and spat at the women as he plowed forward and scattered their sheep.

* * *

In the next town, we walked right into the obstetrics wing of the
People's Hospital and met five female Tibetan obstetricians. I put the
video on wide angle and asked why there were no male obstetricians
here. Jan and the doctors laughed at me. "Cultural barriers prohibit a
Chinese man from being with a minority woman," Jan translated.

A young obstetrician named Dr. Xian did most of the talking. Like
most of the other Tibetan physicians we had met, these obstetricians

could scarcely communicate with their Tibetan patients unless they spoke Chinese. After we compared different methods of abortion, Dr. Xian said that all obstetricians routinely performed abortions and sterilizations. I asked if I could observe an operation.

"*Mei wonti*" (no problem), she said, and told us to return at two that afternoon.

I was so excited that I had a difficult time paying attention to Dr. Xian saying that Amdo had special teams of doctors and nurses that only visited remote areas. These mobile birth-control teams traveled year-round to educate nomads and villagers about diet, contraception, and family planning. The mobile teams performed abortions and sterilizations according to a two-child policy. The procedures were free; women had to pay for medicine.

* * *

Dr. Xian washed and dried her hands with a soiled rag before leading us into a room where a woman lay naked on a table with her legs spread in stirrups. Dr. Xian wore a surgical mask and draped a filthy cloth over the woman's pelvis that exposed her vagina.

Shooting from the hip allowed me to capture the scene in graphic detail as Dr. Xian did a pelvic examination. The nurse handed instruments wrapped in a stained cloth to Dr. Xian. The patient moaned when Dr. Xian inserted the speculum and sounded the uterus with a metal wire. She pinched the cervix with forceps and pulled it up to insert the curette. I began to feel hot. I had gotten so accustomed to cold weather that I now habitually wore silk underwear beneath a union suit, a wool shirt, and the jacket I wore to conceal the camera. I tried to unbutton my shirt and long underwear as discreetly as possible. Sweat beaded on my forehead as Dr. Xian scraped the inside of the uterus and the products of conception sucked through the clear plastic tubing.

When large droplets of sweat began cascading off my forehead and upper lip, I knew I was about to pass out. The woman's moaning made me think of all women in Tibet, and China, who were undergoing these mechanical, unsanitary, coerced abortions. With the blood draining from my head, I staggered white and shaking out of the operating room. I lay down on a bench outside. A Tibetan man there looked at me as though seeing overdressed Western men staggering out of operating rooms on the brink of losing consciousness was normal.

I was sitting upright again when Dr. Xian came out to see what had happened to me. Jan told her that the procedure they used was just the same in the United States, and that I left because I had wanted to respect the woman's privacy.

* * *

As we walked up the hill to town, I realized that I had gathered enough material for my report. I needed to get to Lhasa, and knew that this meant I could no longer keep my promise to not get arrested. Jan realized this too. She agreed to accompany me to Xining by bus, from which I would continue alone to Lhasa.

I stopped to talk with two Tibetan families waiting in a wagon behind a tractor. "*Tashi delek. Nga America amchi yin*" (Hello, I'm an American doctor), I said. Most of the Tibetans on the cart looked at me trying to figure out what I had just said. A woman with two children on her lap understood. "*Lhasa-kay*" (Lhasa dialect), she said, and explained to me that "hello" in the Amdo dialect was, "*Cho day moo, nee ya.*"

I told her that I was thirty-three years old. She said I looked older. When she said she was twenty-nine years old, I said she looked younger. Changing the subject deftly, I asked, "*Chop-chup, doogay?*" (Sterilization, you have?) The woman said yes, she had been sterilized after having her second child at the local People's Hospital.

Although I did not have the Chinese and Tibetan language skills necessary to conduct a thorough interview, this encounter showed me that I could still glean some information on my own. I could also still try to get footage of a sterilization being performed in an operating room. As it turned out, I needed this newfound optimism to enter the land of *mei you* on my own.

When we reached Xining, the travel agent at the hotel said that the road from Golmud to Lhasa was closed: nine Westerners had died when a bus overturned. I abandoned the notion of taking a bus or hitchhiking to Lhasa and instead returned to Chengdu by train with Jan.

* * *

Except for the speakers playing socialist tunes and propaganda at high volume, I loved sleeping on Chinese trains. Even our two compartment-mates, I noticed, seemed to dislike the intrusion. I waited for the two men to step out to smoke; fortunately, we did not have to wait long. Jan guarded the door while I liberated seven three-and-one-half-inch screws before each speaker fell forward and exposed the two essential wires. Clipping them, I felt a momentary surge of nostalgia-inducing adrenaline.

I found an Englishman on the train whom I had met in Dharamsala. He traveled under a Tibetan name, Nema, because he wanted to return to Tibet in the future. Nema shared Lanzhou *pijou* with us and told me the latest traveler stories.

"Two dozen foreigners are stranded in Golmud," Nema told us. "No one is getting through. One Dutchman shaved his head and disguised himself as a monk, but the police caught him and turned him back. The truck drivers are afraid to lose their licenses if they are caught with a foreigner. One Frenchman supposedly hitchhiked to Lhasa. It took two weeks. He was so pissed off when he arrived that he would not speak to anyone for days."

Nema had come to Amdo to improve his Chinese and Tibetan and to buy books. His trip had been a success; he had bought seventy pounds' worth of books, so many that he was having trouble sending them all home.

The barren fields beside the train tracks made me feel detached. Patches of ice reminded me that I had not seen anything green for weeks. Winter was an ugly time to travel in Kham and Amdo.

"When George Bush did his seven-month stint as U.S. ambassador to Beijing," Nema said, "the Chinese had a difficult time pronouncing Bush. They referred to him as Ambassador Bushi, which means 'no' in Mandarin."

* * *

Back in Chengdu, I met Peter, a Canadian probation officer, and Anna, a Yugoslavian tour leader, at a travelers' hotel. They were planning a four-day trip to Lhasa, the shortest possible tour, and asked if I wanted to join them. It sounded good to me, but I had hopes of staying longer.

They said they wanted to stay longer too, but were en route to India. After paying $600 each, which included round-trip airfare, we celebrated at a pub.

There we met a gregarious Tibetan man named Puntso who asked us to sit with him and his *Rinpoche* (revered monk). He explained that the *Rinpoche* was the head of a large monastery in India. This was their first trip to China. Puntso led us to a large man wearing thick gold rings and a pinstriped suit who presided over a group of six Tibetans. The men wore suits. The women wore elegant silk *chubas*.

The *Rinpoche* barely acknowledged our presence when Puntso introduced us by our countries, as "Mister Canada, Miss Yugoslavia, and Doctor America." He gulped a glass of warm Coca-Cola before the ice in it could melt and immediately called out to the waiter for another. When I asked where his monastery was in India he replied, "I hate Americans."

Puntso laughed nervously. "*Rinpoche* does not hate Americans," he said.

"I hate all Westerners," the *Rinpoche* said. "The West sold out Tibet." One of the women burst into tears and pulled her coat over her head.

"If communism can fall in Eastern Europe, it can fall in China," I said.

"Tibet is finished," the *Rinpoche* shouted as he gulped another Coca-Cola. I looked at the angry, overweight man downing Coke and saw a diabetic on the verge of physical, emotional, and spiritual breakdown. I said resignedly that I hoped he was wrong and excused myself before losing my patience. If this had not been the eve of my return to Lhasa, I would have wanted to talk more with the despondent *Rinpoche*.

*   *   *

Once aloft, Peter and Anna each shot a roll of film before we landed in Lhasa. I too was moved by the snowcapped leviathans rising above the clouds, but I knew the mountains would look diminutive in their photos. Instead I pondered what Lhasa might hold for me this time. I wanted to find out what had happened to my patients in the Jokhang

Monastery, especially Champa Tenzin. I was also determined to video-tape a sterilization.

Landing in Gonggar Airport and having to walk through a gauntlet of soldiers with machine guns reinforced my plan to avoid our tour as much as possible. Andy, the English name of our pre-assigned guide, had no trouble picking out the only three foreigners on the flight. He was tall and friendly and fluent in English. He welcomed us to our black luxury sedan with dark tinted windows, the same car government officials used. "For the next three days the driver and I will take you wherever you want," he assured us. During the two-hour drive to Lhasa we learned that going "wherever you want" meant choosing between tours of the Potala Palace, the Ganden, Sera, and Jokhang monasteries, and a carpet factory. We were forbidden to go anywhere without Andy.

"In Yugoslavia we have more freedom than this," Anna said, demanding that Andy stop the car. "I want to take a photograph of that Tibetan village. Is that all right?"

"Whatever you wish," he said, feigning a smile.

"How long have you been in Lhasa?" I asked.

"Too long," Andy said. "First the government told me two years. Five years later I'm still here."

We stopped to take pictures of eleven Tibetans riding on a tractor cart, barley fields, and a gigantic image of the Buddha painted on a boulder. Instead of taking a picture of the Buddha, I photographed a military convoy in desert camouflage coming out of Lhasa: trucks packed with soldiers, more trucks towing artillery and anti-aircraft guns, chauffeured jeeps carrying officers in dark glasses. After the convoy passed I asked Andy what he thought of the Eastern European countries becoming independent.

"Russian communism was a proletarian revolution," Andy said. "The workers revolted because they wanted a higher standard of living. Chinese communism is a peasant revolution. In China, peasants have a good standard of living. Housing is free. So is health care and education. China will not revolt."

"What about Tibet?" I asked.

"Have you been to Tibet before?" Andy asked. I said that I had, but lied in telling him that I had last been here in 1986. He bought it.

"Maybe Tibetans will get independence," he said indifferently. "The longer I am in Tibet the more I want to go home."

We stopped at a military checkpoint outside the city limit. Andy relinquished our passports and permits to soldiers wearing riot helmets and AK-47s. Peter trembled when I aimed my camera from my lap and photographed a soldier peering inside our car. When we drove through Andy pointed out dozens of three- and four-story buildings under construction for Chinese settlers, including a war college campus of forty-three buildings, as though this would impress us.

Peter and Anna started arguing with Andy when we stopped at a sterile cement hotel. "This has nothing to do with Tibet," Anna complained, "and it costs ninety FEC, the same as the Holiday Inn." Andy said that it was too late to change. We should rest for two hours before going to Sera Monastery. I agreed.

When Andy left, I suggested to Peter and Anna that we head over to the Barkhor in the heart of Lhasa. They enthusiastically agreed, but began to look worried as we walked through mile after mile of housing complexes for Chinese immigrants. There were so many more buildings and Chinese in Lhasa since I'd last been here that I lost my bearings.

Finally, we stumbled into the Barkhor Square and its living stream of pilgrims circumambulating the Jokhang Temple. Peter and Anna were enchanted. They stopped so often to take pictures that I made plans to split off and meet them back at the hotel.

A quick stop at the Snowlands, Yak, Kiri, and Banak Shol hotels revealed that a dozen overland travelers were presently legally registered at the Yak Hotel, for only ten FEC a night. I took this information to the police station where I had previously gotten an "Alien Travel Permit." A plainclothes Tibetan man said he was in charge and demanded to know what I was doing in Lhasa. I said that "Golden Dragon" had arranged everything, and he relaxed immediately. I asked him if Lhasa was an open city. At first he said that all foreign guests had to be on a prearranged tour, but after further questioning he admitted, "Technically, Lhasa is an open city. All travel outside the city limits must be arranged in a tour." I thanked him and returned to my cement box of a hotel.

When Andy returned I told him that I needed to rest. He said that I

would feel better tomorrow and whisked Peter and Anna away in the
sedan.

* * *

I waited about ten minutes before heading out, taking a circuitous route
to one of Lhasa's Chinese hospitals. I started walking along the river
until I was sure that no one was following me, then cut through alleys to
the main road. A bicycle rickshaw took me to the emergency room,
where an intern directed me to the run-down women's building. I
entered with the video camera filming from my hip.

A nurse shrieked and ran when she saw me. I followed her and soon
came upon a Dr. Tashi, the oldest of the staff's four female Tibetan
obstetricians. I stuck out my hand and introduced myself in Chinese.
Using a combination of Chinese, Tibetan, English, and sign language,
Dr. Tashi gave me a tour.

We started with the operating room, where three doctors were trying
to start an intravenous line in a pale Tibetan woman's foot. Dr. Tashi
said "hemoglobin" and scribbled a note to herself, "4%," on her hand.
She explained that the woman was having a miscarriage and would have
to have an abortion the next day.

Dr. Tashi led me into the next room, where she stopped at each bed
to give a brief diagnosis that summarized the patient's condition. She
introduced me to patients and their family members as an American
obstetrician. Of the seven women in the room, I understood that two
were there for *chop-chup* and one for *guaco* (abortion).

Some family members of hospital patients were cooking on the hospital's rooftop, where we could see the Potala Palace rising above the
sprawling concrete suburbs. Dr. Tashi's tour ended in the doctors'
lounge. We flirted mildly, comparing our ages and then discussing techniques for abortion and sterilization. She laughed when I said that I was
single. I laughed when she said that she was married. She herself had one
child and used an IUD, she said, but most Tibetan women had *chop-
chup*.

* * *

The next morning, I told Andy that I was too sick to see Drepung Monastery. "I hope you feel better this afternoon," Andy said. "You will like the Potala Palace."

When I got to the Jokhang, the Barkhor was packed with nomads and villagers who had arrived in Lhasa on religious pilgrimages. I also noticed a few Chinese beggars from the mainland. I entered the monastery with a group of Italian tourists who made videotapes of Tibetans prostrating, monks chanting in the central courtyard, and pilgrims offering dollops of yak butter to butter lamps.

I waited to find a familiar face, then finally began wandering down a hall. I eventually came upon Sonam, whom Heidi and I had treated for burns in 1987. He hugged me and pointed to the absence of scars on his face. "*Yakbudoo*," he said, and left to find a translator. He returned with an English-speaking monk named Tenzin, whom I also remembered, and then began talking with manic intensity. Tenzin translated quickly to keep up with Sonam.

"In 1987," Tenzin translated, "the Jokhang had eighty monks. Twenty have since died, some in prison. Some ran away to India. Others are still in prison. Many people worry: in the future, maybe few monks. Maybe someday lost."

"We are workers in a museum," he continued. "We have no true religious freedom. If we had true religious freedom, then monasteries would be like schools. There would be students here, and knowledge persons. Today, people are only allowed to pray and offer butter. After that, nothing. In Buddhism, the most important thing is to learn. The scriptures are very deep. The first time you can't understand. After teaching and meditation you begin to understand. Today people only know how to practice."

A knock made Sonam go to the door, where he received a whispered message. Tenzin laughed when I hid my camera. "Champa Tenzin is waiting to see you," he said. Word of my arrival must have spread through the monastery. Tenzin also said that we had to be careful that spies did not see us. As they had so many times after the riot, monks led me across the many-tiered rooftops to a secluded room.

Grotesque scars covered Champa Tenzin's face, arms, and neck, but his eyes radiated a gentle strength. Before we started talking, he held up a picture of President Bush meeting the Dalai Lama, his smile breaking into an earsplitting grin. Through Tenzin, I learned that Champa's friends had taken him to the *Mendzekhang* several days after the October 1 riot. There the police interrogated him every day. After one month they took him to Sangyip Prison, where he was tortured; his burns proved to them that he was a "splittist agent of the Dalai Clique." The police beat him with cattle prods and put him on starvation rations, but he did not break. After one month they stopped beating him daily. When they let him out after four months he learned that the Panchen Lama had helped win his release.

Tenzin said that I had to leave before any spies noticed me. He told me to come back in two days and Champa Tenzin would have for me a tape recording of prisoners describing their treatment and what they thought of Chinese occupation.

"A Tibetan guard at Sangyip is making the tape now," Tenzin said. "It is important that it get out of Tibet safely."

I agreed and asked if Champa had anything he would like to say to people in other countries. "We need help from the world people," Tenzin translated. "We need freedom. We need independence from the Chinese."

* * *

Later, our sedan broke down halfway up the steep driveway to the back of the Potala. I forgot that I was supposed to be sick and walked ahead, faster than the tour. Peter and Anna listened attentively to Andy's tour-guide perversion of Tibetan history. I surreptitiously ducked under a canvas tarp and followed the sound of women singing down into a dusty courtyard, until my eyes gradually distinguished forms shoveling rubble amid the cloud of dust. This was the real Potala, still under reconstruction after all these years.

I rejoined Andy on the rooftop. He was ordering a Tibetan worker to find the key to the Dalai Lama's sleeping quarters. The worker replied in Chinese that he did not have the key. The man who did had gone for the day. "Tibetans are stupid," Andy said. I made a panorama with the video camera that showed the ocean of new concrete apartment buildings stretching toward the mountains up and down the valley; smokestacks pouring black soot into the air cast a haze in the air that rivaled that of Los Angeles.

I whispered in Tibetan to the worker that I was a doctor who had seen the Lhasa riots in 1987, and that the Chinese occupation was bad. His face brightened and he produced the key to the Dalai Lama's winter quarters from his pocket. When Andy came upon me photographing His Holiness's bed, with his robe folded just as he had left it in 1959, he said, "You must have good karma."

I said that I did, and took the opportunity to ask if I could extend my stay for two more days. Andy said this was impossible; he had already made our plane reservations. I mentioned the police captain who said I could stay at a Tibetan hotel as long as I did not leave the city limits. Andy refused again, but as he did so I noticed he was eyeing my 35-millimeter camera.

"This is a remarkable camera," I said.

"How much did you pay for it?" Andy asked.

I told him the truth: I had bought the camera in Hong Kong two months ago for $100, and I would sell it to him for seventy-five. We shook hands and went straight to the Golden Dragon office. Andy gave Peter and Anna their tickets and changed mine to leave two days later. Then he borrowed American dollars to pay me. All of this happened so quickly that I wished I had asked him for more money.

"Where are you staying?" Andy called as I left.

"A Tibetan hotel," I said.

"Call me if you need a guide."

* * *

A woman in the market recognized me, and as we talked she fought to hold back tears. Her husband had been in prison for two years along with another man I had known. The woman smiled when people greeted her on the street, but her face quickly resumed its sad expression.

"I can't trust anyone," she whispered. "More than a thousand plainclothes police are always on the streets." I wanted to reassure the woman that her husband would be all right, but this was not likely.

A Taiwanese woman doing laundry in the courtyard spoke enough English to communicate to me that she had hitchhiked here from

Chengdu. Every night the police caught her in town and sent her back east in the direction from which she had come. Every morning she got up early and hitchhiked west.

I met an Israeli couple who spoke English, but they were too preoccupied with getting out of Lhasa to help me. Their flight from Kathmandu to Chengdu had landed in Lhasa with engine trouble. The local PSB had questioned them for a few hours, then agreed to let them stay for a week. There were also several German hippies who had hitchhiked in from the Nepalese border. They knew Otto and told me he was due to arrive any week now. Otto still came to Lhasa every year. The passage of time allowed me to remember the wildman's spirit with fondness.

I went to sleep discouraged. However, the next afternoon I was recognized on the street by Rinchen, a Tibetan woman who had heard me address a demonstration at the United Nations in New York City. She asked me what I was doing in Lhasa. Within minutes she had agreed to go with me to the People's Hospital.

* * *

Rinchen gasped as we walked straight into the operating room at the People's Hospital. There we discovered Dr. Tashi putting a bandage over a vertical incision on a woman patient's pubic region. The woman unceremoniously pulled her pants over the bandage and got dressed. "She was just sterilized!" Rinchen exclaimed after talking briefly with Dr. Tashi. I greeted Dr. Tashi and asked Rinchen to inquire how many children the woman had. "One child," she was told.

At the next table blood was pouring from a pregnant woman's vagina. Two doctors were trying to insert a rubber catheter into her urethra. Dr. Tashi explained for a long time in Tibetan before Rinchen translated, "There's some problem with this baby. The mother's got internal bleeding. The doctors feel the best thing to do is cut the whole thing out." At first I thought this meant they would perform a hysterectomy, but it turned out they were talking about a Caesarean section.

"Is this what they would do in the United States?" Rinchen asked. She was not reassured when I said yes. Dr. Tashi said that she had to work. I thanked her and asked if we could see the patients I had seen the other day. "*Mei wonti,*" she said—no problem.

"Isn't she cute," Rinchen said to a young mother and father holding their newborn daughter on the next bed. "It's their first baby," Rinchen told me. "They are in the performance business. He is in the Tibetan opera. She is a violin player. They are allowed to have a second child, but they have to wait three years. Otherwise, there is a 1,000-yuan fine."

Another patient's husband offered us large hunks of boiled lamb. "This man has five boys and six girls," Rinchen said. "Last year the Chinese implemented family planning in his village. They have eleven children. This will be their twelfth. According to the local officials, what is already born is born. Nothing to do. But this new one in the stomach is a problem. There is a fine but no one is sure how much it is. Apparently they are more strict with city folks, especially cadre workers. All of the other families in the room are passing comments like, 'He's going to take it out.' He is reluctant. He doesn't know what to do. He says he wants to have more children, especially if they're sons. His mentality is like counting his herd."

Lying under two blankets in the next bed, a woman told Rinchen that she was pregnant for the second time that year. She had lost the first baby. "She asked the doctors to please let her have this child but they insist that she have an abortion; the doctors say she will die if she has the child." Another woman at the end of the row said that the doctors were pressuring her to abort her second pregnancy. Both women felt well and wanted to deliver.

* * *

When we returned to the Barkhor, Rinchen's cousin was waiting outside her room at the Tibetan hotel. He had come by bus from Gyantse. When Rinchen saw him scratching, she started to pick nits from his head, throwing them over the wall. I went back to my hotel to retrieve a medicated shampoo that I was glad I had not needed to use. Rinchen was still nit-picking when I returned.

Under my direction Rinchen used warm water from my thermos to apply the shampoo to her cousin's head. While waiting ten minutes for the shampoo to work, I told her the lice would walk off by themselves if he stood on his head. Rinchen helped lift her cousin's feet above his head and held them against the wall. Neither he nor Rinchen questioned the *Inji amchi* (Western doctor), even after I said the lice would leave faster if he sang a song. Rinchen realized that I was playing a joke when her cousin started singing, but she did not say anything until he had finished. It was a rare moment of levity during my otherwise bleak return to Tibet.

* * *

There was no one around to translate when I saw Champa Tenzin for the last time to pick up the tape. In Tibetan we told each other that each of us, the Dalai Lama, and Tibet's freedom were all *yakbudoo*. Then we said farewell to each other. I carried Champa Tenzin's smile with me while I waited for my ride to the airport. I had documented more than I ever imagined would be possible; to stay any longer would only increase my chances of getting caught. I tried to assume the countenance of a happy tourist who would someday like to return to Tibet in order to spend more money.

I had enough video interviews to show that China was implementing a two-child family-planning policy for rural Tibetans, and a one-child policy for those in larger towns and cities. To enforce this a host of economic, social, and political sanctions had been established. Although some contraceptives were available, abortion and sterilization were the primary forms of birth control in Tibet. The implications of the mobile birth-control teams and eugenics programs in Amdo were particularly disturbing. I did not know if China was committing genocide in Tibet, but it was my belief that China's family-planning policy, and its colonization of Tibet, were having a genocidal effect on the Tibetans.

* * *

A Tibetan man gave me a ride to the airport at four in the morning in a dilapidated jeep that could only reach a top speed of thirty miles per hour. Tourist buses and Land Rovers passed us continually during the two hours it took to reach the airport. I arrived after the flight's scheduled departure, but found the mob of passengers still pushing to get through customs for our flight.

A soldier looked at my ticket and pointed to the date, which was for the previous day—I had inadvertently overstepped my two-day extension. "*Mei you,*" she said. How well I'd come to know those words.

"Golden Dragon," I said. She smiled and stamped my ticket. She also ordered another soldier to carry my pack.

Soldiers walked back and forth along the line of passengers, who were kept standing outside the airplane for another half-hour in the frigid dawn air. I was the last person to get on the plane and the first to disembark in Chengdu. There, luckily, the customs agents were talking among themselves. I picked up my pack and casually walked past them. Looking back, I saw the agents beginning to search the long line of passengers.

I could not relax until I had cleared a second customs for a direct flight to Hong Kong. I wrote rock and roll titles on my video cassettes and befriended a Canadian couple who spoke Chinese and told me they loved China. They could tell that I was nervous and asked if something was wrong. I said that I had the *douza.*

Soldiers searched my pack thoroughly and found the video cassettes. One looked at the tapes carefully and asked what I had taken pictures of.

"Beautiful people," I said, as he leafed through my passport.

"Did you go to Tibet?"

"It was too cold," I said. The soldier waved me through.

EPILOGUE

B EFORE WITNESSING CHINA'S use of lethal force to
suppress the nationalist demonstrations in Lhasa in the fall of
1987, I had no idea that I would spend much of the next six years
investigating human rights violations in Tibet. Although this has often
been a gruesome undertaking, I feel privileged to have met so many
Tibetans I can characterize only as noble, and to have shared in their
struggle for freedom.

On February 22, 1992, Champa Tenzin was found dead in his room
in the Jokhang Temple. The police claimed it was a suicide. Tibetans in
the Jokhang claimed he was murdered. One of Champa Tenzin's atten-
dants found him in the morning with a rope tied around his neck, covered with blood. The other end of the rope was tied to the leg of the bed.
Neither the bed nor the room were disturbed. The Lhasa PSB officials
who examined the body declared it a suicide and made the head of the
temple sign a document to that effect.

Under Chinese law, the case would be investigated, but none of
Champa's relatives or the Jokhang monks were interviewed. When I
learned all of this from a report by the Tibet Information Network in
London, which never made it onto the international wire or into any
papers in the United States, I immediately suspected that the Lhasa
police had murdered Champa Tenzin. The most obvious sign of a
police cover-up is the near impossibility of self-strangulation, which for
that matter also would not lead to blood loss.

For me, Champa Tenzin's death epitomizes the Tibetan people's
plight. Although China's brutal repression of independence demonstra-

tions throughout Tibet have awakened the world to Tibetan nationalism, the free world continues to prefer doing business with China rather
than hold China accountable for its atrocities in Tibet, and on the
mainland. If China's colonization of Tibet and enforced family-planning policies continue, the world will lose one of its most peaceful cultures. China and the West have much to learn from Tibet; but there is
little time left.

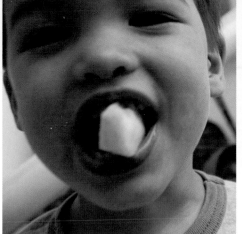

what chefs feed their kids

RECIPES AND TECHNIQUES FOR CULTIVATING
A LOVE OF GOOD FOOD

FANAE AARON

FOOD PHOTOGRAPHY BY VIKTOR BUDNIK

LYONS PRESS
GUILFORD, CONNECTICUT
An imprint of Globe Pequot Press

for cody

Lyons Press is an imprint of Globe Pequot Press.

Food photography by Viktor Budnik
Text design: Nancy Freeborn
Layout artists: Sue Murray and Melissa Evarts
Project editor: Gregory Hyman

Library of Congress Cataloging-in-Publication Data is available on file.

ISBN 978-0-7627-6095-4

Printed in the U.S.A.

10 9 8 7 6 5 4 3 2 1

acknowledgments

I want to acknowledge and thank my husband, Flint, for his patience, his kindness, and his love, and my son Cody, who has been a wonder in both our lives—he is also mostly a pleasure to feed. In writing this book I have come to know so many people. I want to thank the community of people who have been so helpful—all the chefs who have participated in the project for sharing not only their personal recipes but their personal stories with me. I know this topic is as important to all of them as it is to me. I want to thank my dedicated foodie friend Kelley King and my friend Piper Bridges-Fila. I also want to thank Leslie Nichols for all of her insight and encouragement. I want to also thank my friend Mary Ann Marino, who jumped in to help on this book when it was only an idea. I can't thank Sue Bell and all the kids at her school, Giggles and Grass Stains, enough for enthusiastically tasting food prepared from the recipes in this book that I would make and bring in for snacks. I want to acknowledge and thank my agent Jenni Ferrari-Adler and the team at Globe Pequot Press, including my editors Mary Norris and Lara Asher, who have been so encouraging, helpful, and supportive.

contents

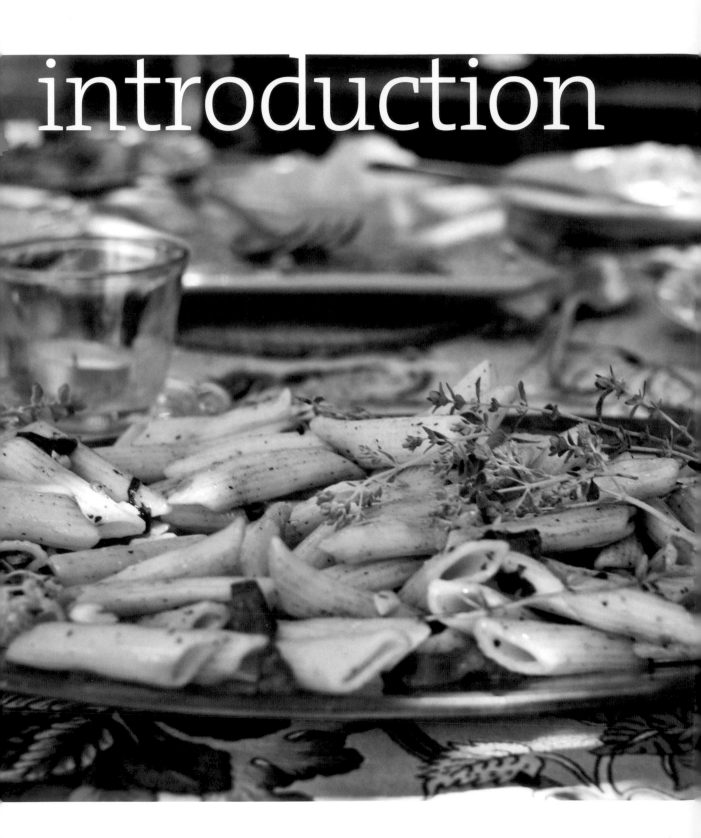

introduction

When it came time to start feeding my son, Cody, solid foods, like most parents I trooped to the store and stocked up on jars of baby food in a variety of flavors. But then when the time came, I popped open a jar and it just didn't seem that appetizing. Instead, I simply gave Cody some sweet potato that I was eating, then some mashed ripe avocado. I liked that he and I could eat the same thing. Even at the very beginning, we could sit and enjoy a meal together. I knew that what he was eating was good, because I was tasting it myself. But I didn't know where to go from there. I had only rudimentary cooking skills and didn't know what to do to add variety, or even if I should. It was easy to mash some sweet potato with a fork, but I didn't know if I should mix it up and try new things or stick to what Cody liked. I wondered if there was a way to feed kids that both nourishes and stimulates them. Our brains are wired to burst to life with new sensations. They light up and chemicals are released in our brains as we experience the pleasure and delight of something new and interesting. Cody did seem to get very excited about the physical sensation of food in his mouth and a spoon in his hand, and he was very pleased when the two met.

I wondered: Would a child raised by chefs enjoy eating even vegetables, which most kids detest and refuse? What kinds of things do chefs do to introduce their children to eating, and are they able to stimulate curiosity about new foods? Do their kids pick out the smallest speck of parsley and call foods "icky" and "gross," just like other children do?

For chefs, every meal is a new beginning—an adventure—and that attitude translates to how they feed their kids. I interviewed lots of chefs all around the country for this book and collected their voices and ideas together. This book illustrates their strategies and their attitudes; it's not just about cooking for your kids. I now enjoy cooking family meals, but the techniques are the same for eating out.

It's about how we can educate kids and eventually enable them, when they are old enough, to make better choices for nourishing themselves.

The recipes in this book are meant to be served as meals for the whole family. Here, the purees are a pared-down part of an overall recipe that the whole family can eat, with suggestions for additions or modifications for older children and adults. Also, the foods in the beginning are more rudimentary and simpler to prepare than the recipes later in the book. Lots of the recipes can be tackled together, with young children doing the measuring and pouring and, later in the book, older children learning about transforming ingredients and the magic of assembling them to make a complete dish together.

The book is organized in chapters by age, recognizing that there are ways that babies and younger children prefer to eat that are different from the kinds of foods that older children gravitate toward. I've tested all these recipes myself and tried to explain some of the trickier parts of recipes and why they are tricky. Some of the ingredients I'd never heard of before—*tamarind? Is it a paste or a fruit?*—and it was a bit of an adventure finding them.

"When people enter the kitchen, they often drag their childhood in with them," says novelist and food writer Laurie Colwin in her book *Home Cooking.* I remember reading her books of essays when Cody was an infant, during his naps. When I look back at those days, I realize that those sweet potatoes became the basis for our relationship and how we experience a meal—cooking together, sharing food together, eating together. We had fun, we learned a lot, and sometimes we struggled. This early foundation still underlies the way we eat and share a meal. Food writer M. F. K. Fisher summed it up when she said, "It seems to me that our three basic needs, for food and security and love, are so mixed and mingled and entwined that we cannot straightly think of one without the others."

recipe list

adolescence { ages eight to eleven }

infancy

A FOUNDATION OF SIMPLE FOOD

ages zero to one

Food is one of the keys to the world of pleasure and adventure in life, according to the chefs I interviewed for this book. It stimulates the senses unlike anything else—and we can impart a desire for that stimulation, as well as a curiosity about new experiences, early in our children's lives by serving them a broad range of colorful, flavorful foods that they can experience with all their senses. Food is about so much more than taste, especially for infants. It's a whole new world for an infant to start eating solid foods, foods that the grown-ups have been eating. Rich with sensory stimulation, food excites infants with its vibrant colors and savory smells. They enjoy putting it in their mouths, rolling it around and tasting it, or just squishing it in their hands and mushing it around the table.

When Do Babies First Experience Flavor?

A baby first experiences flavor in the womb, where taste buds initially develop. "Nourishment and taste buds start in the womb, so what a mother eats is what's in the placenta," says Sally Kravich, a natural health expert. Remarkably, a fetus at fifteen weeks has taste buds that resemble an adult's, and before the end of the first trimester, a baby tastes the flavors of foods by sucking, swallowing, and even smelling amniotic fluid. After birth, a breast-fed baby receives a variety of flavors through the taste and aroma of breast milk, which is constantly changing. Because the foods we eat flavor our breast milk, a breast-fed baby becomes accustomed to those flavors and their variety. "I've never censored or changed my eating, especially while breast-feeding," says Chef Ana Sortun, who wanted her daughter, Siena, to grow to enjoy the same foods she eats. Sortun, who is the chef/owner of the award-winning Oleana Restaurant in Boston, ignored the recommendations of some pediatricians to restrict her diet and avoid a whole host of foods, including garlic, cabbage, and broccoli, while breast-feeding her newborn. "I think from even before she was eating herself, she had a sense of flavor and spices."

The flavor of formula, on the other hand, is bland, sweet, and unvarying from bottle to bottle. It leads to early conditioning for bland, one-note foods. While breast-feeding is far better for infants for many reasons, not every chef's child included in this book was nursed, and feeding infants formula does not at all mean that ultimately they won't eat well as they get older. Nursing a child, as beneficial overall as it is, is just one of many opportunities to teach a child to eat well and acclimate her palate.

Building Blocks of Flavor

When it came time to introduce solids to their infants, the chefs profiled here all started out feeding their kids a foundation of fresh vegetables and simple foods, like building blocks of flavor. Frank Proto, executive chef at Marc Murphy's Benchmarc group of restaurants in and around New York, takes a simple approach, pureeing steamed vegetables. He says, "I want them to experience the pure flavor of foods as they are." Colby Garrelts, chef and owner with his wife, Megan, of Bluestem restaurant in Kansas City, makes purees from fresh vegetables as well, and also offers pureed chicken soup. Chef B. T. Nguyen of Restaurant BT in Tampa points out that babies have palates that are pure and uncontaminated. They need to be given those clean and fresh foods first, she says. Other chefs mention roasting vegetables or fruits to concentrate and sweeten their flavors, and gradually adding another layer of flavor, like lemon or basil.

Perhaps the easiest time to feed a child is at the beginning, when he first starts to eat solid food. My son, Cody, was open and adventurous in the beginning because he had been watching me and my husband, Flint, eat and wanted to participate. The food went into his mouth and, for the most part, didn't come back out. He rolled the food around in his mouth but didn't intentionally reject it—that didn't occur until later.

Taking cues from the chefs I spoke with, when I began to feed Cody solid food, I stayed away from the rice cereal so many books recommended. I didn't want to celebrate such an event with the blandest and least exciting food ever created. It's best to start slow with solid foods and make them liquid and smooth, so I chose to start with a pureed banana. Then I moved on to pureed apple and sweet potato—foods I love, with color and texture. I added other vegetables, like green beans, peas, squash, and carrots. I also made purees from fruits such as peaches, plums, avocados, and apricots. And I mixed breast milk into the purees both to thin them and to help Cody adjust to the new flavors. For babies who are being fed formula, mixing that familiar formula in with new purees will help them acclimate to those new flavors.

I spaced out those first foods to watch for allergic reactions. Cynthia Epps, an infant-feeding specialist in Los Angeles, where we live, recommends doing this, especially if there is a family history of allergies. I began combining foods to keep things interesting. I mixed up Cody's food a lot, and while we had some staples we repeated regularly and frequently, there was always something new on the menu. I often had him on my hip while we were in the kitchen mixing and mashing, giving him tastes of food as I tasted it while cooking. I tried to follow Cody's cues and be sensitive to reflux, gas, and elimination issues, which are common when babies first begin eating solids. I avoided raw fish, like sushi, which can have harmful bacteria, and spicy foods.

I quickly began experimenting. I mixed baked apple puree with herbs like rosemary, tarragon, or

COLBY AND MEGAN GARRELTS have their own restaurant in Kansas City, Missouri, called Bluestem. Colby is the executive chef, and Megan is the pastry chef. Colby was listed as one of the Best New Chefs in 2005 by *Food & Wine*. He was nominated by the James Beard Foundation for Best Chef Midwest Region for 2007 and 2008. For the restaurant, they source their organic produce and meats locally. They serve progressive American farm-to-table fine dining, and they opened a casual lounge next door that serves beautiful bistro french fries with truffle oil, parsley, and cheese. Their daughter, Madi, spends lots of time at the restaurant and knows just where the chocolate bin is in the area where Megan bakes. "I go back there and her cheeks are full of chocolate," says Colby. "She'll go to the kitchen and the cooks will give her things all the time. She's tasting things all the time. She will definitely know food."

Megan Garrelts and daughter Madi : BONJWING LEE

thyme, playing up savory flavors instead of sweet. I mashed carrots and butternut squash together and alternated days of kale and spinach, which I made the way I like them, with olive oil and garlic, so we could eat together. I wanted Cody to eat dark leafy greens, which I love. Cody was born in late March, so when I started giving him solid foods, it was late summer and early autumn. Stone fruits like peaches and plums were fresh at the market, and I roasted them and mixed them into cereals and oatmeal that we all enjoyed together.

After Cody adjusted to eating purees, I began to vary them by texture, color, and flavor and learned from Diane Forley, chef and co-owner with her chef husband, Michael Otsuka, of Flourish Bakery in Scarsdale, New York, to make them flavorful instead of tasteless and boring. She makes fresh soup stock—squash, turnip, rutabaga, and chicken—and adds fresh herbs. "Adding herbs is how I make my food flavorful," she says. "I also use onion to add flavor. Why do people think kids should eat food that's bland? Prepared baby foods are bland. I don't know why there's an assumption that kids don't have taste buds."

Proto agrees. "My daughter loves miso soup," he says. "She loves it! Who would think that a kid would like miso soup?"

Marcia Pelchat, a biopsychologist at the Monell Chemical Senses Center in Philadelphia, explains that infants prefer a salt solution to plain water as early as five months and will enjoy soups and broths.

Most chefs make and keep stocks at home to incorporate in everyday cooking as both a way to make food flavorful and to get multiple meals from

> ⋯⋯⟩ **Babies have ten thousand taste buds compared with adults' six thousand, and many infants have taste receptors not only on their tongue but also on the soft part of their palate and on their cheeks. Marcia Pelchat, a biopsychologist at the Monell Chemical Senses Center in Philadelphia, thinks that's why children are so apt to fill their mouth with food.**

one dish. Premium ingredients can be expensive, and getting the most from them is a good way to economize. Linton Hopkins, executive chef at Restaurant Eugene in Atlanta, makes quick stocks from leftover chicken and bones while he's cleaning up dishes. He'll use that stock for a rice and chicken dish the following night. He'll make a quick broth out of the unused vegetable parts like leek tops. "To me, making a stock is like making a tea," Hopkins says. "People get scared of stocks, but those are the juices that make our cooking better, I think."

Introducing Your Baby to Spoon Feeding

Epps considers infants' oral and tactile development as well as guidelines established by the American Dietetic Association when offering advice on how to go about helping infants learn to eat from a spoon.

The first thing I do is to slowly bring a spoonful of puree toward the child. Children will reach out for it on their own because, developmentally, they are exploring the world through their hands at this age. They'll take the spoon if it's pointing in the right direction and if it's put close to their hands, and they will put it by themselves right into their mouth.

This gets children to participate from the very beginning. When they are feeding themselves, they will naturally eat slower than an adult would feed them and they will intuitively eat an amount that is right for them. Adults who feed infants will be inclined to feed them a whole jar or whole bowlful of food, and that's probably too much for them. At first, the purees should be very liquid and roll easily off the spoon—at eight to ten months you can start to make them thicker. A child at six to twelve months is going through a stage of oral and tactile development that involves passing toys from hand to hand. Giving them the spoon makes their meals part of that development, and it's fun for them.

When babies take the spoon themselves, they will naturally chew on it with their gums and use more chewing pressure than if they were being fed. Allow them to take a spoon and chew and crush on it while they are eating. If, for a few seconds, they get to suck and chew and crush on the spoon, they slow down their eating and become patient. This does two things simultaneously. First, it teaches the child to eat slowly instead of grab food and gulp it down, and second, it lowers the risk of choking because the baby's mouth is developing a chew, crush, swallow, chew, crush, swallow pattern of eating. When an adult feeds a baby, they likely don't leave the spoon in her mouth to give her the opportunity to chew on it, so the baby just swallows the food.

If you allow babies that step of using their mouth to crush on the spoon with their gums, by the time they start to fully feed themselves at ten to twelve months, because they have learned that chewing is part of eating, the risk of choking later when they are eating pieces of food instead of puree is lowered.

The First Bite

Feeding children requires creativity, patience, persistence, and caring, and most children need to be given more than one opportunity to embrace a new food. While Cody was never terribly difficult about trying new foods, I was told many times not to assume he didn't like something until I'd fed it to him a few times. Some babies are slower to take to solid foods; they may have trouble learning to swallow or might be picky from the get-go. Don't give up. Move at a pace that is comfortable for your child and keep trying different foods to find ones he likes. I found myself surprised by many of the foods Cody ended up enjoying.

The first solid food Colby Garrelts gave Madi, his daughter, was carrots. "They are naturally sweeter. We figured she would go towards that first." He was surprised that the vegetables seemed to be the things she liked best. She likes squashes, spinach, carrots, and broccoli. She loves broccoli. "Broccoli stems are sweet," adds chef and cookbook author Peter Berley, and he peels the tough outer skin off and cooks the stems along with the florets.

It is especially important to give picky infants positive experiences with food. I sometimes had to play detective with Cody to figure out which foods he was adverse to and why, and which ones he naturally liked. I built flavor bases from there, giving him a variety that I think helped expand his diet later on. Also, at this early age a different preparation can make a food appetizing. Some foods, such as cabbage and asparagus, have sulfides in them and when cooked can smell bad to children who are sensitive to odors.

Chef, restaurateur, and food scientist Jimmy Schmidt discovered this with his son, Mike, who has difficulties with the aromas of certain foods. "If you look at asparagus, it's a great example because with raw asparagus, the sulfides are not as exposed and aromatic. When you cook it, it tends to get a little stinky. We're used to it, because as adults we like asparagus cooked and we are used to seeing it around. Just from a sheer aroma sense, you smell a raw asparagus and you smell a cooked asparagus, they smell quite different," he explains. "Mike's more open to raw than he is to cooked in the vegetable family. Even when he was a baby, he didn't like pureed peas and stuff like that."

Infants, who have a strong sense of smell, will judge a food on the spoon from a foot away and determine whether or not it's appealing to them. Asparagus, cabbage, broccoli, and cauliflower can be smelly when cooked and served warm. It is possible to cook them so they are soft but serve them cold to minimize their aromas. But even some hearty eaters will ease into eating slowly. As an infant, Cody would never just dig in to a plate of food unless it was a dish he'd had before and recognized. Given a few minutes, he'd take a bite and eventually finish what was on his plate.

I always made sure to give Cody a taste of what we were eating when we ate together. It has established a close bond between us that continues to evolve to this day. Sometimes he takes a bite of a particular food and doesn't like it, but he trusts me enough to take a taste because I have always been sensitive to his eating needs.

"The very first bite for Sasha is a difficult one. She never reacts 100 percent immediately. However, after a bite or two, then, it's like you open up the mouth. At first, she has a squeamish face, then slowly she feels like the comfort zone has arrived. You distract her. Distraction is very important. She needs to be focused. Babies are so busy with everything—if you don't make her focus, baby will not eat."

—Piero Selvaggio, owner of Valentino restaurants in Los Angeles and Las Vegas

Exposing a baby to a wide variety of foods, and consistently adding new foods, helps her eat broadly later as a preschooler and even as an adult. "Children of picky parents, parents who eat a narrow diet, end up just not being familiar with a lot of foods, and all things being equal, familiar foods are liked better than novel foods," says Pelchat. Chef Diane Forley confirms this when she says, "I think we set up and establish cravings in kids by serving certain types of food all the time. We get used to them."

Eat Healthy from the Start

It's easier to give your child a balanced and varied diet later on if you are eating that way while you are pregnant and breast-feeding. The early experience of the flavor of vegetables and other healthy foods has been found to familiarize babies with them, increasing the likelihood that they will accept those foods later when they begin eating them as solids. I saw it as an opportunity to begin building a foundation for Cody to enjoy a healthy, varied diet including vegetables.

Epps teaches her clients to begin feeding infants their first solids with a rotation of green and yellow vegetables and suggests serving fruits only occasionally. Even though so many pediatricians advocate starting with rice cereal mixed with fruit, she points out that rice cereal with fruit is a high-glycemic food. High-glycemic foods cause the blood sugar to rise quickly. Most fast foods are high-glycemic foods because of the added sugars they contain, and anything with the ingredient high-fructose corn syrup is high glycemic. By comparison, proteins, fats, grains, and nonstarchy or sweet vegetables don't impact blood sugar. Getting infants acclimated to eating high-glycemic foods sets them off on the wrong path, toward craving sweet foods. She suggests emphasizing vegetables and then rotating in different whole grains.

Epps proposes starting first with peas, then adding yams and summer squashes like zucchini, then adding a serving of apple before going back to peas again. She also advises staying away from sweetening vegetables or grains with fruits and instead letting those foods have their pure flavor. She recommends small portions, no bigger than the size of the baby's fist. Progressing this way prepares the infant's palate for accepting vegetables and makes it easier later to serve them as finger foods to a toddler, who becomes more difficult to feed.

The biggest problem with feeding children later on as toddlers and preschoolers is getting them to eat foods they are not familiar with—this can be anything that's new, like an avocado or ethnic dishes with unique flavors. Pelchat talks about the benefit of exposing kids to new foods and flavors, both to build familiarity with lots of foods and textures and also to build a tolerance for trying new foods. Scientific

PIERO SELVAGGIO has three grown sons—Giorgio, Giampiero, and Tancredi—and a new young daughter, Sasha. He is the owner of the fine Italian restaurants Valentino and Posto in Los Angeles and Valentino Las Vegas, at the Venetian Hotel in Las Vegas. His restaurant Valentino received the James Beard Award for Outstanding Service in 1996, and the award for wine in 1994. *Wine Spectator* magazine named Valentino one of the top four restaurants in the country in 1996 and again in 2000, and has given its Grand Award for wine to the restaurant every year since 1981. In 1997, the Italian magazine *Gambero Rosso* named Valentino the finest Italian restaurant in the world. Selvaggio was born in Modica, Sicily, and makes his home with his new family in Los Angeles. "I have something I could never have imagined could change my life so sweetly," says Selvaggio of having another child after his three sons were grown. "I couldn't imagine the journey. Interestingly enough, it has been a journey that has taught me a lot. For example, this morning, the highlight of my morning: I took her to the park and put her in the swing because she is a big girl, but the highlight was I made her a one-egg omelette with kale."

literature supports the idea that there is a window of opportunity to introduce children to novel foods that probably closes after they are weaned and before they turn two. Once that window closes, it becomes much harder to condition children to want to eat new things.

"It's important to begin a child with a healthy diet; you start a child not the wrong way but the right way. You put more care into building their taste buds for healthy foods and learning the balance of eating greens and of eating fruit and of eating healthy overall. The earlier you start training your child that this is the way to do things, the better it is," says Piero Selvaggio, chef and owner of Valentino restaurants in Los Angeles and Las Vegas.

"I never really put effort or so much thinking into eating healthy because where I was brought up, in my country, Vietnam, everything is organic and fresh and we don't have processed foods or canned foods. It is still in my mind and on my palate," says Nguyen. "So, I never bought baby food; I made baby food for my daughter. And the meals I made were always balanced. I would make dishes from a protein, a vegetable, and a starch. I would make her a dish of rice, chicken, and carrots, or I would make a variety of beef, rice, potato, and vegetable. I would cook it and then blend it, and if it needed, I put a little bit of milk in just for the consistency."

Part of eating healthy is eating broadly. "There's a lot of variety of foods around, all the time," says Sortun. Colby Garrelts says Madi, his daughter, spends a ton of time at their restaurant, where there are always lots of different things being cooked. "Madi

has known all the cooks and our general manager since she was born. She'll go to the back of the restaurant in the kitchen and the boys will give her things all the time; she's tasting things all the time and I hope she has a great palate. I thought about this a ton when she was first born. Kids here don't because most Americans don't eat this way, but in Vietnam for example infants grow up with fish sauce and curries."

Exposing children broadly includes keeping them around while you are cooking and also while you are eating, surrounding them with the aromas of what you are eating. "Siena, my daughter, is always in the kitchen with me when I am doing stuff," says Sortun. "Madi smells the food, that's a big deal too," adds Colby Garrelts.

try to avoid too many sweet flavors
Babies are naturally inclined to prefer sweet flavors and tend to initially reject sour and bitter flavors, so they may have a tougher time with savory vegetables. Children generally favor those fruits and vegetables that contain the most carbohydrates and sugars, such as potatoes, peas, bananas, and apples. It is believed that the preference for sweet flavors is biologically a protective function—plants with bitter and sour flavors are more likely to be poisonous or contain toxins. Repeated exposure helps kids get accustomed to those flavors and makes it easier for them to enjoy those nutritious vegetables that fall into this flavor range when they are older. Kravich says human beings naturally have a sweet tooth, and sweet is the strongest taste: "If

children have been given sweets and haven't been properly introduced to foods in the weaning process in infancy or predominantly given sweet foods as infants, they're going to develop more of that sweet tooth."

on eating meat

Infants can begin to eat meat as early as eight to nine months of age. Megan Garrelts wanted her daughter, Madi, to eat meat because it contains protein and iron that she thought were important for nutrition. "In the beginning, we couldn't get her to eat meat at all," Megan says. "She would eat other things for protein, but it wasn't the same in our eyes. Then, we were having a bone-in rib eye for dinner, and she just picked the bone up off Colby's plate and started chewing on it because our dog had a bone and she was imitating the dog. From that day, instantly, all she wanted was steak. She was sucking on the meat and the bone and we thought 'oh my god, this is good.'"

Meat can be pureed like other foods, and it's easiest if it's mixed with a soup or a vegetable with a high water content, like tomato. "Most kids seem to like chicken more than anything because it's got a more mild flavor," says Colby Garrelts. Cody loved lamb and other roasted meats, and early on we were eating robustly flavored stews. I loved cooking those foods with him because we could casually prepare everything early in the day and have dinner ready without much immediate predinner preparation. It's also great to come home hungry to a house filled with the aromas of cooking.

the skinny on fat

Healthy babies are born fat. Fat comprises up to 14 percent of their body weight, half of which accumulates in the last five weeks in the womb. Baby fat is evenly distributed just under the skin, unlike adult fat, which accumulates internally around the organs. Healthy babies need fat to keep them warm and, even more important, for brain development and growth, which occur at a remarkable rate all through the first year of life. Seventy-four percent of a baby's energy in the first year of life is devoted to brain development, and that energy comes from fat. Skinny babies often do not flourish because the fatty acids meant for brain development are being used to keep them warm instead. Many of the developmental delays premature babies experience are due to lack of fat.

Healthy infants will continue to accumulate fat up to four times their birth amount during the first year of life. During this year most pediatricians advise giving infants full-fat dairy products, switching to low fat only after the first birthday.

But as children grow and develop, excess body fat causes problems. Sadly, children younger than six have been found to have fatty streaks on their arteries and some narrowing of the coronary arteries. Overweight infants are more likely to become overweight toddlers and stay overweight into adulthood. Studies show that the tipping point that determines obesity can occur as early as when infants are first learning what and how much to eat. Staying away from processed foods and eating healthy foods are critical for infants to learn to eat properly.

Allergies

Food allergies in infants can appear as cold symptoms such as a runny nose, itchy eyes, and a cough, or a rash. Highly allergenic foods include peanuts, milk, and eggs. Epps notes that it's important to remember that an infant's digestive system is different from an adult's. Infants are growing so quickly that the breast milk they consume goes straight into their bloodstream and is immediately used for tissue growth. The digestive system is very sensitive in the first twelve to fourteen months while it is maturing. Epps stresses that highly allergenic food like dairy, including yogurt, shouldn't be given to infants before their system matures, because early exposure to dairy products may actually create an allergic reaction.

Kravich says that children who seem to be chronically congested or who get sick with lots of runny noses, coughs, and colds may not be digesting wheat and dairy foods well. She says eating a fruit or vegetable with foods like starches, dairy, and proteins helps digestion. It's easy to give crackers, Cheerios, and pasta to children, but those foods alone, especially if not whole grain versions, are what Kravich calls "gluey" and "sticky" in the digestive system. She says, "It's like a glue, and it gets built up and it doesn't move through the digestive tract."

"Italians eat tomato with mozzarella; the Portuguese might have pear with a sheep's milk cheese. I started looking at how people eat things, and I realized that when I combine these live foods with dairy, I can digest it better and it doesn't produce mucous," says Kravich. She adds that cheese

"Food is family. There's a culture with Southern food that is all about family, very similar to the European cultures like the Italian culture and the Jewish close-knit community culture. You don't separate food and family. You're talking to a Southerner, and I really believe the South has it goin' on when it comes to food culture and passing recipes through the family. I grew up never eating out; my mom cooked, and my grandfather, Eugene, whom I named the restaurant after, was an outstanding cook. He made vinaigrette every night. He grew up on a farm in Tennessee. And so, you look at the traditions of foods in our South, and that becomes part of how we define ourselves as a family."

—Chef and restaurateur Linton Hopkins
on the culture of food

made from sheep's milk and goat's milk is easier to digest.

Peanut allergies in the United States are on the rise. Because of the severity of the allergic response in an individual with this allergy, parents are understandably concerned about the possibility of their child possessing it. For a long time, pediatricians recommended that infants should not be given peanuts until the age of two. New information suggests otherwise. Parents are left with no clear answers but are now advised to incorporate nuts in an infant's diet and not to wait. Knowing that children who are allergic usually react right away, I nervously gave Cody peanuts for the first time on a Monday morning when I knew

JOAN MCNAMARA founded and runs Joan's on Third, a culinary emporium that includes a much-loved cafe, marketplace, and full-service catering and event-planning company in Los Angeles. Her adult daughters, Carol and Susie, and Susie's husband, Chef Chester Hastings, all work with her. Susie and Chester have a son, Henry, who visits the store for a little bit every day. "I learned how to cook, I suppose, from my mother, the way you learn to walk or learn how to dance. I never took dancing lessons, you just did it, you know?" says McNamara. "When my children were born, I did the same thing with them. I have pictures of both girls standing on a chair—like my grandson now standing on a chair—stuffing the turkey for Thanksgiving. They'd wash their hands, and then I'd let them do it themselves. I always thought that letting them handle food was important, to just say 'look it, this is how you do this, now you do it.' I would watch, but they were allowed to do it themselves."

Joan McNamara and daughters Carol and Susie : MARY ANN MARINO

"I started out with foods that might work together in terms of flavor and consistency, and I let my baby hold the food and play with it, smell it, and then taste it."

—Alejandro Alcocer, New York City chef and epicurean

my pediatrician's office would be open. A new study indicates that peanut allergies may be treatable with a program of controlled peanut exposure that works similarly to a vaccine.

The Importance of Playing with Food

At six months, the age when most parents are just beginning to introduce solid food, an infant is captivated by touching and holding. He is fascinated by his food, and touching and playing with it is an important part of his development. Allowing him to play with his food creates a healthy curiosity and relationship with food. If your baby is reaching for your food, that's a good sign.

As babies grow, they often experience a surge in appetite. They begin to show independence and may want to feed themselves. This can and probably will be messy, so expect plenty of spills and splatters. If

TEACHING YOUR CHILD TO EAT

Teaching your child to eat is like teaching her anything else—it requires a lot of parenting. Here are some tips from chefs for feeding your young child:

•• Take him shopping with you and talk to him, even when he is very young, about the foods you're cooking and eating. Even if he doesn't understand the content of what you are saying, you are building a foundation of communication and teaching about food.

•• Let her watch you prepare her food. Even if she is not eating it, she will smell the aromas and be captivated by watching you mix and stir.

•• Keep him with you when you're eating so he's exposed to the sights and smells of foods you enjoy.

•• Acknowledge from the beginning that there will be challenges—some wasted food and some failures.

•• Don't throw up your hands and give her the one or two things she'll readily eat. If you do, it'll become even harder for you to get her to try something new down the road. Instead, try to use encouragement and games to engage her.

•• Build a repertoire of familiar foods and recipes that you're both happy with.

•• Try to hold off on ready-made meals, fast foods, and sugars until he's older. (Sugars, including those in juice, have a profound effect on a child's brain, concentration, and energy level.) Let his palate develop with the flavor and nutrition of the real food you've made for him. It sets a precedent and a routine at the foundation of his understanding about what to eat.

•• Six months. **Your baby is entering a new world of flavor, texture, and color and is probably ready for solid food. She will revel in the way food feels in her hands, on her face, and—unfortunately!—the way it looks and sounds when it hits the floor. She loves manipulating objects, so let her play with a spoon and experiment with how it goes into the bowl. Make mealtimes part of her exploring time, reminding her to put the spoon in her mouth, too.**

•• Nine months. **At this stage, babies begin to show independence and want to feed themselves. This can be messy, but if you try to control your baby too much, he will sense your displeasure. Give him food that nurtures his curiosity and that he can handle by himself. Don't thwart his efforts or get into a struggle that could lead to a revolt even this early on; it's only a stage, and the pleasure he takes in messing with his food will subside. Expression is good! Touching and handling things is an indispensable preliminary to naming objects. Let him touch it all. His food and his plate and cup have different physical properties, and he will want to explore them.**

•• Twelve months. **By her first birthday, your child wants to explore her environment and test your reactions to it. She enjoys doing things herself, especially things she sees you do, so it's a good time to start tasting lots of different foods: Take a couple of bites yourself and offer her a bite to see what she thinks.**

At this age, a baby can hold a spoon by himself and drink from a cup. He begins to use a pincer grip. He likes to stack things, including food on his plate, and put things inside of other things, sorting them by color or shape. He can follow simple instructions like, "Hand me the napkin," and he understands *no*, but he may not listen.

•• Try to limit saying *no*. **The desire to look, touch, and feel is as urgent for your baby as hunger and as necessary for intellectual development as books will be later. You don't want her to lose her curiosity—you want to foster confidence. If your baby is reaching for your food, take that as a positive indicator of her developmental progress and encourage her exploration.**

you try to control your baby too much at this point, she will sense your displeasure and express frustration that she's not allowed to play. Give her food that nurtures her curiosity and that she can handle by herself.

Remember, these are developmental stages. The pleasure of messing with food will subside, and motor skills will improve. Right now, babies are starting to figure out how the world of objects works—they mush,

they fall, they bounce, they make patterns. Expression is good. This exposure to texture and color is the first step toward understanding objects.

Purees 101

Don't be intimidated by the idea of cooking for your growing baby. Even if you haven't had much experience in the kitchen, you can quickly learn your way

CYNTHIA EPPS is a metabolic nutritionist, board-certified lactation consultant, and infant-feeding specialist in private practice in Los Angeles. She trained at UCLA and the Cedars-Sinai Medical Center in Los Angeles. Her goal is teaching new mothers how to navigate their first year of motherhood.

MARCIA PELCHAT is a biopsychologist and associate member of the faculty at Monell Chemical Senses Center, a science institute in Philadelphia, where biologists, behavioral neuroscientists, ecologists, and chemists explore the science of our senses of taste and smell and how they relate to and affect human health.

around some basic techniques and ingredients. You will increase your confidence by handling these first simple purees.

There is a world of food out there just waiting to be pureed for your baby. Almost every fruit and vegetable can be pureed, thinned out if necessary, and served or frozen in batches and stored for up to six months. Fruits and vegetables can be enhanced with herbs and stocks and combined in flavorful ways, before or after freezing. Pureed food is both efficient and economical. Stored and/or frozen foods are especially handy when you need something fast, and stored favorites can be handy as a backup for meals that are not going over well.

It's a good idea to invest in durable, long-lasting kitchen equipment. A good food mill, for example, will last a lifetime and comes with multiple disks for versatility, whereas specialized cooking gear for infants may be made from plastic and may not be durable. Also, a pressure cooker can save time cooking dried grains and beans in bulk.

Purees can be smooth or a bit chunky. Make sure to remove all seeds. Seeds in fruits, when pureed, can be bitter, and some fruit seeds are not meant for consumption. Apples and pears and similar thin-skinned fruits need not be peeled if they are organic.

Most chefs' pantries are better stocked than most people's home pantries. The ingredients at their fingertips are often the best and freshest. Many times, they are exotic and expensive. While it may be impossible and impractical to replicate a restaurant pantry at home, it is certainly possible to stock your home pantry with different kinds of foods and rotate them to keep them fresh and seasonal.

Keep some ingredients ready to go so that you can concentrate more on the cooking and less on the prep work. Wash all your fruits and vegetables when you get them home from the market, before putting them away. Eric Bromberg, chef and cofounder of Blue Ribbon restaurants in and around the New York area, learned that he could make plain pasta in advance and refrigerate or even freeze it, then refresh it quickly by putting it back in boiling water for a minute or two. Buy cans of organic beans or cook a bag of dried beans to have around. Prepared beans and grains can be easily frozen, either in individual infant portions or family-size portions. Cover with a small amount of

water or stock to prevent freezer burn. Most prepared and fresh foods can be frozen.

raw purees

Some fruits and vegetables, like bananas and avocados, can be pureed easily with a fork. With a basic food mill, you can puree any food that is a bit harder. I carried a small, simple hand-crank food mill with a travel pouch with me to make quick, easy baby meals from foods when we were out. Sometimes, I quickly grabbed frozen peas, lima beans, or fava beans to take with me and then pureed them as needed.

Here are some fresh foods that can be pureed easily: apricots, avocados, bananas, blueberries, cherries, fresh figs, kiwifruit, mangos, melons, nectarines, papayas, peaches, pears, thawed peas, strawberries (after baby's first birthday), watermelon.

boiled purees

Sometimes I blanch long-cooking greens like kale until they are bright green and then take them out of the water to avoid overcooking them. All vegetables can be boiled, but boiling leaches flavor and nutrition out of the food and into the water, so use only a small amount of water or stock and incorporate the cooking liquid in the puree. After cooking, puree in a food processor or blender.

sautéed purees

Sautéing is the process of cooking foods in a pan with oil and/or butter. It's best to cook vegetables in small batches, not crowding the pan. At medium temperature they will brown, get a bit sweeter, and cook quickly in the oil and/or butter. Always use moderate temperatures when cooking with butter, as it can quickly burn (for higher heats with butter, coat the hot pan first with another oil like safflower before adding butter). Add water or broth to the pan after browning and cover with a lid for a minute or so to finish cooking the vegetables if needed. You can also cook them on a lower temperature to soften without browning to get a more delicate vegetable flavor. Herbs and other flavors like lemon can be quickly added at the end after you turn off the heat. Cut leafy vegetables into small pieces and cook for about five minutes. Harder vegetables, such as broccoli and potatoes, can be parboiled in advance. Fresh corn is succulent and sweet; you can simply cut it off the cob and sauté it in butter or oil. Greens like chard and spinach can be sautéed quickly in olive oil and make great purees.

For greens: Cut leafy pieces, discarding the stem, and wash but don't dry them. Add the greens dripping wet to a hot sauté pan with a bit of olive oil in it. Cook greens like spinach for only a few minutes; kale needs to be cooked for about seven to ten minutes. For longer cooking times, you can add a splash of water—or chicken or vegetable stock, for more flavor—to a pan that is getting dry. After cooking, puree in a food processor or blender.

For other vegetables: Cut into pieces and add to a hot pan with oil or melted butter. Stir every now and again to prevent sticking and to ensure the foods cook evenly. Cooking times will vary according to the freshness and kind of vegetable. Test for doneness with a fork. After cooking, puree in a food processor or blender with breast milk, water, or stock.

Vegetables that are delicious sautéed include asparagus, brussels sprouts, broccoli, carrots, cauliflower, corn, fresh fava beans, fennel, green beans, parsnips, potatoes, pumpkin, squashes, turnips, and zucchini.

steamed purees

It's easy to steam vegetables. By steaming instead of boiling, you avoid leaching any of the nutrients into the cooking water. The fruits and vegetables will have a cleaner and truer flavor. If you have a basket steamer, you can simply cut vegetables into small chunks and put them in the basket. Cook in a saucepan with an inch or two of water, with a lid on to keep the steam in. Cooking times vary; you can test for doneness with a fork. Vegetables are ready when they are still bright in color. If you don't have a steamer, you can put the vegetable chunks in a sauté pan with a lid and a small amount of water. Add any herbs and spices just at the end. Incorporate the cooking water into your puree; it will be flavorful and nutritious. After cooking, puree vegetables in a food processor or blender.

Fruits and vegetables that taste great steamed include apples, asparagus, beets, broccoli, carrots, cauliflower, corn, green beans, parsnips, potatoes, pumpkin, squashes, turnips, and zucchini.

baked and roasted purees

The difference between baking and roasting is that baked foods are cooked without any oil. Both baking and roasting vegetables concentrate their flavor; roasting also makes vegetables sweeter. Both baking and roasting are fast, easy, and forgiving cooking methods.

To bake vegetables like beets and potatoes, wash and dry them and wrap them whole in aluminum foil or put them in a roasting dish and cover with a lid or foil. Foods can be baked or roasted whole or cut into chunks for quicker cooking. You can peel them or not. I put a variety of foods in the oven and cook them all at once—baking and roasting. It's a big time-saver.

Put your vegetables in a single layer, uncovered, in separate dishes (they may have different cooking times). To roast, drizzle a bit of olive or other oil over the pieces. (Fresh rosemary is a great addition to roasted vegetables. Mix it in with the oil.) Cooking times vary greatly. I bake beets and potatoes for about an hour at 400°F; smaller vegetables may require only fifteen or twenty minutes. Stir once or twice. After cooking and cooling, puree in a food processor or blender with breast milk, water, or stock.

Foods that are great baked or roasted include apricots, asparagus, beets, broccoli, brussels sprouts, carrots, cauliflower, eggplant, fennel, parsnips, peaches, peppers (green, red, and yellow), plums, potatoes (sweet and white), squashes (butternut and acorn), and turnips.

meat purees

Babies can start eating meat at seven to ten months of age, according to pediatricians, when they've mastered fruits and vegetables. Remember, though, that they don't have molars, so they can't chew pieces of meat the way they chew soft vegetables with their gums.

Any meat or meat dish can be pureed in a food processor. Try extra-small pieces of meatball or a sauce with finely ground meat.

Great First Baby Foods

Sweet potatoes can be cooked in advance and combined in many ways to explore flavors. They can be baked, boiled, steamed, or sautéed. Baking sweet potatoes concentrates their flavor and makes them sweeter.

Combine with: apple, pear, banana, chestnuts, leeks, persimmons, mushrooms, white beans, kale, or grains like oatmeal and brown rice.

Thin out your puree with: orange juice, apple juice, lemon juice, or chicken or vegetable stock.

Add spices like: basil, cilantro, cloves, cinnamon, coriander, cumin, nutmeg, parsley, rosemary, sage, thyme, and garlic.

Peas are also easily combined with other foods. Peas overcook quickly, so boil, sauté, or steam them only briefly. If you are shelling fresh peas, you can make a pea broth from the pods and mix that in for deeper flavor. If the peas are frozen, you can simply defrost without cooking them.

Combine with: arugula, asparagus, carrots, celery, fava beans, leeks, potatoes, or spinach.

Thin out your puree with: carrot juice, lemon juice, chicken, or any other stock.

> **"I even season peas for Henry, my one-year-old grandson, because why not teach what is good flavor?"**
>
> —Joan McNamara, founder of Joan's on Third cafe and marketplace in Los Angeles

Add spices like: basil, chervil, cilantro, coriander, dill, mint, garlic, parsley, rosemary, sage, savory, tarragon, and thyme.

Bananas can be eaten and mashed raw and can also be baked and broiled.

Combine with: apricots, blueberries, cherries, coconut, guava, mangoes, oatmeal, papaya, raspberries, rice, strawberries, or sweet potatoes.

Thin out your puree with: coconut milk, lemon juice, or orange juice.

Add spices like: allspice, cardamom, cinnamon, cloves, and nutmeg.

Apples can easily be baked, sautéed, and stewed.

Combine with: apricots, blackberries, celery root, chestnuts, chicken, fennel, oatmeal, pears, plums, pork, prunes, pumpkin, rhubarb, rice, sweet potato.

Thin out your puree with: apple cider or juice, lemon juice, vegetable or chicken stock, or orange juice.

Add spices like: allspice, cardamom, cloves, coriander, cumin, or nutmeg.

fresh pea and spinach puree

{ COLBY GARRELTS }

MAKES ABOUT 2 CUPS

Make this as a puree for infants, and for the adults, thin puree out with broth or water to make a soup. Add basil, mint, some pancetta, and for infants over one year old, swirl in some cream or top with feta cheese. This recipe works well with summer squash, too.

1 pound fresh or frozen peas
Handful fresh spinach
Reserved cooking water or broth for thinning
  as needed

1. If using fresh peas, shell the peas and steam them for 2 minutes in a steamer basket over boiling water until cooked through and bright green. If using frozen peas, quickly blanch them in a bit of boiling water. Reserve any leftover cooking water to use for thinning out the puree.

2. Puree the peas and the handful of fresh spinach in a blender in batches at high speed. (*Note:* Be cautious about blending hot ingredients in your blender, as this has a tendency to force the top off midblend, splattering the blender contents. Don't fill your blender canister more than half full, and hold the lid down with a folded dish towel while you're operating the blender.) Add the reserved water as necessary to achieve a smooth, thin consistency. You may wish to push the puree through a sieve to get rid of any remaining skins.

3. Cool and store in the fridge for up to 5 days or freeze in ice cube trays.

wild greens puree

{ DIANE FORLEY }

MAKES ABOUT 3 CUPS

Make this as a puree for infants and thin with breast milk, formula, brown rice cereal, stock, or some mashed potato. For older children and adults, the puree can be combined with broth, noodles, and chicken and made into a soup, thinned and made into a sauce and served over noodles, or used to make Poached Chicken with Wild Greens (page 29).

2 cups chopped kale
2 cups chopped collard greens
2 tablespoons olive oil
1 teaspoon salt
1 cup plus 2 tablespoons water, divided
½ cup fresh flat-leaf parsley leaves
¼ cup fresh basil leaves
2 cups chopped spinach
Breast milk, formula, rice cereal, stock, or cooked white potato as needed for thinning

1. Add kale and collard greens into a saucepan with olive oil, salt, and 2 tablespoons water. Cover with lid and let steam over medium heat, stirring occasionally, until greens turn bright and soften, about 10 minutes.

2. Add parsley, basil, and spinach and cook 5 more minutes to wilt spinach and herbs.

3. Let cool. Transfer to a blender and puree with the remaining cup of water.

4. Serve thinned with breast milk, formula, rice cereal, stock, or cooked white potato as needed, and portion remainder into ½-cup servings and freeze in resealable plastic bags.

millet cauliflower puree

{ PETER BERLEY }

Make this as a puree for infants, but for toddlers it can be mashed instead. Add the crispy caramelized onions for older children and adults.

Millet Cauliflower Puree:
1 small head cauliflower, cored and roughly chopped (about 3 cups)
1 cup millet, washed and drained
½ teaspoon salt
3 cups water

Crispy Caramelized Onions:
1 cup olive oil
2 medium onions, very thinly sliced into crescents

For Millet Cauliflower Puree:
1. Combine the cauliflower, millet, salt, and water in a heavy saucepan.

2. Bring to a boil over high heat.

3. Reduce the heat to low and simmer, covered, for 25 to 30 minutes, until the water has been absorbed.

4. Mash the millet and cauliflower until smooth.

For Crispy Caramelized Onions:
1. Heat the oil in a wide sauté pan over medium heat.

2. Add the onions and sauté slowly for 20 to 30 minutes, until the onions are a deep golden brown.

3. Regulate the heat to prevent burning. Stir often for even browning.

4. Drain the onions and reserve the oil.

5. To serve, drizzle a bit of the oil over the mash and top with a mound of crispy onions.

wild greens soup with noodles

{ DIANE FORLEY }

SERVES 4

Noodles with soup is a fast and easy standard in our house—a big dollop of greens puree mixed in the soup adds a big nutritious boost and a subtle earthy flavor. Sometimes we add delicate slices of poached chicken (page 29).

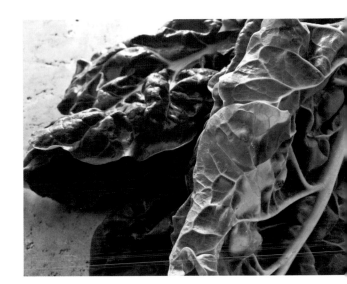

2 cups Wild Greens Puree, more or less to your liking (page 21)

4 cups chicken broth

1 package ramen, soba, or udon noodles, cooked according to package directions (break into small pieces for infants first)

1 tablespoon butter (optional)

Sprinkle of Parmesan cheese

1. Combine puree with chicken broth in a saucepan and bring to a simmer.

2. Add cooked ramen noodles to warm broth mixture.

3. Finish with butter and sprinkle with Parmesan cheese.

pumpkin soup with coconut, peanuts, and scallions

{ B. T. NGUYEN }

SERVES 4

Pumpkins are not just for jack-o'-lanterns and pies. Good choices for cooking are sugar pumpkins and heirloom varieties such as the gray-skinned Jarrahdale, the white-skinned Cucurbita, or a delicious cheese pumpkin that has a pale orange skin. When selecting a pumpkin, remember that a fresh pumpkin or squash will be a lot easier to peel and more flavorful than one that's been on the shelves for a while.

Cody and I play guessing games when cutting up fruits and squashes about what color the insides will be. This is a warm, comforting soup and the peanut and scallion garnish livens it up for older children and adults and adds a welcome and surprising crunch. Use less broth or water to make a thicker puree that is more like baby food.

4 cups vegetable or chicken broth

3 cups pumpkin (½ small pumpkin—approximately 2 pounds) or butternut squash, peeled and cut into 2-inch cubes

⅓ cup sliced galangal (see note at right)

8 ounces coconut milk

2 tablespoons soy sauce, Maggi or other quality brand

1½ teaspoons raw or other sugar

1½ teaspoons sea salt

¼ cup roasted peanuts, finely chopped or crushed

3 scallions, white and light green parts only, chopped fine

1. In a medium saucepan over medium heat bring broth to a boil.

2. Add pumpkin and galangal (in cheesecloth to remove quickly and easily; see note below) and simmer over medium heat for 25 minutes or until the pumpkin is soft (fresher pumpkins will cook faster).

3. Turn heat down and add coconut milk, soy sauce, raw sugar, and salt and stir until combined and sugar is dissolved. Turn the heat off and let cool; remove the galangal.

4. Puree for babies and freeze leftovers. For adults and older babies, serve with finely chopped roasted peanuts and scallions sprinkled on top.

Notes: Galangal is a mild type of ginger. It has a floral aroma and is a bit tougher to cut than ginger. Try going to an Asian market to find it. Some people recommend substituting ginger, but ginger at the same quantities is too pungent. You can make the soup using ginger sparingly or make the soup without it. Using butternut squash will make the soup sweeter than using pumpkin.

Wrapping spices and herbs in cheesecloth is a great way to give flavor to soups and a pot of beans and is easy to remove when the cooking is finished. Another great trick is to put them in a refillable tea bag. Try it here with the galangal, which is a bit too fibrous to puree with the soup and is better removed after cooking.

cannellini bean dip

{ PIERO SELVAGGIO }

"I was amazed," says Chef Piero Selvaggio of his daughter dipping bread into a cannellini bean dip one night out for dinner. "Sasha, who is ten months old, devoured the first little morsel, the second little morsel, and I thought, 'It makes so much sense—it's simple and so flavorful and it's good—and it's healthy.'" Selvaggio says this dip is similar to hummus, but the use of cannellini beans, popular in Italy, makes it Italian in spirit. You can use dried beans cooked with rosemary and other herbs for a richer flavor. Serve pureed beans with a poached egg nestled on top for a complete meal or as a dollop atop Diane Forley's Ratatouille with Balsamic Vinegar, Honey, and Basil (page 55). Use the best-quality fruity extra-virgin olive oil you can to drizzle over the dip.

1 can cannellini beans or white kidney beans, drained and rinsed
1½ teaspoons white wine vinegar
1 clove garlic, chopped
1½ teaspoons Worcestershire sauce
Kosher salt to taste
Pinch black pepper
¼ cup good olive oil
1 tablespoon chopped chives
Italian bread or other bread, or breadsticks warmed for serving
Cucumber sliced into sticks
Carrot sticks

1. In a food processor puree the beans with the white wine vinegar, garlic, Worcestershire sauce, and salt and pepper. Gradually add the olive oil with the machine running and puree until smooth.

2. Serve the dip in a bowl with chives sprinkled over the top and with warmed Italian bread or breadsticks, cucumber, and carrot sticks.

scrambled eggs and kale

{ PIERO SELVAGGIO }

SERVES 4

Piero Selvaggio says that kids love egg whites, so he adds more whites than yolks when making scrambled eggs. Kale can have a strong flavor, and sometimes we add a small bunch of fresh basil that Cody likes. If you are holding off on serving dairy, you can make this without the cheese. Serve with toast, fresh berries, and a side of yogurt.

2 large eggs

5 egg whites

1 teaspoon olive oil

6 ounces kale (cavolo nero preferred), parboiled and finely chopped

2 ounces fresh mushrooms, sliced

4 ounces mozzarella cheese, shredded or chopped if fresh

Sea salt

Black pepper, optional

1. In a bowl, mix the eggs and egg whites with a splash of water to combine.

2. Heat the olive oil in a nonstick pan over medium heat. Add the eggs and cook, stirring, until the eggs come together. Add the kale, mushrooms, and mozzarella. Stir together and cook just until the cheese melts. Sprinkle with salt and pepper and serve.

roast chicken with potatoes and kale

{ PIERO SELVAGGIO }

SERVES 4

I was always looking for ways to incorporate greens like kale into meals for Cody because they are so rich in nutrients. I love the flavor of kale when it's cooked right, but its earthy flavor can make it a tricky addition to dishes. While kale is sweeter in the wintertime, it is available year-round at markets. I like using the kale that has long, thin, dark blue green leaves, called Lacinato or dinosaur kale. If your child has never had kale before, start with adding a bit less to the recipe. If you are preparing this for infants or babies still learning to chew or unfamiliar with meat, chop chicken into very small cubes and make sure not to overcook, because the meat will be too chewy and dry. Kale and squash are a wonderful combination, and you can substitute any winter squash for the potatoes. To puree, remove the chicken from the bone and puree with the vegetables and a bit of chicken stock.

½ pound fresh kale, washed, stems removed, and
    chopped
½ pound small potatoes (or winter squash like
    butternut or acorn), chopped
1 onion, chopped
2 tablespoons olive oil
Sea salt and fresh pepper
3 chicken legs
Pinch of paprika
½ lemon, juiced

1. Preheat the oven to 450°F.

2. Spread kale, potatoes (or squash), and onion onto a large pan. Drizzle the oil over the vegetables, sprinkle with salt and pepper, and mix to evenly coat the vegetables. Cut the chicken legs halfway through at the joint between the thigh and drumstick. Rub salt and pepper and paprika all over the chicken and set atop the vegetables. Cover the pan with foil and bake for 20 minutes.

3. Remove the foil and continue to bake for another 20 minutes or until the chicken is cooked through and tender. Cut the chicken into small pieces for infants who can chew and add a squeeze of lemon. Serve alongside the vegetables.

poached chicken with wild greens

{ DIANE FORLEY }

When poached chicken is cooked right, it has an incredible and lovely silky texture, perfect for infants first learning to eat meat. But if the chicken is just a bit overcooked, it will get rubbery. One way to save time in the kitchen on busy days is to have poached chicken ready in the fridge to dice up for an older baby's snack or to add to soup, or for older kids and adults to make chicken salad or sliced chicken sandwiches. Use this chicken in Diane Forley's recipe for Wild Greens Soup with Noodles (page 23).

2 boneless, skinless chicken breasts
Broth or water to cover
Salt and pepper
1 cup Wild Greens Puree (page 21)

1. Clean and dry the chicken breasts.

2. Pound the chicken breasts so that they have an even thickness throughout and are no more than ½-inch thick, for even cooking.

3. Put enough broth (makes the chicken more flavorful) or water to cover the chicken breasts in a saucepan and heat to a low simmer.

4. Add chicken breasts and poach over low heat, skimming off and discarding any foam. Poach chicken until just cooked through, about 5 minutes. Watch the chicken carefully so as not to overcook.

5. Remove chicken to a cutting board and reserve the broth to thin the puree or for another use. Season the chicken with salt and pepper to taste and let rest for a couple of minutes.

6. Warm Wild Greens Puree in a pan over low heat, adding broth as needed to thin.

7. Slice the chicken and serve topped with warmed puree.

lemongrass chicken curry

{ B. T. NGUYEN }

Curry is a traditional Vietnamese comfort food. This is not an actual curry; it is more like a stew. The dish can be pureed and thinned with broth or breast milk if necessary or pureed with plain cooked rice or potatoes. When cooking, the chili powder should be put in toward the end of cooking, after the baby's portion is removed. I like prepping everything the night before so it is ready. Chef B. T. Nguyen recommends serving the curry soupy with freshly baked French bread. I often entice Cody to taste things by first dipping in some bread.

Marinade:

¼ lemongrass stalk, tough outer leaves removed and stalk chopped

1 shallot, chopped

2 cloves garlic, chopped

1 teaspoon chopped galangal or ginger (use less for infants) (see note on page 24)

1½ teaspoons chopped fresh cilantro

2 tablespoons coconut milk

1 tablespoon chopped fresh basil

2 green onions, white parts only, sliced (reserve green parts for curry)

1 tablespoon lime juice

Curry:

2 boneless, skinless chicken breasts, cubed

¼ cup vegetable oil, divided

1 pound potatoes (or batata), peeled and evenly chopped

½ onion, chopped small

2 medium carrots, peeled and evenly chopped

½ cup chicken stock or coconut water

7 ounces coconut milk (about half a can)

¾ stalk lemongrass, tough outer leaves removed and stalk pounded to crush and soften

1 teaspoon best-quality fish sauce

1 teaspoon palm sugar or golden granulated sugar

Salt and pepper

½ teaspoon chili powder (eschew for infants, adjust for children)

Small bunch cilantro

Small bunch basil

2 green onions, green parts only, sliced

For the Marinade:

Grind the lemongrass in a spice or coffee grinder. Add the rest of the marinade ingredients and process until smooth. Rub onto the chicken cubes, massaging a bit to coat evenly. Marinate covered and refrigerated overnight or at least 3 hours. Remove from the refrigerator an hour before cooking.

For the Curry:

1. Heat 2 tablespoons of oil in heavy-bottomed pan over medium heat. Add potatoes, onion, and carrots and cook, stirring occasionally, until evenly browned, about 5 minutes. Transfer browned vegetables to a plate.

2. In the same pan heat the remaining 2 tablespoons oil and add marinated chicken. Cook to brown for 5 minutes, turning occasionally to brown on all sides.

3. Add stock or coconut water, coconut milk, and crushed lemongrass stalks and return the potatoes and carrots back to the pan. Mix well and bring to boil.

4. Add fish sauce, sugar, salt and pepper, and chili powder (if using); simmer on low heat for 35 to 40 minutes, or until potatoes are soft.

5. Portion onto plates and sprinkle cilantro leaves, chopped basil, and green onion on top to serve.

Note: Lemongrass stalks have a lovely elusive flavor but are fibrous and can be hard to prepare correctly, especially for young children. It works best to cut the yellow section of stalk into thin slices and grind them in a mini grinder/chopper or food processor that handles small quantities, adding a bit of water or oil if necessary. For very small amounts pound them into a paste with a mortar and pestle.

after purees

THE BEGINNING OF ADVENTUROUS EATING

ages one to two-and-a-half

It's true toddlers are fun and silly. They are experimenting and learning new things constantly. Chefs tap into and embrace their curious nature in the way they feed their children at this age by enthusiastically introducing them to the whole world of food, its wondrous colors and shapes and interesting flavors and textures. There's almost nothing a toddler can't eat, and chefs don't hold back, offering them tastes of everything in the pantry, on the stove, or in the market.

Bring Them to the Table
While many parents slip into a routine of feeding toddlers separate meals of bland foods like pasta with butter, chefs bring their children to the table with them, introducing them early on to foods with the complex textures and flavors that they themselves enjoy. "Our kids went right from eating purees to eating what we were eating," says Eric Bromberg, chef and cofounder of Blue Ribbon restaurants in New York City.

Alejandro Alcocer, epicurean and founder of Green Brown Orange (Green Catering, Brown Café, and Orange Épicerie) in New York City, rattles off a list of the unusual things he feeds his toddler, Joaquin: "Shrimp, lobster, asparagus, and oysters. He eats what we're eating. We sit down together and cut what we're eating into small pieces, and he eats with his hands." Feeding children expensive and exotic ingredients is not necessary, but feeding them a wide variety of foods is. At this age it's important to make sure they are learning to like the flavors of healthy foods, including vegetables and whole grains, and are learning to like the experience of eating foods with new flavors—both of which can be tricky.

repeatedly offer a variety of flavors
Toddlers, like babies, have an abundance of taste buds that are spread around their mouths, including on the inner surfaces of their cheeks. They have an amazing ability to decipher flavors. Cutting-edge science at the Monell Chemical Research lab helps us to understand that all babies are born with a preference for sweet flavors and can distinguish between different types of sweet foods. A taste for bitter flavors—like the flavors of some vegetables—is learned. Children

33

"Cooking . . . I find that it's a good time to spend with your kid. . . . We got Zen a play kitchen, and every morning she's like, 'What do you want for breakfast, Daddy?' We got to the point where as long as I don't have to get to work super early, she'll want to make me breakfast. . . . It's becoming really fun; I always show her that, too. You've got to make it fun. I don't want to be serious all the time. I certainly don't want to be serious with a two-year-old . . . I just think you have to make it a fun experience for the kids. If you don't, you're kind of missing out."

—Zack Gross, chef and owner of Z Grille
in St. Petersburg, Florida

grow to like foods by eating them repeatedly. Studies show that toddlers who are given lots of different vegetables do learn to enjoy them, and those children also end up liking vegetables they haven't previously tasted more often. Science suggests that children have a critical learning window—from when they begin eating solid foods until about two years old—to adjust to eating a wide variety of foods.

Chefs teach their children early on to enjoy a variety of flavors by repeatedly offering them a diverse selection of foods and foods that have unique flavor characteristics—earthiness, richness, bitterness, pungency, and sourness.

"One of the things that we continuously do is just keep introducing things to Madi. When Meg's parents were down here for New Year's—when she was about a year and a half old—I shoved a spoonful of caviar in Madi's mouth. She chomped it down and ate it. A lot of times kids don't like certain things because they are too strongly flavored and they like more sweet

and mild food, but for Madi, I just go full bore on it," says Colby Garrelts, chef and co-owner with his wife, Megan, of Bluestem restaurant in Kansas City.

Chefs agree that learning to eat a variety of foods as a toddler is critical to eating and enjoying a broad range of foods later on. "Bring your kids into the lives you lead," Marc Murphy, owner and executive chef of Benchmarc restaurants in New York recommends. "We just cut up whatever we are eating into small enough pieces so they don't choke. Whatever we make is what they'll eat."

"Babies can taste so many different flavor profiles," says B. T. Nguyen, Tampa chef and restaurateur. "So let them eat what you eat. They will open up to it. But if you say 'my kids only eat chicken,' you know what, you are not opening them up to let them experience other flavors."

take your kids to a farmers' market
Diane Forley, chef and co-owner with her chef husband, Michael Otsuka, of Flourish Bakery in Scarsdale, New York, says that her daughter, Olivia, can identify a lot of foods and ingredients from having shopped with her at an early age at the farmers' market and the grocery store: "She can identify arugula."

Alcocer describes going to farms and introducing his sons to "the whole process. I've gotten involved with some local farmers, and worked with them to learn about organic farming. Through visiting these people, Constantin is able to appreciate and understand where food comes from." He also talks about taking Constantin to Africa, where "we see people prepare food with a fire in a hut. He sees that people can

> **"Introduce as many new things as possible without overwhelming the child. I think children can very easily get overwhelmed with flavors and tastes."**
>
> —Cathal Armstrong, chef and co-owner of Restaurant Eve; Eamonn's, a Dublin Chipper; and The Majestic in Alexandria, Virginia

gather foods and just eat them. He sees that they have no access to sugar and processed foods. He knows that there are people in the world who don't have so many choices."

don't emphasize your own food dislikes

Chefs also agree that it's important not to convey your own distaste for certain foods to your children. "Don't ever say you don't like something in front of your kid," Murphy advises. "It will influence them. They either won't like the thing you say you don't like, or they'll use it as an opportunity to create their own dislikes." Frank Proto, executive chef with Murphy of Benchmarc restaurants in New York, says, "My wife doesn't like peas, but she doesn't say so in front of the kids."

establish your own mealtime routines

Though many chefs' schedules make it difficult for them to have regular meals with their children, they acknowledge that it does make a difference to sit down to a meal together. Cathal Armstrong, chef and co-owner of Restaurant Eve; Eamonn's, a Dublin Chipper; and The Majestic in Alexandria, Virginia, says that his children's eating suffered during a time when both he and his wife, Michelle, were working long hours and not able to eat dinner together with their children. Because chefs typically work during dinner hours and on weekends, many devote time in the morning to cook breakfast together with their children.

Children at this age love familiarity and routines. They begin to make associations between foods and experiences. Zack Gross, chef at Z Grille at St. Petersburg, Florida, reminisces about how his mom cooked tacos when he was a child or made "amazing" French toast for him. "I loved the way she made it and loved her for making it." While Gross admits it's not the healthiest snack food, he relishes eating cotton candy at the baseball game with his daughter, Zen.

Cook Well and Give Kids Options

Armstrong explains that cooking well is important for children because "if the food tastes good, they are much more likely to eat it. I do think being a good cook is an important part of introducing food to children, especially when you want to introduce challenging foods like brussels sprouts instead of carrots. Carrots are easy because they are sweet. Brussels sprouts are a much more difficult challenge. It's just a matter of getting them to try a little bit; try a quarter and chances are they are going to hate it the first couple of times. Seasoning, too, is an important part of food," adds Armstrong. "Cooking things they recognize and want to eat is also important."

"Giving kids a choice and not always deciding everything for them—especially at two, when they go through that independent phase—is important; they can be really cranky during the terrible twos. I think allowing them those independent choices even at a young age is crucial," says Armstrong. "Food is one of the ways you can do that," adds Megan Garrelts. "They eat what they like from what

ZACK GROSS AND HIS WIFE, JEN, have a busy urban restaurant, Z Grille, in St. Petersburg, Florida, that is both elegant and edgy. It serves adventurous, casual-yet-gourmet fare that is both playful and decadent, like his Dr Pepper–fried Ribs or his Cornflake Sage Fried Chicken served with a bacon waffle. In 2009, he was nominated for the James Beard Award as Best Chef in the South. They have a daughter, Zen. Zack says, "I like to go home and make a nice piece of chicken with some cooked rice with gravy—something that's very comforting—that's what I like to eat at home. . . . I want to spend time with my kid and I want to get her to eat and make sure she enjoys eating and gets pleasure out of it. Cooking with her is getting her to enjoy it more. I find that it's a good time to spend with your kid, too. My mom taught me how to cook."

Chef Zack Gross and daughter Zen : JEN GROSS

we cook and we don't force them to eat what they don't like," says Murphy.

"I'll give her a choice, like, 'You can have one of these three things.' She's at an age where she can choose," says Ana Sortun. "For lunch today, I asked her if she wanted a ham sandwich or a hot dog or whatever. She'll tell me what she wants. We'll do the same thing for breakfast. 'Do you want oatmeal, do you want cold cereal, or do you want eggs?' She loves eggs and waffles. Sometimes she'll want that, and sometimes she'll choose oatmeal."

Cooking braises, and more forgiving stews, is an easy way to make flavorful food for a toddler. "I definitely go traditional at home. I roast chicken and make corn on the cob and grill steaks, but in the winter when we are not outside as much, we'll braise lamb and roast some root vegetables and things like that," says Colby Garrelts.

I took Colby's suggestions and often made braises and stews for our family's dinner when Cody was at this age. The meat was easy to chew and flavorful. I made short ribs and lots of tender roasted meats like pork tenderloin. Since Cody napped best at home, I would take advantage of this and start a dish while he was napping in the middle of the day. I'd brown the meat and add onions and other vegetables, broth, and wine and then let it cook slowly. I liked that we had something already prepared to come home to and could avoid a hectic rush to make dinner. And I liked that the house always had the delicious aromas of slow-cooked foods. I'd open the lid so Cody could peek at what was cooking, and as a bonus, there would usually be enough to freeze some for a future meal.

Some dishes were too much for Cody. I would try to modify the stronger flavors of these by adding cheese, cream, or butter or adding a starch like potatoes. Many modern chefs use herbs and lemon to brighten and crisp the flavors of dishes. "You know little kids, they can't take a lot of spices and flavorings—they like it simple," says Peter Berley. "Sometimes I'll make a kid version of what we're eating that's a bit simpler than ours," says Forley. "But if we're having something we know they'll like—for instance, baked chicken—then I won't adjust the menu for the kids; we'll just all eat the same thing." With kids, it's about finding the right balance between introducing new flavors and foods and adjusting those recipes that may still be a bit overwhelming for them.

Enjoy Eating and Cooking with Your Kids

It's fun to be silly with a toddler, and eating with your toddler should be enjoyable. "I love food. That's why I do what I do, so I don't want to come home and eat boring food," says Colby Garrelts. I agree, and I wanted Cody to eat well so we could enjoy meals together. I liked making special things for us to eat and enjoy as a family.

Lure children into eating by setting an example and enjoying food yourself, and by having them participate and play in the kitchen. Keeping your kids in the kitchen with you is important at this age. Not only are they continuing to become familiar with the sights and smells of all the foods you are cooking, but they are naturally curious and will want to watch you at work. They will want to imitate you, and giving them

"**I've moved my cutting board out of the normal spot where it was, over by the sink, and I've created a little square over by the stove. . . . Zen can watch everything. I put the *mise en place* in front of her and then she can dump it in the pan, or I help her do it. 'Oh, I cooked it!' she'll say. And she has more of an appreciation to eat things.**"

—Zack Gross, chef at Z Grille in St. Petersburg, Florida

some tools to play with will make them feel like they are involved. Cody played intently with the salad spinner, a bag of beans, and a wooden spoon while in the kitchen with me. Every now and again he'd pop up to help mix something, and then he'd go back to playing. Sometimes he pretends he's cooking pasta in a little pan that I give him, and he asks me to taste it.

Sally Kravich, a natural health expert, says, "What we feed our kids is so important. And so is their connectedness to it. That's why I teach kids about planting seeds and letting them grow. They get connected to the plant itself. It's why I always had them make messes and play in the kitchen, putting their hands in it and creating lots of different things, because then they are a part of it. Saying, 'Taste this, taste that. Let's see what this thing tastes like.'"

Cody and I planted a simple herb garden together so we could both dig in the dirt and take care of something and watch it grow. Planting our garden gave us an opportunity to smell, taste, and identify herbs. We would go out together and pinch off some basil or parsley. Having the experience of growing and picking the herbs helped Cody like those flavors. Sortun gets most of her produce from her husband's farm, Siena Farms. Siena, their daughter, spends a lot of time

there. "She likes watermelon radishes and arugula. She knows where they come from. That's a big part of it," says Sortun. Sortun organizes field trips for Siena's school, and she realized that kids would eat and enjoy foods growing at the farm that their parents swore they wouldn't eat at home.

Picky Eaters

While toddlers will fully join in and eat all the interesting foods you eat, quirky food phases and picky eating also begin for lots of kids at this age. Colby Garrelts says of his daughter, Madi, "She's not always a real good eater, and it seems like she's been going through different cycles or times when she'll eat better than others." Quirky eaters might relish a food one day and completely refuse it the next, ask enthusiastically for something and then play with it but not eat it. They may eat only tiny portions or not eat at all. Trying to reason with any toddler doesn't work particularly well, but distraction and silliness are good strategies to get them eating and enjoying their food. Toddlers sense what's important to you; they will follow your lead because they want to keep you happy. "The first time we gave Eve potatoes she spat them out," says Armstrong. "And then I gave her a little bit and I said, 'Don't spit it out.' Then I gave her a little more, and now she's older and she says, 'Please can I have some mashed potatoes for dinner?'"

Picky eating is very common among toddlers. Some picky eaters may be born that way. Scientists have found that the ability to taste may be genetically related to the number of taste buds on a person's tongue. While adults have six thousand taste buds, babies have up to ten thousand. The so-called genetic "supertaster" is not necessarily a picky eater and vice versa. He may have as many as eleven hundred taste buds per square centimeter of tongue compared to as few as eleven taste buds in the same size area, creating a vastly different experience and response to flavors like sweetness and bitterness. "Sweet and sour are two tastes that kids do like as they are developing," says Berley, "but things like spicy and bitter, more complex flavors, really develop much, much later for the taste buds."

"Spicy food is hot, and it hurts to eat it," adds Otsuka. "Kids probably don't have the ability to discern that pain from any other pain. They are still developing. And any kind of pain is bad from a kid's perspective." In fact most children even from cultures known for their spicy cuisine dislike the burning sensation from eating spicy foods. Science shows that the brain actually thinks the tongue is on fire, and even adults who enjoy eating spicy foods experience them as painful. While there is no correlation between age and tolerance for spicy foods, finding spicy foods palatable is learned, and at some point it just clicks that feeling that the burn on the tongue is stimulating and pleasurable.

All foods can be sweetened a bit without adding sugars. Roasted meats can be cooked with red onions that add sweetness or they can be served with gravies or fruit sauces and relishes. Vegetables can be roasted to caramelize their natural sugars and make them sweeter. Vegetables like carrots and corn are sweet on their own. Alternatively, some vegetables can be baked or served in a cheese sauce, which usually goes over well with kids.

Although Cody was never a truly fussy eater, he did have picky phases that were both surprising and frustrating. It's hard to be motivated to cook for a picky eater, and sometimes it's best to keep things simple. There were times when I resorted to easy favorites at home for dinner, like nachos made with black beans with some Greek yogurt for dipping and some avocado on the side. Cody always enjoys these nachos, and I knew overall it was a pretty healthy dinner.

Children can become fussy eaters for a number of reasons. They may develop sensitivities to certain tastes, smells, or textures, or they may be imitating parents' fussy eating habits. There is "a family resemblance in broad attitudes in things like food neophobia—fear of trying new foods," explains Marcia Pelchat, a biopsychologist. "So if you have parents who are suspicious of food, worried about food, with a lot of anxiety about food, you are going to notice that also in their children." Fussy eating habits are also more likely to develop when parents punish or reward their children's eating behaviors.

Chefs' children are no exception, and chefs agree that it's important to keep trying, even when your child refuses a food. Some children need more time to get used to the various textures, colors, and tastes of new foods. The biggest challenge with feeding young kids—especially picky ones—is novel foods and new flavors. Studies show that approximately one quarter of parents with infants and toddlers think their children dislike a food after serving it only twice. "When I introduce a food to my one-year-old and he doesn't like it, I

"They love broccoli, then all of a sudden they don't like broccoli anymore. It's just phases. Like anything else with raising kids, it's a full-time job. You have to keep at it. You can't slack off. Otherwise they develop those bad habits. It's your job—it's your duty."

—Andrea Curto-Randazzo, Miami chef

keep trying, even in the same meal," says Susie, Los Angeles cafe and marketplace owner Joan McNamara's daughter. Chefs emphasize that it's important to "go with the flow" and rely on what's working at any given time, without discontinuing the process of trying new foods. Studies show that children who do dislike a particular food or ingredient at this age will accept and enjoy that food after repeated exposure. In other words, for most of us, enjoying the flavors of a variety of foods is learned, and it requires patient conditioning to teach toddlers to like those foods, too.

Forley says, "It's a daily investigation between parents and kids. There are no hard-and-fast rules. My daughter, Olivia, used to like certain things, and now she's gone off them. Maybe her taste for the things she is rejecting will come back, but for now we have to work with what she'll do and what she won't." Still, it's important not to give in to a toddler's preference for an overly simplified and limited diet.

Keep in mind that children at this age probably won't remember a food they've eaten from one sitting to the next. They will certainly recognize distinct foods with colors and shapes that appeal to them, but most children will not immediately remember foods they've disliked. Gross says of his daughter, Zen, "When she doesn't want it, she says 'no, please'—she's got that one down. And then, I don't force her to eat it. It's just going to lead to a bad experience. I just wait and try it again later."

Getting toddlers to try things and take that first bite can be difficult. "She loves fruit. So as long as there's fruit on the plate, in a bowl, next to her, I know she'll eat that. . . . You just have to put something new next to something she recognizes. She needs that push through," says Gross. He also finds things he knows she likes and then "mixes in a few things." I tried this and found it to be true for Cody. I'd also make bites for Cody on the fork and feed them to him so he could taste ingredients together. I'd tell him that meat with sauce on it tastes really good, or that asparagus with melted Parmesan cheese on top is yummy together. Studies also show that children begin to associate foods with experiences. Children who are fed a new food followed by something sweet, like peaches, are more likely to accept the new food—they will build an association between the new food and the pleasant experience with the sweet peaches.

There are many other strategies for dealing with a picky eater. Most important is remembering not to struggle over food. If you find yourself getting frustrated, it's best to retreat for the moment. Children of all ages respond badly to what they perceive as bullying and shaming. A child may decide she doesn't like a food because she associates it with an unpleasant experience. Try to stay good-humored and lighthearted when you talk with your children about food.

Avoiding Food Wars

As adults we eat conscientiously, thinking about health, but kids are notoriously picky eaters and simply won't eat things that don't appeal to them. They are too young for reasoning, and it is not a strategy that works well. Also, kids at this age quickly learn the power of refusing a food, and the classic "picky eater" struggle can ensue because they begin to assert their independence. "They need to be able to control their world," says Cynthia Epps, an infant-feeding specialist. I've always relied on making things fun with Cody and using games and distraction, knowing that bribing and begging would be counterproductive, unpleasant, and uncomfortable for both of us. Many of our meals start off with "no" but end with an empty plate.

Sortun gets creative by playing upon her daughter's imagination. This is a very imaginative age, and one day her daughter called a cucumber stick "yucky" even though it has been a repeated staple that they grow on their farm and that she loves. Instead of taking the challenge head-on, Sortun playfully said, "It's not a cucumber, it's a bridge." Seeing the cucumber as something fun motivated Siena to pick it up and start eating it.

Nguyen creates a feeling of trust with her son, James: "I say 'try it once, if you don't like it, spit it out,' and I hold my hand out for him to spit it into. With every new dish, I say, 'James, here's a little piece, try it. Here's my hand, if you don't like it, spit it out.' Every once in a while he says, 'OOOH, I like it.'"

"They are very strong-willed little people," says Gross. "I decided that my daughter and I have a better relationship because I don't talk to her like she's two. I talk to her like she's twenty-two, and it seems to work out really well for me. I don't get nearly as upset about things. I just tell her like it is," he says.

"Food is the very first opportunity toddlers have to control what they do. It's not that they don't like the food you put out in front of them; they just rather you don't put food on a plate right in front of them. Instead, put an empty plate in front of them and a serving plate with food just beyond and let them pick and choose family style," explains Epps. Toddlers are learning that they are separate beings and can affect their world, and so they embrace and test this power constantly. It's best to give toddlers control of the space right in front of them—what's in arm's reach when they sit at the table. It doesn't work to simply put a plate in front of them and expect them to comply. Epps suggests that a more clever way to acknowledge this new power they have to exert control is to instead play on their curious nature by putting things within their reach and allowing them to take for themselves.

"Knowing how to get around food wars is key. . . . It's knowing how to keep them on track, how to stay cool, how not to fight with them," says Epps. She teaches that a parent has the responsibility for what, where, and when the child eats, but the child is responsible for whether or not he is going to eat and how much he eats. "As parents, it's real hard to back off and allow that to happen," continues Epps. "What you need to know is how you get into a rhythm of breakfast, snack, lunch, snack, dinner through the day so that if any one of those breaks down, there's a snack or a meal coming within a couple of hours." She defines a snack as the leftovers of the previous meal or a substantial food instead of the easy to grab but nutritionally incomplete prepackaged foods like cheese puffs or dried cereal.

"Sometimes, I get a little frustrated with Madi when she hasn't eaten all day, and I find myself falling into that trap of trying to get her to eat more than she

ALEJANDRO ALCOCER was born in Mexico and has worked in renowned restaurants all over the world. He infuses the food at Green Brown Orange, his tiny, upscale neighborhood cafe, catering company, and marketplace on Manhattan's Lower East Side, with an eclectic mix of earthy, local flavors and worldly nuance. Alcocer loves to travel around the world with his children. He is a single father of two boys: Joaquin Cristobel in New York and Constantin in Berlin. Alcocer says of being around restaurants, "It's a lifestyle. We grow our own produce. The restaurant is an offshoot of a catering business and a place to showcase what we do."

wants. But if she eats only two bites at dinner, she eats only two bites. Then, at breakfast, I'll make her some eggs and give her a banana, and she'll go to town on it—I think that's what you need to do. Parents get frustrated that kids won't eat what they want them to at dinnertime, and they think, gosh, they can't go to bed without eating," says Colby Garrelts. Sortun says of her daughter, "She is not a big eater—she snacks a lot . . . she's a grazer, she doesn't eat a lot at once." Even if kids don't eat a lot, it's important for children at this age to learn to sit at the table, because "eating around the house and roaming, they become grazers. We want to make sure we are not starting a bad habit early on," says Kravich.

Getting Kids to the Table and Trying Foods

Some fussy eating is rooted in behavior—children at this age prefer to play rather than sit and eat, and they have a hard time stopping a fun game. Many toddlers have trouble making transitions between activities, and going from playtime to mealtime is no exception. To help Cody get to the table to eat, I encouraged him to bring things that he was playing with, like his toy dinosaur, to the table with him—"because he's hungry, too," I would say playfully. I would ask his dinosaur, "Are you hungry, dinosaur?" Sometimes, to get Cody focused on eating, I'd ask his belly if it was hungry. "Knock, knock, Cody's belly, are you hungry?" I'd then exclaim, "Your belly's hungry, he just told me, he wants some soup."

To get kids to eat, chefs also talk about how important it is to convey the sensory appeal of foods to kids. McNamara says, "There's a way of holding food, showing it, and enjoying watching your kids look at it and try it," she says. Otsuka adds, "I talk about colors with my daughter. She understands what she likes by colors. Green needs to be on the plate." And if his daughter doesn't like something, he says, "I'll just step away from it for a few days, and then maybe bring it back and try again later." For Cody, I expanded the basic

> "It's tough with the little ones because most of the not eating stuff is psychological until they get to that age where they feel more comfortable trying things."
>
> —Andrea Curto-Randazzo, Miami chef

repertoire of food bite sounds to include racecars and rocket ships.

Sometimes peer pressure helps. If your child observes that an unusual or exotic food is desirable to others, he'll be more likely to try it. Alcocer relates a story about visiting Mozambique with Constantin, where everyone ate a certain fatty and smelly fish. "It was a completely different fish experience than Constantin was used to. But he saw that the local children and their parents were enjoying it—so he began to enjoy it, too."

We have to balance our kids' training between two main points they must learn: to listen to their own bodies to know when they are hungry or full, and to eat regularly according to the schedule of meals that we eat as a society—breakfast, lunch, and dinner. "I don't want to tell James to eat when he is not hungry," says Nguyen.

"When Madi is hungry, she eats," says Megan Garrelts.

"It's not always going to be at the same time that we are all hungry, but she eats the stuff I want her to eat when she is hungry," adds Colby Garrelts.

"Some days, like yesterday, she came home from preschool and wanted cereal for lunch and

MARC MURPHY's cuisine is thoughtful but casual and includes rustic Italian dishes and French bistro fare at his three New York–area neighborhood restaurants: Landmarc Tribeca, Landmarc Time Warner, and Ditch Plains. Murphy is one of the frequent judges on the Food Network show *Chopped* and has competed on *Iron Chef*. Murphy has two daughters, Callen and Campbell. He says proudly of Callen, "One of her favorite things to eat when she was four was fennel salad with smoked oysters." They go to the market together and see what's good, and that's what they cook at home.

that's what she wanted," says Megan. "You know we go through that as adults, too. Some nights I come home and I want oatmeal for dinner or something out of the ordinary. I remember sometimes my mom would make us breakfast for dinner, like pancakes and eggs, just because that was the fun. Even though they are just little people and they don't communicate very well, kids still have cravings and wants just like we do as adults."

TIPS FROM CHEFS ON FEEDING TODDLERS

- **Share your food.** Toddlers mimic and model their behavior on you. They are naturally interested in the foods you're eating. "It's like learning how to talk: They talk like we talk. They eat what we eat," says Chef Marc Murphy.

- **Toddlers like to be helpful and involved.** Let your child help shop for and prepare a meal, and talk about the fruits and vegetables as you go: what's fresh, what looks good, how you will combine them. Let him help you pick the apples from the bin in the market. Ask him what he wants to eat, both at the market and at home. At home, give him a safe and kid-friendly task like washing the vegetables. When he becomes more coordinated, let him mix, measure, pour, and grate.

- **Kids learn by doing.** Murphy has a special children's stepstool, designed for the kitchen, called a "learning tower." It allows his daughter to climb up and be at a safe height to stand at the stove. They make omelettes together.

- **Make food fun.** Chef Joan McNamara says food should be all about "fun and love." Boys are often interested in cars, trains, and airplanes, so use the age-old game of "here comes the train." Do train bites with train sounds, car bites with car sounds, and plane bites with plane sounds. Chef Alejandro Alcocer plays an octopus-eating-shark game at the table with his son. I like to bring a toy dinosaur to the table and have the dinosaur ask Cody to take a bite.

- **Be open and experimental.** Try new things. Chef Eric Bromberg says, "We make our own pancakes and let them put in any ingredients they want. Sometimes the pancakes are green and disgusting, sometimes they're black and stick to the pan, and sometimes they're light and fluffy. It's all part of experimenting: seeing what you like and how you make stuff. It adds a whole new level of interest—that food is a cool thing. It's entertaining!"

- **Play smelling games.** Chef Michael Otsuka takes his daughter, Olivia, into their garden to smell and identify herbs. They incorporate those herbs into their meals. Experiments suggest that the sense of smell accounts for up to 90 percent of our perception of flavor and lots of flavors, like vanilla and tarragon, are purely smell. While taste preferences are inborn, according to Marcia Pelchat, a biopsychologist, aromas seem to be learned and preferences are a matter of culture and experience. It's fun and surprising to shake and sniff, or scratch and sniff, foods like cinnamon sticks, fennel seeds, and cumin. Warming foods releases their aromas. Take, for example, the difference between raw garlic and garlic that is sautéed.

- **Hold off on ready-made meals, fast foods, and sugars.** Let your child's palate develop from the flavor and nutrition of the food you make for him. It establishes a foundation for her understanding of what constitutes "good" food. The processed chemical flavors of candy, soda, and junk food easily overwhelm the simple flavors of real foods like corn and broccoli.

- **Talk about it.** Chefs constantly discuss ingredients, menus, and recipes with their children. This kind of exposure is a form of education. McNamara enthuses, "We love talking about food!"

- **Eat at ethnic restaurants.** "Dining in those restaurants is a different experience from dining in a fine-dining restaurant where the formality of the meal is a little more precise," says Chef Cathal Armstrong. "There's a variety of unique flavors with each cuisine and it can be good exposure." Also, kids will often try new and more adventurous things when dining out because it's part of the experience. "I don't know if it's because that place has such different things, she feels comfortable trying it, but she'll go, 'Yeah, I'll try that.' She's always a little more adventurous when we go to that specific restaurant," says Chef Andrea Curto-Randazzo.

- **Distract them.** Not talking about the problem at hand can be a useful tool. Occasionally Cody will say his food is "yucky" when we sit down to dinner, and then he'll say, "I don't like it." I just eat my dinner and talk about something else. He'll stall and wait to see if he gets a reaction, and then slowly on his own he'll start to eat. I can also break into singing his favorite song and he'll smile and forget all about yucky. Another game I play is "open your mouth and close your eyes and I will give you a big surprise." We'll try to guess what food from his plate was on the bite. I tell him, "You have to chew and swallow to figure it out."

- **Introduce the food to them.** When there's soup that Cody's hesitant to eat, I give him toast to go with it and I make a big silly surprise face and dip the toast in the soup. He'll eat the toast, then jump in to eat some of the soup. I'll also start counting the carrot pieces floating in the soup, and we'll play a numbers game of swirling them and getting them on the spoon.

- **Use quality ingredients.** The better your ingredients, the simpler and less time-consuming your food preparation can be and the more flavorful your food will be. Produce that is old loses its flavor and tastes starchy and wooden.

- **Try to avoid being a short-order cook.** Feed your kids what you eat, or make simplified versions of adult foods. It's easier and more efficient than cooking to order, and it creates a nice sense of family and togetherness.

Healthy Eating

What we eat plays a big role in how we feel. Sugars, including those found in fruit juice, have a profound effect on our bodies, affecting brain concentration and energy levels. Chefs know that a child who is ingesting sugary snacks and drinks is going to behave differently. "Joaquin is starting to go through the terrible twos," says New York chef Alcocer. "We're careful about what he eats. We keep him away from sugar. We give him a nonsugary cereal in the morning. At night we give him starch and vegetables so it's easier for him to transition into sleep."

Most chefs don't consume fast food on a regular basis, and they pass their attitudes down to their children. "My kids don't like McDonald's," says Forley. "It probably rubbed off from us; I'm sure we've said bad things about McDonald's in front of them." Forley doesn't keep packaged or precooked food in their house, knowing that ready-made foods taste different than foods we cook ourselves and are usually made from ingredients that are lower in quality and freshness. Prepackaged foods contain more sugar, salt, and chemicals to flavor and preserve the food. Staying away from those foods is a great way to stay healthy.

It's not just a matter of limiting sugar and fast food. Even cooking at home has changed. "I'm not allowed to use butter anymore," Murphy says ruefully. "My wife has informed me that the butter part of our relationship is over. The idea of a healthy breakfast has changed. When we were kids, it was eggs, toast with butter, orange juice, and bacon. We've learned so much more about what's bad for us. The first couple

of years are when kids build up their fat cells. So we really limit the fatty or fat-producing foods. We have to be careful."

While I know using a stick of butter in a pan to cook mushrooms is way too much fat to be healthy, I still serve Cody butter on his toast and even put a small amount in our home-cooked dishes and even on vegetables from time to time. Kravich says, "I use some butter on vegetables like butternut squash for kids so that it feels creamy and it tastes yummy. As far as dessert goes, we'll make things like an apple crisp; I just don't put a lot of sweetening in it." Kravich also advises parents to feed their children whole grains instead of white rice and breads and pasta made from white flour. Those foods aren't good for the digestion, she says. She advises feeding kids different-colored rice like red rice and black rice or rice that has a variety of colors mixed together.

Berley made lots of quick pickles with vegetables like string beans and cauliflower for his children. Pickled foods are not cooked but are preserved in vinegar and contain the same nutrition as raw vegetables. Kids love pickles, they are crunchy and salty and you can make quick refrigerator pickles at home in different flavors by adding different herbs and spices, or you can keep them plain if that's what your kids prefer.

Processed foods usually include flavoring agents that make them taste differently from home-cooked foods. Becoming too accustomed to these unnatural flavors can make it harder to appreciate the flavors of wholesome foods. Keep use of processed foods to a minimum and teach your kids to be flexible eaters with discerning palates. "I'd rather give my

PETER BERLEY is the former executive chef of the renowned vegan restaurant Angelica Kitchen in New York City. He is not a vegetarian himself but is known for his savvy about vegetarian cooking and won a James Beard award for his book *The Modern Vegetarian Kitchen*. He has two other popular cookbooks and also works as a culinary educator. He is knowledgeable about macrobiotic eating and raised his family on its principles. He has two adult daughters, Kayla and Emma. Berley says, "I study about food, I've never been into studying nutrition. I've been very skeptical about the science of nutrition only because a lot of it is so much based on one book that analyzes nutritional components in food—there's only one book that everything is based on—all the how much vitamin C is in something, how much vitamin A is in something—that all comes from only one source, which is really not very accurate. That's part of it. The other thing is, I found that to think that way is very analytical and very cerebral, and I've always felt that it's best to see how you feel with what you eat."

Chef Peter Berley and daughter Kayla : CAM CAMAREN

son a bar of good chocolate than something that is rainbow-colored and has high-fructose corn syrup in it," says Nguyen.

Megan Garrelts is the pastry chef at her and her husband's restaurant. How does she moderate the amount of sweets Madi eats? "I try to not have too many conversations. I just tell her no and we move on. I'll change the topic," says Megan.

Eating at Restaurants

"I think it's important to expose your kids to restaurants," says Megan Garrelts. "When Madi was an infant even, we brought her in all the time—she would sleep in her car seat. I don't think it's appropriate to take infants out to twelve-course tasting menus every night, but, at the same time, if you shelter them from ever being in normal day-to-day restaurants and socializing with people on that level, you're adding fuel to the fire."

Children learn table manners and etiquette at restaurants. "Madi's very good at restaurants," continues Megan. "She always wants a napkin because she sees everyone around her with a napkin. It's funny because we didn't teach her that. When we eat in the lounge at the restaurant, the server will bring her a napkin and silverware, and she has to have that stuff before we eat. She understands everything that goes into having a meal, sitting down and waiting for her food."

"When we go out to a restaurant, we're there to eat," says Chef Andrea Curto-Randazzo. "I remember when I was growing up, you went out to eat, you sat in your seat, you weren't climbing everywhere or you got *the look*. I think, also, when I was little I had an

> **"The earlier you bring them out with you, the better they will be at knowing that this is how you are supposed to act."**
>
> —Megan Garrelts, pastry chef and co-owner of Bluestem restaurant in Kansas City

appreciation for food—I remember telling my dad, 'I want the big person's size.' It would always be, 'Baby, you can have whatever you want.' I was excited about that. I try to make my children feel the same way. They are super excited to go out to dinner; they know it's a treat and it's special, so we are there to eat. The baby is into the sugar packets, but she's two and a half, so you gotta give in to a little something."

Eating at restaurants is a good time to try new foods. Pelchat paints a picture of how parents she has known may have conditioned their children to become picky. She says, "While they were willing to eat at a Brazilian restaurant, they didn't order the *feijoada,* the scary dish. They ordered steaks or something. Both of them sent their food back several times with minor complaints. Plus, they didn't eat with their kids. That kind of made sense to me that their son would end up being picky."

Try to make eating out an opportunity for your family to try new things. Make a point of ordering something adventurous—even if it's only a side dish or an unusual appetizer. Try ordering a number of smaller plates that you can all taste and share.

chicken and rice with vegetable gravy

{ ZACK GROSS }

I love chicken and gravy. This gravy is easy to make and so delicious. Lots of gravies are made with flour, but this gravy with cream has a satisfying rich and delicate flavor. Chef Zack Gross suggests serving with jasmine rice.

4 chicken breasts, bone in and skin on
Salt and pepper
1 tablespoon olive oil
1 onion, peeled and chopped
2 carrots, peeled and chopped
2 stalks celery, chopped
¾ cup chopped mushrooms
2 cups chicken stock
2 tablespoons fresh thyme
2 tablespoons fresh rosemary
¼ cup heavy cream (or crème fraîche or a pat of
    butter—but not milk)

1. Preheat oven to 325°F.

2. Season the chicken with salt and pepper. Heat a large straight-sided, ovenproof skillet over medium-high heat, and when the pan is hot, add the oil. Brown the chicken skin-side down in batches if necessary so as not to crowd the pan, about 5 minutes each side. Remove browned pieces to a plate as you brown the next batch.

3. When all the chicken is browned, turn the breasts skin-side up and snuggle them all together in the pan. Add the chopped vegetables to the pan in and around the chicken, and put the pan in the oven, uncovered, for about 15 minutes.

4. Remove the pan from the oven to the stovetop and remove the chicken to a plate. Spoon out or pour off all but a tablespoon or so of fat, leaving the vegetables in the pan.

5. Put the pan back on the stovetop, over low heat, and pour the chicken stock into the pan, stirring and scraping to incorporate any browned bits off the bottom of the pan. Add the fresh herbs and cream (if using butter, mix in at the end, off heat) to stock. Raise the heat and reduce the liquid by about half, until thickened, about 8 to 10 minutes.

6. When thickened, pour the gravy into a food processor or blender and pulse until smooth. If using a blender, leave some room at the top and pulse the blender without the very top piece on to let the steam escape. Finally, season with salt and pepper and pour the gravy over the chicken and serve.

Note: You can easily make this with skinless, boneless chicken breasts also.

chicken cassoulet with white beans and bacon

{ COLBY GARRELTS }

A cassoulet is a deeply flavorful and satisfying meal. Usually it is cooked and then allowed to rest overnight to deepen the flavors before reheating and serving. I find myself making this dish on a Sunday afternoon when we feel like being homebodies, playing board games or reading lots of books. Any leftovers are delicious the next day for lunch with a salad or mixed into some broth. Done right, the flavors meld together and the beans are soft and creamy. Cody likes the tomato-y beans, and sometimes we serve this with wheat toast and call it "beans on toast." If you have sausages on hand instead of bacon, go ahead and use them or any other meat you have around.

4 slices French bread or other similar bread, cut into small cubes

3 bacon slices, coarsely chopped into ¼- to ½-inch pieces

1½ pounds chicken breasts or thighs, cut into ¾-inch-thick cubes (pound breast to an even thickness before cubing)

1 tablespoon olive oil

1 medium shallot, chopped

3 garlic cloves, chopped

2 teaspoons chopped fresh oregano

2 teaspoons chopped fresh thyme

¼ teaspoon dried crushed red pepper (optional)

1 cup chicken stock

1 15-ounce can great northern beans, drained

1 14½-ounce can diced tomatoes in juice

3 tablespoons tomato paste

½ teaspoon ground allspice

Salt and pepper

2 tablespoons olive oil

½ cup freshly grated Parmesan cheese

2 tablespoons chopped fresh parsley

1. Preheat oven to 200°F. Spread the bread cubes out onto a baking sheet and bake until dry and crumbly, about 10 minutes, stirring halfway through. Remove from oven and when cool, crush in your hands to make coarse crumbs.

2. Cook bacon in a medium-size, heavy ovenproof Dutch oven (or straight-sided skillet with a tight-fitting lid) over medium-high heat until brown and crisp, about 4 minutes. Using a slotted spoon, transfer bacon to a bowl.

3. Add chicken to pot to brown, but do not cook through. Using a slotted spoon, transfer the chicken to the bowl with the bacon. Pour off the fat from the pot.

4. Turn heat down to low and add the olive oil, shallot, and garlic to pot and sauté until beginning to soften, about 10 minutes. Stir in oregano, thyme, and red pepper. Add chicken stock and beans and then turn up the heat until liquid is reduced below beans and is thickened, about 15 minutes.

5. Turn oven up to 350°F.

6. Stir in tomatoes with juices, tomato paste, and allspice. Return chicken and bacon to pot. Season cassoulet with salt and pepper. Taste to test for flavor and add more salt and pepper if needed. Bring to boil.

7. Cover pot and transfer to preheated oven; bake 30 minutes. Remove pot from the oven.

8. If making to serve at a later time, uncover pot and cool the cassoulet 1 hour at room temperature. Then refrigerate, uncovered, until cold. Once cold, cover and keep refrigerated. When ready to use, rewarm, covered, in 375°F oven about 40 minutes, adding more broth if necessary.

9. Increase oven temperature to 400°F. In a bowl, mix bread crumbs with Parmesan cheese and season with salt and pepper. Sprinkle over warm cassoulet. Bake until bread crumb topping is golden brown, about 10 minutes covered and another 5 to 10 minutes uncovered. Sprinkle cassoulet with parsley and serve.

Note: If you have leftover chicken that is already cooked, you can use that in the recipe instead of raw chicken. Cut the chicken into cubes and skip the step of browning; add cooked chicken cubes to the bowl with the cooked bacon.

hot dogs with homemade relish and carrot sticks

{ ZACK GROSS }

SERVES 4

Hot dogs are a swift, unfussy, hit-the-spot lunch or dinner. Chef Zack Gross says he likes Hebrew National hot dogs and potato rolls. He boils his dogs, and then keeps them warm in the water while he makes the relish. It's worth the extra time to cut the onions and pickles very fine, especially for kids. I can't stop looking for a snack to have with this relish when I make it, and when my friend Piper comes over, we cut the hot dogs lengthwise and then into small folded bites that we eat like pretty canapés with a dollop of relish in the middle.

¼ cup finely chopped red onion
¼ cup finely chopped yellow onion
1 tablespoon red wine vinegar
1 tablespoon brown sugar
2 tablespoons water
¼ cup finely chopped dill pickles
1½ teaspoons mustard or more to your liking (yellow, Dijon, or brown)
4 best-quality buns
4 best-quality hot dogs, cooked
Bunch of carrots, peeled and cut into sticks, for serving

1. To make the relish, heat a small sauté pan over medium heat and cook the onions with the vinegar, brown sugar, and water until the onions are soft and most of the water is absorbed, about 10 minutes. Remove from heat to a bowl and combine with the pickles and mustard.

2. To steam the buns, put the heated hot dogs in the buns and put them back into the bun bag and tie closed; let stand about 2 minutes. Remove to a plate and serve carrot sticks on the side.

steamed black cod with ginger broth, lime, and noodles

{ COLBY GARRELTS }

SERVES 4

This is Chef Colby Garrelts's favorite meal in the world. Mine, too. The broth is fantastic and even better if you make the stock yourself, which is as easy as throwing some fish bones (or shrimp shells) in a pot with water and an onion and some of the other ingredients from the list below for 20 minutes. Don't boil the water, or the stock will get cloudy. We bring both the soy sauce and the sesame oil to the table, so Cody can pour a bit extra into the soup himself. The same recipe can also be made with chicken stock and boneless chicken breast, but omit the fish sauce.

I also like Colby's clever method of using a pie dish to steam the fish in the pot with the broth.

6 ounces rice noodles

1½ cups snow peas, ends trimmed

1 cup shredded carrots

4 cups good quality fresh fish stock (clam juice or even chicken stock can be substituted)

1 tablespoon grated peeled fresh ginger

1 tablespoon toasted sesame oil

1 tablespoon soy sauce

1 teaspoon fish sauce, Three Crabs brand recommended (optional)

5 tablespoons fresh cilantro, divided

4 5-ounce black cod or halibut fillets

Salt and pepper

2 tablespoons chopped green onion

2 tablespoons fresh lime juice

1 tablespoon chopped fresh mint

1. Gather a large pot with a lid to make the soup, a steamer that can fit inside the pot, and a 9-inch pie dish to place the fish in.

2. In a second pot, boil the noodles in salted water for 3 minutes. Place snow peas and carrots in a colander, drain noodles over them, and rinse and divide among 4 bowls.

3. In the large pot, place the fish stock, ginger, sesame oil, soy sauce, fish sauce, and 3 tablespoons cilantro; bring broth to a boil.

4. Add steamer rack or basket to pot. Place the fish in the glass pie dish, sprinkle with salt and pepper, and place pie dish on top of steamer rack. Cover pot and steam fish just until opaque in center, about 6 minutes for cod and 8 minutes for halibut. Serve with sauce and noodles; garnish with 2 tablespoons cilantro, green onions, lime juice, and mint.

Note: It's worth getting Thai rice noodles. Rice pasta cooks in a different way.

red bean and walnut spread

{ ANA SORTUN }

SERVES 8

At her restaurant, Oleanna, in Cambridge Massachusetts, Chef Ana Sortun serves this popular dip with homemade string cheese and bread. To prepare it, Sortun spreads the dip out on plastic wrap, tops with herbs, pomegranate molasses, and pomegranate seeds, and rolls the whole thing up. She then serves it in slices. We make the dip plain, spread it on Wasa Lite crackers, and use the herbs and pomegranate seeds on top. Cody didn't like it right away, but the next day he asked for it, talked about how much he liked it, and wanted more.

1 cup dark red kidney beans, soaked overnight and
   rinsed well
3 cups water
¼ white onion, minced
1 bay leaf
¾ cup walnuts
4 tablespoons butter
½ teaspoon chopped garlic
Salt and pepper to taste
2 teaspoons chopped dill
2 teaspoons chopped mint or basil
2 teaspoons chopped flat-leaf parsley
2 teaspoons pomegranate molasses (you can find this
   at Whole Foods or similar markets)
Bread, crackers, and string cheese for serving
Garnish for older children and adults: toasted walnuts
   and pomegranate seeds

1. Combine beans, water, onions, and bay leaf in a saucepan and bring to a boil. Turn heat down to low and simmer until tender, about an hour.

2. Heat oven to 350°F. Spread the walnuts out on a baking tray and toast for about 8 to 10 minutes, stirring once, and checking frequently until toasted.

3. Drain beans well and discard bay leaf. In a food processor fitted with a metal blade, puree the beans with walnuts, butter, chopped garlic, salt, and pepper until smooth and creamy.

4. Mix chopped herbs together and put aside a small amount for garnish. Blend the rest into the beans and add a splash of water if the mixture is too thick.

5. Season with salt and pepper and serve on warmed bread slices or crackers. Drizzle with pomegranate molasses and sprinkle with herb mix.

6. Serve next to some string cheese. For older children and adults, top with walnuts and pomegranate seeds.

ratatouille with balsamic vinegar, honey, and basil

{ DIANE FORLEY }

SERVES 4-6

This dish is just delicious—the balsamic, honey, and basil are unique additions.

1 onion, diced
1 eggplant, diced,
1 red pepper, diced
2 zucchini, diced
¼ cup olive oil
1 tablespoon ground fennel seed
1 tablespoon ground coriander seed
1 tablespoon salt
1 cup tomato sauce
2 tablespoons balsamic vinegar
2 tablespoons honey
1 bunch basil leaves (15 leaves), chopped

1. Preheat oven to 375°F.

2. Toss vegetables with olive oil, spices, and salt; place on foil-lined baking sheet and bake until vegetables are browned, about 45 minutes to 1 hour, stirring often to cook evenly.

3. Remove vegetables from oven and transfer to medium-size pot. Add tomato sauce, vinegar, and honey and let cook over low heat until mixture softens, about 10 minutes.

4. Remove from heat and add chopped basil and serve.

nori chips

{ PETER BERLEY }

Chef Peter Berley's children grew up on these tasty nori seaweed chips the way most kids grow up eating potato chips. Nori are thin sheets of dried seaweed commonly used for wrapping sushi. Nori has lots of protein, and few other foods contain as many vitamins and minerals. They can be found in the Asian section of the grocery store. Nori chips are super fast and easy to make. I like them with sesame oil brushed on after baking. You can store them for several days, but when we make them, we never have any left!

5 nori sheets (one package)
1 teaspoon olive oil
Salt for sprinkling
Sesame oil (optional)

1. Preheat oven to 300°F.

2. Lay the nori sheets out on a baking tray—you can cut some in half to fit your baking tray. Brush them lightly with olive oil and sprinkle lightly with salt.

3. Bake for 15 to 20 minutes, until crisp like a potato chip. Brush lightly with sesame oil if you like. Break into bite-size pieces and serve.

Tip: You can make incredibly crunchy and delicate kale chips the same way, at the same time, but keep a close eye on them so they don't burn.

macaroni and cheese

{ JOAN MCNAMARA }

SERVES 10

"My grandson eats our macaroni and cheese, that we have here, that was my mother's recipe. ...I would make that for my kids," says Joan McNamara, founder of Joan's on Third cafe in Los Angeles. She says she learned to cook from her mother, who would encourage her cooking and tell her just not to be afraid, "just go ahead and try." Her macaroni and cheese is unlike any other. She explains: "Most people do a roux (a cooked mixture of flour and butter) in macaroni and cheese—and this one doesn't. It's just everything thrown in the pot—you boil the noodles, then put in milk and butter and any kind of cheese you want, put it in the oven, and it's done. My mother would say, 'just add the milk'— it would be swimming in milk. *Swimming!* It looked like you had put all that macaroni in this pool of milk, and she'd say, 'Don't be afraid to put in too much, it will absorb into the thing,' and sure enough it did."

1½ tablespoons salt
1 pound pasta (elbow macaroni, fusilli, or any shape desired)
2 ounces (4 tablespoons) butter
3¾ cups whole milk
6 ounces ricotta or small curd cottage cheese
3 ounces cream cheese
12 ounces Monterey Jack cheese, shredded
20 ounces Old Amsterdam Gouda (see note at right), shredded, divided
Salt and pepper to taste

1. Preheat oven to 350°F.

2. Bring a large pot of water to a boil. Add 1½ tablespoons salt, and when the water returns to a boil, add the pasta and cook until just tender. While the pasta cooks, measure and put in a large bowl the butter, milk, ricotta or cottage cheese, cream cheese, Monterey Jack cheese, and 12 ounces of Old Amsterdam Gouda (reserve the rest for the topping). When the pasta is tender, drain well and add warm to the other ingredients. Season with salt and pepper. Gently mix everything together, leaving some chunks of cheese visible.

3. Pour the mixture into 9 x 11-inch baking pan. Top with the remaining Gouda. You can store this in the refrigerator until you are ready to cook. Bake for 30 to 40 minutes, or until beautifully golden.

4. Serve hot or at room temperature.

Note: Aged Gouda cheeses have a more intense butterscotch-caramel flavor than regular Gouda cheeses. Old Amsterdam is an award-winning brand of Gouda cheese, aged 18 months and known for its rich flavor. It is rich, but not dry or salty like other matured cheeses. It can be found at fine cheese shops as well as places liked Trader Joe's. If you can't find Old Amsterdam, you can substitute with half the quantity of another high-quality aged Gouda.

Tip: Try making this in muffin wrappers in a muffin pan for smaller portions and easy serving at a party.

whole grain sesame scallion pancakes with tofu

{ DIANE FORLEY }

I sometimes make these as part of Cody's packed lunch, and sometimes we make them together and shape them like dinosaurs with a cookie cutter. Cody doesn't always like the texture of the soft tofu in the pancakes, even if I chop the tofu small, so we occasionally add chicken or fresh soybeans, called edamame. These can be made with leftover plain grains or leftover rice from a flavored rice dish—omit the soy sauce or make the grains fresh.

2 eggs

2 cups cooked grains: rice, barley, or quinoa

2 tablespoons soy sauce (if using plain grains)

1 tablespoon sesame oil

1 tablespoon sliced scallions, white and light green part only (optional)

½ cup flour

Salt and pepper to taste

1 cup cubed tofu

3 tablespoons olive oil

1. In a bowl, beat eggs with a fork.

2. Add grains, soy sauce if using, sesame oil, scallions if using, flour, salt, and pepper. Gently mix in tofu.

3. Heat olive oil in an 8-inch nonstick skillet over medium heat. Scoop small portions, flatten into pancakes, and place in the pan. Cook until brown on one side, about 5 minutes. Flip carefully with a spatula and finish browning over low heat until cooked through. The pancakes can also be baked in oiled muffin tins in a 375°F oven for 20 minutes.

cauliflower and parmesan macaroni

{ JIMMY SCHMIDT }

This is so creamy and decadent—it's a wonderful treat. You can make it in muffin tins to serve in small portions or to serve easily at a party. Parmesan cheese has a strong flavor; substitute a milder cheese for children who prefer blander flavors.

1½ tablespoons salt

2 cups elbow macaroni (preferably whole wheat or high fiber)

1 large head cauliflower, core removed, brown spots, if any, scraped off, and florets separated

1 cup half-and-half (more if necessary)

2 cups finely grated Parmesan cheese

Sea salt

1. Bring a large pot of water to a boil. Add 1½ tablespoons salt, and when the water returns to a boil, add the pasta and cook until just tender. Meanwhile, place the cauliflower florets in a colander set atop the pasta water and cover to steam the cauliflower while the pasta cooks. Turn the heat down a bit to keep the water boiling but not boiling over.

2. When the cauliflower is tender, remove it from the colander and pour it into a food processor. When the pasta is tender, drain and transfer it to a bowl.

3. Preheat oven to 400°F.

4. Puree the cauliflower with the half-and-half until smooth, then blend in 1¾ cups Parmesan cheese till smooth and thick, saving ¼ cup to sprinkle on the top before baking. Adjust seasonings as necessary with sea salt.

5. Pour the cauliflower and cheese mixture into the bowl with the pasta and fold until thoroughly combined. Adjust the texture to be slightly wet as necessary with a little additional half-and-half.

6. Pour into a casserole dish and dust the top with the remaining Parmesan cheese. Cover with foil and bake in the oven for 20 minutes. Remove the foil and bake for another 5 minutes or so, until browned on top.

spring pea risotto with barley

{ PETER BERLEY }

SERVES 4-6

Sometimes kids need something fun to do at the table before they will settle in to eat. For this dish I gave Cody the block of Parmesan and the grater. He grated some cheese on top, mixed it in, and then started eating. This is a fast, easy meal for a babysitter to do also.

1 cup pearl barley, soaked in water to cover by 2 inches for 4 to 6 hours
½ cup finely chopped onion
1 tablespoon extra-virgin olive oil
Sea salt and freshly ground black pepper
4 cups vegetable stock
1 cup fresh peas
½ cup finely grated Parmesan cheese
1 tablespoon butter
1 teaspoon finely chopped basil or other fresh herbs (optional)

1. Drain the barley.

2. In a 2- to 3-quart saucepan, sauté the onion in olive oil with a pinch of salt over medium heat 5 to 7 minutes or until soft and translucent.

3. Stir in the barley and stock and bring to a boil. Reduce the heat and simmer for 35 minutes, stirring occasionally until most (but not all) of the liquid has been absorbed and the barley is tender.

4. Stir in the peas and cook 3 to 4 minutes or until tender. Stir in the cheese, butter, and basil. Season with salt and pepper and serve.

noodles with tahini dressing

{ ANA SORTUN }

**This makes a tasty and filling packed lunch. The
dressing can also be used as a dip for broccoli,
carrots, or cucumbers or any flat bread like pita.
For a thicker dip, use less water.**

1½ tablespoons salt

½ pound spaghetti (can use buckwheat noodles, rice
    noodles, or spaghetti)

¼ cup tahini

3 tablespoons warm water (or more for consistency)

¼ cup extra-virgin olive oil

1 teaspoon rice wine vinegar or white balsamic vinegar

2 teaspoons freshly squeezed lemon juice

½ teaspoon sugar

½ teaspoon ground cumin

1 tablespoon Greek yogurt or mayonnaise

Kosher salt to taste

Sesame seeds and finely chopped red pepper or
    cucumber to garnish, optional

1. Bring a large pot of water to a boil. Add 1½
tablespoons salt, and when the water returns to a boil,
add the pasta and cook until just tender. When cooked,
drain into a colander and rinse under cool water.

2. Meanwhile, make the tahini dressing by whisking
tahini and warm water together in a bowl until
smooth. Stir in the oil, vinegar, lemon juice, sugar,
cumin, yogurt or mayonnaise, and salt. The dressing
will last for 3 to 5 days in the refrigerator. Serve cold
or at room temperature.

3. Mix the tahini dressing into cooked and rinsed
pasta. Add more water if the sauce is too thick.
Sprinkle the sesame seeds and chopped red pepper
or cucumber on top if using and serve.

toasted mochi snack with maple syrup

{ PETER BERLEY }

{ PETER BERLEY }

SERVES 4

It's nice sometimes to have a quick sweet something without a whole lot of mess and preparation. This is both healthy and delicious. Another option for spreading on the *mochi* (and dipping!) instead of maple syrup is apple butter. Mochi is a popular Japanese food made from special sweet rice. It's made by steaming then pounding the rice into shapes and is surprisingly chewy. In Japan it is served grilled or toasted, used in soup or in desserts—soft thin sheets wrapped around ice cream are delicious. The mochi in this recipe is made with brown rice and comes in a thick sheet. When baked it puffs up so it's crispy on the outside and chewy on the inside. It can be found in a Japanese market or markets like Whole Foods or in health food stores. I like to cut the pieces up small so they are more crunchy than chewy.

1 12½-ounce package mochi
Maple syrup for drizzling and dipping

1. Preheat oven to 450°F.

2. Cut half the mochi into 1- or 2-inch squares and store the rest for future use. Spread pieces at least 1 inch apart on a baking sheet and bake 8 to 10 minutes until puffed up.

3. Drizzle on maple syrup or serve on the side for dipping.

strawberry pancakes with strawberry maple syrup

{ ZACK GROSS }

SERVES 4

"Nobody has time to make pancakes from scratch with a toddler!" says Chef Zack Gross, and it's true—sometimes using a mix makes pancakes doable on a busy school day. I finally bought a double-burner skillet so I can make lots of pancakes all at once. It's fun to add strawberries or other seasonal berries, and sometimes we even add frozen cherries to ours. Gross says, "I like to put a couple of sliced strawberries into the pancake before flipping them; you can make faces and designs, whatever keeps your child's attention." He recommends Bisquick brand; I like using the different kinds of mixes from Bob's Red Mill. This sweet, buttery compote is a tasty change from maple syrup. There's no need to butter the pancakes before pouring on the sauce.

Pancake mix for at least 4 servings
4 tablespoons butter, divided
1 pint strawberries or other seasonal berries, washed and sliced, divided
2 tablespoons sugar
Juice of ½ orange, about 2 tablespoons
½ cup real maple syrup
Whipped cream (recipe below), optional

1. Follow the package instructions to make the pancake batter for at least 4 servings.

2. Ladle batter onto a hot skillet, buttered with a teaspoon or so of butter, and then gently tap the strawberry slices into the pancakes before flipping, using about ¼ of the pint.

3. In a separate pan, melt remaining butter with sugar. Add in the rest of the strawberries and the orange juice, and cook a couple of minutes.

4. Add the maple syrup and stir to combine. For special breakfasts, top with whipped cream.

Whipped Cream:
1 cup heavy cream
1 cup powdered sugar
¼ teaspoon vanilla extract

Combine all ingredients in a medium bowl and whisk until your arm hurts (or until the cream forms soft peaks).

preschoolers

EMERGING INDEPENDENCE

ages two-and-a-half to five

All the chefs I spoke with about the preschool years agreed that this is when their kids became quirky, opinionated, and particular about the foods they ate and the way they ate them. "Children's palates change dramatically as they grow—they change as they are changing," says Chris Cosentino, executive chef at Incanto restaurant in San Francisco. "A year and a half ago, Easton loved oysters and he would down them like nobody's business. Now his palate has changed; he doesn't enjoy oysters anymore. He didn't like wasabi before; now he likes wasabi." Children at this age make decisions about eating for themselves, and it can get tricky.

Chefs' children may limit the foods they like to eat, but the foods they choose are surprising and remarkable—not at all the foods typically represented on most children's menus. Cosentino's son, Easton, loves sardines, arugula, asparagus, and sushi. Andrea Curto-Randazzo's daughter's favorite dish is rack of lamb. Siena, acclaimed Boston chef Ana Sortun's daughter, eats salads and watermelon radishes and, to Sortun's surprise, adores spicy greens. She says of her daughter, "She doesn't think any food is weird, and I love that."

It's classic that a two-year-old who eats everything will suddenly become hesitant and idiosyncratic at three years old, and about half of all children at this age do go through a tough time with food. According to Marcia Pelchat, a biopsychologist, food neophobia—when kids really don't want to eat anything new—peaks at age three and then gradually declines throughout life.

Lots of preschoolers take to eating only "white" foods like bread, pasta, potatoes, and french fries. Most, somewhere along the line, learn the word *yucky*. "It's as if children go through a tunnel at around three years old, where feeding them becomes challenging," says Floyd Cardoz, chef at New York's Tabla restaurant. "And then at five years old, they come out and are more open." It's a good time to serve more traditional and familiar foods that kids find appealing or cook meals made of simple, separate foods. Serve meals family style so kids can help themselves to the foods they are willing to eat. Miami chef Andrea Curto-Randazzo says of feeding her three daughters, "I stick to the traditional, because I'm a firm believer in those family recipes, and that stuff is simply so good. Granted, if we are having chicken chili, I might whip up my own cheddar cornbread or something." Sally Kravich, a natural health expert, advises that those starchy white foods, because they have no fiber, can be like glue in the digestion. It can make children become unhealthy. She suggests making little changes like using whole grain pasta such as those made from rice or quinoa, which are more nutritious than white-flour pasta and better for the digestive system.

How Chefs Make Food an Adventure for Their Kids

I asked chefs why their kids eat such interesting foods, and if they think there's a way that they're cooking that makes foods like vegetables palatable. The simple answer is that chefs take their children into their world of food, and, in doing so, they pass on to their children their own sense of pleasure and enthusiasm. Instead of heading to the supermarket to grab boxes and bags off of shelves, they go to the farmers' market, where kids meet farmers, taste samples, and explore interesting things like squash blossoms and dragon fruit. They visit local farms and orchards where children can pick food in the field—it is deeply satisfying to forage and eat a freshly picked strawberry or an apple right off a tree. They shop fresh from butchers and fishmongers, where there are curiosities like crabs—it's not just grocery shopping; it's an adventure.

Chefs teach their children, cook with them, and they cook well, using quality ingredients to make the food they cook taste better. They allow their kids to be creative with them in the kitchen, mixing their own

ingredients for making things like savory waffles with different flavors and topping combinations. Given a broad range of ingredients to choose from, children can surprise us with what they opt to eat. An example is Benchmarc executive chef Marc Murphy's daughter, who visits his restaurant regularly. Murphy says, "When my daughter was three years old, she'd go into the kitchen, look at the *mise en place*, and pick up whatever she'd want, as if she were at a buffet. That's where she ate her first endive."

"One of the most important parts, I think, is getting children excited about food," says Cosentino. "It promotes more questions, more interests in different things on a regular basis . . . you make them more inquisitive. My son Easton has been going to the farmers' markets since the day he was born; he's been a part of that system ever since the beginning. It's been a pretty interesting dynamic for us. He knows what things are in season, he waits for certain things, and he gets really excited about it. He loves apples, but apples are done for him right now because berries are in season. He looks forward to asparagus, but then he's done with it after a while."

Cathal Armstrong, chef and co-owner of Restaurant Eve; Eamonn's, a Dublin Chipper; and The Majestic in Alexandria, Virginia, grows vegetables in a tiny greenhouse at home. "The kids participating in that element makes them a little more interested in trying foods they wouldn't normally eat because they see them," he says. "They participate in planting the seeds, the excitement of having the first sprouts come out of the ground, seeing the fruit come up. That makes them considerably more interested in trying something than if you go to the grocery store and pick up a bunch of radishes—most kids won't eat them. If the kids plant radishes, they produce fruit within a few weeks." Kravich says she planted seeds in her garden with her kids. They watched them sprout and grow, which "connected them to the earth and was symbolic to how they looked at life and creation," she explains.

Chefs all agree the preschool years are not a time to narrow their children's diet. The goal with pre-schoolers is to get them to continue to eat broadly. Vegetables, it's no surprise, are the foods most often rejected by this age group. When I asked Chef Linton Hopkins why his children love vegetables, he said, "I don't overcook vegetables. Overcooked, bland food, no one likes, especially kids." In the wintertime, he regularly cooks greens in a skillet for his kids. "I've found the kids really don't love the real slow-braised-style green, so we get the skillet really hot and add a little bit of fat and just hit it real hard in the pan, and it gets bright with a little acid—sometimes that's a pepper vinegar we have. If it's bright, fresh food, regardless of what kind it is, I think kids are going to enjoy it. The one thing I find with home cooks—I don't think they season enough to make a dish sharpened and focused to where it makes your mouth water."

It's not surprising, given hectic lifestyles and fussy children, that home cooks tend to revert back to the handful of recipes they know well and cook them repeatedly. Chefs, though, don't have limited menus and tend to cook creatively and experimentally. Diane Forley and Michael Otsuka, chefs and owners of Flourish Bakery in Scarsdale, have a strategy where they only bring foods into the house that they love to eat, or want to eat. They prepare foods from scratch and make sure that there's a range in terms of nutritional value. They believe food should taste good, and they prepare foods that they, themselves, want to eat. But then the kids lead them from there. There's a basis from which they start, but the developing likes and dislikes of the kids require them to simplify, eliminate, and adjust the meals and menus a bit as they go.

The menus in Cardoz's house were always mixed. "We wouldn't do the same thing every day," he says. "I just wanted them to be used to a lot of flavors. . . . The food always had some amount of spice in there or herbs in there. You know, lots of salt is bad for kids, but there would be some amount of salt in there too, just so that they understood what it was. . . . I did not do anything that was not recognizable, that was not familiar to them, like, there wouldn't be snails or chicken feet or tripe, things like that that kids don't like."

You can also entice kids by the way you describe a particular food or dish. Hopkins says, "A lot of times my wife will say, 'Kids, this is my famous turkey chili,' and they're like, 'Wow! Famous turkey chili!' You know, we'll describe a dish like that, and they want to be a part of the famous turkey chili!" Chefs agree that children have to see you enjoy food, too. If they see you enjoying something, they want to know what it is.

Chefs use a lot of patience with their children in regard to food. "It's very easy to say he's not eating anything, I'm just going to give him mac and cheese from a box," says Cardoz. "Instead, we've made mac and cheese from scratch. My son, when he was five,

> **"Those early experiences of them eating well have really affected their whole lives."**
>
> —Peter Berley, cookbook author and New York City chef

would ask me to make a five-cheese omelette for him for breakfast . . . and he was involved in grating the cheese, mixing the cheese, cracking the eggs. Yes, there was a mess in the kitchen and he cracked the eggs, but it was his omelette so he wanted to eat it."

Culture, History, and Family

Children at this age are highly impressionable; they will take the aromas of the foods we cook most often deep into their psyche. They create robust memories of what they see and do at this age. Cardoz says it was important for him when cooking with his children to always connect food with stories of how he grew up, "so there was some sense of culture and history and family with everything we did. I would tell them, 'My father would love to eat steak with potatoes,' and I would make those potatoes for them."

Curto-Randazzo says, "Probably the most popular dish among all of my kids is chicken cutlets—the chicken, thin, with seasoned bread crumbs, and I panfry it . . . then put a little lemon on it. It's something my grandmother would make, too. It's great the next day in the refrigerator. It's a very Italian thing to do, have chicken cutlets around." She mostly cooks Italian food at home because "that is my upbringing and my husband's upbringing, too . . . so there's always the Italian theme going on. . . . That was my comfort food. I'll make escarole soup with the little meatballs and white beans, homemade chicken soup with some pasta, or pasta with lentils."

Cookbook author and chef Peter Berley says that his children appreciated having had specially made lunches, like sandwiches made with good bread and

nori rolls with brown rice. "They both say now, "These were the foods you made, that we loved, and we did feel really different and special." Cosentino's son, Easton, asks to go to a place they frequent together that he refers to as their "special noodle place." His son also loves cooking shabu shabu at Korean restaurants. Cosentino says eating foods from different cultures fosters curiosity about those cultures and makes learning interesting. He says, "History, food, and culture are not just about stuffing food into your stomach to get energy—there's more to it. History is behind everything."

Sortun sometimes makes meals fun by serving them away from the kitchen, at the coffee table where Siena, her daughter, is playing, "So that I can coax her out slowly, so that it doesn't seem like dinner is a punishment," she says. "Changing it around really helps me. Sometimes to make it fun we'll have breakfast in her tent in her room. . . . She's still kind of playing, but I'm getting her to focus on eating. I think there are a lot of distractions, and kids will play and think that eating is boring."

Cooking Strategies for Busy Families

For working parents and families who are really busy, it's good to have a perspective on what's important and a strategy for putting meals together. Making batches of foods and freezing portions can make dinner much easier. Meatballs, soups, and sauces can easily be frozen, as can cooked beans, fresh pasta, and cooked rice. Berley says his and his wife's schedules were always chaotic and unpredictable because they were both freelancing. He was working in restaurants and catering when his children were young. "Sitting down to eat was more important than cooking together . . . simply because I wasn't around—I was working a lot. . . . It didn't always work that we could cook dinner together. What I would do a lot of times is tell my wife what to start cooking—I would coordinate with her, like, why don't you start this [put the rice up for example], and I'd come home and finish up dinner real quick, and we'd sit down to eat. My real desire was to get them to eat as well as possible at home, as often as possible with us."

Sortun's strategy is to prepare a week's worth of food basics when home on the weekend. "I'll pick one day where I'll cook a few days' worth of meals—I make three or four meals," she says. "I'll make soup, I'll make chicken salad, I'll make a grain, and a chickpea and quinoa salad. That way there's stuff for lunch and dinner . . . there's always something to start from, so they can have a good balanced meal. My husband is good at cooking too, so I never have to worry, but it's a time issue. Trying to get them fed by a certain time can be a challenge. It makes it easier for them for the week when I'm not there for dinner—I'm usually working when they are having dinner. That way I know they are getting something good for dinner while I'm away."

Most chefs when cooking at home make only one meal—the family meal that everyone will eat. It happens in different ways at different chefs' homes. Some chefs plate the meals, others put food out and children and adults serve themselves from a dish, family style. For dinner, Blue Ribbon restaurants executive chef/co-owner Eric Bromberg and Armstrong both make a protein, a starch, and a vegetable,

> "We have said from the beginning, our family meal is a family meal. So we really don't create special meals based on individual likes and dislikes. My children get input. . . . We'll talk about it ahead of time; when we go to the farmers' market on a certain day, we'll give them some money and they'll pick some things, so they're proud to bring those vegetables that they bought. And I think that's a great way to include them in the choices."
>
> —Linton Hopkins, executive chef at Restaurant Eugene in Atlanta

and everyone chooses the foods they would like to eat. Sortun creates a design on the plate with the food, like bridges and tunnels and that sort of thing.

Eating Preferences— How to Cook for a Preschooler

"What we do is introduce a flavorful dish that is something they are going to be more familiar with, like pizza," says Armstrong. "We'll make it ourselves. From that platform, you can start to build ingredients like garlic and olive oil and basil and start to get more aggressive with flavors. You have to start with a foundation that kids understand." Cardoz agrees: "It's easier to put something in with something they already like. Some kids love shrimp—you can easily get kids to eat shrimp with rice if they don't like rice. Putting a dish together, I would never put all the strange things together, because I know my kids are going to be afraid of it." Curto-Randazzo adds, "If you put something on the table they really do like, you have a greater possibility of getting them to try something they might not."

ANDREA CURTO-RANDAZZO and her husband, **FRANK RANDAZZO,** are executive chefs of the Water Club in Miami. Previously, at Wish restaurant in Miami, Curto-Randazzo was named one of *Food & Wine*'s Ten Best Chefs. Randazzo was a contestant on *Top Chef*. They have three daughters, Isabella, Gia, and Lilli. Curto-Randazzo says, "I do want my kids to appreciate food because it's a beautiful thing, it's what I do, it's a big part of me. As chefs, my husband and I want them to appreciate all kinds of foods. And I always stress trying new things. For me, the person who got me to try new things was my grandfather. I'm sure by five or six, I was eating everything. He had me try pigs' feet, tripe, whatever. It was because he was my buddy, I wanted to be with him and be like him; so every time he gave me something new to try, I was all about it."

Lots of children who are three to five years old dislike spice, but Cody sometimes goes full force at something surprising like Dijon mustard and other times can't handle something as simple as herbs in eggs. Sometimes he says it smells funny, and it's a bigger challenge to convince him to take a bite. Cardoz advises parents to stay the course and be patient, and for his children he turned to more traditional family foods: "Which kid doesn't like meatballs?"

For other chefs, talking about ingredients and how they go together becomes important. To make his food flavorful and palatable for Zen, St. Petersburg chef Zack Gross uses a particular brand of smoked bacon: "For me, Nueske's bacon . . . that's something I don't skimp on. It adds so much to the dish. I love to have that wafting smell. Just to have that smell—smoky bacon—coming out of my oven first thing in the morning."

We learned from Bromberg to put mushrooms under the skin when roasting a chicken, and it is true, in our house, like his, a roast chicken will always go over well. For Tampa chef B. T. Nguyen, raw carrots, celery, and broccoli are staples. "Those are the three vegetables my son, James, loves, that I pack for him and have in the refrigerator all the time so he can snack on them."

Berley wasn't so concerned with teaching his kids about cooking or ingredients, "I was more concerned that they just enjoyed what they were eating—that was my main concern. I wanted them to have a good feeling and develop an attachment to eating real food. And, if they could develop that, then I figured if they got curious, the more they got curious, the more they'd want to know—and that's what happened."

For children who prefer pasta dinners, Berley suggests using semolina pasta, which is more nutritious because it has "a higher protein than pasta made from, say, a basic wheat bread flour." Whole grain durum wheat pasta, which is the whole durum wheat made as pasta, is another option. When you get whole wheat pasta from Italy, that's what you are

> "There's got to be something they like that they can hang their hat on and say, 'Okay, I get it.'"
> —Floyd Cardoz, New York City chef

getting. Berley suggests, "You can eat pasta with beans or meats and fishes and get even more nutrition in there."

"Yucky," "I Don't Like It," "I'm Full," and How to Change the Game

We do hear lots of "I'm not hungry" from Cody just as it's time for dinner, or at the table, things are frequently called "yucky" and "icky." Lots of kids will reject anything green, regardless of whether they consider the food to be otherwise palatable. With this age group, it's important to distinguish what is, in fact, about the food and what is about something else—like Cody's wanting control or feeling moody. Control issues around food are big at this age, instructs Cynthia Epps, a Los Angeles infant-feeding specialist. Not only do kids like to sort food so they themselves can control what they are eating, but they want to test the kind of control they can exert at mealtimes. All kids will experience this in some form or other. For some it is a quick and passing phase; for others it can be a prolonged and disruptive period of time.

How much we allow Cody at this age the independence of declaring he is or is not hungry has been a big question for us. The downside of letting the meal end when Cody says "he's full" is that sometimes he eats only a few bites of his meal and can get cranky from hunger later. Sortun says, "They know when they are full and when they have had enough. We are not sticklers for that kind of stuff as long as she's had a balanced meal." Nguyen sums it up when she says, "You have to give them the freedom to choose, but at the same time you have to focus them, expose

them." Gross keeps it all in perspective. He says, "I believe they have to make their own decisions. You try to teach them what you believe, but you can't fully make 'em do it. That's what I've realized. It's not worth getting upset about either. There's not enough time I spend with my daughter to want to be upset because she didn't want to eat something that I made for her." We would all be a lot happier if we relaxed a bit and had some fun.

Practically half of preschoolers aren't consistently hungry at mealtimes. One in four frequently refuses to eat; one in five asks for particular foods and then won't necessarily eat them. Statistics also show that half of all preschoolers try to end a meal after only a few bites. Cody has learned and frequently uses the phrase "I'm full," which we take to mean he's not engaged and we need to pay more attention to him during meals. At four years old, Cody went through a phase where he would *always* say, "I don't like it" when he first sat down—to everything. Giving him ways to participate helped, like letting him grate a little Parmesan cheese over his risotto or grind a bit of pepper into his stew. It's enough of a distraction for him to change the topic, and he forgets the fuss and eats.

Children at this age also begin to use language purposefully, and it creates tricky situations. They start to construct stories and learn catchphrases in order not to eat. Cody says with conviction about not eating his preschool packed lunch, "I was saving it for later." At home, when he says he's not hungry before mealtimes, I offer him an alternate truthful scenario, like suggesting he may not want to eat

CHRIS COSENTINO is the executive chef for Incanto, his San Francisco restaurant. Also, he is cocreator of Boccalone (www.boccalone.com), an artisanal salumeria, or cured-meat shop, also in San Francisco. Cosentino has a strong commitment to sustainable principles and humanely raised meats and is an avid researcher of ancient cooking techniques and culinary lore. He gained national acclaim as a leading proponent of offal cookery—cooking every part of an animal. The practice stems from a belief that no part of an animal slaughtered for food should go to waste.

Cosentino was raised by a single mom, but they lived close to his grandparents and all shared a weekly Sunday dinner. He firmly believes in the importance of that social family time. Of his son, Easton, he proudly says he can tell if strawberries are "too watery" or if the asparagus is not in peak season. "He always hangs around with the cooks in the restaurant; it's created a very interesting dynamic of taste and palate." Cosentino believes the most important thing is to be honest with kids, not to trick or lie to them to get them to try something. "It may not be the result you want right then and there, but the long-term result will be better."

Chef Chris Cosentino : NANCY NEIL

> **"My three-year-old is interested in beans from the vine—cooking them and eating them. We poach them and keep them crunchy, or sometimes we overcook them and make them mushy. He likes to play with them. So he's learning about how they can be different depending on how they're prepared."**
>
> —Alejandro Alcocer, New York City chef

because he would like to play instead. I know then that I need to make the meal a bit more fun to help engage him, and I propose a fun game we can play after eating.

Epps says that at meals "the most important thing you do is to not put anything in front of them at all." She explains that children's psychological boundary is the space right in front of them, at their fingertips, and that's the space they want to control. So it's better to serve food family style in the center of the table rather than putting the food directly on everyone's plate. Then, if they see you taking a serving of something and enjoying it, it will pique their curiosity and they're more likely to try it themselves, because it's their own idea to take some. "So set the food on a plate and only bring out the two things you want them to eat—set it down out of their reach," says Epps. "Sit down next to them and say, for example, 'we are having chicken and we are having asparagus.' Pick up a piece of chicken and start to eat and say, 'How was preschool today, did you see the clouds, it's raining outside?'—in other words, talk off topic."

Bromberg didn't worry too much about times when his children would go through phases, because they ate well most of the time. Nor is he overly concerned about the order of dishes. If his children are excited to eat a scoop of ice cream when they first sit down and doing so allows them to eat their broccoli and chicken after, then he's fine with that. "My wife and I both are of the 'clear your plate' generation," says Bromberg. "And that didn't really serve us well. We thought a different approach would be more successful, so we let them eat at the pace they're comfortable with and

try and give them options at mealtime. Yeah, we had challenging times; at one point our daughter only ate blueberries. I'm not kidding! She ate a pint of blueberries a day and nothing else."

Beginning to Cook

"What I did at three or four years old to get them involved in food was to cook with them," explains Cardoz. "I would sit them on the counter and make it so that it was fun. Make it so that they were involved. I would do things that were kid friendly. We'd make homemade chicken nuggets. . . . They like sushi, so we made sushi together. We've made meatballs together. We've made burgers together. We've made pasta sauce together. We've done everything."

Cooking is a wonderful activity for children of all ages, and all the chefs I spoke with cook with their kids at this age. Now, most children can measure, pour, and stir. An example of how savvy some chefs' children are in the kitchen at this age comes from Alejandro Alcocer, who says, "My five-year-old can cook pasta, roast tomatoes, and make a sauce. We have an electric induction stove, so he can't burn himself unless he touches the bottom of the pan. He's very careful when he lifts out the basket from the hot water. He mashes his roasted tomatoes and puts them on his pasta. He says 'I'm cooking!' It makes him a very confident little boy and gives him a sense of independence to know he can feed himself."

Marc Murphy's daughter uses a special stepstool called a Learning Tower so she can cook with him and be safe and comfortable at counter height. He taught

TIPS FROM CHEFS ON FEEDING PRESCHOOLERS AND SOME HELPFUL RULES

Make rules clear and be "patient and persistent," says Chef Cathal Armstrong. Rules do work better if you stick to them and aren't mean about it. Also, the earlier you set them the better. Of course kids will test the boundaries, but I find a lighthearted approach to enforcing them works. I continue playing a game with Cody where bites have vehicle sounds. Once, Cody cleverly replied to the car-sound bite, "Tunnel's closed for construction"; my reply was, "They're on a lunch break," and he took the bite.

•• Keep trying. **Studies show that you may have to offer preschoolers a new food ten to sixteen times before they'll accept it.**

•• Children must taste the food before rejecting it. **Chef Floyd Cardoz says, "If you don't like it that's fine, but you have to taste it." This, actually, is not as hard as it sounds if you set the rule and stick to it.**

•• Relax and make meals fun. **Make mealtimes about eating and socializing, and don't be afraid to have fun. You can be silly and still have good table manners! No playing with food—throwing food or spitting food included—but that doesn't mean you can't be playful. Try a game to engage your child (or distract him if he's acting up): "Open your mouth and close your eyes and I will give you a big surprise! Guess what bite it is: zucchini bite? Rice bite?"**

•• Dipping. **I put toast rectangles alongside Cody's soup for dipping. I can convince him to taste the soup by dipping the bread in or even floating pieces of bread in the bowl of soup that he can fish out with his spoon. You can also count the bread bites. Counting is big fun in our house.**

•• Mixing bites. **A new food goes over better in the company of a familiar food. Some foods together are just so much better than separately.**

•• Try a different preparation. **Foods that are rejected may be enjoyed if prepared differently. Foods that are strongly disliked shouldn't be pushed. Chef Diane Forley says, "I don't sneak things in because she knows!"**

•• Talk about flavors. **Help your kids learn which foods are salty or bitter or rich or sour to build a vocabulary around food. I know Cody really enjoys the authority of tasting and declaring something is sour.**

•• Make only one meal. **No one wants to be a short-order cook in her own home. Make only one family meal and let everyone eat the parts of it that appeal to her.**

•• Get saucy. **Like dipping, sauces can be an incentive to eat. Chefs try different sauces with foods and let their children make their own combinations. We dip chips in yogurt and carrots in yogurt mixed with tahini. We also try mixing in herbs and spices.**

- Serve small portions on small plates. **"I use miniature cups for Siena so she can finish the whole cup," says Chef Ana Sortun. "We want her to drink water, and we have better success if she's not overwhelmed by the size of the cup. It looks like she can accomplish something. She can handle the amount of water that's in that cup. And I keep filling up the cup. Those kinds of things work. I never give her a huge plate of food."**

- Use cool plates and spoons worth mentioning. **Cody particularly likes a colorful Asian soupspoon from my mother. He will eat more because he likes the spoon.**

- Eat with friends whose kids eat well. **Cody was a model participant in this program, and many kids would eat double their normal four-bite intake in his company. Of course, it goes the other way too, as we are learning now at four and a half.**

- Children must sit down at the table and stay at the table while the meal is going on. **"You don't need to eat, but you need to sit" works well for us to get Cody to the table; talking about things he's interested in helps keep him there.**

- Don't give up. **"It's really easy to give up and say, 'Okay, here are chicken fingers'. And every once in a while you do that because of the exhaustion, but you have to keep at it and keep on them because there are going to be chicken fingers forever," says Chef Andrea Curto-Randazzo.**

- Grow a garden. **"Let the kids participate in growing their own food, and they tend to be much more excited about trying it," says Chef Cathal Armstrong.**

- Talk to your child's preschool teacher. **Suggest starting a small vegetable garden in pots at school. Also, ask the teacher to help the kids eat lunch. Many children will not eat their lunch at preschools if, instead, they are allowed to play.**

- Don't reward with sweets and chocolates. **Instead, reward and treat your children with activities and love.**

- Read books. **Sally Kravich, a natural health expert, used to read *In the Night Kitchen* by Maurice Sendak to her children to inspire them to cook with her. Together they would make healthy versions of cakes and pies with fruits and nuts.**

her to make an omelette. "She takes the fork, brings in the edges from all sides. She learns by doing. I teach her about heat. When the pan is hot, I have her hold her hand above it so she can feel the heat. She'll say to me, 'Daddy, that's hot. That's too grown-up for me to touch.' She looks at the knives and says, 'That's a grown-up knife. I can't use that.' She knows that I'm an adult and she's a child. She knows she's learning."

"I've created a little square over by the stove," says Gross. "I put things in bowls that Zen can dump in the pan, getting her excited about cooking. And she has more of an appreciation to eat things."

REASONS FEEDING A PRESCHOOLER MAY BE HARD

•• They can be quick to dismantle something and eat only the part they want.

•• They learn the word *yuck*, and it's an easy way to reject stuff.

•• They are creatures of habit and create associative memories. If they've had candy or a treat at a store while shopping, they will want that same treat the next visit because they associate the two together. Although this is true of younger children also, at this age they are more outspoken and insistent.

•• They love a colorful, crinkly package. For us, this meant a foray into the world of snack packages and trying to figure out moderation. Sometimes, group playdates can end up being snack fests because everyone generously shows up with a big bag to share and the kids overindulge.

•• They want what their friends have. If they spot ice cream anywhere in the vicinity, they want one too, and at school they want the foods their friends have. "It is difficult at that time. It all depends on what their friends are eating and how often they hang out with their friends—and what their friends eat at home," says Floyd Cardoz.

•• They are persistent and persuasive. Saying "no" repeatedly can be difficult.

•• Getting food in their mouths is only half the battle. Preschoolers love to spit out food, let it fall out of their mouths, swing food around that is only partially in their mouths, and throw food. Also, I still fork feed Cody things to try. Sometimes, he's just as likely to spit it out.

•• They know the word *treat*, and it can be difficult to ensure that they eat sugary foods in moderation.

CATHAL ARMSTRONG, a native Dubliner, was honored as one of *Food & Wine*'s Top Ten Best New Chefs in 2006. He was a nominee in 2007 for the James Beard Award Best Chef Mid-Atlantic for his four restaurants: Eve; The Tasting Room at Eve; Eamonn's: A Dublin Chipper; and The Majestic, in Alexandria, Virginia. He and his wife, Michelle, have two children, Eve and Eamonn. "I always get the kids involved in making the dinner, picking the herbs, peeling the garlic, chopping the garlic, and things like that—with a garlic crusher, not with a knife; they are not ready for knives yet. I think it's really important to be involved in the preparation of the meal and the cleanup of the meal because it develops good habits and good sensibilities in general," he says.

Cathal and Michelle Armstrong, daughter Eve, and son Eamonn : STACY ZARIN GOLDBERG

> "What's important, I think, is to keep the variety around Siena and get her involved in the cooking thing. Not to do it professionally, just as a skill to have, to feed herself well."
>
> —Ana Sortun, chef/owner of Oleana restaurant in Cambridge, Massachusetts

When chefs cook at home, they don't plan menus and make shopping lists. Instead, they cook spontaneously. "I'm a skilled chef—this is what I do. I would pick something up on the way home, bring something from the restaurant, and convert it into something else—it was very much on the fly," says Hopkins. Chefs know instinctively how the flavors of foods will go together, and, unlike most of us, can improvise meals. They use their senses along the way to make creative adjustments. They expose their children to the experimental way of cooking.

As a home cook, I don't have the same resources or know how to cook like chefs do, but, for Cody and me, cooking is a still a fun way to experiment and get creative, even if sometimes we make something that's not so good. We talk about being open to trying something new and it's okay if things don't go so well.

Armstrong's children "have little chef uniforms. They'll put them on and get involved in making bread and cakes and stuff. They love that kind of thing."

Lunch at School

"We talk about lunches. For instance, today I asked him what he wanted for lunch, and he told me he wanted a tamale, some raspberries, applesauce, and rice cake," says Cosentino, who says son Easton always eats his lunch.

I started talking with Cody, too, about lunch, but noticed when he attended a new preschool for the summer, when he was four, that his lunch would come home having been only nibbled at. Cody has always eaten his lunch, whether at home, at restaurants, with friends on lunch dates, or at his regular school. As it turned out, the children at his school who are finished with their lunch have free play, so, of course, Cody would rather play with his friends than sit by himself and eat lunch. I began to pack lunches that were simpler and quicker to eat. I think children in preschool are too young to be left to their own devices at school when it comes time for lunch. It's very stimulating for them to eat with all their friends, and they need some guidance about the importance of eating lunch.

I know that when Cody doesn't eat his lunch at school, he is hungry right when I pick him up, and any after-school plans get put on hold until he eats. I am usually caught off guard, and all I have are some simple snacks, when what he really needs is protein. It's too hard to pack a lunch and then bring a whole other meal for after school.

"I'll give her cold chicken cutlets to take to school. She'll eat it. Typically, we pack the lunch for her—turkey sandwiches are really popular, so I can't say we get too creative there. She'll eat the heck out of a turkey or peanut butter sandwich," Andrea Curto-Randazzo.

Notes about Foods and Health

Food stimulates the senses and provides sustenance, nourishment, and comfort. It should make you feel good; it should be adventurous but not gluttonous. Eating a variety of foods is key and so

ANA SORTUN opened Oleana, her Cambridge, Massachusetts restaurant in 2001. She also has a bakery and cafe called Sofra. The *New York Times* called her cooking "deeply inventive." In 2005 the James Beard Foundation named her Best Chef Northeast. She favors Mediterranean cooking—including lots of beans and purees. She published a cookbook, *Spice: Flavors of the Eastern Mediterranean*. Of her daughter Siena's eating she says, "Her mom's a chef and her dad's a farmer—there's a lot of variety all the time. She's really into the stuff my husband grows, and she eats stuff right out of the field, stuff that I think she's not going to like, like spicy greens. She knows where it comes from. That's a big part of it."

Ana Sortun, husband Chris Kurth, and daughter Siena : MICHAEL PIAZZA

is moderation. I was once told that the best thing to teach your child was delayed gratification, and I would add moderation. I had kept Cody away from candy up until now, but at four I took him for a chocolate. It was actually a chocolate-covered salted caramel. We got a package or two from a special shop where we could sit outside on a bench under a tree. He watched me carefully unwrap the package, and I gave one to him and had one myself. We stared at each other, eating them slowly, bite by bite. They were so delicate and decadent that when we were done we just sat quietly for a moment, letting the flavor and the joy of it sink in. There are some things that are special and the experience of indulging in them is embraced. Foods that are decadent should be enjoyed consciously and those times acknowledged as special occasions.

What is health about at this age? Active four-year-olds need a surprising number of calories, and nutritionists say that eating a variety of foods is critical. For us, most of our food is homemade and moderate in its decadence, and it includes lots of vegetables and a good mix of whole grains. I admit to putting a pat of butter in our tomato sauce and an extra sprinkle of cheese on pasta. We forgo donut shops and candy from supermarkets and instead from time to time make our own cookies, cakes, and ice cream. We stay away from processed, overly sugary, overly salty foods. We do find ourselves occasionally buying a crinkly bag of something in a rush on our way to a playground playdate. Most chefs do, too. Paul Virant, executive chef at Vie restaurant in Chicago, says he didn't want his children to have to feel different from their friends

because of the foods they were eating. Likewise, I allow Cody a big, crinkly-bagged, relatively healthy snack from time to time so he can fit it. Also, Murphy suggests that having too strict a policy leads to sneaking overindulgences.

Epps believes that restricting sugary foods during the first twelve to fourteen months sets what she calls a "near sensory response," and "if you have laid down a solid foundation with not too much exposure to overly sugary foods, children then, when they have these [sugary] foods are going to be just like kids— they're gonna try them, they will dive into the cake like the other ones, but then, they will push away from the table and go off and play. They are able to self-limit. It doesn't get out of hand." She believes that without the early exposure to candy and other overly sweet foods as a preschooler "real, real, sweet food tastes too sweet."

I find this to be true for Cody. We go for ice cream after school on hot days from time to time, and we've even eaten decadent cookie ice-cream sandwiches and make cakes and other treats, but he never overindulges. Interesting to me is that while I know he relishes every last spoonful of chocolate ice cream, he doesn't ask for it more than once a month. Further, if he asks for a treat and I say no, he's okay with that.

Epps warns, "Taste buds can be influenced by exposure. . . . It's just brain chemistry." She explains that children who have too much early exposure to foods that are continuously sweet and overly sweet can be easily triggered into craving those foods. "They experience strong cravings and will salivate at seeing them in the hands of another child or in a shop window. That's not limited to just infancy, it has a lot to do with eating disorders," she explains.

It's unfortunate to have to mention that some foods that should be so healthy and wholesome end up with chemicals and pesticides that none of us want our children eating. Dr. Charles Bembrook, the chief scientist of the Organic Center (www.organic-center .org) says that for families to limit chemical pesticide exposure, they should eat certified organic produce at least for their favorite fruits and vegetables. In summertime soft fruits and berries are better purchased as organic; in the fall, apples. I rely on the environmental working group that has a great list of produce to be wary of eating because of a potentially high concentration of chemical pesticides. Conventionally grown apples and nectarines are at the top of their list. Their list also includes cherries, peaches, pears, raspberries, imported grapes, strawberries, bell peppers, celery, potatoes, and spinach. Fruits and vegetables least likely to be contaminated with chemical pesticides are bananas, mangos, pineapples, corn, onions, avocados, peas, and cauliflower. It's often thought that peeling fruit will eliminate the pesticides from those fruits, but the flesh of a peach with its soft skin is riddled with pesticides, which is why it often tops the list of produce to avoid unless it is organic. Also consider that peeling an apple will remove about a third of the apple's nutrients.

Kids this age don't know between white bread and wheat, and instead of making chicken soup with rice—à la our favorite Maurice Sendak book—we make chicken soup with barley.

turkey meatballs with orecchiette pasta and tomato sauce

{ DIANE FORLEY }

SERVES 4-6

Making meatballs is an act of love. They are always a bit time-consuming to craft, and they require a tender patience to make them just right. I make them for Cody because he gets excited for meatballs. They are the perfect thing to have in the freezer for a babysitter to make. On nights we go out, I like leaving Cody with something he knows is still homemade just for him. So I make a double batch. Sometimes I put them in a chicken soup with pasta, chard, and a good shaving of Parmesan cheese that Cody does himself at the table.

We also love them over pasta with sauce (see my recipe at right for tomato sauce). In general, the longer you cook tomato sauce, the more the acidity mellows out and the sweeter it becomes. Here, the sauce cooks for only 20 minutes, but a caramelized red onion creates that sweetness.

Note: Orecchiette pasta is a small shell-shaped pasta that holds the sauce like a little bowl would and makes a perfect mouthful.

Meatballs:

3 tablespoons extra-virgin olive oil, divided

2 shallots, peeled and minced

3 cloves garlic, peeled and minced

Kosher salt and freshly ground black pepper

2 tablespoons water

1 tablespoon chopped fresh rosemary (or 1 teaspoon dried)

1 tablespoon chopped fresh oregano (or 1 teaspoon dried, crumbled)

½ teaspoon honey

2 tablespoons sour cream or plain yogurt

1 tablespoon Dijon mustard

1 egg, lightly beaten

2 teaspoons paprika, Hungarian sweet preferred

1 tablespoon dry mustard, preferably Colman's

1½ pounds ground turkey

¼ cup plus 1 tablespoon bread crumbs

Pasta:

1½ tablespoons salt

1 pound orecchiette pasta

Fanae's Quick Tomato Sauce:

1½ teaspoons olive oil

½ red onion, chopped

1 28-ounce can whole peeled tomatoes

½ cup tomato puree

1 tablespoon butter

8 basil leaves, optional

Salt and pepper

Pinch sugar, if needed

1. For the meatballs, heat a small skillet over medium heat and warm 2 tablespoons of the oil. Add the shallots, garlic, a big pinch of salt, and a good grinding of fresh black pepper and cook just until the oil begins to sizzle, about 2 minutes. Add 2 tablespoons water and cook until the shallots are soft and the pan dry, about 5 minutes; set aside to cool.

2. For the pasta, bring a large pot of water to a boil. Add 1½ tablespoons salt. When the water returns to a boil, add the pasta and cook until just tender. Drain.

3. In a large bowl, combine the shallot mixture, rosemary, oregano, honey, sour cream or yogurt, Dijon mustard, egg, paprika, and dry mustard and mix well. Add the turkey and season with ½ teaspoon salt and mix until combined. Add the bread crumbs and mix again until combined. With a rounded teaspoon or tablespoon, measure and scoop the mixture into small meatballs, the size of a quarter in diameter, onto a plate. You can also form by hand; keep your hands wet to prevent the meat from sticking to your hands.

4. In a medium saucepan over medium heat, add the remaining tablespoon of olive oil and brown the meatballs in batches, turning gingerly so as not to break them apart. Cook until browned on all sides; then remove them to a plate while making the sauce.

5. In the same saucepan, make the sauce. Add the olive oil or butter and the red onion and cook, stirring occasionally, until the onions are soft and lightly browned, about 5 minutes. Chop the tomatoes or squish with your hands into the saucepan with the juice from the can and the tomato puree. Stir to combine and add the meatballs back into the pan to continue cooking. Stir occasionally, being careful not to break the meatballs, and simmer for 10 minutes.

6. Add the butter to the tomato sauce. Turn off the heat and add the basil leaves; taste for seasoning and add salt and pepper and a pinch of sugar if necessary.

7. Divide the pasta into bowls; top with the meatballs and sauce.

Notes: The best way to freeze meatballs is to brown them first in the pan and freeze them half cooked. After spacing them out on a tray or plates so they are not touching, put the tray or plates in the freezer for an hour. Once set, the frozen meatballs can be placed in a freezer bag without clumping together and used as needed for up to one month. When ready to cook, add frozen to cook in the simmering sauce. An easier way to make meatballs is to turn the meat mixture out onto a long piece of plastic wrap and then form into a log. Unwrap and cut slices and form into meatballs.

boccalone sausage and beans

{ CHRIS COSENTINO }

SERVES 4

Chef Chris Cosentino has a shop in San Francisco, called Boccalone, that sells cured meats and sausages. This dish is especially good with the Italian sausage from his shop.

1 pound dried cannellini beans
Water to cover
3 quarts pork stock
6 cloves garlic, peeled and crushed, divided
1 whole carrot, peeled
1 whole fennel bulb, split
1 whole peeled onion
1 14½-ounce can plum tomatoes, chopped
1 tablespoon olive oil
1½ pounds Italian sausage links, cooked or uncooked
4–5 fresh sage leaves
Salt and freshly ground black pepper

1. Sort through the dry beans, removing any stones, then rinse under cold running water. Place beans in a large pot and cover by at least a couple of inches with cold water. Let soak for at least 4 hours or overnight. Alternatively, bring to a boil, cover, simmer for 5 minutes, then turn off heat and let rest covered for 1 hour.

2. Drain the beans and return to pot. Add pork stock, 2 of the garlic cloves, carrot, fennel, onion, and canned tomatoes. Bring to a simmer over medium heat and then lower the heat so that the beans are barely simmering and cook 1 to 2 hours, or until beans are just tender. Note that the fresher the beans, the shorter the cooking time. Remove from heat and let cool in cooking liquid. Remove the whole vegetables.

3. Heat olive oil in a large, heavy-bottomed skillet over medium heat. Add the sausage links and remaining crushed garlic cloves. Do not crowd the pan, or the sausage won't brown well. Once the sausage is brown, cut in half on the diagonal, add the sage leaves, let sizzle, then add the reserved beans in their cooking liquid, stirring occasionally until slightly thickened, about 5 minutes.

4. Season to taste with salt and pepper. Simmer a few minutes longer, stirring gently, until sausage is cooked through and the sauce has thickened. Be careful not to break up the beans.

Note: This recipe calls for preparing dried beans. However, you can skip steps 1 and 2 in the recipe by substituting 3 15-ounce cans of beans, rinsed and drained.

baby lamb chops

{ DIANE FORLEY }

SERVES 4–6

These are fast and easy to prepare for a quick dinner with children next to you in the kitchen. Chef Diane Forley recommends serving them with Ratatouille with Balsamic Vinegar, Honey, and Basil (page 55).

8 double lamb chops
Kosher salt and freshly ground black pepper
4 tablespoons olive oil

To cook the lamb, heat two large sauté pans over medium-high heat. Season lamb with salt and pepper. Add 2 tablespoons of the olive oil to each sauté pan and add the chops. Brown the lamb on all sides, turning every 2 to 3 minutes, about 7 minutes total for medium rare. Cut a small slice in the chop to check for doneness. Transfer to platter and allow to rest for about 5 minutes before serving.

spiced beef sandwiches

{ CATHAL ARMSTRONG }

SERVES 4

The meat in this recipe marinates in spices all week in the fridge but is well worth the wait. A perfect early weekday dinner: warm sandwiches on whole wheat toast spread with the sauce left in the pan and horseradish. We had pickles on the side, and Cody couldn't decide whether he wanted his very last bite to be a sandwich bite or a pickle bite. After the last bite he suggested we lie down and take a nap on the couch, but we ended up playing at the table, trying to decide if his toy dinosaurs were meat eaters—and would've liked the sandwich meat—or plant eaters.

½ teaspoon ground cloves
½ teaspoon freshly ground black pepper
½ teaspoon ground allspice
½ teaspoon ground cinnamon
½ teaspoon ground mace
1 tablespoon brown sugar
2 tablespoons salt
2 teaspoons molasses
2 pounds boneless tied rib roast of beef
6 ounces Guinness beer
Water
Horseradish, optional

1. Mix all of the spices, sugar, and salt together. Add the molasses and rub the mixture all over the beef. Place in a nonreactive container in the refrigerator for 7 days. Every day, turn and rub the beef.

2. Place the beef in a pot and add Guinness and water to cover. Bring to a simmer and cook for about 3 hours until tender but not falling apart. Let cool in the cooking liquid. When cool, remove the beef and refrigerate until cold before serving.

3. Serve with wheat or pumpernickel bread. Horseradish can be added to taste.

delicate root vegetables

{ CATHAL ARMSTRONG }

SERVES 4

It's handy to have vegetables ready in the fridge to whip up quickly on a busy night. We do a lot of roasting of root vegetables in our house, but have found that preparing them this way gives the vegetables a nice, more subtle flavor. If you're getting your vegetables fresh from the farmers' market, you may not need to add the sugar.

4 baby carrots
4 baby turnips
4 baby parsnips
Water to cover
Salt
Sugar
1 teaspoon butter
Pepper

1. Peel and cut the root vegetables into even-size chunks. Place the carrots, turnips, and parsnips in separate small pots (they have different cooking times) and cover with water and season with salt. Add three parts sugar for each part salt to the water. Bring to a simmer.

2. When tender, drain and cool the vegetables by running cold water over them. Set aside in the refrigerator until ready to serve. This step can be done up to a day in advance.

3. In a small sauté pan, warm the root vegetables with a little butter. Season with salt and pepper.

simple leafy greens

{ PETER BERLEY }

SERVES 4

"From the time they were three years old, practically daily, they've been eating leafy green vegetables, hearty winter greens from the fall through the spring and lettuces in the summer," Chef Peter Berley says of his children. We eat these all the time at our house, too. Sometimes we eat them plain like this, and other times we add them to pasta or rice with some Parmesan cheese on top. They are great on spinach ravioli that has nothing else but a light sauce of chicken stock with a bit of butter.**

1 pound winter or fall greens—chard, kale, and
    collard greens are all good choices
1 tablespoon olive oil
Salt and pepper

1. Bring a large pot of water to a boil. Wash and chop the greens, removing any tough stems. Add the greens to the water and cook until they are just a bit soft and bright green—all greens have different cooking times; chard is quick and kale takes a bit longer. They will shrink quite a bit. Don't overcook them; they should still be bright in color.

2. Once cooked, strain the greens, discarding the water.

3. Heat a large sauté pan; once hot, add the oil. When the oil is hot, add the greens and add salt. Stir and cook quickly until tender.

4. Add a grind or two of pepper, to your taste, and serve.

carrot salad with ginger

{ ANA SORTUN }

SERVES 4

Chef Ana Sortun makes this tasty salad for Siena for lunch. She suggests serving with pita bread cut into shapes, brushed with olive oil, and toasted. I made a batch to send one day to school for Cody and his friends to eat, and the bowl came back empty.

1 pound carrots, peeled and cut into 2-inch lengths
Water to cover
2 tablespoons extra-virgin olive oil
2 teaspoons white balsamic vinegar
1 teaspoon honey
¼ teaspoon ground ginger
Kosher salt to taste

1. Place carrots in a sauce pot with enough water to cover. Bring to a boil and simmer for about 20 to 25 minutes, until carrots are tender when squeezed with a pair of tongs.

2. Drain well and place carrots into a small mixing bowl.

3. Coarsely mash them with a whisk or a fork. Add the other ingredients and season with salt to taste.

curried chickpea salad

{ JOAN MCNAMARA }

SERVES 4

This dish is surprisingly good considering the ingredients are so simple, and it's a cinch to make. It's better to eat the same day, once you stir in the fresh herbs.

4 teaspoons best-quality olive oil
1 cup diced onions
½ teaspoon turmeric
½ teaspoon cumin
½ teaspoon coriander
¼ teaspoon cayenne pepper (optional)
2 15-ounce cans chickpeas, drained and rinsed
4 teaspoons lemon juice, or to taste
¼ teaspoon salt
Pepper to taste
2 tablespoons chopped fresh cilantro or parsley

1. Heat a sauté pan large enough to easily hold the beans over medium heat. When hot, add the oil to heat, then add the onion and sauté until deeply colored, about 6 to 8 minutes, stirring periodically.

2. Add the turmeric, cumin, coriander, and cayenne pepper, if using, and continue to sauté until the spices are aromatic and a bit toasted, about 3 minutes.

3. Add the chickpeas, lemon juice, salt, and pepper and cook for another 5 minutes to blend the flavors.

4. Remove from heat and cool. Store in the refrigerator, or mix in the fresh cilantro or parsley and serve immediately.

deviled eggs with tuna

{ ANA SORTUN }

SERVES 4 WITH ACCOMPANYING DISHES

Chef Ana Sortun suggests making this as part of a packed lunch along with Carrot Salad with Ginger (page 96). Assembled this way the tuna is milder tasting. For a treat use fresh tuna instead of canned.

½ cup minced celery

Large pinch curry powder

½ teaspoon paprika

1 6-ounce can water-packed tuna, drained, or 6
　　ounces fresh tuna

2 teaspoons extra-virgin olive oil

4 hard-boiled eggs, split in half lengthwise, with yolks
　　removed and whites set aside

1 cup mayonnaise or half mayonnaise/half plain yogurt

Salt and pepper to taste

Cupcake wrappers for packing in a lunchbox (optional)

1. In a small sauté pan, sauté the celery, curry powder, paprika, and fresh tuna (if using) in olive oil for about 3 minutes, until the tuna is just cooked through. Cool, drain well, and chop by hand. If using canned tuna, just sauté the celery with curry and paprika in oil until the celery softens, then combine with the canned tuna in a bowl.

2. In a small mixing bowl, mash egg yolks with a fork. Stir in mayonnaise or mayonnaise/yogurt combination and tuna mixture. Season to taste with salt and pepper.

3. Fill centers of egg whites with a heaping spoon of tuna filling and serve or pack in cupcake wrappers for lunchboxes or picnics.

cannellini and yellow wax bean salad with shaved radish

{ CHRIS COSENTINO }

SERVES 4-6

The beans in this recipe soak overnight twice, which makes them especially tender and flavorful. In a pinch, add the olive oil when you first cook them, cook the beans a bit longer, and skip the second overnight soak, says Chef Chris Cosentino. When he makes this salad, it's beautiful with half rounds of onion and large chunks of radishes; here it calls for smaller kid-size bites.

Salad:

1½ cups dried cannellini beans

Water to cover

½ yellow onion

1 celery rib

1 carrot

Kosher salt and fresh black pepper

2 tablespoons extra-virgin olive oil

⅓ pound yellow wax beans, ends trimmed

¼ cup Zinfandel Vinaigrette (recipe below)

¼ red onion, sliced and chopped into small pieces

3 red radishes, chopped small

2 tablespoons chiffonade-cut basil leaves, preferably piccolo fino verde

Zinfandel Vinaigrette:

2 tablespoons Zinfandel vinegar, or good-quality red wine vinegar

¼ cup plus 2 tablespoons olive oil

2 tablespoons extra-virgin olive oil

Kosher salt

Freshly ground black pepper

Splash of lemon juice

1. Soak the dried cannellini beans in water for 4 hours or overnight in the refrigerator. Alternatively, place beans in a pot covered with 3 inches of water, bring to a boil, cover, and simmer for 5 minutes, then turn off heat and let rest, covered, for 1 hour.

2. Drain the beans, discarding the water, and place in a medium saucepan with whole peeled onion, celery, and carrot. Cover with cold water, bring to a simmer, and let cook until tender (about 2 hours). Remove the vegetables and season beans with salt and pepper and a good helping of extra-virgin olive oil. Let cool and set in the refrigerator overnight.

3. The next day, blanch yellow wax beans in a pot of salted boiling water until colorful but still crunchy (about 2 minutes) and shock in salted ice water to stop the cooking. Remove the beans from the ice water as soon as cold. (The beans will absorb water and lose flavor, so limit the time immersed in water if possible). Once cool chop beans into bite-size pieces.

4. For the vinaigrette, pour vinegar into a mixing bowl, then gradually whisk in the oils. Once the oils are incorporated, season with salt and fresh black pepper. To help with final balance, squeeze in a bit of lemon juice.

5. Strain the cannellini beans and place in a mixing bowl with the yellow wax beans, onion, and radishes.

Season with salt and pepper to taste; then dress with the desired amount of Zinfandel Vinaigrette. Sprinkle with basil leaves. Taste, adjust seasoning if needed, and serve.

Note: This recipe makes a good quantity of Zinfandel Vinaigrette. Keep any extra in the refrigerator for up to 1 week and use it to dress any cold vegetable or leafy green salads.

spaghetti pancakes

{ MARC MURPHY }

This is a clever pancake version of macaroni and cheese. It's fun to make with kids, who always like noodles.

4 teaspoons salt
1 pound spaghetti
4 eggs
½ cup grated Parmesan cheese
½ cup grated pecorino cheese
½ cup grated Swiss cheese
4 slices American cheese, cut into quarters
Salt and pepper to taste
2 tablespoons olive oil

1. In a large pot bring 4 quarts of water to a boil. Add the salt, then add the pasta and cook until tender. Drain but don't rinse, and set aside to cool.

2. Meanwhile, mix the eggs and grated cheeses in a large bowl. Season with salt and pepper to taste and add the pasta.

3. Heat a large nonstick sauté pan on medium heat and add the oil. Put pancake-size messy scoopfuls of the spaghetti mixture in the pan and flatten each out. Lay the slices of American cheese on top and layer and flatten another smaller scoopful of the spaghetti mixture on top. When the bottom is golden brown, flip like a pancake and cook the other side, about 5 minutes a side, and serve warm.

yogurt panna cotta

{ BARBARA LYNCH }

SERVES 4

This is a simple luscious pudding made with gelatin, so it sets softly once chilled. Sometimes I pour it to set into old mismatched china teacups, but it's beautiful set into glasses with layers of fruit or compote or unmolded on a plate topped with berries. Cinnamon or other spices can be added, or it can also be served with chocolate sauce or caramel sauce.

¾ cup heavy cream
1 cup full-fat Greek-style yogurt, such as Fage Total
¼ cup sugar
¼ teaspoon pure vanilla extract
Kosher salt
1 teaspoons powdered gelatin
Fresh fruit or compote (optional)

1. In a medium saucepan, combine the cream, yogurt, sugar, vanilla extract, and a pinch of salt over medium heat just to dissolve the sugar.

2. Sprinkle the gelatin over ¼ cup cold water in a small saucepan and let it sit for 5 minutes to soften, then heat it over low heat until it becomes a clear liquid. Whisk this into the cream mixture and pour through a fine-mesh strainer.

3. Divide among 8 4- to 5-ounce ramekins or parfait glasses, cover with plastic wrap, and refrigerate until set, at least 4 hours, preferably overnight.

4. Serve the cold panna cottas garnished with fresh seasonal fruit or your favorite preserve, jam, or compote.

Note: These will hold, refrigerated and covered with plastic wrap, for 2 days.

honey roasted nuts and fruit

{ MEGAN GARRELTS }

SERVES 4

We serve this to friends, and no matter how much we make, it's gone by the time they leave. Scrape into a container before it cools completely, because it does gets stuck to the pan or bowl pretty quick once it's cooled.

2 cups mixed nuts

1 teaspoon kosher salt

½ teaspoon freshly ground black pepper

Pinch cayenne pepper (optional, for kids who like a little spice)

⅓ cup honey

1½ teaspoons fresh chopped herbs: rosemary, sage, thyme

2 tablespoons golden raisins

2 tablespoons chopped dried figs

2 tablespoons chopped dried apricots

2 tablespoons chopped dates

1. Preheat oven to 350°F.

2. In a large bowl toss together the nuts, salt, peppers, and honey.

3. Lightly spray a baking sheet with nonstick cooking spray and spread the honey-coated nuts onto the sheet.

4. Bake the nuts for about 8 minutes, until they are evenly toasted, stirring and rotating the baking sheet within the oven during the baking time.

5. Once toasted, remove the nuts from the tray and transfer back into the large bowl. Toss the warm nuts together with the chopped herbs and dried fruit.

6. Allow the nuts to cool to room temperature and serve.

7. Place the nuts and fruit in an airtight container and store in the refrigerator for up to 2 weeks.

honey ginger ice cream

{ MEGAN GARRELTS }

YIELDS 1¼ QUARTS ICE CREAM, PLENTY FOR 4
SERVINGS PLUS EXTRAS

The ginger in the ice cream is subtle, and it makes a delicious and irresistible ice-cream flavor that leaves you wanting another scoop. This is great with Chef Megan Garrelts's Sugar Cookies (page 111) crumbled on top. She recommends serving the ice cream alongside her Warm Roasted Nectarines (page 112).

1 pint heavy cream
1 cup whole milk
½ cup brown sugar
½ cup Missouri honey (or *your* favorite local honey)
1½ teaspoons freshly grated gingerroot
6 egg yolks

1. In a large saucepan, combine cream, milk, brown sugar, honey, and freshly grated ginger. Warm over medium heat to infuse the honey and ginger into the cream.

2. Place the egg yolks in a stainless steel bowl and whisk to combine together.

3. Slowly whisk the hot cream into the egg yolks.

4. Strain the mixture through a fine sieve and chill over an ice bath.

5. Once the ice cream base is chilled, process in an ice-cream machine according to the manufacturer's instructions.

6. Serve and freeze any extra in an airtight container.

milk chocolate walnut ice cream

{ MEGAN GARRELTS }

YIELDS 1¼ QUARTS ICE CREAM

Making your own ice cream with friends over beats going to the store for ice-cream cones any day. Cody and his friends hover around the mixer and watch it churn before their eyes. This was the very first ice cream Cody and I made together, and it was the creamiest and most delicious chocolate ice cream I've had.

1 pint heavy cream
1 cup milk
1 cup sugar
6 egg yolks
6 ounces milk chocolate, melted
¼ cup toasted walnuts, coarsely ground

1. In a large saucepan combine cream, milk, and sugar. Warm over medium heat until tiny bubbles are visible along the edge of the milk, next to the side of the pan.

2. Place the egg yolks in a stainless steel bowl and whisk to combine.

3. Slowly whisk the hot cream into the egg yolks.

4. Whisk in the melted milk chocolate.

5. Strain the mixture through a fine sieve and chill over an ice bath.

6. Once chilled, process in an ice-cream machine according to the manufacturer's instructions.

7. Place the churned ice cream into a chilled bowl and fold in the toasted walnuts.

8. Serve and freeze any extra in an airtight container.

banana bread

{ MEGAN GARRELTS }

MAKES 1 LOAF

This makes a beautiful, high-rising loaf that is moist and flavorful on the inside and has a delicious crisp and crunchy crust. It's not the hearty or heavy banana bread with walnuts we're all familiar with. It is a special treat when served with Chef Megan Garrelts's Butterscotch Sauce (page 110).

2 cups flour
2 teaspoons baking powder
½ teaspoon salt
2 teaspoons cinnamon
½ teaspoon cardamom
½ teaspoon nutmeg
6 ounces unsalted butter at room temperature
1 cup sugar (plus some extra for coating the pan)
2 eggs at room temperature
2 teaspoons vanilla extract
1 cup milk
¼ cup buttermilk (see page 109)
Zest from 1 lemon
2 ripe bananas, mashed

1. Preheat oven to 350°F.

2. Sift the dry ingredients and set aside. Use whisk to make sure the dry ingredients are all mixed together, and you won't get an odd bite of baking soda in the bread.

3. Cream the butter and sugar; add eggs one at a time and vanilla.

4. Add the dry ingredients to the butter mixture alternately with the milk and buttermilk.

5. Mix in the lemon zest and mashed bananas—do not overmix.

6. Butter a loaf pan, then coat with sugar by adding a tablespoon or so to the pan and shaking it around. Pour the batter into the pan.

7. Bake in preheated oven until golden brown and firm to the touch and a toothpick comes out with crumbs, about 40 to 50 minutes.

Note: Creaming the butter and sugar gives baked goods a light airiness—they will be more delicate. Start with the butter soft, at room temperature, and beat with the eggs, also at room temperature, for several minutes, long enough to create tiny pockets of air. If you've forgotten to leave your butter out at room temperature to soften, you can use your microwave. Warm the butter on low in 10-second intervals and watch it carefully so it doesn't melt. To cream, place the softened butter into the bowl with the sugar. I use a wooden spoon to crush and mix the butter together with the sugar. In the end, the butter and sugar together should be fluffy.

⋯⋯⧽ Quick buttermilk can be easily made by mixing 1 cup milk with 1 tablespoon lemon juice or vinegar, which clabbers the milk. Let the mixture stand for 10 minutes, and it will thicken and clump up a bit. I actually like making pancakes and such with the lemon juice version; it gives them a brighter flavor. White vinegar (not cider vinegar) is flavor-neutral and clabbers the milk nicely without adding any fruit flavor. If you clabber your own milk, mix it alternatively with the milk so as not to also clabber the other milk called for in a recipe.

butterscotch sauce

{ MEGAN GARRELTS }

MAKES 1 CUP

Chef Megan Garrelts suggests drizzling this decadently over her Milk Chocolate Walnut Ice Cream (page 106) or spreading it on her Banana Bread (page 108).

1 cup brown sugar
1 cup unsalted butter, cut into pieces
½ cup cream
1 teaspoon lemon juice
½ teaspoon salt

1. In a saucepan, combine all the ingredients.

2. Whisking constantly, bring the mixture to a rapid boil and cook until it is a deep caramel color.

3. Strain through a fine sieve and keep warm.

sugar cookies

{ MEGAN GARRELTS }

MAKES ABOUT 30 SMALL COOKIES

Delicate, with a hint of lemon and a satisfying crunch, these butter cookies are perfect. Make them by the sloppy tablespoon or use cookie cutters. Chef Megan Garrelts uses the dough to top her Summer Stone Fruit Cobbler with Crème Chantilly (page 114) and her Warm Roasted Nectarines (page 112).

2¼ cups flour
1½ teaspoons baking powder
1 teaspoon salt
2 sticks plus 2 tablespoons unsalted butter
1¼ cups sugar
1 teaspoon vanilla extract
½ lemon, juice and zest
1 egg

1. Sift the dry ingredients and set aside.

2. Cream the butter, sugar, vanilla, lemon juice, and lemon zest together.

3. Add the egg to the creamed mixture and mix well.

4. Add the dry ingredients in thirds, mixing each time.

5. Turn the dough out onto a piece of plastic wrap on the counter. Top with a second piece of plastic wrap and roll the dough into a flat disk about ¼-inch thick. Chill the dough until firm or store in the freezer for later use. (To store for making sugar cookies, gently roll dough in plastic wrap into an even log, about 2 inches in diameter, and store wrapped in aluminum foil or a re-sealable plastic bag in the freezer. Slice and bake straight out of the freezer, as needed, in a 350°F oven.) Bake until slightly golden, about 10 minutes.

warm roasted nectarines

{ MEGAN GARRELTS }

SERVES 4-6

These are great on their own, with a scoop of Honey Ginger Ice Cream (page 105) or with a dollop of yogurt in them. We use thick Greek-style yogurt. You can also drizzle some honey over the yogurt. Make them in the middle of the summer, when the fruit is deliciously ripe. As a special treat, make Sugar Cookies (page 111), crumble them, and sprinkle them over the top before serving.

4 nectarines
2 tablespoons brandy
¼ cup sweet white wine (or white grape juice)
¼ teaspoon vanilla extract
4 tablespoon sugar
1 tablespoon unsalted butter

1. Preheat oven to 350°F.

2. Split the nectarines in half and remove the pit.

3. Place the nectarines face up in a buttered roasting pan.

4. Mix the brandy, sweet wine, and vanilla together in a small bowl.

5. Pour the wine mixture over the nectarines (there will be some left over). Sprinkle the sugar over the fruit and dot with the butter.

6. Cover the pan with foil and roast the fruit in the oven until the fruit is tender but still holds its shape, about 30 minutes, depending on the ripeness of the nectarines.

7. Serve warm with desired accompaniments.

summer stone fruit cobbler with crème chantilly

{ MEGAN GARRELTS }

MAKES 1 9-INCH ROUND COBBLER

We make this in summer and bring it along for summer-evening picnics. Instead of making one big cobbler, we bake individual servings in cupcake wrappers in a muffin tin. This can also be made without the cookie crust for a simpler treat.

Note: **The Crème Chantilly can be made in advance and kept in the fridge for several days.**

Cobbler:

2 nectarines, cubed

2 peaches, cubed

1 cup assorted fresh berries, washed and hulled

2 tablespoons sugar (more if fruit is out of season and/or unripe)

¼ teaspoon cinnamon

¼ teaspoon cardamom

¼ teaspoon nutmeg

½ orange, juice and zest

¼ teaspoon freshly grated gingerroot

½ tablespoon cornstarch

½ batch sugar cookie dough (page 111)

¼ cup cream

¾ teaspoon ground cinnamon

2 tablespoons granulated sugar

Crème Chantilly:

1¼ cups heavy cream, well chilled

1 tablespoon confectioners' sugar, sifted

¾ teaspoon vanilla extract

1. Preheat the oven to 350°F.

2. To make the cobbler, combine the cut fruit in a large bowl and toss with sugar, spices, orange juice and zest, ginger, and cornstarch. Taste the mixture; you should be able to taste each flavor you added. Depending on the flavor of the fruit, you may need to add more spices, sugar, or cornstarch. Cornstarch should lightly coat each piece of fruit.

3. Mound the fruit mixture in a buttered and sugared cobbler dish or into cupcake wrappers in a muffin pan.

4. Cut chunks of sugar cookie dough and place on top of the fruit to cover most of the surface.

5. Mix the cinnamon and sugar. Brush cookie dough with cream and sprinkle cinnamon and sugar mixture on top.

6. Bake in the oven until the cookie dough is golden brown and the fruit begins to bubble, about 30 minutes.

7. Meanwhile, begin making the Crème Chantilly. Whip cream, sugar, and vanilla until stiff, then chill.

8. To serve, mound slices or spoonfuls of warm cobbler onto plates and top with Crème Chantilly.

big kids

DEVELOPING A PALATE

ages five to eight

Many children grow out of their fussy eating sometime between the ages of five and eight. It's common for younger children to resort to dietary quirks, such as separating foods so they don't touch on the plate and eating things like chicken and pasta without any sauce. Miami chef Andrea Curto-Randazzo says at this age her kids started to like dipping bread in olive oil and having sauce all over their pasta. She thinks children during this time "mature a little, they get a little more comfortable. . . . It's that age when they get a little more adventurous and start to enjoy food." She mentions that her daughter turned around at six years old and now loves fresh mozzarella, prosciutto, and salami. While kids are certainly a bit more adventurous at this age, some flavors will appeal to them more than others, and their willingness to try new foods may depend upon what you offer them and how you present it.

Introducing New Flavors

New York's Tabla restaurant executive chef and co-owner Floyd Cardoz says, "As children get older, it's all about making foods with contrast in flavors and texture. Not over-the-top bitter, over-the-top salty, or over-the-top spicy; you can't have all those things for kids." His children at this age began to eat things that, honestly, I don't even eat as an adult—like tripe. When they eat dim sum at a local Chinese restaurant, "they have a blast with chicken feet, snails, and clams. Things like that," he says, "my kids love them now." Celebrated Boston chef Barbara Lynch, says of her daughter, Marchesa, "She's slowly getting a palate. She still doesn't like pepper, it's too strong for her, so anything spicy she doesn't like and she loves bitter foods."

Children can begin to taste the subtleties and complexities of food, but they still prefer certain foods based on the diet they have been exposed to. "Her own palate, I don't know," says Lynch. "She's eating what we're eating. If I was cooking a lot of Indian food and Indian spices, she'd be eating that, but I don't do that often." Eric Bromberg, chef and cofounder of Blue Ribbon restaurants in New York, talks about a time before he had his own children and being with his sushi restaurant partner, Toshi: "His kids were five and seven years old and were eating raw squid and raw tuna. . . . At first it was just really startling, like,

> **"If they see you enjoying something, they want to know what it is."**
>
> —Floyd Cardoz, New York City chef

wow! That's unbelievable! And then we were thinking, well, that's what their dad gives them and that's how they learn what food is."

Five is a fun age also because, for the first time, I can just ask Cody outright something like, "Do you want some Brie cheese on your bread?" and there's a good chance he will give a straight—and even affirmative—answer without there being more complicated issues involved. It goes over better if it's something we can share. At this age, finally, he's more open, just thinks it over, and lets me know what he wants. His mannerisms and speaking patterns at five are almost like an adult's in many ways—he's descriptive and articulate.

Some children remain hesitant about trying foods and eating vegetables. Chef Cathal Armstrong, of Alexandria, Virginia, says, "From what I understand, kids don't taste food the same way we do, so if they find something offensive today, a month from now they may not. . . . Once you find things that they like, you build on it from there. If they won't eat a vegetable, try it again at a later date. Eventually they will come around to it as their palates grow and develop."

Cardoz says he tries foods repeatedly, but "I'll put it [on their plate] after they've forgotten about it."

It's important to note that chefs don't hide vegetables as purees in other foods for their children. "It's best for kids to understand food in its natural form and recognize it for what it is and eat it because they enjoy eating it and not try to trick them and play games with it," says Armstrong.

Chef and award-winning cookbook author Peter Berley says kids will just turn up their noses at

something and won't want to eat it, but there are vegetables that can be palatable for children, like broccoli and green beans because they are not bitter. "Broccoli stems especially have a sweetness to them because there is a carbohydrate in there. Peel the stalks and steam them or blanch them along with the florets. Children also love cooked onions because they are sweet." He acknowledges that children, being children, have food preferences. He lists other foods kids love: "any grain because grains are loaded with carbohydrates; anything milky; tofu, which is bland; sour tastes—they love pickles! They love lemon on things, salty tastes and sweet tastes. . . . Later they start to get into spicier foods and the bitter greens." He says you have to wait until they are ready for bitter flavors. "You can't force it on them." When his daughters were six or seven years old, "they started eating bitter greens like crazy. They ate lots of vegetables, including kale, collard greens, mustard greens, broccoli, and cauliflower."

Linton Hopkins's children also enjoy vegetables. He says, "We buy organic vegetables. . . . We try to buy what looks great and alive at the grocery store, and then with the kids I'll go and visit the farms. . . . They know the farmers, so they're proud to say, 'Hey, that kale is from Joe and Judith!' and there's a pride in eating it. . . . You have to buy the best ingredients and treat them simply, and then season correctly, not overcook vegetables. You cook them until they're just done so they're still bright green and alive and there's a little 'toothsomeness' to them. I think people don't know what to do with raw vegetables. I think

"We'll introduce aspects of the salad, like tomatoes. We'll get her to eat that. Then we'll try a piece of onion, and she'll try that. Gradually you just build the whole thing into a salad over a period of time."

—Cathal Armstrong, chef and co-owner of Restaurant Eve;
Eamonn's, a Dublin Chipper; and
The Majestic in Alexandria, Virginia

there's a real inability to approach them simply, like sautéing fennel in olive oil until it's just cooked the right way and then adding fresh lemon and parsley. It is something my kids will eat and love, but it's fresh and cooked right."

Lynch also prepares vegetables simply for Marchesa, who at six still likes to separate her foods. "If it's tomatoes, no basil on them. Maybe when she's seven she'll have basil on them."

Paul Virant, executive chef at Vie restaurant in Chicago, says that frozen vegetables are just as nutritious as fresh vegetables. Frozen broccoli, for example, is frozen one day off the farm, whereas some supermarkets have produce that, while fresh, has been off the farm for weeks. Vegetables lose their nutrients the longer they sit in trucks and on shelves.

For more challenging vegetables, like okra, Cardoz makes soup. He says his kids would never eat okra because "okra is a very hard thing to like. They tried it once and said, 'We don't like it,' and that's fine. So I made gumbo. I put the okra in there, and they ate it. They loved it. So much so, that now my eldest son loves okra."

Cooking at Home

The way chefs cook at home for their families varies. Berley cooked foods that his family found comforting and familiar—simple, healthy staples that were easy to prepare. He says kids aren't bothered by eating the same foods repeatedly because "they love repetition. . . . They don't like variety because it's scary. It's new, it's different. They think, 'Will I like this thing?' When they see the same thing that they like, it's comforting.

It's like reading children a story; they want to hear the same story every night. They know every word of the story, but they like to hear it."

But Lynch brings up an important point when she says, "If you're not cooking all the time and you're just making the basics . . . you get into a rut or a routine. So I kind of think it's important, on the weekends, just to experiment a little bit, get the kids involved."

"Kids are still kids and it has to be a pleasant experience," says Armstrong. "It's okay to battle from time to time. Once a month I'll cook something that they are not familiar with and they haven't tried before, and it's going to be a little bit of a challenge with them. For the most part I cook things I know they want to eat and maintain the dining experience as a pleasant experience." Of course chefs have a larger repertoire than most of us, and the variety of foods their children are familiar with and enjoy are also much greater than most families' handful of staple recipes.

I find Cody gets overwhelmed if we are constantly trying out too many new recipes, especially if they are exotic foods or foods that are completely out of his comfort zone. If he has had a week of eating dishes he likes, trying something new is a welcome and fun adventure.

Virant says, "One of the things that's interesting is when I cook at home it's never the same. I think that there's something good about that, and there's

> **"If kids have a bad experience with food, they are not going to eat it. My son, for the longest time, wouldn't eat shrimp because my mom made it once with extra salt. I had to convince him to just *try* a piece of shrimp, that it was not salty. And when he finally got over the fear, he started eating it again."**
>
> —Floyd Cardoz, New York City chef

something bad about that. I think that it's important for kids to have memories of certain foods. . . . My mom would make chicken and dumplings and pot roast—I can still taste those dishes, and they were always the same. I think there's something to be said for creating food memories." For him, cooking at home means improvising with ingredients on hand, and even if his children really like the meal, he can't necessarily re-create it. His wife is the one who uses recipes, so her dishes turn out the same way each time she makes them.

Food Associations

This age can be tricky because kids can make strong memorable associations with food. It's one thing to try to convince a toddler to try something; it's another thing altogether to convince a strong-willed six- or seven-year-old. Children can get ideas about food and develop dislikes from their friends or even from characters in movies and on television. I have a friend whose daughter suddenly refused to eat tomatoes, saying only, "I hate tom-ah-toes" in a pretend English accent by way of explanation. Eventually my friend discovered her daughter was modeling the behavior of a TV character who says that very thing in just that way.

I make Lynch's Japanese Pancakes (see page 154) a lot because it's a fun, fast dinner we all like. Once, however, I was trying out a different batter and a different method, using forms that shaped the pancakes into perfect circles. I didn't use the forms correctly, though. I put too much batter in, and the resulting pancakes were thick and a bit mushy in the

middle. The new batter wasn't great either. Usually I would say something like, "Well, it's not as good, but try it with sauce." We'd find a way to salvage it, because that's the meal I had prepared and I don't like throwing away food. But at this age, kids remember negative food experiences like that, and after one bad batch of pancakes, Cody doesn't want them at all anymore. I have a hard time convincing him that although something we tried one time wasn't good, it is good this time.

Fortunately, making memories with food goes the other way, too. Cardoz says cooking with kids, making foods they enjoy, like homemade macaroni and cheese, creates positive food associations.

Teaching Children the Culture of Food

At this age children are conversational, and it's likely that they are spending most of the day at school and then with friends. Eating meals together takes on more significance and becomes family time. "When all four of us are home together, it's an important time," says Hopkins, "and we sit down and talk and we share. I really believe in the etiquette of sitting down and having a meal together. Even if it's just twenty minutes." Armstrong believes in the importance of "being able to sit around the table and discuss social issues and current affairs, homework, school friends, and books." He calls it "the social notion of food," where eating a meal together is a pastime.

Executive chef at San Francisco's Incanto restaurant Chris Cosentino says, "My mother was an amazing single mom, and my grandparents were very close to us. We spent every Sunday sitting down as a family, sitting there having supper, and that's a big deal. I think that's part of our culture that's missing these days. That meal period with three generations sitting together is going away, and I think that's a sad part of our generation, missing out on that. We do Sundays at my house now, spending that time is really, really key. Without that, things backfire—you don't have that social family time."

Inspire Kids to Eat—with Enthusiasm!

"You put food on the table, they're gonna find their way," says Hopkins. But it is hard to watch your child refuse food, and it's hard to have to throw away uneaten food. Not every meal at this age will go well, and my husband likes to quote a funny scene in a *Desperate Housewives* episode where the culinarily high-minded Bree brings out a sumptuous

---

BASIC FIXES FOR COOKING MISTAKES

Good-tasting food is balanced, meaning not too sweet, salty, bitter, or sour. It is possible to fix dishes with simple additions to make them taste better. Add "fix ingredients" in small amounts, then taste and keep adjusting, if necessary.

•• Too salty: Add a bit of sugar and/or some lemon juice or vinegar (balsamic vinegar will add both at the same time).

•• Too sweet: Add salt and vinegar or lemon juice. You can also add a bit of butter or cream if appropriate.

•• Too sour: Add a bit of salt and sugar.

•• Too rich: Add a bit of vinegar, lemon juice, wine, or even tomatoes.

•• Too spicy: Add something sweet like sugar, honey, or maple syrup, or something creamy, like yogurt or sour cream, to make spicy food taste less spicy.

•• Too gamey: Add or serve with something sweet, like roasted apple or roasted squash.

Overcooked foods are inevitable from time to time in busy households where it's hard to concentrate on cooking times. And they are trickier to rescue. Meat that is overcooked won't ever become tender or succulent, but it can be made palatable. You can use overcooked meat in a soup in small pieces, or try resting very thin slices in a sauce before serving. Another option is to make a filling for something like tacos— you can add lots of fresh vegetables to contribute moisture. Whip together some chicken salad with your overcooked chicken. Puree your overcooked vegetables for a side dish or cream soup by adding some herbs and spices, cream, and/or butter. Alternatively, they can be added to a potpie or quiche.

BARBARA LYNCH is regarded as one of the country's best chefs. Her culinary empire in the Boston area includes 9 Park, named Best New Restaurant by *Food & Wine* magazine the year it opened, and she has a handful of other restaurants, a wine bar, a drink shop, a butcher shop, a modern diner, a catering company, and a cooking demonstration kitchen called Stir. She is a 2003 James Beard Award winner as Best Chef Northeast and was awarded *Food & Wine*'s 10 Best New Chefs Award. In 2009, Lynch was honored to receive the Crittenton Women's Union's Amelia Earhart Award. Past recipients include Doris Kearns Goodwin and Julia Child. Lynch's first cookbook, *Stir: Mixing It Up in the Italian Tradition,* received a prestigious Gourmand award for Best Chef Cookbook for the United States. She has a daughter, Marchesa. Lynch says, "I'm always cooking. I'm either at home cooking or we're at a gathering and I'm cooking. I make Marchesa try everything.... She eats oysters, shrimp cocktail, artichokes, and fried calamari. When she's with me in the different restaurants, with another friend, she's much more adventurous."

Chef Barbara Lynch : DEBORAH JONES

"gourmet" meal she's prepared to her family, waiting hungry at the dinner table. Andrew, her teenage son, says, "Can't we just have a hamburger and get it over with?"

Chefs inspire their own kids to eat in lots of different ways. Virant brings his family and friends to his restaurant on nights when it is closed, to cook then eat together. Lynch makes it fun for her and Marchesa to cook together and says "I got her to eat quail one night. I said, 'Look at this, this is such good chicken, this is chicken for little kids, look you can eat the whole thigh and the drumsticks.'"

Healthy Eating and Teaching Kids about Foods That Are Good for Them

Food plays a central role in children's healthy development. At this age children need to be taught not just about what healthy food is but also about not eating too many sugary foods, which profoundly impact their mood and their ability to concentrate. Kids love sugary foods.

"Taking as much sugar as possible out of the diet is important because kids already get enough sugar from other sources," says Armstrong. He is careful about the foods he buys for his household and says one of the biggest challenges as a parent is the eating habits children form outside the home. "School meals consist of sugar mixed with sugar seasoned with sugar," he says.

Lynch prefers giving her daughter, Marchesa, honey. "I love honey. I'd rather have her eat honey than mounds of sugar," she says. Sally Kravich, a natural health expert, adds that honey is actually very healthy for the body. She also suggests using a bit of date sugar or molasses or even stevia, an alternative plant-derived sweetener, instead of white sugar.

Bromberg tries to avoid serving sweet breakfasts and instead serves eggs or toast and every now and again bacon. He says, "I think there's an enormous impact to how my kids act and deal with the day based on what they're eating and how they're energized—and how they process the energy."

"It's important to get off sugar because that will create more moodiness," says Kravich. "What they all need are those fatty acids, like fish oil, that help balance hormones and calm the brain. Sugar is anti-hormone. Calcium is literally and figuratively your body's support—it emotionally supports, it keeps calmness, and it helps build bones. Dairy and fish are both good sources of calcium; almonds have calcium, too. The vegetable with the highest amount of calcium is bok choy. It is important to feed children at this age foods high in calcium, but because we can't get enough from our food, it's a good idea to also give them calcium supplements. Kids who are more hyperactive or have ADD burn calcium at a faster clip and need more calcium than the average child. The energy needs to be redirected, too, in physical activities like karate or gymnastics."

I teach Cody about the foods we're eating. I tell him proteins like beans and meats make him grow strong; vegetables, especially the green ones, make him feel good and keep him healthy; and carbohydrates like pasta and bread give him energy for running around.

ERIC BROMBERG and his twin brother, BRUCE, have built a small empire in New York's restaurant scene with their casual and eclectic Blue Ribbon restaurants, which include a sushi bar, a bakery, and a popular cafe serving American fare. Their restaurants are neighborhood favorites and have won a slew of awards. Bromberg is coauthor of *Bromberg Bros. Blue Ribbon Cookbook*. He is the father of three children: Leah, Jason, and Brett. "I love everything about food and cultures, and I'm more interested in food from different places than anything," he says. Of his children's eating, he says, "They'll taste anything, some things they'll spit out and say, 'that was disgusting,' but they'll try just about anything." Jason, Bromberg's son, says, "Sometimes the best thing is the thing that looks horrible. I remember my first time trying asparagus, I'm, like, 'Ew, I don't wanna try that!' and then, when I tried it, I found out that it was really good!" Bromberg adds, "Jason had seaweed soup and thought it was going to be gross, and he didn't try it the first time at all. And then the second time, he tried it and decided it was pretty cool. We order anything; I am as adventurous as I can be."

Eric Bromberg and son Jason at Blue Ribbon : MARY ANN MARINO

Bromberg says his children "actually often ask, 'What's good for me?' and 'What's not good for me?' . . . And we do our best to suggest that everything is essentially good for you, it's just a question of quantity. So sugar isn't bad for you, but too much sugar is bad for you. Salt's not bad for you, too much salt is bad for you. Fat isn't bad for you, it's too much of it that is." Jason, Bromberg's son, says he went through a phase in which he wanted to have strawberry milk for all his meals. "I'd never really eat anything, I'd have strawberry milk and say, 'I'm full!'" says Jason. It was a learning experience says Bromberg. "We talked about it and he chose that—that's what he wanted to eat, and we did that for a while." But then Jason got a cavity. "We just told him if he kept drinking strawberry milk, then he was going to get more cavities. . . . Something happened and he kind of learned it. It just seems to me to be a much more successful way of teaching. . . . So, I take that approach with most things." Jason, at the end of the story, proudly says, "I don't drink any type of flavored milk except for plain, just plain milk."

Children at this age can learn about the importance of reading labels at the grocery store and making decisions about what to eat and not eat, what's fun and what looks fun but isn't wholesome or healthy food.

"I'm a firm anti–high fructose corn syrup guy," says Cardoz. "I look at all my labels. We have only organic unsweetened ketchup at home, there's no Heinz ketchup. My kids are allowed to have a soda only once a week at home. . . . When their friends come over, it becomes an issue, and it gets a little hard. Instead, at home my kids drink fresh orange

"I know some parents who don't allow their kids to have any candy and with some success. They don't allow it in any form. But I think it's pretty complicated, especially when a kid isn't with you and candy is available. I think it just creates a really weird relationship. So we let our kids have, pretty much, what they like to eat, and I think it encourages them to eat other things that they don't know whether they're going to like. And they'll always, especially Jason, try anything."

—Eric Bromberg, chef and cofounder of New York City's Blue Ribbon restaurants

juice—we squeeze it ourselves. They eat fruit . . . there's always fruit in the home. And there are always vegetables. There're going to be times when they fail, and you have to let them, in moderation. You've got to help them make right choices."

Five-year-olds can be stubborn about eating, Kravich says, and sometimes a psychological way of talking works. She tells a story about a five-year-old girl she was working with. Like many young children, she had a preference for sugary breakfast cereals, and her mother had a hard time convincing her to eat things like oatmeal. "I talked to the little girl about a lot of different things, but the first thing I said was, 'Are you the mommy or is she the mommy?' She said, 'She's the mommy, silly.' So I said, 'Mommies need to

> "We're focused on food tasting good and on having the right amount of food that makes you feel comfortable and not feel sick after eating and simplifying meals at home, so there's not a conflict or a battle."
>
> —Eric Bromberg, chef and co-owner of New York City's Blue Ribbon restaurants

show you what to do so *you* can grow up to be a good mommy.'" Kravich adds that parents are sometimes too permissive with their kids, allowing their kids to determine the foods they eat without any real regulation or guidance or even allowing them to eat too many snack foods in lieu of meals for example.

Cardoz, like most chefs, stays away from fast food. His son, Peter, was seeing lots of McDonald's advertising on children's programs and wanted to eat there all the time. "We didn't cut it off totally," Cardoz says. "I felt Peter would not be too happy, and it was the right way to go about it. We cut it down tremendously. We would give it to them occasionally but not often . . . these things are not taught to kids. I feel it's up to the parent to make sure and teach what is acceptable and what is not." Cardoz doesn't buy many processed foods either and says, "Sometimes my son wants to have one of those breakfast things, Pop-tarts, that you put in the toaster oven. And we let him have that because all the kids in school are having that. We don't ban it totally. Occasionally the kids are allowed to have them."

Armstrong says what's important for him is to "maintain that they eat a balanced diet: some proteins, some carbohydrates, some vitamins, some minerals." Lynch calls herself a healthy eater, "so it's important that whatever I'm feeding myself and my husband, we feed Marchesa the same. It's important because we want to eat together." When Berley's children were young, "We tried to emphasize home-cooked food. We never told them what to eat when they weren't at home with us, so there was nothing for them to rebel against. Not wanting to stigmatize them or make them feel like there were taboos on food . . . when they were on their own they ate whatever they wanted." Armstrong points out that children at this age have a tendency to rebel against their parents, "so I've really tried not to be overly aggressive with any information I'm giving them, but just to show them."

B. T. Nguyen, chef and owner of Restaurant BT in Tampa, believes it was important to carefully nurture and develop her children's palates through their infancy and younger years because it would make them choose to eat good, healthy foods when they began to make their own decisions about eating. She says when her children were about seven or eight years old, "they wanted control over what they wanted to eat, and I gave it to them. Okay now you want to take over—go ahead. I think *you* should have that experience."

Some kids still don't eat a lot at mealtimes. "When she's full, she's full," says Lynch of her daughter, Marchesa. "She noshes all day, but it depends if she has gymnastics or lots of activities at school that day. It depends if she's going through a growth spurt, too."

PAUL VIRANT grew up in Missouri, where his grandmothers took him to the local smoke-house and farmers' market and taught him how to preserve fruit and pickle vegetables. He is the chef/owner of a restaurant just outside Chicago named Vie, which means "life" in French. He says of his restaurant, "I wanted to create an extension of my home, where people can come and enjoy good food and drink in the company of the people whom they care about. And I want them to enjoy every morsel and drop of life." His awards include being named Best New Chef 2007 by *Food & Wine* magazine. He has competed several times on the Food Network's *Iron Chef* and is the father of two boys, Zane and Lincoln.

Paul Virant and his sons, Lincoln and Zane : LINDA BERGONIA

Chef Paul Virant recommends similar strategies for feeding big kids as for little ones. As children grow and develop, they take more in from, say, a visit to the farm, and they can take on more responsibility in caring for a garden. Utensils are no longer just toys; they can handle a knife to cut their own food.

- **Mix it up. Serving a variety of foods is important, including a broad range of ingredients, flavors, and fine foods.**

- **Cook foods simply. Make a simple chicken dish and add a flavorful relish for the children to taste and the adults to enjoy.**

- **Be accommodating. It's important to take the kids' preferences into account when making meals.**

- **Teach. Exposing children to all stages of food production from seed to table is important. Take a trip to the farm or plant a small garden.**

- **Serve family style meals. Put food on large plates in the center of the table and let everyone take what they like.**

- **Get special utensils. Give kids fun forks or a special kids' knife like the Kuhn Ricon Kinderkitchen kids' knife or colorful one-piece learning chopsticks.**

Table Rules

For Virant, dinner lasts about a half hour. His table rules are to sit up straight and keep your napkin on your lap, and he still has to remind his kids frequently.

"I think the most important thing for parents," says Armstrong, "is to be confident, consistent, and patient." All chefs agree that mealtimes require patience. Taking time out for dinner is important, but sometimes children need to be reminded repeatedly about things like using utensils and staying seated.

"Our biggest thing," says Hopkins, "is you can't leave the table until you've tried at least two bites of everything. But sometimes they're just not hungry; they may have a yogurt before dinner that really fills them up. So they may just eat five or seven bites and they're done."

Lots of children need help to focus on eating. Children do best when dinner is served early. They get hungry around five and want to eat. Eating snacks before dinner is common, and Lynch limits bread before meals so Marchesa eats more of the prepared foods. Bromberg says, "We have dinnertime, and when you get up from the table and you're done, that's your dinner and then you do a couple of things and you do your homework and you get ready for bed. At bedtime you don't say, 'I'm hungry, I didn't have anything for dinner.' Ninety-nine percent of the time that gets the message across that you eat what you're hungry for and that's it. It's not just a casual thing where if you feel like you're hungry at eight o'clock when it's time to go to bed you can have another dinner. That doesn't mean that we don't have late-night snacks as well sometimes . . . like an apple or a banana. We definitely make it so they don't eat before bed, 'cause that always kind of has a rough-night's-sleep effect."

If Cody is not engaged in the cooking process, but is playing by himself, and I call him to the table and just put a plate of food down in front of him, then eating is not something he will want to do. He'd rather not be interrupted, even for meatballs—his favorite. If I connect him in some way to the meal preparation, it goes better. When he's participated, he feels he has more of a say and he's included. I find if I sit with him where he's playing and talk to him for a couple of minutes before I start cooking and tell him what I'm thinking of making for dinner, he'll wander over to the kitchen himself for a bit while I'm cooking. He'll drive his toy car over and jump up on a stool to see what's in the pan. I make room for him and let him mix, pour stuff into the pot, or grate cheese if he wants to.

"We get through the point of one kid saying, 'Oh, I hate that,' when the other two like it or he liked it last week. As long as you're not really engaged [in] that part of the conversation when they're sitting at the table anyway, then eventually they settle down, they get hungry, and they'll eat what they like or what they want," says Bromberg.

Shopping with Kids

The experience of grocery shopping with kids can be challenging. They see endless aisles stacked top to bottom with colorful bags, boxes, and jars, and it seems like a free-for-all to reach for anything they want and throw it in the basket. It's very stimulating for Cody, and in every aisle he randomly grabs

> **"We go to the supermarket together, and that's a really positive thing. We always go through the vegetable section and the meat section and the fish section, and I ask them what this vegetable is or that vegetable is and they know almost all the vegetables."**
>
> —Eric Bromberg, chef and co-owner of New York City's Blue Ribbon restaurants

things within his reach. He is constantly asking for things that look fun or that he recognizes from being with his friends. Of course he likes all the cartoons on the cereal boxes, and he doesn't understand why we buy what we buy, and it raises a lot of questions. Sometimes we turn it around and draw large pictures of animals like panda bears and elephants to cut out and put on our more homely looking breakfast cereal boxes. We make up our own names and stories as we're eating breakfast.

Chefs have an advantage because they navigate grocery stores looking for raw ingredients like vegetables and meats, or unflavored and unprocessed ingredients like pasta or rolled oats. Preparing most of their meals from scratch simplifies shopping because they can avoid the aisles of processed foods, which are usually packaged to draw the attention of children, with designs of cartoon characters and colorful pictures. "Lunchables are a very good example of marketing to kids," says Hopkins, "and I swear even now my kids walk by and they're like 'Lunchables!'

DIANE FORLEY and **MICHAEL OTSUKA** were co-executive chefs of the critically acclaimed restaurant Verbena. Forley was named one of America's Hottest Young Chefs by the *Wine Spectator* and is the author of *Anatomy of a Dish*. Forley's influences include her parents' Egyptian, Guatemalan, and Hungarian ancestry. Otsuka has a Japanese American father and a Viennese Jewish mother. He learned to make traditional Japanese dishes with his paternal grandmother. They now have bakery in Scarsdale, New York, called Flourish Baking Company. Forley and Otsuka have lots of ethnic spices in their pantry and bring foods into the house that they love to eat. They prepare foods from scratch, and they believe food should taste good. Their two children have different eating behaviors. When Otsuka used to go fishing, his daughter, Olivia, who is a super smeller and a more discerning eater, was fascinated with the fish he brought home. She'd want to look it over and touch it, but she wouldn't eat it. But Adam, their son who eats lots of different things, loves to eat fish.

Diane Forley and Michael Otsuka with daughter Olivia and son Adam : Mary Ann Marino

and I say, 'Are you kidding me? No way!' They're starting to fade away from asking that every time."

Hopkins teaches his children about foods when he helps them make selections at the store. "Avery made a choice. We usually get just plain applesauce, and she actually got the stuff with cinnamon, and I was fine with that as long as it was still all natural, organic applesauce with no sugar added. The big thing for us is a lot of added sugar. We put a cap on the number of grams of sugar a cereal can have per serving, and there can be no high-fructose corn syrup in anything. We really try to control things that way." And Hopkins adds, "I'm not the bad guy. The label is. So, if they see ingredients on the label that they don't know how to pronounce, we're not eating it."

Kravich says that MSG, a prevalent food additive and common flavor enhancer in fast foods and packaged and manufactured foods, can overwhelm taste buds. And it's true that kids who continually munch on BBQ potato chips have a hard time transitioning to more sophisticated and wholesome flavors.

Kravich points out that MSG oftentimes isn't listed on food ingredient lists as such and may be listed as "natural flavorings," hydrolyzed protein, or even simply as "spices."

"The first thing we hit is the vegetable section, always," Hopkins says. A good reason to start there is that it's so colorful. Kravich points out that kids are associative in their thinking, and if you take them to the vegetable section first, it becomes first in their consciousness. Also, she says, kids have a limited attention span, so if you're hitting the important things first, that's what they'll see. It satisfies Cody, who helps pick the vegetables and fruits that fill the basket. "Children want to participate in the process," says Hopkins, "and letting them helps them learn in little steps . . . the whole culture of going through a grocery store where kids are saying, 'I want.' You know, it's not just long lists of 'I want,' and you get everything you want down every aisle."

Cardoz allows his children to select things they want, and then they go home and cook them together.

chicken with lemon, artichokes, and parsley

{ JENNIFER VIRANT, CHEF PAUL VIRANT'S WIFE }

SERVES 4

This is a shockingly fast dinner to cook and so surprisingly good it's become part of our regular repertoire. It's equally tasty with either boneless chicken breasts or bone-in, skin-on breasts—the skin is perfectly cooked and the meat tender and full of flavor. For bone-in, simply increase the cooking time by 5 minutes.

3 skinless, boneless chicken breasts
Salt and pepper
2 tablespoons butter
1 14-ounce can artichoke hearts (packed in water),
   drained and quartered
¾ cup chopped, loosely packed Italian parsley
½ lemon, juiced

1. Pound breasts a bit so they are no more than 1-inch thick and season with salt and pepper on both sides. If using bone-in, rub salt and pepper on the skin on bottom sides.

2. Preheat a large saucepan to medium heat and, when hot, add butter.

3. Add chicken to the pan to brown smooth-side down or skin-side down if using bone-in. Cover with a lid, and cook for about 5 minutes, or an extra 3 minutes longer for bone-in.

4. Flip chicken over, add artichoke hearts, and cover again to cook for another 3 minutes, or an extra 5 minutes for bone-in; then add the parsley and lemon juice. Cook uncovered for 1 minute more and serve.

braised chicken with farro, tuscan kale, tomatoes, and parmigiana reggiano

{ PAUL VIRANT }

SERVES 4

This is made in one pot—a true masterpiece dish, both beautiful to serve and deeply satisfying to eat for a nice stay-at-home dinner. The chicken is succulent, and the skin gets perfectly crisped. It feels like a very elegant meal, even though it is quite simple to make.

Note: Farro is a healthy whole grain that can be found at Whole Foods or similar markets. It has a hearty, rustic, nutty flavor and is served like rice.

4 chicken leg and thigh quarters
Salt and pepper
¼ cup plus 2 tablespoons extra-virgin olive oil
1 sweet onion, sliced
7 cloves garlic, sliced
2 teaspoons sweet smoked paprika
¾ cup farro
1 tablespoon chopped thyme
1 cup Italian white wine (Pinot Grigio)
¼ pound Tuscan kale, stems removed, leaves chopped small
1 cup diced tomatoes
3 cups chicken stock
2 tablespoons chopped Italian parsley
Parmigiana Reggiano

1. Season legs and thighs with salt and pepper. Over medium-high heat brown the chicken in ¼ cup olive oil in a Dutch oven, about 5 minutes per side. Remove chicken to a plate. Add onions, garlic, and paprika to the Dutch oven and cook a few minutes.

2. Preheat oven to 350°F.

3. Add farro and thyme, cook another minute. Add white wine; bring to a boil and cook until the liquid has reduced and its flavor has concentrated. Add kale and tomatoes, cover, and cook for 5 minutes.

4. Place chicken back in the pot, add chicken stock, bring to a boil, and place in the oven. Cook uncovered for 45 minutes in the oven, until the farro is done and most of the liquid has evaporated.

5. Remove from oven and add parsley and remaining 2 tablespoons of olive oil; season with salt and pepper.

6. Arrange farro and Tuscan kale on a serving platter, place chicken on top. Garnish with a generous amount of grated Parmigiana Reggiano, and serve.

chocolate fillet of prime beef

{ JIMMY SCHMIDT }

Chef Jimmy Schmidt uses certified Angus beef, which is a premium meat that boasts superior flavor and tenderness. He suggests a simple melted chocolate sauce.

For adults, try sautéing half an onion and some garlic in butter, then adding half a cup each white wine and water, reducing, then adding the chocolate and seasoning with salt and pepper.

Steaks:

1½ teaspoons natural cocoa powder
½ teaspoon sea salt
1½ teaspoons sugar
4 fillets of prime tenderloin of beef, about 4 ounces each
1 teaspoon safflower oil

Glaze:

4 ounces milk chocolate, melted
Chocolate milk as necessary for consistency

1. Preheat broiler on the lower setting, about 460°F.

2. Mix the cocoa powder, salt, and sugar together in a bowl. Rub the steaks with safflower oil and then roll the steaks in the spices to coat all surfaces lightly. Tap to remove any excess.

3. To make the glaze, melt chocolate in a small pan over very low heat. When melted add enough chocolate milk to make it into a sauce.

4. Place the steaks in an ovenproof pan and put under the broiler. Cook until seared but not heavily browned, about 6 minutes. Turn over and continue to cook, approximately 4 minutes for medium rare, depending on the heat of your broiler and thickness of your steak. Remove the steaks from the oven, brush with glaze, and let rest for a couple of minutes.

5. After the steaks have rested, cut into easy-to-eat slices and arrange in a fan on a serving plate; drizzle the remaining sauce over them.

kaffir lime leaf shrimp

{ B. T. NGUYEN }

Kaffir lime leaves are incredibly fragrant, and the use of them removes any fishy smell from the shrimp. I like making this with kid-size shrimp. Serve these shrimp with rice. This recipe calls for using sugar cane sticks as skewers. It's delicious to chew a bit on the skewer, and the heated sugar cane releases a burst of sweet juice, says Nguyen. We get them at the local farmers' market, where they sell fresh sugar cane juice, but it can be found canned too. Sugar cane is loaded with essential nutrients and has many health benefits. While eating refined white sugar zaps energy, sugar cane boosts energy and is actually healthy to eat. You can also use bamboo skewers.

6 fresh whole Kaffir lime leaves
1 tablespoon finely chopped garlic
1 teaspoon palm sugar
1 teaspoon pepper
1 tablespoon roasted sesame seeds
2 tablespoons pure sesame oil
2 tablespoons fish sauce
20 shrimp, peeled and deveined
4 7-inch lengths sugar cane sticks or bamboo skewers

1. Mix Kaffir lime leaves, garlic, palm sugar, pepper, sesame seeds, sesame oil, and fish sauce in a bowl; set aside.

2. Skewer 5 shrimp onto each sugar cane stick; brush shrimp skewers with Kaffir lime mixture and refrigerate for 2 to 3 hours.

3. Grill for 3 minutes on each side. (Do not overcook shrimp, or they will get chewy.) Serve with a vegetable of your choice.

sweet ginger baked tofu

{ PETER BERLEY }

SERVES 4

Cody likes this flavorful tofu a lot. We make a bunch to keep around to put in salads, have for lunch, or snack on after we've been running around. This can be served simply as an accompaniment with cold soba noodles or cut up and simmered in miso soup. If your kids are resistant to trying something new, like tofu, try to engage them in a guessing game about the ingredients. What do they taste—ginger? Honey? Sesame?

1 pound extra-firm tofu
¼ cup soy sauce
¼ cup rice vinegar
¼ cup apple cider or apple juice
2 tablespoons sesame oil or olive oil
2 tablespoons honey
1 small clove garlic, minced
1½ tablespoons minced fresh ginger

1. Preheat oven to 375°F.

2. Slice tofu ½-inch thick. Lay the tofu between two clean cotton dishtowels. Put a plate on top and a weight on the plate (a couple of cans of beans or tomatoes will do). Set aside for 15 minutes.

3. Whisk the remaining ingredients together in a bowl.

4. Lay the tofu snug together in a single layer in a rimmed baking pan. Pour on the marinade and bake on the middle shelf of the oven for 30 minutes or until the tofu is well browned and the marinade has been absorbed.

broccoli with olive oil and sea salt

{ BARBARA LYNCH }

This is how Chef Barbara Lynch makes broccoli for her daughter, Marchesa. Adding good-quality olive oil and specialty salt to the vegetables makes them especially delicious. It's also a good basic preparation for other vegetables like carrots, cauliflower, and green beans. You can quickly cook a small handful of vegetables this way for an easy kid-size vegetable snack or to put in a lunchbox. Vegetables can be steamed if you have a steamer or quickly blanched in boiling water. The trick to the recipe is to use good ingredients and to cook the vegetables just right so they are still bright in color and either just cooked through or with a bit of crunch still in them, depending on your preference. Young children will enjoy drizzling the olive oil and sprinkling the sea salt. It may help get them to take that first bite.

2 heads broccoli, chopped into small florets, stems peeled and chopped
2 tablespoons best-quality extra-virgin olive oil
Good-quality sea salt

1. Steam the broccoli until just cooked through and remove to a serving plate.

2. Drizzle the olive oil over and sprinkle with sea salt.

Note: Traditional *fleur de sel* is a type of hand-harvested sea salt from France that imparts a flavor much better than that of regular table salt. Specialty salts have different shapes and have a bit of a welcome and surprising crunch. Fleur de sel has a higher mineral content than table salt and smells like the sea. It dissolves quicker than regular salt and is sprinkled on food just before serving. Try some on chocolate ice cream!

broccoli and cheese curds

{ PAUL VIRANT }

SERVES 4 AS A SIDE DISH

Cody liked both the cheese and the broccoli but started to separate them, saying that he liked them apart. It sparked a conversation about the way things go together and that sometimes things taste better together. We talked about BLTs being tastier because the flavor of the bacon mixes in with all the other flavors in the sandwich, like the juicy tomato and crispy lettuce. I asked him to take a mixed bite and tell me what he thought. He agreed that the cheese was good together with the broccoli.

1 tablespoon butter
½ pound broccoli (fresh or frozen), cut into florets
    and stems chopped
Salt and pepper
¼ pound cheese curds (preferably from Wisconsin)

1. Preheat oven to 400°F.

2. Heat the butter in a 10-inch skillet (preferably cast-iron) and add frozen or fresh broccoli.

3. Cook on medium-high heat until the frozen broccoli is warmed and any water evaporates. If using fresh broccoli, cook for about 3 minutes, add 1 tablespoon of water, and cover to steam for 3 to 5 minutes, until the broccoli is tender.

4. Season with salt and pepper, sprinkle curds on top, and bake for 10 minutes. Serve.

Notes: Fresh cheese curds have a mild, slightly milky flavor and a characteristic "squeak" when eaten. Unfortunately, cheese curds rapidly lose their freshness, and they should be eaten very quickly.

winter gratin of potato, onion, and cabbage

{ PETER BERLEY }

SERVES 4

We like serving this with sausage. It's not rich or fancy—it makes a great casual meal. The potatoes get tender and a bit sweet from the onions, and the cabbage is a bit tart. I usually don't go for bread crumbs, but these I find myself picking off first to eat, just like Cody.

4 slices sourdough bread, cut into small cubes

¼ cup extra-virgin olive oil, divided

1½ teaspoons unsalted butter

1 cup thinly sliced onion (about 1 large onion)

2 garlic cloves, finely chopped

1½ teaspoons caraway seeds

Pinch red pepper flakes

Sea salt or kosher salt

1 pound potatoes, peeled and thinly sliced crosswise

Freshly ground black pepper

¼ small head green cabbage, halved, cored, and sliced crosswise ⅓-inch thick (about 3 cups)

½ lemon, juiced

½ cup vegetable or chicken stock or water

¼ cup finely grated Parmesan cheese (about 2 ounces)

¼ cup coarsely grated Gruyère cheese (about 2 ounces)

1. Set a rack in the middle of the oven and preheat to 200°F. Spread the sourdough cubes out on a baking tray and bake for 10 minutes or until dry, tossing halfway through. Remove from the oven and let cool. Crush with your hands to break up into crumbs.

2. Turn oven up to 400°F.

3. Warm 1½ teaspoons of the olive oil and the butter in a small straight-sided ovenproof skillet, preferably cast-iron. Add the onion and cook, stirring occasionally, until lightly browned, 5 to 7 minutes. Add the garlic, caraway seeds, red pepper flakes, and pinch of salt, and cook, stirring, for 1 minute. Transfer the mixture to a bowl.

4. In another large bowl, toss the potatoes with 1 tablespoon of the olive oil, and season with ½ teaspoon of salt and a generous grinding of pepper. In a third bowl, toss the cabbage with 1½ teaspoons of olive oil, lemon juice, and a pinch of salt.

5. Layer half the potatoes in the skillet. Layer in half the cabbage, then half the onion. Repeat, finishing with the onion. Pour in the stock or water.

6. In a bowl, toss the bread crumbs with the remaining olive oil and both cheeses, and season with salt and pepper.

7. Spread the bread crumb mixture over the vegetables. Place the pan over medium heat and bring the liquid to a simmer.

8. Cover and transfer to the oven and bake for 35 minutes. Remove the cover and continue to bake until the vegetables offer no resistance when pierced with a fork and the topping is crisp and golden, about another 5 minutes. Let the gratin rest for 5 to 10 minutes before serving.

spicy tomato soup with crispy grilled cheese

{ BARBARA LYNCH }

SERVES 6

This is a delicious early weekday dinner or rainy-day lunch—the grilled cheese sandwiches are great for scooping up bites of soup. These sandwiches are a bit more work, but they are so delicious they are worth it! If you like your sandwiches extra crispy, cook them a bit longer.

Soup:
2 tablespoons extra-virgin olive oil
1 small onion, sliced
1 pinch crushed red pepper flakes (up to ½ teaspoon more if you want it spicy, as I do)
2 28-ounce cans plum tomatoes
1½ cups water
¼ cup fresh basil leaves
Kosher salt and freshly ground black pepper

Grilled Cheese:
Good country, French, or Italian bread
8 tablespoons (1 stick) unsalted butter, at room temperature
½ pound mozzarella cheese

1. To make the soup, heat the olive oil in a large, heavy saucepan over medium heat.

2. Add the onion and red pepper flakes and cook, stirring occasionally, until the onion is tender, about 7 minutes.

3. Add the tomatoes and water and cook, stirring occasionally, for 30 minutes.

4. Add the basil, season lightly with salt and pepper, and let cool briefly.

5. Puree the soup in a food processor, in batches if necessary, and pass through a fine-mesh strainer, pressing the solids with a ladle. (Save the pulp, if you like; though it has no place in this soup, it's great on crostini or baked eggplant.) Keep the soup on medium-low heat if you plan to serve it right away.

6. To make the grilled cheese, stick the bread in the freezer briefly; it will be easier to slice when cold and firm. With a serrated knife, cut the bread into 12 exceedingly thin slices—as thin as you can without making the bread fall apart.

7. Melt the butter in a skillet over medium heat.

8. Heat the oven to 400°F. Have ready two heavy baking sheets of the same size so that one can nestle into the other. Line one with a sheet of parchment paper.

9. Slice the cheese thinly. (How thin is not as crucial here, as the cheese melts so thoroughly that it practically disappears into the bread.)

10. Brush 6 of the bread slices with the melted butter and lay them butter-side down on the parchment-lined baking sheet. Top each with a single layer of cheese and then top with another slice of buttered bread to make sandwiches.

11. Put the sandwiches on the prepared baking sheet, leaving some space between them. Cover the sandwiches with a piece of parchment and stack the second baking sheet on top of the first; this will cook the sandwiches on both sides without the need to flip them and will also flatten them a bit.

12. Bake until the sandwiches are golden brown and crisp, 15 to 20 minutes.

13. Carefully peel away the top layer of parchment, transfer the sandwiches to a cooling rack, and serve warm or at room temperature. If there are any ragged bits of baked cheese hanging off the sandwiches, just trim them away by hand; you'll want to eat these, so go ahead.

sweet red pepper linguine

{ JIMMY SCHMIDT }

This is a great dish for children who prefer very plain foods. The colorful pepper stays nicely crunchy. Sprinkle cheese on top at the table. We like serving this cold for lunch, and we use a bit less Parmesan cheese.

Sea salt

¾ pound linguine (whole wheat or high fiber preferred)

3 red bell peppers, cored and cut into fine julienne to mimic the size of the noodles

4 tablespoons unsalted butter, melted

½ cup grated Parmesan cheese, divided

1. Bring a large pot of water to a boil. Add 1½ tablespoons salt. When the water returns to a boil, add the pasta and cook until just tender.

2. Add the red peppers to the cooking pasta for 1 minute to warm and slightly soften. Scoop out a cup of pasta water and set aside. Drain the pasta and peppers into a colander and transfer to a large bowl. Add the melted butter and half the Parmesan, tossing to coat well. Adjust the seasoning with salt as necessary and add some of the pasta water if the pasta is dry.

3. To serve, twist the noodles into a mound in the center of each plate. Sprinkle the rest of the cheese on top at the table.

penne with bacon, peas, and lemon

{ JENNIFER VIRANT, CHEF PAUL VIRANT'S WIFE }

SERVES 4

Like all kids, Cody loves bacon, and in this dish, three of his favorite foods are brilliantly combined. Try adding mint or parsley at the end and sautéing vegetables like broccoli, asparagus, sliced brussels sprouts, or Swiss chard in the pan with the bacon fat before adding the peas.

Salt
¾ pound penne pasta
½ pound bacon, about 4 thick slices, diced
1 shallot or ½ onion, chopped
¼ cup olive oil
Juice and zest, grated, from 1 lemon
1 cup frozen peas, thawed
Salt and pepper

1. Bring a large pot of water to a boil. Add 1½ tablespoons salt. When the water returns to a boil, add the pasta and cook until just tender.

2. Meanwhile, cook the bacon in a large straight-sided skillet, and when crisp, spoon off all but approximately 1 tablespoon of the fat from the pan. Add the shallots or onions and cook until tender, about 5 minutes.

3. When the pasta is tender, before draining, scoop out a cupful of liquid and set aside. Drain the pasta.

4. Add the olive oil, lemon juice, and lemon zest to the pan with the bacon, scraping and mixing in the browned bits off the bottom of the pan.

5. Immediately add the drained pasta and the peas to the pan, stirring to combine.

6. Season with salt and pepper and add a splash of the pasta liquid if dry, and serve.

delicate ricotta gnudi

{ BARBARA LYNCH }

SERVES 4

Gnudi **are the light, cloud-like cheese fillings of ravioli made to be served without their pasta sheath. Here they are prepared with a bit of flour—making them easy to work with and a great way to introduce kids to making their own pasta. They go well with lots of sauces, including a simple one of butter and sage. They need not be perfectly shaped to be tasty, so have some fun! They can be stored for several days or frozen.**

½ pound ricotta, drained if very wet
¼–½ cup all-purpose flour, plus more as needed
1 large egg, lightly beaten
3 tablespoons finely grated Parmigiana Reggiano
2 teaspoons kosher salt
¼ teaspoon freshly ground white pepper

1. In a large mixing bowl, combine the ricotta, ¼ cup flour, egg, cheese, salt, and pepper. Use a wooden spoon to mix ingredients together well.

2. Lightly flour your work surface and a baking sheet for holding the shaped gnudi. With floured hands, knead the ricotta mixture briefly; it will be quite wet and sticky at this point. Dump the mixture out onto your work surface.

3. Cut off a piece of the gnudi dough and try rolling it into a ¾-inch-thick log. If you can't get it to roll, add a little more flour to the dough and try again. You want as little flour as possible to keep these together so the resulting gnudi will be light and ethereal.

4. Cut the log into 1-inch pieces and then roll into little balls. If you have a gnocchi board, hold it at a 45-degree angle over your floured baking sheet and roll each ball down the length of it to give the gnudi grooves. As the gnudi nears the end of the board, let it drop onto the baking sheet. If you don't have a gnocchi board, hold a fork, tines facing down, and roll the ball down the length of the tines. Repeat until all of the dough is rolled and cut.

5. Freeze the gnudi, about 1 hour. (Because they are so soft, they are much easier to handle frozen, so do this even if you plan to use them soon.)

6. To serve, bring a large pot of well-salted water to a gentle boil. In batches, drop the gnudi into the water and cook until they float, about 1 to 2 minutes. As each batch cooks, remove gnudi with a slotted spoon and keep them warm or transfer them directly to the sauce they are being served with.

creamy risotto-style brown rice with spring greens and asiago

{ PETER BERLEY }

SERVES 4–6

Try this recipe instead of risotto. It's healthy and delicious. We often make a big batch to serve when Cody's friends stay for dinner.

Sea salt or kosher salt

9 ounces mixed spring greens, such as tatsoi, baby mustard greens, lamb's quarters, and arugula (about 9 cups)

1 tablespoon extra-virgin olive oil

1 large bunch scallions or ramps (wild leeks), trimmed and thinly sliced (about 1 cup)

1 teaspoon finely chopped garlic

2¼ cups cooked brown rice, preferably basmati, from 1 cup raw rice

1 tablespoon unsalted butter

2 ounces finely grated hard Asiago cheese (about ½ cup), plus additional for serving

Freshly ground black pepper

1. Bring a large pot of water to a boil. Add about 1½ tablespoons of salt and return to a boil. Add the greens and blanch until they are just wilted, about 1 minute. Use a spider or slotted spoon to transfer the greens to a colander and let cool slightly; reserve the cooking water.

2. Press the greens to remove excess water, then transfer them to a board and chop roughly.

3. In a large skillet over medium-high heat, warm the olive oil. Add the scallions, garlic, and a pinch of salt, and cook, stirring, until softened, about 2 minutes.

4. Stir in the rice, chopped greens, butter, and 1½ cups of the reserved cooking water and cook, stirring, over medium-high heat, until the water is almost absorbed, 3 to 4 minutes. Stir in the cheese and season with salt and pepper.

Note: Do not use fresh Asiago cheese; it's unpleasant when melted in this dish.

japanese pancakes

{ BARBARA LYNCH }

"I make Japanese pancakes, which are a Japanese crepe almost," says Chef Barbara Lynch. "I put raw shrimp, uncooked broccoli, carrots, and kale in the batter—all raw, but it actually cooks in the pancake. I make them because they are little snacks for me, and Marchesa absolutely loves them. I think she loves them because they are round. She gets to use her chopsticks, which she loves, and we dip them in a little soy sauce. It is always fun to serve with chopsticks!" If you have pancake rings, use them to make perfect circles or other fun shapes but don't make them too thick. And if you're looking for something a bit less salty than soy sauce, try the dipping sauce I created below, which is slightly thicker and has other flavors to temper the soy sauce.

Pancakes:
1 teaspoon canola oil for skillet
1 cup all-purpose flour
½ cup water or Japanese dashi broth
1 egg
1 cup grated cabbage or pureed yam
Pinch table salt
Dash white pepper
¼ cup raw kale, stemmed and chopped small
¼ cup grated carrots
¼ cup finely chopped scallions
¼ cup boiled and chopped shrimp
Dash hot sesame oil
Pinch cumin seeds

Dipping sauce (such as a good soy sauce or make your own tangy sauce, such as Fanae's Homemade Dipping Sauce)

Fanae's Homemade Dipping Sauce:
½ cup Worcestershire sauce
¼ cup sugar
¼ cup soy sauce
¼ cup ketchup
1 tablespoon Dijon mustard
½ teaspoon ground allspice

1. Heat a skillet over medium heat. When hot, add oil.

2. Make the pancake mix by combining flour, water or dashi, egg, cabbage or yam, and salt and pepper.

3. Sprinkle the vegetables and shrimp into the batter and add sesame oil and cumin seeds (to taste).

4. Pour ¼- to ½-cup portions into the skillet. Cook pancakes, flip to finish cooking.

5. To make Fanae's Homemade Dipping Sauce, combine Worcestershire, sugar, soy sauce, and ketchup in a small saucepan. Cook over low heat, stirring, until the sugar is dissolved and the mixture reduces a bit. Stir in the mustard and allspice. Cool and serve, or store for several days, refrigerated.

6. Serve pancakes with dipping sauce.

wild rice soufflé

{ DIANE FORLEY AND MICHAEL OTSUKA }

I love the exotic, earthy flavor of wild rice. Baked as a savory and sweet loaf, it is a perfect food for anyone wanting to eat whole grains and avoid gluten. You can serve this warm next to a main dish, but its flavor really comes out when it's cooled off. We eat toasted slices for breakfast when it's cold and wintry out.

5½ cups water, divided

¾ cup plus 2 tablespoons wild rice, divided

½ teaspoon salt

¼ teaspoon allspice

¼ teaspoon ground cloves

¼ teaspoon nutmeg

½ teaspoon coriander seed

2 tablespoons grits, polenta, or cornmeal (whole grain is best)

1 teaspoon butter

Salt and pepper

½ cup raisins or dried cranberries

3 eggs

1. Heat 3 cups water and ½ cup wild rice in a saucepan and bring to a boil. Add salt, turn the heat down low, and simmer, uncovered, until soft, about 45 minutes. When the wild rice is tender, drain any remaining liquid and set aside, covered, until ready to use.

2. Meanwhile, in a coffee grinder or spice mill, grind the remaining wild rice and the spices together until dry and powdery. Place in a bowl and blend in the grits, polenta, or cornmeal.

3. Heat 2½ cups water in sauce pot until just about to boil. Slowly whisk the ground wild rice mixture into the hot water. Turn the heat down to low and continue to stir intermittently until the mixture thickens into a porridge, about 20 minutes. Turn off the heat and stir in butter. Season with salt and pepper and taste, adding more salt if necessary; it should taste a tiny bit salty.

4. Pour the porridge mixture into a large bowl and mix in the cooked wild rice. (This mixture can be stored in the fridge to continue the next day.)

5. Preheat oven to 375°F and thoroughly butter a medium-size loaf pan.

6. Add the raisins or cranberries to the wild rice mixture and stir to combine.

7. Separate the eggs, placing the whites in a medium-size metal bowl and the yolks in a small bowl. Beat the yolks with a hand mixer on high or whisk until thick and pale, about 3 minutes, and then, using clean beaters, beat the whites on high until they have soft, glossy peaks, about 2 minutes.

8. Gradually mix egg yolks into the wild rice mixture, stirring throughout, then fold in beaten egg whites.

9. Scrape into the buttered loaf pan and bake until a toothpick comes out clean and the soufflé is browned on top, about 60 minutes. Remove from the oven and let rest for 5 to 10 minutes. With a knife, loosen the soufflé from around the edges of the pan before removing. The soufflé can be served warm or, once cool, stored in plastic wrap.

savory waffles

{ LINTON HOPKINS }

SERVES 4

"One thing my kids really love," says Chef Linton Hopkins, "is when it's raining outside at lunchtime and we make a batch of savory waffles. Instead of sugar and syrup, we just fold in Parmesan and Gruyère, if I have some sitting in the refrigerator, and salt and pepper. We use that as a complement to a bunch of soups, like tomato soup. We have a waffle iron that has shapes of animals and a barn, so I ask my kids, 'Do you want to be the pig today? Or the chicken? Or have a cow?'" If you have some sliced ham, you can fold the waffle and make a fun ham sandwich with the waffle as the perfect crispy bun, and in springtime you can add sautéed and chopped asparagus to the batter.

Try adding herbs and other seasonal produce, like pumpkin puree, to the batter instead of cheese. Hopkins makes his waffles from scratch, but you can use your favorite ready mix. We like the multigrain mix from Bob's Red Mill.

2 cups waffle and pancake mix

2 eggs

2 cups milk

2 tablespoons vegetable oil

Salt and pepper

¾ cup grated good Parmesan cheese

½ cup grated Gruyère or similar cheese

1. Preheat oven to 200°F and place a waiting plate to warm inside. Heat a waffle maker until a flick of water beads and bounces around.

2. Prepare the waffle mix, adding eggs, milk, oil, salt, and pepper, and mix until just combined, adding more milk if the mix is too thick. It should be the consistency of pudding. Then fold in the cheeses.

3. Lightly butter the waffle maker and spoon judicious dollops of the mix onto the center of the hot waffle iron and spread just a bit. The mix will spread when the lid closes and expand as it cooks, so adding too much will be a bit messy as it bubbles out the sides.

4. As the waffles finish, use a fork to lift them off and put them in the oven to stay warm while the rest are made. Waffles are best served warm. Freeze any leftover waffles to enjoy later.

chickpea panisse with carrot ginger butter

{ PETER BERLEY }

SERVES 4

Peter Berley says *panisses* are a perfect snack for kids. Spread with the Carrot Ginger Butter and topped with toasted almonds, they are especially delicious. You can also simply dust them with sugar or for adults sprinkle them with salt and cracked black pepper. Sometimes we add cardamom and cinnamon while the chickpea flour is cooking, and mix in a teaspoon of honey before it cools.

You can make fingers and bake them as below or cut into rounds. You can also try frying them in ¹/₂ inch of hot oil (put them in when snakelike patterns appear in the oil). Whichever way you decide to make them, serve right away.

Panisses:
1 cup chickpea flour
2⅔ cups cold water
¾ teaspoon salt
3 tablespoons butter
Vegetable oil
1 tablespoon olive oil
½ teaspoon salt
⅓ cup sliced almonds (optional)

Carrot Ginger Butter:
12 ounces carrots, peeled and thinly sliced
2 cups plus 1 tablespoon water, divided
2 teaspoons peeled and finely chopped ginger
¼ teaspoon sea salt
1 tablespoon honey or light brown sugar
1 tablespoon lemon juice
Sea salt and freshly ground white pepper

1. To make the panisses, combine the chickpea flour and water in a bowl and whisk until smooth. Strain the mixture through a strainer into a heavy medium saucepan to remove any lumps. Add the salt and butter and cook over high heat, whisking continuously, until the mixture is smooth and thick. Reduce the heat as low as possible and simmer, covered, for 20 minutes.

2. Uncover and whisk again until smooth. Pour into a 7 x 11-inch baking dish or a 10-inch pie plate and refrigerate until set (about 40 minutes). This can be done up to 3 days ahead. Store in the refrigerator sealed with plastic wrap.

3. Meanwhile, begin making the Carrot Ginger Butter by combining carrots, 2 cups water, ginger, salt, and honey or brown sugar in a pan and simmering, covered, until tender. Uncover the pan and cook until liquid has evaporated.

4. Preheat oven to 375°F.

5. Transfer the carrot mixture to a food processor, add the lemon juice and 1 tablespoon water, and puree. Season with salt and white pepper.

6. Lightly brush a heavy baking sheet with vegetable oil. Spread the sliced almonds on a separate ungreased baking sheet and toast in the oven for about 7 minutes, watching carefully so they don't burn and stirring once midway.

7. Meanwhile, run a thin knife around the edge of the panisse and unmold onto a cutting surface. Slice into bite-size squares or rectangles or cut with cookie cutters. Transfer the shapes to a large bowl and brush (or gently toss) them with 1 tablespoon olive oil.

8. Spread the panisses over the prepared baking sheet and bake for 20 minutes until crisp and golden.

9. After cooling slightly, spread each with Carrot Ginger Butter, top with the toasted almonds, and serve immediately.

adolescence

THINKING AND EATING FOR THEMSELVES

ages eight to eleven

Eric Bromberg, chef and co-owner of New York City's Blue Ribbon restaurants, says that at this age his kids will try almost anything. His children are as curious and bold as he is about tasting different foods, though they still initially display the kind of hesitancy and trepidation that most kids will. Most of the chefs I interviewed have cultivated a culinary curiosity and openness in their children, and their children easily and confidently rattle off their likes and dislikes, their knowledge about ingredients, and even simple cooking strategies. They can instantly discern quality and freshness and articulate it in detail. Bromberg's son, Jason, says excitedly that he likes when chicken is roasted with mushrooms tucked under the skin.

When his children were younger, Floyd Cardoz, chef at New York's Tabla Restaurant, embraced cooking more traditional family meals. At their present ages he cooks an extensive repertoire at home for family meals, including pasta with truffles and osso bucco, and even interesting side dishes like a salad with pine nuts, olives, and anchovies.

Focusing on Nutrition

The focus of all chefs with children this age is trying to manage nutritional balance for their children. At eight, children are still moody about food and go through phases of coveting favorite foods.

"It's important to recognize the parents' role in teaching and educating the kids about food, about society and social aspects," says Alexandria chef Cathal Armstrong. "I really try to maintain that they eat a balanced diet—some proteins, some carbohydrates, some vitamins, some minerals. Just consider a balanced diet and not worry too much about 'Well, we had broccoli yesterday, we can't have broccoli again today.' If it's a vegetable they like and will eat, give them more of it."

Armstrong's daughter, Eve, who was a hesitant eater during her preschool years, now enjoys a broad culinary repertoire. She especially loves eating fish and meat. Favorite family dinners include roast chicken, roast pork, and ribs. Armstrong says she is still at times reluctant to try new foods, but a patient approach does eventually bring her around.

> "My children have a really good relationship with food—that's the point. They know how to enjoy it, they know how to prepare it for themselves, and I'm just really grateful for that. The legacy I can leave them is that you can really nourish yourself."
>
> —Peter Berley, New York City chef and award-winning cookbook author

Both of Josiah Citrin's children pick through their meals, separating and reassembling what's on their plate for themselves. Citrin, chef and owner of Los Angeles restaurant Melisse, considers himself lucky, though, saying, "My kids like eating healthy things—they like eating broccoli, they eat carrots, and they eat salad every night." His approach is to give them the foods they like to eat, like Mexican food or Korean food, but to make sure the foods are flavored authentically and not Americanized, and also that they're made with quality ingredients.

"Real food's the most important thing," says Linton Hopkins, chef and owner of Atlanta's Restaurant Eugene. "I don't change the way I think about food—being at home or being in the restaurant." His approach is to get ingredients both local and fresh, putting them together in simple ways. Flavor comes from the ingredients he selects, enhanced with careful preparation and the addition of simple sauces. The food is regionally traditional in its ingredients and made from scratch.

About cooking at home for his family, Hopkins says, "I really don't try to 'gussy up' the food by putting too many ingredients in—as a professional cook, I've learned that more and more I'm pulling items out of a dish and making a recipe that's under five ingredients—I'm just trying to select the best of those ingredients. So that roast chicken really tastes like roast chicken. I just maybe squeeze some lemon on it at the table; I use citrus fruit a lot in cooking because we want to have that good acid balance." Roasting a chicken is easy, and he says, "I think my total prep time on roasting a chicken is about two minutes. I turn on the oven and put a chicken in an iron skillet with salt and roast it for forty-five minutes."

Hopkins speaks warmly of growing up with home-cooked meals prepared by both his mother and his grandfather, Eugene. Chef and cookbook author Peter Berley expresses a similar sentiment when he says, "What became the most important thing was eating together as much as possible—we were completely dedicated to eating dinner together. That was like a rock—we ate dinner together all the time, every night." Every chef I interviewed agrees: Family time at this age is important, and so is eating well together.

It's much easier to get your kids to sit at the table and eat, and to eat well, if you started when they were young. If you started at the beginning, feeding them vegetables, talking to them about healthy foods, and sitting with them together at meals, then at this age, these things are part of their routine.

Healthy Strategies for Picky Eaters

Citrin says that at his house, his wife limits after-school snacks and then will steam broccoli for their children before dinner. "We always start them off with the vegetables before as an appetizer, so they eat them when they're hungry," he says.

Chef Jimmy Schmidt did start early feeding his children healthy foods, but his oldest son, Michael

Blu, is still a picky eater. Schmidt, chef at Rattlesnake restaurants in the Midwest, attributes this to his highly developed sense of smell. "So to a foreign smell, his immediate response is, 'this is weird.'" Of the vegetables he likes, he prefers them raw to cooked. "I'll be making dinner, and he'll come in and say 'That's stinky. It smells like rotten eggs. He's right—there are sulfides in asparagus." Sulfides are also in broccoli, cabbage, onions, peppers, cauliflower, brussels sprouts, rutabagas, and turnips. "It's been tricky since he was a baby," say Schmidt. "He didn't like pureed peas or other vegetable purees. He'll eat cooked carrots, but he prefers them raw; most vegetables he prefers raw. Cauliflower is blander, and I'll use purple and orange cauliflower, which he thinks is cool looking."

Citrin says of his children, "They weren't as picky in the beginning, and then they got picky." Augustin, Citrin's son, will taste anything in the kitchen while playing chef in the restaurant during the prep hours, but it's hard to get him to eat a whole meal, says Citrin. But Augustin likes the artichoke soup at the restaurant, as well as the crab cakes and the onion soup. He also likes caviar and sautéed *foie gras* with pineapple—a gourmet treat that is undoubtedly a perk of owning a restaurant.

Both of Citrin's children enjoy eating salads, broccoli, carrots, turkey sausages, and pea soup, but neither likes cooked tomatoes. He incorporates foods they like into new dishes with other foods, and he cooks at-home variations of dishes they like from their weekly outing to their favorite local Korean barbecue restaurant. Citrin says, "That's why I eat at Manpuku once a week. They eat everything. He loves

that place. He eats the beef. I don't know what it is about that place." There his son adores the seaweed salad, the avocado rolls. He loves the daikon and purple carrot salad so much that the waiters bring him a plate of it as soon as they see him coming in the door.

Fitting in with Food

This is an age where friends are important, and so is fitting in and being cool. It's an age of secret codes and inside jokes and made-up languages, and kids have a strong need to belong. Eating cool things is part of that, and no kid wants to feel weird. Virant says he doesn't want his children to go to a friend's house and feel like they are the "weird" kids because they don't eat what their friends eat. "Food's kind of a cool thing. And my oldest daughter just did a report for class on Japan and food in Japan. She did it on her own, and at first she was kind of embarrassed and scared because she thought all the other kids were gonna think it's gross to eat octopus and fish eggs. It turned out everybody liked it—her eyes were opened, and she was like, 'Wow, that was really cool!'"

Bromberg thinks his openness in allowing his children to eat freely what they like "promotes them to eat other things that they may be hesitant about trying" He says he prefers his children not to eat things like candy, but, "I think it's pretty complicated, especially when your kid isn't with you all the time and candy is available. I think it just creates a really weird relationship." It's a trade-off, he says.

Bromberg calls himself an experimental eater, and his kids have learned to follow suit. "We'll go to Chinatown and they'll eat jellyfish," he says of his children. "I mean, some things they'll spit out and say that was disgusting, but they'll try just about anything." Jason, Bromberg's son, tells me, "Sometimes, the best thing is the thing that looks horrible." He mentions asparagus as an example of something he initially thought of as "ew" but turned out to be "really good." "It seemed like that seaweed soup was disgusting, but then when I tried it, it was delicious," he adds. Bromberg explains that the first time, Jason didn't try the soup at all. Then the second time he did try and decided it was pretty cool. Bromberg says, "We order anything, and I'm as adventurous as I can be. I love everything about food and cultures. Whenever we go somewhere, we try and focus on the foods that are native to that region. We're in a restaurant that's on the ocean, so we should have things that come from here that are in the ocean, and likewise when you're at a Holiday Inn in Iowa, you don't necessarily want to have the shrimp cocktail!"

Exposing his children to real eating is important, and he says, "Maybe it's silly, from an economic point of view, but if they want to eat a lobster when we're out to dinner at a restaurant, we let them order a lobster, and the three children share it." He says, "If that makes it a positive dining experience in a restaurant for them, then it makes more sense to me than if they have the kids' hamburger and fries or fried chicken fingers and fries."

Palates expand with age, and Schmidt's son continues to open up to new foods. Schmidt helps that process along. He says, "I use different types of sea salt for different dishes. I also use flavored sea salts

with herbs and stuff in them. My children don't pick up on it, but they are getting a broader flavor profile." Schmidt says of Michael Blu, "As he gets older, he learns to navigate his senses better. His eating will expand when he's able to assimilate unusual smells or new smells and associate them with foods that actually taste good to his palate, like fish. We don't put any pressure on it." Schmidt says Michael Blu is "setting his own pace on how he's expanding his food." He will try foods his friends like to eat and will come home asking for foods his friends say they like eating. At this age kids are acutely aware of what is going on with their friends and classmates. "It's his opportunity," says Schmidt, who makes sure those opportunities are taken advantage of. "I do collect their feedback, like with Michael on his aroma issue. You got to look at it from his perspective—is there something else here that's triggering this effect? Then I try to expose them to new things."

Engage Kids in the Process and Preparation
Making the kitchen the family zone is a good way to engage kids with cooking, too. Even limited participation connects them to the food. "Usually they're doing their homework right there on the sort of bar/ledge next to the stovetop and see us cooking," says Hopkins. "I made a curry, and Avery wasn't a huge fan of the smell, but she actually liked the flavor."

Buying fruits and vegetables at the store is not as deeply gratifying and rewarding as picking them yourself. Being out in a field, seeing how vegetables grow and picking them yourself, is a way to open kids

JIMMY SCHMIDT is a three-time James Beard Award winner and owner of the Rattlesnake Club restaurants in Denver and Detroit. Celebrated chef, restaurateur, food scientist, and innovator, he focuses on traditional cooking methods to create simple, rustic, and healthy dishes. His numerous awards include the James Beard Award for Best Chef Midwest, *Wine Spectator*'s Award of Excellence and *Gourmet* magazine's America's Top Tables and America's Best Restaurants. Schmidt is also involved in developing nutritional products for athletes who need to eat efficiently for stamina and focus and has his own products, LifeForceV and Life2Go. He has also served as the director of sports nutrition for GM/Corvette Racing and has coordinated catering services for the "24 Hours of Le Mans" race in France since 1999. He is the father of three boys: Michael Blu, Jasse Sonic, and Cadet Bar. He says of feeding his family, "The big thing at the end of the day is that food is seasonal and as pure as possible—it's not manufactured—it doesn't have ingredients in it that you don't know what they are."

Jimmy Schmidt : MARSHALL WILLIAMS

JOSIAH CITRIN uniquely crafts his menu at Melisse, his refined French restaurant in Santa Monica, with seasonal finds from the local farmers' market. He left an early career as a tournament surfer to travel to France and learn to cook. Melisse earned two stars from the Michelin guide, #1 for Top Food in Los Angeles (2006, 2008, 2009) and #1 American-French Restaurant for Food in Los Angeles (2003–2010) by Zagat Guide, Four Stars by Mobile Travel Guide (2001–2009), *Wine Spectator* Best Award of Excellence (2001–2008), and Top 40 Restaurants by Gayot .com since 2006. Citrin has a son, Augustin, and a younger daughter, Olivia. Augustin has a discerning palate and can be vocal about his disappointments. Citrin finds himself teaching life lessons like, "When the bacon's overcooked, it's overcooked, it is what it is—part of life." He says, "I wait for the day when I can go to a 2-star and 3-star restaurant in France with my kids. Or a bistro and order *tete de veau*—I think I will get that day with them, they'll get there."

Josiah Citrin in the kitchen at Melisse : MARY ANN MARINO

up about vegetables so they become more than foods on a plate they are being pestered to eat. A small child might try spinach and other greens if told those foods are what make their favorite superhero strong, but older children need more intellectual stimulation and hands-on involvement. Schmidt tells a story about when Michael Blu visited his grandparents who live in Northern Michigan, where he went wild-blueberry picking. While he liked blueberries before, his earthy experience picking them himself made them more delectable. They also go every fall as a family to local orchards to pick apples. They eat them right there off the tree, crisp and sweet. "We try to hit as many local farms to experience it. We go to different farmers' markets to see different fruits and vegetables and they try things."

Virant makes a ritual winter jaunt into the forest with his children to see the sugar maple trees tapped for making maple syrup. They hear a naturalist talk about the syrup-making process and visit a little hut to see sap for the syrup boiling down in an iron kettle over a crackling wood fire. At home, they make hot cereal and use that syrup.

Simple Home Cooking

Hopkins says the methods of home cooking are a lot simpler than cooking in his restaurant. He explains the difference this way: "At Restaurant Eugene, we'd take a chicken and make chicken four ways on the same plate—we'd get the breast that we would have sautéed and then bring it up in like a bucket poach, and then we'd have the skin that we'd take off and recrisp so we'd have a sheath of chicken crackling,

and then we'd make confit from the leg to pack in ravioli, and then we'd have a reduction of sauce from the bones and the gizzards and the liver that would be the sauce. So, it's a much different intent at home; I'm not going for that kind of flavor. At home you don't have that team of cooks and that time, so at home it's being able to know how to roast a chicken." He says, "I really don't spend more than thirty minutes. Roast chicken, for example: It's two minutes to get that chicken in the oven. I know that the meal itself will take forty-five minutes, but to put on a pot of rice, to get the chicken roasting in the oven, and then clean the salad greens and have a vinaigrette, my total prep time is probably twelve minutes. And then I just wait for the chicken and the rice to finish and then plate up is another five."

He explains his methods: "What we'll do at home is take the roast chicken and we'll eat all the meat off in one night. Then I'll make a stock from those bones while I'm cleaning up from dinner, and then we'll have chicken soup and rice the next day. So, we try to make things using methods to get multiple meals from one item and not have a culture of throwing foods away. My kids love how when we buy a roasting chicken, we'll pull the liver out and just fry that up and eat the liver. They see us do it first—we don't throw it away. I really don't think of a food as gross, in its raw state—and my kids see that philosophy around food; they are raised in our culture of food. So instead of using just the bottoms of the leeks, we use the tops and make a leek broth. And then we incorporate the stocks as much as we can. We incorporate the

JIMMY SCHMIDT ON NUTRITION AND HEALTH FOR CHILDREN

"The refined carbohydrates (white pasta, white rice, white bread, or anything made with refined white flour or white sugar) are not very nutritious—they're not good for you. Technically what they do is spike your blood sugar to high levels that cause your body to dump insulin into your bloodstream. Your blood sugar spikes first, then crashes. There's no doubt gyrations in blood sugar and insulin are the source for diabetes—a great concern.

"At this age my children are so active, they are not storing fat, any of them—they are converting all their food into running around and growing. My kids are super lean. My focus is getting the protein and the carbs in them because they're so active. Protein should be an important part of kids' diets—meat, eggs, dairy, cheese, chicken, steaks, roasted pork. But if you look at what kids eat—the pizza, the pasta, the french fries—you start to add up a whole lot of carbs and not a lot of protein. It is also relative to their mood, their energy levels, and how often they get colds and get sick. Amino acids are the building blocks of proteins; they're real essential nutrient components that kids can't always assimilate in food easily, especially if they have picky diets.

"Trying to get everything in your bloodstream to fire most efficiently is pretty hard to do. Balanced blood sugar is essential, and the low glycemic index is the more stable environment for it. Kids have more stable energy too when they eat low-glycemic foods—they don't run into crashes, or mood swings. For Le Mans, where they have twenty-four-hours-straight car racing, I do their whole menu to specifically keep them away from refined carbs, because if you see a driver eat a candy bar after he's been up fourteen or sixteen hours, his blood sugar spikes, insulin kicks in, and he will be sleeping over a tire, and it will kill him.

"When I cook at home, if I use butter, I use really good butter, but everything is in moderation. I cook a lot of things in olive oil. I use jellies that are made with cane syrup instead of high-fructose corn syrup, and I use organic peanut butter. My kids eat a reasonable amount of whole-protein pastas like those from Bionature. Sometimes I add in vegetables; I'll julienne the zucchini so it looks like the pasta, just a different color. At the end of the day, the big picture is that I'm serving food to my children that is seasonal, as pure as possible, and not manufactured—it doesn't come from a box and have ingredients in it that you don't know what they are."

stocks in everyday cooking—I really believe that helps with flavor."

To make the stock, he says, you take the leftover roast chicken and bones and you put it in a pot with just enough water to barely cover it, and you've got a stock in an hour. When cooking at home, he says he thinks about making things spicy that he likes but his children are hesitant about. "If I do a sauté like a stir-fry of chicken, I'll put fresh peppers like serranos or little Vietnamese chiles on the side for my wife, Gina, and me to fold into our meal. We do put Tabasco and Crystal hot sauce on the table, which my children love putting on their eggs. We want them to start slowly in adding that sense to their taste."

Bromberg takes a similar approach to home cooking. He says, too, that he cooks simple things at home and mentions roast chicken and sautéed spinach. Some nights he says are just vegetarian—good rice and beans or grains. About roast chicken, he says, "It's the simplest thing to do, and it's not like red meat, where it has to be cooked properly and it's no good when it's reheated. Also, you can make an awful lot of things out of a roast chicken! And if you have it already cooked, it's a breeze."

Hopkins says, "Mostly at home it's vegetables as a side dish. So it'll be this tomato fondue, and then there'll be a big sauté of some bok choy we picked up at the market, and then there'll be a bowl of rice and then our protein and then maybe a little sauce."

One way chefs manage to cook their meals so efficiently is by having some foods prepped and ready to go. Hopkins says, "It's really trying to roll your basic prep into multiple meals. . . . Sometimes we'll

roast a chicken, and that'll become chicken salad. Or that leftover roast chicken becomes shredded into a pasta the next day." That kind of cooking comes from experience. It saves time because meals are not started from scratch, and it is much more economical. Starting meals from scratch every day is not only time-consuming, but it's also much more expensive.

I was given the *Joy of Cooking* as a gift by my mother-in-law when I first got married, but I didn't cook much then. I learned to cook when we had Cody and became a family. Family cooking is a much different sport than cooking for, say, a dinner party or a meal for two at home. Learning from the chefs interviewed in this book, I am a much more efficient cook, and I see beyond one meal in my cooking. I buy and make a whole chicken instead of just the breast or thigh so that I can have leftovers. I am creative with prepped foods and use them as ready ingredients in making meals, and don't just reheat the same dish the next day, which nobody really wants. When I do buy just chicken breasts, I buy and cook a couple of extra.

Hopkins also cooks strategically. "For example, when we make tomato sauce, we'll make a big batch that's enough for two or three meals, and then we can freeze leftovers if we don't want to eat it the next day," he says. Dinner in the summertime is fast, he says, because, "we're really out on the grill a lot."

It's true that cooking fish or steak on the grill can be very easy and fast. Lots of chefs mentioned using the grill to cook summertime meals. If you're starting with very fresh fish or meat, it takes only a bit of seasoning and technique to make it delicious. Hopkins says he also resorts to simple things like a

FLOYD CARDOZ was born in Bombay and is executive chef and co-owner with restaurateur Danny Meyer of Tabla in New York City. He is the author of *One Spice, Two Spice*, where he shares many personal stories and his unique cross-cultural blend of Indian and French cuisines. He has two sons, Justin and Peter. He says of dinners at home, "We always have greens with our meals, like a few weeks ago I made osso bucco—real osso bucco. But I couldn't figure out how to get the vegetables in it because the dish was so different, so I made a green bean salad. I know my kids love olives and pine nuts, so I put olives and pine nuts and anchovies in the salad, and they enjoyed it."

baked potato and salad night. He lists risotto and stir-fries as other simple family meals that he loves making at home. He says, "My wife doesn't like when we do breakfast for dinner, but occasionally I love that. I've got some bacon and eggs lying around and some toast, so it can be very quick!"

Citrin says he keeps *queso fresco,* the Mexican cheese, around that his children like. He makes a quick meal of corn tortillas with rice and beans, some chicken, and the queso fresco. I make tacos for Cody and myself for dinner out of almost anything—leftover slow-roasted beef is very satisfying in a taco.

Also, it's worth investing in some simple tools to help with prep. A proper cutting knife that is sharp will be a lot faster to use when chopping vegetables like carrots or potatoes than struggling with a small paring knife. Hopkins says, "The speed that professional cooks work at is unknown at home. . . . I can clean/break down an entire kitchen at home in ten minutes. All dishes, all done, in the dishwasher, sink clean, oven wiped down, done." While sometimes I like the slow meandering pace of cooking and cleaning after a hectic day, I learned from Hopkins that when I am focused and organized, I can be much faster and more efficient at getting meals cooked, dishes done, and all put away. Sometimes, it works out that I can clean everything up the last ten minutes while dinner is cooking and before I even put out the food.

Eating One Family Meal

Schedules are hectic at this age. Citrin admits that his date night with his wife and his son's guitar lessons have interrupted the ritual of their special Monday cooking nights. At every age the family dinner table changes, but all the chefs interviewed for this book agree about the importance of sharing meals and social time together. "I have breakfast or lunch together with my daughter every Tuesday. I take her to John O'Groats," says Citrin. They also have ritual weekly family outings to Manpuku, their favorite local Korean barbecue.

At home, even though eating preferences can differ for every member of the family, it is more important than ever at this age to share a collective, if not a cohesive, meal. "We try to find the perfect meal for our kids as opposed to saying 'this is our family meal,'" says Armstrong. Meals that work for

"I remember celebrity chef Jacques Pepin saying that he didn't have any food rules at the table, but you know, as a parent, how can you have that? There is always some kind of rule that comes out of your mouth. A big rule is what ingredients are allowed in the house—that seems to be the biggest rule. And before you get seconds in anything, you have to have eaten everything at least once. You have to eat that first plate completely. Also, you can't leave the table until you've tried at least two bites of everything. They may eat just five or seven bites of something and they're done, the portions are smaller. Look at the size of their stomachs, they're just smaller. Also, the kids set the table. That's a thing in our house. They have to get the napkins, the glasses of water, and the knife and fork. Gina, my wife, teaches them about it—what side the fork and the knife and the spoon go on. You can't just throw the napkin on the table at the place setting; it goes on a certain area on the place setting. There are so many lessons around the table that are just great. No one just dives in until we say a little blessing together. Thanks for our food, and then we begin. We pass and share, and that's the sort of culture we want to teach our children."

everyone can be constructed by using simple strategies like serving sauces and condiments on the side and offering foods family style so each person can select the foods she prefers.

"The whole attitude of 'I don't want that for dinner' is off-limits at our house. . . . They get input. We'll talk about it ahead of time, when we go to the farmers' market on a certain day, and we'll give them some money, and they'll go pick some things up so they're proud to bring home those vegetables that they bought. And I think that's a great way to include them in the choices," says Hopkins. "Our priority is making sure they're included in the raw food choices, like, 'Hey! Do you want to have spinach tonight or asparagus?' We frame it in a question like that."

Armstrong agrees and says, "I think it's important to feed kids what they want to eat." He says his kids enjoy eating vegetables because he initially introduced them patiently in small amounts.

Cooking with and for Kids

Chefs' kids begin cooking for themselves through curiosity. They see their parents playfully mixing, combining, and tasting, and they want to do it, too. They experiment: "Why don't we just take a little of this and a little of that . . . this is how you cook. I've learned that cooking is what happens between the lines of a recipe. If you just put me in a space with ingredients, I'm gonna come up with forms and shapes from those ingredients," says Hopkins. And he adds, "I find having a sauce in your food really helps. You know, a little pan drippings left over from the roast chicken to put on your rice. I'll make simple little meals like chicken with mushrooms and will bring the stock around and actually create a sauce."

His daughter, Avery, at eight years old enjoys sauces on her foods, too, to spread on and to dip into, and she began making her own concoctions. "Avery calls it 'cobbydo'—a little sauce she made," says Hopkins. "I just let her go to the refrigerator with a little ramekin and she makes a soy, Worcestershire, and mustard mayonnaise. Because it has soy in it, she calls it a 'Chinese cobbydo. . . .' We'll have roast chicken, so she'll dip her chicken into it, and it's really good! It's great with fish; you can use it on salmon, too."

And his son tries new things with food, too. "There was a period with my son where'd he'd just chop everything up together and mix it into this weird mash, a horrible looking . . . indescribable thing," Hopkins explains. "He did it once with a Mexican meal with tortillas. It turned into something horrid, and he couldn't eat it. We teach him not to just junk it up too much on the plate."

Hopkins believes in foraging for the best ingredients and then cooking them simply. "I'm an ingredient-based cook, and we try to really be an ingredient-based household," he says. To teach his kids, he says, "We don't go the store with recipes, saying, 'This is what we have to get.' We have certain staples and go-tos, our vegetables, and our meat, and bread we get from our own bakery. Let's just get the good ingredients in the house and then we'll just cook. If I have a little flour and cornmeal around, we'll make little johnnycakes, or maybe I'll just have cornmeal and fold in a little butter to it. I always have buttermilk in my refrigerator—it's a great thing for the whole world of quick breads and for folding into soups. Kids love little pancakes and quick breads—they are always a hit. So we have cast-iron skillets and griddles going all the time. I'll have some ground pork, and we'll have citrus fruit, always, on hand. I love having mustards and coating chicken before it goes on the grill. Buttermilk's always a great marinade. We really try to celebrate the ingredients."

An important role parents can play in that part of their children's education is to get them to participate in meal preparation. "I always get the kids involved in making the dinner," says Armstrong. "Picking the herbs, peeling the garlic, chopping the garlic, and things like that—with a garlic crusher, not with a knife; they are not ready for knives yet. I think it's really important to be involved in the preparation of the meal and the cleanup of the meal, because it develops good habits and good sensibilities in general," he says.

Josiah Citrin adds, "When I make fish with breading or something, then it's good 'cause my children can help me do it." Bromberg points out that stoves are awkward things for kids even at this age, and he tries to do things away from the stove.

"One of the tremendous things about the kids participating in cooking is the participation starts with this comment: 'Turn the television off. Let's go work in the kitchen,'" says Armstrong. "Just get them to participate in something with their mother or father, just that part itself, is really important."

What's a "No"?
"Nothing's a 'no'—not even McDonald's," says Citrin. "It's a balancing act, and I don't want to have any no's, because no's just lead to—sneaky." His approach has been to build a repertoire of healthy foods his children enjoy, like Dover sole with lemon; lemon chicken that he broils; pork cutlets with lemon on them, a particular favorite; and turkey chili.

LINTON HOPKINS opened Restaurant Eugene, named for his grandfather, with his wife, Gina, who is the restaurant sommelier, in 2004. His menu reflects his strong ties to local farmers, with dishes that combine his traditional Southern upbringing with formal French techniques and showcase his knack for culinary experimentation. He was one of *Food & Wine*'s Best New Chefs in 2009 and was also nominated in 2009 for a James Beard Award for Best Chef Southeast. He is the father of a son, Linton, and a daughter, Avery. He says of his children, "They are raised in our culture of food, that's how they think about it. You know, they take the lead from us without a doubt. . . . Of course, in our household, we talk a lot about food."

Linton and Gina Hopkins, daughter Avery, and son Linton : BEALL & THOMAS PHOTOGRAPHY

Fast food is a big issue for chefs' families. It embodies the antithesis of the kinds of food and appreciation for food that they embrace. "We need to know about why we don't go to McDonald's," says Hopkins. "I love cheeseburgers, so I'll cook cheeseburgers at home. I don't believe cheeseburgers are bad for you. Good meat and real cheese and bakery bread, that's good for you. I teach that distinction about what is bad food and what is good food."

Armstong says of his children, "Their friends go to McDonald's, and my children say, you know, we just don't eat that. I would tell them, don't be rude about it; there's no reason to be offensive about it—my children just won't eat anything that comes from McDonald's. They know what's in it, they know what the truth is, and they won't eat it."

It's tricky, Armstong admits, because there's definitely a tendency for children to rebel against the ideas of their parents. "So I've really tried not to be overly aggressive with what we are feeding them or with any information I'm giving them," he says. "But just to show them. They are well aware of the effects of industrialized mass-produced sugars on the well-being of children across the nation. They know about

it. They've seen it in the media, too. It's not just Dad on another crazy rant."

Cardoz says, "I tell my kids what's in food. I tell them how it's processed. I tell them to read labels. My eleven-year-old reads labels on boxes himself now."

Armstrong and his wife are particular about snacks for the kids because they are mostly packaged foods, frequently loaded with ingredients like chemicals and refined sugars. He admits no child wants to eat "health food," and his strategy is to seek out healthier options like fruit leathers without chemicals and preservatives. "They don't have snacks available to them that are not healthy. They don't drink soda, but we use soda as a good reward, like if we are on vacation somewhere, they are allowed to have soda. Other than that they don't drink soda, and they are not that interested in soda." Of his kids Berley adds, "We never had soda in the house—ever. We never bought soda—it just didn't exist. Maybe they had soda when they were outside with their friends. They didn't have it at home."

Schmidt believes children crave sugary snacks, candy, and soda when they eat a lot of refined carbohydrates, and that moderation comes from not eating a lot of refined carbohydrates like white flour, white sugar, white rice, and low-protein white-flour pasta. He explains that when you eat refined carbohydrates, you burn through them, your sugar level drops, and you immediately crave more carbohydrates. He says that it takes four or five days of cutting back on eating refined carbohydrates for the body to assimilate the proteins and such differently, and then you won't crave those foods any longer. He keeps his children on a diet of low-glycemic foods and says of his kids, "They like their sweet stuff, but neither of them has a sweet tooth—they'd rather have fruit than a big chocolate cake or something like that."

When Hopkins makes biscuits, he uses lard, because as a Southerner, raised on biscuits, that's what belongs in biscuits. He says, "It's just a matter of, is it good lard? Were these happy pigs? My definition of good food is—well, ice cream is good for you. I don't really see a problem with real cream with farm eggs. We don't really serve dessert with our meals at home, but I have no problem with real ice cream or real cake or real cookies. I like my milk to be a single ingredient—on the back of the carton it reads 'milk.'"

Lunches—The Lure of Nuggets

"A kid will not eat broiled chicken every day," says Bromberg, "but she will eat nuggets five times a week!" Bromberg admits that lunches are complicated for him because at school the food is generally unhealthy, and while his children like eating some of the things served at school, some they don't. It's a balance, and he lets them choose. "Sometimes Jason likes triple-decker ham and cheese sandwiches with the crusts cut off. We make him those. My daughter, Leah, if she doesn't like her lunch, she just doesn't eat it. She'll come home from school, she'll say, 'I'm starving.'"

Bromberg's approach is to let them choose what they're going to do while offering guidance. His children read the school lunch menu that's published for the week, and together they focus on choosing the

B. T. NGUYEN is one of Tampa's most talented and best-known chefs. She sums up her culinary approach in three words: authentic, healthy, and fresh, and her hip French Vietnamese restaurant reflects her sensibilities, using local sources. She has a daughter, Trina, and a son, James. She says, "My daughter grew up in the restaurant business. We started as a very small restaurant, and I took Trina with me since she was a baby—she's always been around food. Her good eating habits started when she was young."

B.T. Nguyen and son James : Norman Batley

school lunches the kids like without too much focus on the nutritional aspect, because Bromberg recognizes that lunches in school are a social function. His children want to participate with their friends. Bromberg says, "They're in school and that's what's going on and they need to sit with everybody and go through the line. . . . There's a lot of peer pressure for so many things, and food is definitely one of them, especially because they all eat together as a group in school. There's only a small list of things on the school lunch menu that Leah will try."

Chef B. T. Nguyen says of her daughter, Trina, "She started packing her own lunch. But she wants to be cool. Like anybody she doesn't want to be controlled by her mother in what she eats. But she finds that the food at school is not good—it's canned food or frozen food. Her palate is extremely sophisticated. She eats raw oysters, raw tuna. She wants her beef medium rare. She really loves food. As much as she's trying to be cool, to fit in."

"For breakfasts, we kind of make it a variety of stuff," says Bromberg, "but we don't generally go for muffins and cakes and that kind of breakfast, because they kinda get really hyped up and then before lunch happens at school they're falling asleep or running around, crazy."

"You know people ask me about when my son used to have a peanut butter and jelly sandwich for school every day for lunch. That's what he used to like to eat. People say, is it true? Doesn't he get sick of it? Yeah, he liked that . . . it was a good peanut butter and a good jelly," says Citrin. He packs his kids school lunches. "I give them what they like," he says. "Today

SALLY KRAVICH is one of the leading natural health practitioners in the country. She holds a Master of Science in holistic nutrition and is currently completing her Ph.D. Her background spans a lifetime of studies, and she combines extensive global studies, firsthand experience of historical and cultural remedies, and a vast knowledge of food as medicine to support clients on the path of wellness and healthy living. Her unparalleled career provides guidance for uniting body, mind, and spirit. Widely regarded as an authority on health, vitality, and wellness, Sally's advice has been cited in *Harper's BAZAAR, W, Essence,* and many other magazines. She has been featured as a nutritional expert for pregnancy with Aleta St. James on NBC's *Dateline.* Her specialized programs integrate practical wisdom with modern methods for achieving vibrant, radiant health. Her approach is outlined in her book, *Vibrant Living: Creating Radiant Health and Longevity.* She also has a DVD series and is working on a cookbook for preparing fast, easy, healthful, delicious meals.

•• Use sauces. **"I find having a sauce in your food really helps,"** says Chef Linton Hopkins. He explains that at his house a little pan drippings left over from a roast chicken spooned on a side dish of rice goes over well. Sauces provide that delicious umami flavor to foods and can be a bit rich or a bit sweet.

•• Feed them when they are hungry. **Kids tend to eat what's put in front of them more when they are hungry—not overly hungry but hungry.**

•• Set a timetable for dining. **Children need consistency in general, explains Chef Cathal Armstrong. He says that schedules are really helpful when raising children. Dinner is at six o'clock. It always has to be ready at six o'clock. He finds that when something's happened and dinner is pushed back, it's too late; his children are really too hungry, and they get cranky, making dinnertime difficult.**

•• Control snacking. **If children are eating dinner on a set schedule consistently, it's easier to control what time they have their snacks. If dinner becomes late, the first thing kids reach for are snacks that contain sugar, because sugar is the fastest source of energy, explains Armstrong. Then they have a sugar high, and then they crash again. It's all a big mess, he says.**

•• Include important nutrients. **Health expert Sally Kravich recommends calcium, B vitamins, and fish oil for children at this age, who are growing, beginning puberty, and consequently may have acne or become moody. She advises eating vegetables like bok choy, which are high in calcium, and supplementing with additional calcium and other helpful nutrients. She says to try to limit sugar, because it makes children more nervous and off balance.**

what I did, I had some nice salami, I put some salami in his lunch, a bottle of water, I did a sliced cucumber for him, some carrots, some grapes—it's enough for him to choose."

This age is a gateway to being teenagers—children begin to read and acquire their own information and so formulate their own opinions. They begin to feel grown up and want to think for themselves and want to have some control over their lives. They still need real adult guidance, but having them participate in the choices and preparation of meals is even more important. It gives them a way to feel their choices and input are valued.

Hopkins says, "I'm trying to get them to pack their own lunch so that they start learning about choices. I'll watch what they pack and augment it with whatever I see it's lacking. My daughter loves tangerines and my son loves kumquats, so we make sure those are always available, and we'll invariably have around some kind of crackers and cheese. They can make sandwiches for themselves—peanut butter and jelly or turkey and cheese sandwiches. Yogurt is also popular. Radishes and little carrots and those kinds of things seem to be the most popular items."

potato chip–crusted chicken tenders

{ JOSIAH CITRIN }

SERVES 4

Chef Josiah Citrin recommends this recipe because it is interactive and the kids enjoy helping. They like the potato chips, so it's fun for them. Citrin suggests trying out different-flavored potato chips and trying them on pork cutlets and even crab cakes. The cutlets come out really crispy—crispier than when using bread crumbs. He recommends serving them with a salad of grated vegetables that the kids can also prepare or string beans. Leftover chicken makes great lunch sandwiches, or it can be frozen for a later date for heating quickly in the oven. I make extra to freeze for Cody on nights when we have a babysitter prepare dinner.

Hawaiian or other light-colored nonsalted potato chips
Egg white
3 chicken breasts
Lemon wedges or Mayonnaise Sauce (see page 181)

1. Grind up the potato chips by spreading them out on a cutting board and rolling over them with a rolling pin until they are finely ground. Consider placing them in a large, sealable plastic bag to keep the crumbs contained.

2. Place the egg white in a bowl (save the yolk for the Mayonnaise Sauce).

3. Cover each chicken breast with plastic wrap and pound it down with the smooth side of a meat mallet so it is a consistent thickness.

4. Preheat oven to 375°F.

5. Cut the cutlets into "tenders" and brush on the egg white.

6. Coat the chicken pieces well with the ground potato chips and bake in the oven on a foil-lined baking sheet until crispy, about 15 minutes, depending on the size and thickness of the chicken pieces.

7. Squeeze lemon on top or serve with Mayonnaise Sauce (recipe at right).

Mayonnaise Sauce:

1 egg yolk

1 teaspoon Dijon mustard

½ lemon, juiced

1 cup olive oil (do not use extra-virgin, it will become
   bitter)

Water as necessary

1 ripe Roma tomato, diced

1. Combine egg yolk with mustard and lemon juice in a
bowl big enough to whisk all the ingredients together.

2. Slowly add the olive oil and whisk together until
the sauce gets thick, adding drops of water if it gets
too thick. Continue adding the oil in small quantities
and whisking until thick and blended.

3. Mix in diced tomato.

Notes: If you're concerned about the fat in the potato
chips, try cornflakes or coat only one side—cook
crusted-side down first.

You can cheat on the Mayonnaise Sauce by adding
Dijon mustard and lemon juice to a big dollop of jarred
mayonnaise.

kalbi steak

{ JOSIAH CITRIN }

This is the favorite meal at the Citrin household and a lunchbox hit. We make this for dinner and sometimes serve it in bowls and other times serve it with large lettuce leaves to make wraps and bundles at the table. I pack the leftover rice, steak, and vegetables for the next day's lunch for Cody. The marinade also works for pork and chicken.

Please note that this recipe calls for marinating the steak for several hours or overnight; plan accordingly.

Kalbi Marinade:

½ cup soy sauce

¼ cup water

2 tablespoons sesame oil

2 tablespoons rice vinegar

2½ tablespoons sugar

3 cloves garlic, pressed, crushed, or minced

2 teaspoons minced fresh ginger

2 tablespoons coarsely chopped onion

Steak:

16 ounces rib eye or NY strip or skirt steak, sliced ¼-inch thick

1 cup rice

1 tablespoon toasted sesame seeds, as garnish (optional)

2 green onions, as garnish (optional)

Vegetables such as shredded carrot or cabbage, thinly sliced daikon, or cucumber, for serving (optional)

1. Whisk all the marinade ingredients together until blended and the sugar has dissolved.

2. Pour a portion of the marinade into a smaller container and save for a dipping sauce. Combine the rest of the marinade and the steak slices in a nonreactive glass or plastic bowl to marinate for 2 hours at room temperature or 4 hours to overnight in the refrigerator.

3. Cook the rice according to the package instructions.

4. Heat a grill pan or a griddle over high heat and quickly grill each steak slice, keeping a close eye on them—the sugar in the marinade will burn quickly.

5. Once cooked, arrange the steak on a platter and sprinkle with the toasted sesame seeds and green onions. Arrange the rice in a serving bowl and the vegetables on another platter. Let each person construct a bowl of their own, with steak and vegetables atop the rice. Have the reserved marinade in a bowl at the table for dipping.

Note: To pack for lunch, arrange the sesame seed– and green onion–sprinkled steak alongside the rice and other vegetables, or pack them in separate containers, depending on what kind of containers you have available. If packed in a single container, items can portioned and separated with cupcake wrappers. The reserved marinade dipping sauce should be packed in a separate sealed container.

shaking beef

{ B. T. NGUYEN }

Chef B. T. Nguyen makes this dish, one of the most highly requested at her restaurant in Tampa, with good-quality beef and recommends using a Courvoisier cognac. Sometimes I buy the small single-serving bottles of cognac or other alcohol to use in recipes that call for small quantities of good-quality alcohol that I wouldn't necessarily have around for drinking. You can have the butcher cut the steak for you, or if you are doing it yourself, cut it when the meat is cold, with a sharp knife, and it will cut easier. While tasty made last minute, the dish is far better if you marinate the meat overnight—the meat gets a much deeper flavor. Double the marinade and save half to cook last minute in the wok for extra sauce. Serve with steamed jasmine rice. This recipe does require a bit of concentration and focus to get just right. I love watching my friend Piper make it—she tenderly watches and turns each piece of beef as it browns with chopsticks. The trick to this recipe is to cook the dish in small batches so that the beef gets seared on the outside and stays tender on the inside. Otherwise the pan or wok gets too crowded and beef will simmer in the sauce instead.

Note: This recipe calls for marinating for several hours or overnight; plan accordingly.

Marinade:

4 cloves garlic, finely chopped

1 tablespoon soy sauce

1 tablespoon fish sauce

1 tablespoon sugar

½ teaspoon freshly ground black pepper

Beef:

1 pound filet mignon or other similar tender cut, cut into bite-size cubes

1 tablespoon vegetable oil

1 tablespoon butter

Salt and pepper

¼ red onion, finely sliced

1½ tablespoons good-quality cognac

2 fresh ripe tomatoes, sliced

2 cups watercress (or arugula)

1. In a nonreactive bowl or container large enough to hold the beef, mix together all the marinade ingredients. Add the meat, mix to coat evenly, and let sit refrigerated for several hours or overnight.

2. Heat a large heavy-bottomed pan or wok until very hot, then add half the vegetable oil and swirl to coat the pan; next add half the butter. Turn and swirl the pan as the butter foams and turns a light

brown. Do not let the butter burn. Add half the beef cubes and toss with the oil by shaking the pan. Season with a pinch of salt and pepper. Let the meat sear for 2 minutes, then turn with tongs. Add half the sliced red onion and continue to cook the beef until seared on all sides but still a tender pink in the center. Repeat the steps with the other half of the ingredients.

3. Add the cognac for the last minute of cooking and shake the pan to release and coat the beef. Remove from heat.

4. To serve, arrange the tomato slices on plates and pile the watercress around or on top of the tomato slices. Place the beef in a mound on top of the tomatoes and watercress.

goan caldo verde

{ FLOYD CARDOZ }

SERVES 6

"We always have greens with our meals," says Chef Floyd Cardoz. "If I want them to eat kale, I do a soup with kale. . . . I use chorizo with potatoes and chicken stock, and then I puree the whole thing so it has the flavor of the chorizo and the flavor of the potato and so the kale is palatable."

When we make this soup we don't always puree it, and sometimes we add pasta because Cody, like most kids, loves pasta. He will eat only a little soup on its own, but he will fish out every last piece of pasta in the soup and, in the process, eat a good half bowl. Then, I pour the soup into a small cup so he can drink it. He thinks it's fun that way.

Chorizo has many varieties and all add a distinctive flavor to a dish. In Los Angeles the varieties readily available are either Spanish or Mexican, although chorizo also comes from South America, Portugal, Philippines, Dominican Republic, Puerto Rico, and Goan, India. Spanish chorizo is usually a cured smoked sausage, red from the dried smoked red peppers mixed in with the pork. Its flavor is distinctive, and it's usually eaten sliced without further cooking. Mexican chorizo is usually raw, with the texture of ground beef. It is also red from its high chile and spice content.

For added flavor, boil the kale in chicken or vegetable stock instead of water. You can save the stock afterwards to use again.

2 tablespoons canola oil

3 cloves

Bay leaf

1 tablespoon cumin seeds

1 teaspoon whole black peppercorns

½ cinnamon stick

½ cup sliced onions

5 cloves garlic, sliced

2 cups chorizo or similar sausage, sliced

2 cups canned diced tomatoes

1 cup diced celery root

2 cups peeled, diced potatoes

2 quarts chicken stock

Salt

Pepper

½ pound kale, washed, stemmed, and cut into thick strips (or substitute spinach)

Pasta (optional)

1. In a heavy-bottomed 6-quart Dutch oven or soup pot, heat the canola oil over medium heat. Add the cloves, bay leaf, cumin, black pepper, and cinnamon stick and cook until fragrant, about 3 minutes.

2. Next, add the sliced onions and garlic and cook over medium-low heat for 5 minutes, until softened and transparent.

3. Add the sausage and when browned, add the tomatoes and celery root and cook for 4 minutes more.

4. Add potatoes and the stock, bring to a boil, reduce to a simmer, and cook for 30 minutes, until tender. Season to taste with salt and pepper.

5. Bring a medium pot of water to a boil, then add 1 tablespoon salt. When the water returns to a boil, add the kale a handful at a time and cook for 2 to 3 minutes until the kale is tender but still bright green. Remove with a spoon and cool. Continue to cook each batch this way until all the kale is cooked.

6. Remove the bay leaf from the soup. You can either stir in the kale and serve with pasta (optional) or puree and serve.

baked halibut with potatoes and tomatoes

{ JOSIAH CITRIN }

This is a great way to introduce kids to fish. Halibut has a delicate flavor and the cornflakes sprinkled on top give it a crunch that kids will love to pick off and eat. Sometimes children need a way into a dish, and the familiar crunch of the cornflake topping gives them just that. A child serving is half a fillet. Chef Josiah Citrin recommends serving with jasmine rice.

12 or so fingerling potatoes
Butter for coating the baking dish
4 6-ounce halibut fillets (or any mild white fish),
    skinned and deboned
Salt and pepper
1 lemon, juiced
1 tablespoon olive oil
Approximately 1 cup water
12 cherry tomatoes
5 fresh basil leaves, chopped
1 teaspoon Dijon mustard
¼ cup cornflakes crushed into large crumbs

1. Boil the potatoes until just tender, about 15 minutes depending on their freshness, and slice ½-inch thick.

2. Preheat oven to 350°F.

3. Butter a baking dish large enough to hold all the halibut fillets in one layer, and lay the fillets in the dish, leaving a bit of room between the fillets and around the edge of the dish. Sprinkle the fish with salt and pepper and squeeze the lemon juice over the fillets.

4. Drizzle the olive oil and add enough water to the pan to come halfway up the thickness of the fish. Scatter the potato slices and the whole cherry tomatoes along the edge of the baking dish and sprinkle the basil leaves all over on top.

5. Cover with parchment paper or aluminum foil and put the baking dish in the oven to bake slowly for 15 to 20 minutes, until the fish is just cooked through and still moist.

6. Remove the dish from the oven and brush the top of the fish with mustard and sprinkle lightly with the cornflakes (do not cover the whole fillets). Place the dish quickly in the broiler for just 20 seconds for the crumbs to get crunchy but not burnt.

goan shrimp curry

{ FLOYD CARDOZ }

SERVES 6

I always welcome making an interesting one-pot dish like this shrimp curry. Make sure to shake the can of coconut milk before opening and pouring it in the dish.

2 pounds peeled shrimp

Salt

½ teaspoon black pepper

1 teaspoon cumin

1 cup shredded coconut

6 cloves garlic

4 cups shrimp stock or water, divided

1 teaspoon turmeric

2 tablespoons tamarind paste

2 tablespoons canola oil

¾ cup onion, sliced

2 fresh chile peppers, split (Anaheim work well)

1 can coconut milk, well shaken before pouring

Sea salt

1. Season the shrimp with salt and let stand for between 15 and 30 minutes in the refrigerator.

2. Grind the pepper and cumin in a spice grinder until finely ground.

3. Combine the coconut and garlic in a blender cup with 1 cup shrimp stock or water. Blend until smooth and combine with the mixture of spices, the turmeric, and the tamarind paste.

4. Place a medium-size pot over medium heat. Add the canola oil; when hot add the sliced onions and sauté for 3 to 4 minutes. Next add the spice paste and cook for 2 to 3 minutes. Add the remaining 3 cups of stock or water, chiles, coconut milk, and sea salt and cook over medium-low heat, stirring and not letting the liquid boil, for 10 to 15 minutes.

5. Cook the shrimp in the sauce until just done and still tender, approximately 10 minutes, stirring every now and again.

Tip: If you have a bit of time, make your own shrimp stock from the shells. Simply peel the shrimp and add the shells to a pot with water (for 2 pounds shrimp use 2 quarts water). Add an onion; some celery and carrot; and some herbs, like parsley, thyme, and a bay leaf. Make sure to skim the surface as the stock cooks. It will take about an hour to cook, but it smells delicious and will add much more flavor to the dish.

lemongrass snapper

{ B. T. NGUYEN }

"The fresher the ingredients, the better the food," says Chef B. T. Nguyen. If you prep the fish so it's ready to go in the morning or the night before, this is a superfast dinner served simply with rice or with Lemongrass Risotto (page 198).

Note: **This recipe calls for marinating for several hours or overnight; plan accordingly.**

1 3-pound whole red snapper or yellowtail, or 2 smaller fish, preferably butted, cleaned, and deboned

1–2 stalks fresh lemongrass, tough outer leaves removed and discarded, interior chopped fine or pureed

1 dried bay leaf, crumbled, or 1 fresh bay leaf, chopped

1 teaspoon grated fresh galangal or ½ teaspoon grated fresh ginger

1 garlic glove, sliced

1½ teaspoons mild curry powder

1½ teaspoons vegetable oil

1½ teaspoons soy sauce

1 teaspoon sugar

⅛ teaspoon black pepper or more to taste

1. Clean the fish, including the cavity, in fresh water and pat dry. Make three medium cuts on the outside of both sides of the fish and set aside.

2. In a small food processor or mortar and pestle, mix the lemongrass, bay leaf, galangal or ginger, garlic, curry powder, vegetable oil, soy sauce, sugar, and black pepper and pulse or pound into a paste. The lemongrass stalks are fibrous, so make sure to pound well until softened or puree well.

3. Using your hands, rub the spice mixture into the cavity of the fish and into the cuts on the outside of the fish.

4. Wrap the fish tightly in plastic wrap and marinate in the refrigerator for at least 3 hours.

5. When ready to cook, heat oven to 450°F. Unwrap the fish and bake on a tray or in a ceramic dish in the oven for 25 minutes or until done.

Note: Lemongrass stalks have a lovely elusive flavor but are fibrous and can be hard to prepare correctly, especially for young kids. It works best to cut the yellow section of the stalk into thin slices and grind them in a mini grinder/chopper or food processor that handles small quantities, adding a bit of water or oil if necessary. For very small amounts, pound with a mortar and pestle. If preparing in a soup, the lemongrass will soften as the soup simmers.

gratins of squash

{ LINTON HOPKINS }

SERVES 4 AS A SIDE DISH

Most gratins are baked with cream or milk and lots of cheese. In the summertime, when squash is so abundant, Chef Linton Hopkins makes lighter gratins with summer squash simply dressed with olive oil, onion, and Parmesan cheese. The squash stays brightly colored and is tender without being overcooked and mushy. Sometimes we add garlic with the onion or add a layer of tomatoes to the gratin, or sometimes we add some fresh basil or marjoram.

1 pound yellow or green summer squash, thinly sliced
1 teaspoon kosher salt
1½ teaspoons olive oil, divided
½ Vidalia or other sweet mild onion, chopped
Salt and pepper
½ cup grated Parmesan cheese, divided

1. Lay the sliced squash in a colander; massage the salt onto the squash, and let sit for 20 minutes, until beads of sweat form. Rinse the squash under water and pat dry.

2. Preheat oven to 350°F.

3. Heat a sauté pan over medium heat, and, when hot, add 1 teaspoon olive oil. Add the Vidalia onions and sauté until soft and translucent, about 4 minutes. While onion cooks, in a bowl combine and mix the squash with remaining ½ teaspoon olive oil plus salt and pepper.

4. To assemble the gratin, cover the bottom of the baking dish with about ⅓ of the sautéed onions. Arrange about ⅓ of the squash slices on top, and sprinkle about ⅓ of the cheese over the squash. Repeat layers two more times and top with a thicker blanket of cheese.

5. Bake uncovered for 25 minutes, until the squash has softened, the cheese has melted, and the top has turned a golden brown.

Note: Vidalia onions are sweet yellow onions grown in Georgia. They are juicy and flavorful and sweet enough to be eaten raw. Buy what you need and use them quickly, as they don't store well.

summer tomato fondue

{ LINTON HOPKINS }

SERVES 4 AS A LIGHT SIDE DISH

"We really try to celebrate the ingredients," says Chef Linton Hopkins. He makes a tomato fondue all the time in the summer, when tomatoes are piled high at the markets and incredibly flavorful. Tomato fondue can be served on toast, over fish or lentils, or plain on a plate, next to some meat or fish. It can be cooked long and slow to make it richer and thicker; butter and roasted garlic or herbs can be added to round out the flavor.

2 tablespoons olive oil

¼ onion, chopped

3 pints cherry tomatoes, cut in half or quarters, or use another fresh ripe tomato cut in pieces

Salt and pepper

Sugar to taste

Fresh basil or other fresh herbs like parsley or tarragon, chopped (optional)

1 tablespoon butter (optional)

1. Heat a medium sauté pan on medium-low heat; add the olive oil to warm. Add the chopped onions, stir, and cover to soften the onions but not brown them, about 5 minutes.

2. Raise the heat, add the tomatoes, and cook for several minutes over moderately high heat until the tomatoes have cooked down and the juice has thickened a bit, about 5 minutes.

3. Season the tomatoes with salt and pepper, add a sprinkle of sugar if needed, and mix in herbs and butter, if you like.

cast-iron charred cherry tomatoes and squash blossoms

{ CHRIS COSENTINO }

SERVES 4

Cody had never eaten squash blossoms, and I'd never cooked them before. I admit I was a bit scared to eat them; they are unusual looking. Cody, too, was hesitant. To encourage him to try these, I made a fun game out of it—we would count to three and then eat. His eyes got wide with surprise—and so did mine—at how good they tasted, from the blossom to the crunchy stem. We ate them all that way, down to the last one, which we split. This will become our springtime favorite. Have all your ingredients together, as this cooks very fast. The goal is to char the tomatoes without having them break apart. You will need a very hot burner to cook this on the stovetop.

1½ pints mixed cherry tomatoes
12 squash blossoms with stems attached
1½ teaspoon extra-virgin olive oil
Maldon sea salt or other sea salt
2 tablespoons basil (piccolo fino preferred)
Black pepper

1. Heat a large cast-iron pan over the center of a fire or on the highest setting of the hottest burner on your stove.

2. While the pan is heating, wash the tomatoes and squash blossoms, being sure to leave the stems on the blossoms (they're delicious), and remove the stamen from the center of the squash blossoms.

3. Once the pan is screaming hot, add the olive oil, then throw in all the cherry tomatoes and blossoms, season with Maldon salt, and then add the basil. Once the basil is added, remove from flame, season to taste with black pepper, and serve immediately.

corn cakes

{ LINTON HOPKINS }

Corn cakes, also known as johnnycakes, are a simply made down-home savory cross between corn bread and pancakes, delicious served with chili or soup or fancied up with lemon zest and honey and served warm with crème fraîche and jam or fresh berries. Chef Linton Hopkins makes them by adding buttermilk to cornmeal with a touch of salt. There's no one way to make corn cakes. Instead it's better to flavor them as needed for what you're serving. Add some chives and fresh corn for serving with sour cream as a side dish for a dinner entree, or make them sweeter if serving for breakfast.

Tips: Wipe out the pan between batches when cooking to remove any burned butter, which has an unpleasant taste. See page 109 for a quick substitute for buttermilk.

½ cup cornmeal

½ cup flour

1 teaspoon salt

¾ teaspoon baking powder

¼ teaspoon baking soda

½ cup buttermilk (plus more for thinning)

2 tablespoons honey or sorghum molasses

1 egg

1 tablespoon butter

1. Whisk together cornmeal, flour, salt, baking powder, and baking soda in a bowl. In a saucepan, heat the buttermilk and honey or molasses together over low heat until the honey is melted. Pour the mixture slowly over the cornmeal mixture, whisking to prevent lumps. Add a bit more buttermilk to thin the batter if necessary; then add the egg.

2. Butter a large skillet or griddle and heat to medium heat. Grease a spoon with a bit of oil and scoop tablespoons of batter into the pan; spread and flatten a bit with the back of the spoon.

3. Let the cakes gently cook until they are a deep golden brown on the bottom and a bit firm on the edges, about 2 or so minutes depending on how thick and big they are, and then turn them over like regular pancakes.

4. Spread a bit more butter on the griddle and on each cake before turning them over and cooking for another 6 minutes (or longer), until they are a deep golden brown and cooked through. Corn cakes are best served warm, but they can be added to lunchboxes or refrigerated for another snack or meal.

lemongrass risotto

{ B. T. NGUYEN }

This risotto is uniquely made without cheese. The shiitake mushrooms add a wonderful flavor, and you don't miss the creaminess the cheese would add otherwise.

Note: Lemongrass stalks have a lovely elusive flavor but are fibrous and can be hard to prepare correctly. It works best to cut the yellow section of stalk into thin slices and ground them either in a food processor or pound them until soft with a mortar and pestle. If preparing in a soup or risotto, as for this recipe, the lemongrass will soften as it cooks.

6 cups chicken, fish, or vegetable stock
Salt and pepper
3 tablespoons canola oil, olive oil, or butter
1 large onion, diced
3 stalks fresh lemongrass, finely chopped
1 carrot, diced
1 cup leeks, diced
1⅔ cups Arborio or jasmine rice
¾ cup dry white wine
1 cup shiitake mushrooms, stems removed and tops sliced
1 tablespoon fish sauce

1. In a medium saucepan, heat the stock, season with salt and pepper if needed, and keep warm over a very low flame.

2. Heat oil or butter in a large nonreactive saucepan, add onion, lemongrass, carrots, and leeks; cook over high heat for 3 minutes.

3. Add rice and sauté for 3 more minutes.

4. Once the rice starts to become translucent, add the white wine and shiitake mushrooms and stir. Cook until the wine is all absorbed; then add the stock ladle by ladle, making sure the liquid is absorbed before adding the next ladle, and stirring constantly. Continue until the rice is al dente, about 20 to 25 minutes, stirring frequently until all the liquid is absorbed.

5. Add fish sauce, mix well. Taste for seasoning, add salt and pepper as necessary, and serve.

risotto with pumpkin, ginger, and sage

{ PETER BERLEY }

SERVES 4 WITH LEFTOVERS

I'm always looking for ways to cook pumpkin in the fall when Halloween is all around—it always feels festive and comforting. If pumpkin season has passed, try using sweet potatoes or winter squash.

2 tablespoons extra-virgin olive oil

1 cup finely chopped leek (white part only)

3 cups peeled pumpkin or winter squash, cut in
   ½-inch cubes (about 1 pound)

1 tablespoon peeled and minced fresh ginger

5 cups water or vegetable stock

Sea salt

Freshly ground black pepper

1 tablespoon finely chopped fresh sage

1½ cups Arborio rice

½ cup dry white wine

2 tablespoons unsalted butter

½ cup finely grated Parmesan cheese

3 teaspoons finely chopped parsley

½ cup toasted pumpkin seeds (recipe at right)

1. In large sauté pan, heat the olive oil over medium heat and, when warm, add the leeks, pumpkin or squash, and ginger and sauté for 5 minutes.

2. Meanwhile, heat the water or stock in a pot and season with salt and pepper if needed; keep warm over a low flame.

3. In the sauté pan, stir in the sage and rice. Once the rice starts to become translucent, add the white wine and stir. Cook until the wine is all absorbed; then add the stock ladle by ladle, being sure the liquid is absorbed before adding the next ladle, and stirring frequently. Continue until the rice is al dente, about 20 to 25 minutes.

4. Add the butter and cook, stirring with a wooden spoon, for 1 to 2 minutes, then stir in the cheese.

5. Turn off the heat and let the risotto rest, uncovered, for 3 minutes before serving.

6. Add sea salt and freshly ground pepper to taste. Serve sprinkled with parsley and Toasted Pumpkin Seeds (recipe follows).

Toasted Pumpkin Seeds:

½ cup pumpkin seeds (shelled)

½ teaspoon extra-virgin olive oil

Pinch fine sea salt

1. Preheat oven to 375°F.

2. In a bowl, toss the seeds, oil, and salt together. Spread the seeds on a cookie sheet and toast in the oven for 15 minutes. Cool until crisp.

homemade ranch dressing

{ LINTON HOPKINS }

MAKES ABOUT 1 CUP

This dressing thickens up after a bit in the fridge—perfect for dipping veggies in. For an even thicker dressing, add extra sour cream and use a thick Greek-style yogurt.

1 small clove garlic, minced

¼ teaspoon salt

¼ cup sour cream or crème fraîche or thick plain yogurt

¼ cup mayonnaise

2 tablespoons buttermilk (plus more for thinning)

½ teaspoon white wine vinegar or lemon juice

1 tablespoon chopped fresh parsley

½ tablespoon chopped fresh dill

½ teaspoon chopped chives

Salt and pepper to taste

1. Mash the minced garlic and salt with a mortar and pestle to make a paste.

2. In a bowl, combine the garlic paste with the sour cream, crème fraîche, or yogurt; mayonnaise; and buttermilk. Add more buttermilk to thin for a pourable dressing or less for a dip.

3. Add the vinegar and herbs and season with salt and pepper. The dressing will store refrigerated for several days. The flavors will meld and get better; stir again before serving.

lemon bars

{ JOAN MCNAMARA }

MAKES 9 BARS

These lemon bars are signature treats at Chef Joan McNamara's Los Angeles food emporium, Joan's on Third. It's hard to resist these pretty lemony treats, dusted with sugar and just the right balance of tart and sweet. She says she always had lemon bars in the freezer ready for her kids when they had friends over. It made hers the favorite house to visit.

½ cup (1 stick) butter, melted
1¼ cups flour, divided
Pinch salt
½ cup sugar
½ teaspoon baking powder
2 eggs, slightly beaten
¾ cup honey
2 teaspoons lemon zest
5 tablespoons fresh lemon juice
Powdered sugar for dusting the bars

1. Heat oven to 350°F.

2. To make the crust, combine the melted butter with 1 cup flour, salt, and the sugar in a medium bowl and mix until a dough forms. Press dough into an 8-inch square pan, leaving a thicker edge to make a sturdy crust for the filling. Bake until lightly browned, about 18 minutes. Remove from the oven and cool. Leave the oven on.

3. For the custard filling, mix together the remaining ¼ cup flour and baking powder in a medium bowl. In another bowl, beat together the eggs, honey, lemon zest, and lemon juice. Whisk the egg mixture into the flour mixture until combined. Pour into the baked crust and put back in the oven to bake for 20 to 25 minutes, until the filling is set. Remove and cool.

4. When cooled completely, dust lightly with powdered sugar and cut into bars.

Note: Lemon bars will keep in the refrigerator for 1 week, or can be frozen on a baking tray and then stored between layers of parchment or waxed paper in an airtight container. Simply defrost and serve.

Tip: You can easily make just the right amount of your own powdered sugar by putting regular granulated sugar in a blender or food processor.

metric conversion tables

Metric U.S. Approximate Equivalents

Liquid Ingredients

METRIC	U.S. MEASURES	METRIC	U.S. MEASURES
1.23 ML	¼ TSP.	29.57 ML	2 TBSP.
2.36 ML	½ TSP.	44.36 ML	3 TBSP.
3.70 ML	¾ TSP.	59.15 ML	¼ CUP
4.93 ML	1 TSP.	118.30 ML	½ CUP
6.16 ML	1¼ TSP.	236.59 ML	1 CUP
7.39 ML	1½ TSP.	473.18 ML	2 CUPS OR 1 PT.
8.63 ML	1¾ TSP.	709.77 ML	3 CUPS
9.86 ML	2 TSP.	946.36 ML	4 CUPS OR 1 QT.
14.79 ML	1 TBSP.	3.79 L	4 QTS. OR 1 GAL.

Dry Ingredients

METRIC	U.S. MEASURES	METRIC		U.S. MEASURES
2 (1.8) G	1/16 OZ.	80 G		2⅘ OZ.
3½ (3.5) G	⅛ OZ.	85 (84.9) G		3 OZ.
7 (7.1) G	¼ OZ.	100 G		3½ OZ.
15 (14.2) G	½ OZ.	115 (113.2) G		4 OZ.
21 (21.3) G	¾ OZ.	125 G		4½ OZ.
25 G	⅞ OZ.	150 G		5¼ OZ.
30 (28.3) G	1 OZ.	250 G		8⅞ OZ.
50 G	1¾ OZ.	454 G	1 LB.	16 OZ.
60 (56.6) G	2 OZ.	500 G	1 LIVRE	17⅗ OZ.

index